Rhetorical Public Speaking

Rhetorical Public Speaking: Civic Engagement in the Digital Age, Third Edition offers students an innovative approach to public speaking by employing the rhetorical canon as a means of constructing artful speech in a multi-mediated environment. It provides a foundation to guide students in understanding, constructing, and delivering messages that address matters of public concern. This edition features contemporary as well as historical examples to highlight key concepts and show how rhetoric works in practice. Each chapter includes speech excerpts, summaries, and exercises for review and retention. Students of public speaking are encouraged to employ their new skills as engaged citizens of society.

Nathan Crick is Associate Professor of Communication at Texas A&M University. His publications include *The Keys of Power: The Rhetoric and Politics of Transcendentalism* (2017), *Rhetoric and Power: The Drama of Classical Greece* (2015), and *Democracy and Rhetoric: John Dewey on the Arts of Becoming* (2010).

Rhetorical Public Speaking

Civic Engagement in the Digital Age

Third Edition

Nathan Crick

Routledge
Taylor & Francis Group

NEW YORK AND LONDON

First published 2017
by Routledge
711 Third Avenue, New York, NY 10017

and by Routledge
2 Park Square, Milton Park, Abingdon, Oxon, OX14 4RN

Routledge is an imprint of the Taylor & Francis Group, an informa business

First Published by Pearson Education, Inc. 2011, 2014

Library of Congress Cataloging-in-Publication Data
Names: Crick, Nathan, author.
Title: Rhetorical public speaking / Nathan Crick.
Description: 3rd edition. | New York, NY : Routledge, 2017. | Includes index.
Identifiers: LCCN 2016058274 | ISBN 9781138292772 (hardback) |
    ISBN 9781138292796 (pbk.)
Subjects: LCSH: Public speaking.
Classification: LCC PN4121.C745 2017 | DDC 808.5/1—dc23
LC record available at https://lccn.loc.gov/2016058274

ISBN: 978-1-138-29277-2 (hbk)
ISBN: 978-1-138-29279-6 (pbk)
ISBN: 978-1-315-23252-2 (ebk)

Typeset in Warnock Pro
by Apex CoVantage, LLC

Visit the eResource: www.routledge.com/9781138292796

Printed and bound in Great Britain by
TJ International Ltd, Padstow, Cornwall

Contents

6 The Rhetorical Situation   137

10 Eloquence   235

Preface

The purpose of this book is to give students a practical understanding of how public speaking can function as a rhetorical intervention—as an act of persuasion designed to alter how other people think about and respond to public affairs that affect their lives. The audience for this book is the **engaged citizen**—that individual who is an active participant in the democratic process of debate, deliberation, and persuasion as it relates to issues of public concern.

▶ NEW TO THIS EDITION

This new edition has been updated and expanded to provide students with the tools they need to be effective public speakers. The following lists specific changes to the new third edition:

- ▶ More diverse and contemporary examples of rhetorical artifacts from politicians, social movement activists, citizens, and celebrities to show public speaking in action

- ▶ An introduction to media theory that articulates the relationship of rhetoric to written, electronic, and oral communication

- ▶ Expanded and simplified chapters exploring the different canons of rhetoric that will allow any student to learn the essentials of public speaking quickly and easily

- ▶ New chapter exercises that provide methods for impromptu speeches, debates, group exercises, take-home assignments, and recording short videos of public speeches outside of class

The guiding rationale for this book is that the success or failure of democratic social life depends on the cultivation of engaged citizens, each of whom has the capacity to act rhetorically in the public sphere. In other words, democracy suffers when we base our educational system on the naïve faith that individuals instinctively possess the skills of public advocacy. The reality is that citizens are made, not born. Part of that educational process involves instilling in people the belief that free speech is their right and individual expression is their duty. The other part of the process is to give them the knowledge, skill, and confidence to perform that duty and to judge the performances of others when the situation demands it. One unique function of a class in public speaking is to provide a structured and supportive environment in which to develop these skills in preparation for an active life. This textbook is designed to facilitate that process by providing the tools—understood as methods—that promote the creative expression of engaged citizens.

The speaker in rhetorical public speech is therefore something more than just a person who says words in the presence of others. A rhetorical public speaker is called a **rhetor**, meaning a conscious instigator of social action who uses persuasive discourse to achieve his or her ends. Being *conscious* implies that a rhetor is not simply one whose speech happens to have consequences. All acts of communication have the potential to influence people and events, but rhetorical public speech is unique in having been created specifically for that purpose. That is what makes it an art rather than a product of luck. Being an *instigator* means that a rhetor intentionally behaves in such a manner as to cause others to think and feel in new and different ways. We instigate not only when we prompt, originate, and begin something, but also when we do so in the presence of others who may be reluctant to follow. An instigator makes people act in ways they might not otherwise have done if not prodded to do so. Finally, what is instigated is a *social action*, meaning that the effects of a rhetor's persuasive discourse are determined by how they alter and impact the behaviors of other people with respect to some end, or some goal or interest that functions in response to an exigence. A rhetor thus represents a person willing to stir, motivate, challenge, and even confront audiences in order to make them think and act in such a way that addresses a shared problem.[1]

It is from this methodological and pedagogical perspective that examples have been chosen which represent strategies for generating social change within certain historical moments of crisis. Methodologically, a historian of public speaking finds the most interesting examples of rhetoric on the margins of culture. Understandably, this does *not* mean that these strategies were particularly *effective* or *virtuous*; it means only that the strategy was explicitly and creatively employed in such a way that makes it useful for the purpose of elaboration. Instructors and students who do not find their own views expressed in the examples of the book should bring them to the table during the span of the course to generate productive discussion through engagement.

The controversial nature of these speeches also provides an opportunity to discuss the ethics of rhetoric. By "ethics," I do not refer to whether a speaker's beliefs match up to some formal catechism or obey some polite convention. The **ethics of rhetoric** are determined by how well the speaker has fully considered the broader consequences of his or her actions beyond the immediate moment and has acted conscientiously with respect to that evaluation. Part of the responsibility of rhetorical theory is to make speakers aware of just how much impact a single speech might have in a complex and interconnected world in which "good intentions" are not enough to produce desired consequences. The ethical study of public speech helps people to avoid getting trapped into such a situation by providing the tools to survey a broader social environment before acting. Based on this "holistic" ethical ideal, a large part of what distinguishes this book from other texts on public speaking is its continual emphasis on the speaker as a part of a larger social whole.

I have tried, in this book, to reconnect public speaking with the rhetorical and wholly democratic tradition of eloquence—of the act of appearing before others to express one's truth with beauty and excellence. Toward this end, I have emphasized that aspect of public speaking which is often quickly passed over by textbooks in haste to present the latest in flowcharts and moral catechisms—the act of appearing before others. Throughout this book, I will emphasize public speaking as an action that occurs in the company of others who share experience on matters of common concern. Although rhetorical public speaking is arguably about the act of persuasion, it is more importantly an action of gathering together people to appear before one another in a shared space of their common world.

Finally, the book emphasizes that public speaking is an art. As an art, it is learned through practice. Nothing replaces the pure experience of simply talking in front of others. This experience cannot be quantified or measured. The value of any conceptual material, therefore, must be judged with respect to how it enriches and broadens the experience of the student in the act of speaking. The Roman rhetorician Quintilian wrote, "An art consists of perceptions consenting and cooperating to some end useful to life" and involves "a power working its effects by a course, that is by method"; consequently, "no man will doubt that there is a certain course and method in oratory."[2] A successful course in public speaking will seek to educate students in a method of channeling the power of the spoken word toward ends that are useful in life.

▶ NOTES

1. For the relationship between rhetoric and citizenship, see Robert Asen, "A Discourse Theory of Citizenship," *Quarterly Journal of Speech* 90, no. 2 (2004), 189–211.

2. Quintilian, quoted in *The Philosophy of Rhetoric*, in *The Rhetorical Tradition: Readings from Classical Times to the Present*, ed. Patricia Bizzell and Bruce Herzberg (Boston: Bedford Books of St. Martin's Press, 1990), 329.

Introduction

The goal of rhetorical public speaking is the transformation of a collection of individual hearers into a common and committed audience through the power of the spoken word. Every metaphor, every gesture, and every argument must be directed toward this act of turning the many into the one, at least for a moment. This basic fact was recognized by nineteenth-century orator and philosopher Ralph Waldo Emerson, who wrote more than one essay on the subject of "eloquence." Of the orator, he says the following:

> That which he wishes, that which eloquence ought to reach, is not a particular skill in telling a story, or neatly summing up evidence, or arguing logically, or dexterously addressing the prejudice of the company,—no, but a taking sovereign possession of the audience. Him we call an artist who shall play on an assembly of men as a master on the keys of the piano,— who, seeing the people furious, shall soften and compose them, shall draw them, when he will, to laughter and to tears. Bring him to his audience, and, be they who they may,— coarse or refined, pleased or displeased, sulky or savage, with their opinions in the keeping of a confessor, or with their opinions in their bank-safes,—he will have them pleased and humored as he chooses; and they shall carry and execute that which he bids them.[1]

Although Emerson's language expresses something of a tyrannical tenor ("Do my bidding!"), he nonetheless emphasizes the essential characteristic that sets public speaking apart from other mediated forms of communication, such as writing or video—the fact that experience of being in the same place at the same time to listen to a single person speak can be a very powerful experience indeed. This is because, as Walter Ong later pointed out, "spoken words are always modification of a total, existential situation, which always engages the body. . . . In oral verbalization, particularly public verbalization, absolute motionless is itself a powerful gesture."[2] When we watch someone on a screen or read his or her words on paper, silence may bore us and we can always turn our attention to other things, but when we are present together to listen to a speech that captures our attention, we commit ourselves completely to the experience.

However, it is natural to ask whether Emerson would have had held oratorical eloquence in such high regard if he lived in our modern technological age of the Internet, television, smart phones, digital video, photography, movie, radio, and all the other technologies from the past hundred years. Indeed, one might argue that modern technology will soon make the art of oratory obsolete altogether. Why, after all, give an informative speech about the history of the civil rights movement when one can forward a PDF file? Why bother making introductory speeches to every person in a new workplace when one can post to a Facebook group? And why get everyone in the same room to hear a sales pitch when they can do it by videoconferencing? In an age where communication via electronic technology is the first choice for most people in their busy lives, one must have a clear reason for gathering people together in the same space at the same time to hear a speech. Consequently, any book that purports to teach public speaking as oratory must address the unique quality of oral performance that makes it something to take seriously despite the pervasiveness and attractiveness of new media.

The best place to find evidence of the continued vitality of the oratorical tradition is simply one's everyday experience. On the one hand, it is undeniable that new media have effectively challenged or even replaced many communicative interactions that previously had relied on face-to-face contacts. One can imagine a time when the university classroom, the corporate boardroom, and the local merchandise store will all go the way of the door-to-door salesperson and the colonial-era town hall meeting, and when a "friend" will refer simply to a relationship one has with a digital picture and associated text messages. On the other hand, the science fiction projections of a time when human beings will be content simply sitting alone in a room surrounded by video screens and constant chatter are really meant as amplifications of isolated tendencies in society rather than serious predictions based on human nature. For the fact remains that despite our ability to communicate through media as never before, there is a very basic need in every human being for intimate human contact that comes from simply being with others in the same place at the same time and recognizing and welcoming one another's presence. There is simply no way that any form of media will replace the necessity to be present together at births and at deaths, during weddings and wakes, in celebration and in tragedy, and to achieve communion and to resolve crisis. In short, even as the amount of time spent communicating through new media increases mathematically, the importance of those moments when we must come together and share the experience of eloquence increases geometrically. We may not speak to one another in person as much as we have in the past, but that only means that we must be prepared to do so with passion and with power when the moment calls.

Moreover, although the inventions of our time are certainly new additions to the world, the challenge of adapting our forms of communication to new technology is a very ancient one. In the age of Classical Greece in the fifth century B.C.E., the new technology was writing and the new medium was papyrus. We might think this an archaic medium by our standards, but at the time it was highly disruptive to the traditional oral community. In the *Phaedrus*, Plato has Socrates complain that writing will

> introduce forgetfulness into the soul of those who learn it: they will not practice using their memory because they will put their trust in writing, which is external and depends on signs that belong to others, instead of trying to remember from the inside, completely on their own. . . . And they will imagine that they have come to know much while for the most part they will know nothing.[3]

Although a writer himself, Plato wanted to limit the scope and influence of writing because he believed it would interfere with the pursuit of wisdom through what he called "dialectic," which was a method to use face-to-face dialogue to seek out truths of both the world and of the soul through living speech. For him, writing threatened to replace that which was real and vibrant with that which was artificial and mechanical.

But just as every first generation has its Plato, whose job it is to warn us of the dangers of being seduced by new technology, every second generation has its Aristotle, whose job it is to adapt our method of communication to our available media. Although a student of Plato, Aristotle did not look upon writing with such anxiety. He simply recognized that each medium required its own unique form, and that "each kind of rhetoric has its own appropriate style."[4] In his mid-fourth-century B.C.E. treatise *Rhetoric*, Aristotle gives us perhaps the first extended treatment of the differences between the written and spoken word:

> The written style is the more finished: the spoken better admits of dramatic delivery—alike the kind of oratory that reflects character and the kind that reflects emotion. Hence actors look out for plays written in the latter style, and poets for actors competent to act such plays. . . . [However, speeches made to hear spoken] look amateurish enough when they pass into the hands of a reader. This is because they are so well suited for an actual tussle, and therefore contain many dramatic touches, which, being robbed of all dramatic rendering, fail to do their own proper work and consequently look silly. Thus strings of unconnected words, and constant repetitions of words and phrases, are very properly condemned in written speeches: but not in spoken speeches—speakers use them freely, for they have a dramatic effect.[5]

Aristotle points out perhaps the most essential quality of the spoken word—its unique suitability to capture the emotional character of a situation with only a few words or gestures, and to do so in such a way that powerfully brings an audience together through shared experience. Whereas writing must reproduce every single aspect of a situation through words, thus necessitating lengthy and detailed narration and argumentation, oral performance can accomplish the same task with a simple turn of phrase or wave of the hand. And even perhaps more importantly, Aristotle recognizes that the spoken and written word are not in competition; each is suited for its own unique purpose and has its own unique form.

The difference between these two media was emphasized again much later by philosopher John Dewey in the twentieth century, who made an effort to recover the importance of the face-to-face community that he felt was being threatened by rapid changes in both transportation and mass communication. At the time, many people were arguing that the only way to sustain democratic life was to abandon the oral tradition and instead concentrate on disseminating massive amounts of print material that would inform citizens about every single aspect of the world so that they could make educated decisions about matters of political and economic affairs. What Dewey recognized was that although the written word was certainly important to deal with complex matters, it was not sufficient to sustaining democratic life. He wrote:

> Signs and symbols, language, are the means of communication by which a fraternally shared experience is ushered in and sustained. But the winged words of conversation in immediate intercourse have a vital import lacking in the fixed and frozen words of written speech. Systematic and continuous inquiry into all the conditions which affect association and their dissemination in print is a precondition of the creation of a true public. But it and its results are but tools after all. Their final actuality is accomplished in face-to-face relationships by means of direct give and take. . . . The connections of the ear with vital and out-going thought and emotion are immensely closer and more varied than those of the eye. Vision is a spectator; hearing is a participator. Publication is partial and the public which results is partially informed and formed until the meanings it purveys pass from mouth to mouth.[6]

For Dewey, written speech has a linear pattern and logical coherence that makes it suitable for effectively arranging and disseminating complex ideas, whereas oral speech tends to emphasize the total quality of shared experience that makes it more suitable to sustain relationships and to create connections among diverse groups of people. Written speech highlights the power of language to create a network of causal relationships, to weave together a web of meanings, and to project possibilities into the future based on knowledge of the present and past.

In effect, written speech gives order to a complex world, as exemplified in the scope and power we grant to the discourses of science, religion, economics, and history. He thus relates writing to "vision" not only because one has to literally look at the words, but also because it creates the experience of being an observer from a distance. By contrast, by connecting via the ear, oral speech tends to create the experience of being surrounded by and immersed within an environment. Oral speech made in the presence of others brings ideas and possibilities to life within the objects, people, and events of one's surroundings. When successful, oral speech draws people together to share what is created in that moment, an effect that is often associated with ritual ceremonies and celebrations. In short, genuine community can only exist within the spoken word. Dewey's democratic ideal would therefore strike a balance between the two media. A harmonious relationship between written and oral speech would bring about the best of both "spectator" and "participant" experiences, thereby allowing people to stand outside a situation and contemplate it from a distance while also, periodically, immersing themselves in the shared life of a community.

The introduction of even newer electronic media of communication has not refuted this ideal as much as supplemented it. The phrase "electronic media" is taken from Canadian media theorist Marshall McLuhan, who used it to denote any technology of communication that used any form of electricity to disseminate messages immediately across a potentially global field and/or reproduce auditory sounds or visual images with great accuracy and the potential for playback. The term *electronic media* therefore includes both traditional "mass media" such as the television and radio as well as newer "digital media"—everything accessible through modern computers, such as e-mail, the Internet, and digital photography and video. Starting with the telegraph in the nineteenth century and extending up to and beyond modern smart phones, electronic media far surpass the invention of the printing press and introduces the utopian possibility of immersing ourselves in the total life of the planet in a single moment. This creates opportunities for expanding the horizon of one's experience to distances unheard of a century ago. Social networking sites and global communication systems now create the possibility of reaching thousands if not millions of people instantaneously.

Yet despite all of this, we still demand the detached solitude of the literate life and the tactile experience of partaking in the spoken word. Each medium serves its own function and must be appraised by that function. In order to guide judgments about what medium of communication is appropriate for what types of situations, this introduction will define three different speech contexts: the context for written speech, the context for online communication, and the context for public speaking.

▶ THE CONTEXT FOR WRITTEN SPEECH

Written speech, as it is used here, refers to the primary media of print rather than handwriting insofar as print privileges sequential ordering of parts, a specific point of view, an explicit logical progression, a complex arrangement of information, and a spirit of objective detachment. According to McLuhan, printed speech is marked by isolation, reflection, distance, specialization, and fragmentation. In writing, one does not participate together in a shared moment; one composes or reads in private, taking each word and each sentence at a time, and threading together a total sequential narrative that often has a sense of past, present, and future. McLuhan observes that

> writing tends to be a kind of separate or specialist action in which there is little opportunity
> or call for reaction. The literate man or society develops the tremendous power of acting in

any matter with considerable detachment from the feelings or emotional involvement that an illiterate man or society would experience.[7]

By "acting without reacting," McLuhan means the ability to reflect on ideas or situations—not with just an overt, physical response—but by quietly writing down one's thoughts in logical or poetic form.

Writing, that is to say, makes possible the monk, the poet, the scientist, and the philosopher. Written speech refers to those objects that we wish to study in private, to dwell over and reflect upon, to use as a reliable guide for judgment. Objects of written speech include annual business reports, scientific journal articles, the Bible, handwritten letters, diaries, legal judgments, novels, the U.S. Constitution, technical manuals, poetry anthologies, new procedural guidelines, to-do lists, biographies, economic projections, and philosophies. Because of the nature of the medium, the context for written speech tends to be of a much broader scope than that of oral or electronic communication. A written document takes time to compose and to publish in the promise that the message it contains will retain relevance for some time to come. For instance, sometimes it is better to provide a written manual rather than to explain a procedure, to print out an article rather than send it by e-mail, or to document the reasons for a judgment rather than argue them in a public setting. To put it succinctly, written speech is the best response when we wish to give an audience material to "take home and study." Whenever we want someone to reflect upon a message in private and be able to return to it later, written speech is the ideal medium.

Perhaps the paradigmatic case of written speech as a rhetorical response to a complex and enduring problem is the publication of "reports" produced by research committees and commissioned by government or industry to provide frameworks for action based on careful research into the current situation. Ideally, these reports are then studied by relevant authorities, after which time they present their judgments on how to act. "Reports" are the way that specialist groups such as scientists, judges, economists, theologians, and historians actually function rhetorically in the broader political environment. Even though their intention may not have been specifically to "persuade," the publication of their research acts to guide judgments about public affairs in a powerful and convincing way. From a rhetorical perspective, situations that call for a persuasive response through written speech tend to possess the following qualities:

- ▶ A pervasive problem that endures across durations of time and breadth of space
- ▶ Sufficient time to deliberate upon a proper response without the need for immediate action
- ▶ Significant resources to draw upon in analyzing the problem
- ▶ An audience with the willingness and capacity to deliberate over a period of time upon a single issue

Given this type of situation, rhetoric that takes the form of written speech generally attempts to accomplish the following goals:

- ▶ Provide a distinct perspective on a situation that offers a useful point of view
- ▶ Give order and coherence to a disordered and chaotic condition
- ▶ Replace short-sighted fears and desires with far-sighted judgment
- ▶ Replace overheated involvement with cooler forms of detachment
- ▶ Encourage delayed individual reflection over immediate group response

> **DISCUSSION**
>
> The best way to understand the unique character of written speech as a print form is to compare the same text presented in two different media types. What is the difference, for instance, between checking out a book from the library and reading it as a PDF file online? What is the difference between writing and receiving a handwritten letter and just sending an e-mail? And when do you feel you need to "send a card" with writing inside of it versus simply sending an e-card?

▶ THE CONTEXT FOR ELECTRONIC COMMUNICATION

Although electronic forms of communication include many technologies of the mass media, most of us will primarily make use of online forms of electronic communication, such as e-mail, teleconferences, website postings, and text messaging. **Online communication** is thus meant to refer to text, image, audio, and video messages sent and received by individuals on computer-aided technologies and capable of being received simultaneously by an infinite number of users, and also being recalled by those users at any time. As indicated by McLuhan's analysis, online communication tends to foster mobility and decentralization and at the same time creates a sense of constantly being "in touch" with other people. In addition, it tends to favor messages that have an iconic or mosaic form over those that feature more primarily linear narratives or arguments more fitting to written speech.

There are several specific features of online communication that make it unique. First, it allows for multiple messages to be sent and received simultaneously and at rapid speed. This creates an enormous competition for time, as it creates an almost permanent backlog of messages awaiting consideration. In this environment, messages are naturally developed to capture one's immediate attention and be received and understood in a short amount of time. Second, the capability of multimedia messaging further heightens the competition for attention, such as a simple e-mail supplemented with embedded images, attached files, and background graphics or sound. Third, it creates a situation of receiving a message in private at the same time that it is capable of being broadcast to a group. This reduces the sense of "privacy" that written speech tends to produce while at the same time allowing a message to be freed from its situational context. Fourth, the capability of saving and resending messages allows them to spread widely and rapidly, thereby allowing both successes and mistakes to be immediately broadcast to all members of a group, from a group of friends to a global audience. Fifth, it creates the possibility of anonymity if the message is sent with a blind or disguised sender, thereby liberating the message not only from context but from authorship.

The majority of our online communication tends to be informal in quality—despite the intended content. Even in organizational settings, official e-mails are often laced with personal observations, jokes, compliments, or complaints that have a conversational tone. E-mail, in particular, fuses composition and production in one function, thereby fostering a type of discourse that is loose and impromptu rather than formal and reflective. In addition, online communication makes ease and entertainment permanent features of its use. Even governmental websites are designed to be appealing to the eye. On the one hand, this makes online communication ideal for situations that require readily accessible information or the rapid dissemination of striking ideas, events, or images. Whereas websites are there to present information or perform a function for anyone who needs it at any time, e-mails and text messages allow individuals to send specific messages to anyone in an instant. On the other hand, online communication tends to lack durability. As quickly as messages are produced, they are destroyed or replaced. Also, online communication tends to lack a sense of shared or situated context. Whereas even a book needs to be read somewhere, online communication has the sense of being received everywhere and nowhere.

But does electronic communication dominate every aspect of our lives simply because it is available? That question can only be answered by looking more closely at the unique qualities of each type of media. If we take the writing of Marshall McLuhan as a guide, the Internet exaggerates all the characteristics of previous electronic media, such as the telegraph, radio, movie, and television, which appear to eclipse the function of both written and oral speech. McLuhan writes that

> it is the speed of electric involvement that creates the integral whole of both private and public awareness. We live today in the Age of Information and of Communication because electric media instantly and constantly create a total field of interacting events in which all men participate.[8]

McLuhan associates the following qualities with the electronic age: **decentralization**, or the ability for organizations or groups to operate without any central organizing structure; **implosion**, or the impression that everything far away can be brought close to you in an instant; **mosaic form**, or a mode of presentation that places multiple things next to each other simultaneously, as in a hyperlinked website; and **immersion**, the sense that everybody is deeply involved in everyone else's lives and activities all at once.

However, whatever the utopian hopes and terrifying fears generated by the appearance of the Internet, little indicates that online communication has made the book and the speech obsolete. The Internet has certainly created that sense of being a "global village" that McLuhan prophesized, breaking down the stark divisions among peoples by creating a sense of being connected as a whole. However, although the rise of electronic communication has permanently affected almost every aspect of our personal, cultural, and political lives, it has not obliterated (except with a few exceptions, like papyrus and the telegraph) older forms of communication. For instance, despite the ability to reach the whole nation online, political candidates still spend ever-increasing time and money speaking at rallies, community centers, and special events where supporters eagerly gather to listen. Televangelists have been around for decades, yet millions of Americans still travel to places of worship every week to gather together in shared praise. Commemorative events like the Fourth of July or the presidential inaugural address are now streamed online at any time, and yet people will even endure harsh natural elements to be able to say that they were there in person. And while telecommuting and teleconferencing have increased the scope and efficiency of business, the rituals of the board meeting, the national convention, the interview, and the sales pitch remain staples of corporate culture.

Once again, nothing denies that online communication may also transmit complex information that functions similarly to written speech in certain contexts. It only indicates that the medium is more suitable to respond to more immediate situations. Rhetorically, online communication plays a particularly significant role within social movements, both in terms of its organizational capacity during rallies and protests as well as in terms of maintaining an actively interested support based on mass e-mails, videos, text messages, and other media that keep relevant "current events" in the consciousness of the audience. Online communication has made organized movements possible that are of global scale and that can act almost immediately anywhere in the world. As with the written word, then, there are particular situations that are suitable for online communication and those that are not. Rhetorical situations that call for a persuasive response through online communication thus possess the following qualities:

▶ Dealing with an event that is of short duration and requires immediate response

▶ Widespread interest in that event, which produces heightened emotional tensions seeking expression

▶ A rapidly changing situation that makes people desire the latest information

▶ Little time to dwell upon the complexities of the situation or reflect upon its past or future

▶ A communication environment where many messages are competing for attention

Rhetoric that takes the form of online communication generally attempts to accomplish the following goals:

▶ To communicate with individuals in a diverse population across a wide area

▶ To signal, or call attention to, a specific event, object, person, or quality

▶ To direct action in the immediate present, often in the form of a command

▶ To stimulate the senses and satisfy emotional cravings

▶ To generate a common interest in a particular subject matter

> **DISCUSSION**
>
> When have you been without access to online forms of communication for an extended length of time? What did you feel you were missing? What functions did you feel unable to perform? Did that give you a sense of peace or were you actually more anxious? What does this experience tell you about your relationship to online communication?

▶ THE CONTEXT FOR PUBLIC SPEAKING

If written speech tends to invite individual cognitive reflection in solitude while online communication heightens the feeling of collective immersion in an immediate event, public speaking generates an atmosphere of shared experience within a dramatic situation. For **public speaking** is not so much about the words spoken as the fact that they are spoken *publicly*—which is to say, spoken within a shared space that includes both the words and the total environment in which they are uttered. Public speaking is different from mass communication. **Mass communication** disseminates a message, but it is received in a different environment than that in which it was produced. It reaches a "public," as an organized body of acting citizens, but it is not a *public* speech. A **public speech** is an oral communication delivered by an individual to a public audience gathered in a shared physical environment to listen collectively and respond to that message in the present.

Even a speech videotaped and rebroadcast is not the same as the speech heard by those physically present. A public speech is a shared event that often has a past and a future. The speech includes all the events that led up to it (including the travel required for people to reach the same place, the time it takes to gather together and to wait, and any preceding events that introduced it) and the actions that follow it (including conversation with others about the speech, any proceeding events, and the final departure of the guests). The public speech is not separate from its history. It *requires* its history to be meaningful. Those who watch a speech on television may remember certain words or phrases used, and perhaps an image of the audience flashed before the screen, but their memory of watching the speech is tied up with the physical context of where it is watched—a living room, a bar, a classroom, and the like. For the people actually present, the speech is an event that is a part of a larger drama, even if it includes merely the conversation with co-workers before and after the boardroom meeting.

For McLuhan, the dominant aspect of the spoken word is therefore the creation of "audience participation," not just in the understanding of the words but in the comprehension of the total speech situation that "involves all of the senses dramatically." In oral speech, "we tend to react to each situation that occurs, reacting in tone and gesture even to our own act of speaking." When we speak, we are not just conveying information; we are forming relationships between ourselves and the audience, the audience members with each other, and everyone with the total environmental context. At each word spoken, one must manage a delicate process of adjusting to constant **feedback**, or the return messages that are constantly being sent by the other people involved in the communicative process. Oral communication is thus a means of inviting people to participate in a shared, **tactile** experience that involves what McLuhan calls the profound and unified "interplay of the senses."[9] In other words, being present at an oral performance is a whole-body experience that we feel "in touch with" in a way that cannot compare to the experience of watching the same speech on a video recording (and this includes even speeches that are incredibly boring; nothing makes you more intimately aware of your chair as a bad speech).

What makes it so difficult for those versed in the language of written or online communication to appreciate the uniqueness of public speaking is the habit of isolating the message from its context and judging it as if it were just a pamphlet or an e-mail. But the unique thing about public speaking is not the content or even the style of the words; it is the fact that the words are spoken in the company of others in a common, shared space. This almost intangible quality is more easily experienced than explained. It is the difference between being part of a graduation ceremony and receiving the diploma in the mail, between going to a place of worship to hear a sermon and reading a religious text at home, between making a toast at a wedding and sending a card of congratulations, between hearing an inspirational speech before a big game and receiving an e-mail of that speech, or between announcing the birth of a child before one's family at Thanksgiving and distributing a video of that speech online.

The fact is that public speaking is a unique and complex experience that cannot be reduced to the simple content of the message. For instance, despite the fact that written communication allows for more complicated factual and logical argumentation and online communication makes possible more sophisticated multimedia presentation, McLuhan observes that oral communication tends to be far more complex in terms of its ability to comprehend and bring together a diverse number of environmental elements into a coherent whole. He notes that dominantly oral communities "are made up of people differentiated, not by their specialist skills or visible marks, but by their unique emotional mixes."[10] Therefore, although oral communication is certainly less capable of precise diagnosis than written speech and is more restricted in scope than online communication, it is far more powerful in situated settings to bring about a feeling of meaningful group participation in a dramatic moment. These kinds of settings often are more capable of producing distinctly memorable events with the possibility of generating lasting relationships and commitments. Although occasions for public speaking may occur less frequently than occasions for written or online communication, they are far more capable of producing monuments of shared experience that act as a firm ground on which further written or online communication is built.

Perhaps the best way to appreciate the unique functions of a public speech is by experiencing the opposite—speeches that attempt to perform functions better performed by written or online communication. Particularly in organizational settings, so-called informative speeches are often given that really just summarize what is already written on paper. One has, during these speeches, the feeling that the speaker should have just "sent a memo on that." Alternatively, people often launch into speeches that try to re-create the experience of seeing a movie or a video that is better shared by simply being forwarded electronically. The reaction to such speeches is the proverbial, "I guess I needed to be there." A public speech should never be used as a replacement for a medium of communication that can do the job better. But the inverse is also true. Given the ease of sending e-mails, we often assume that a quick message can perform the job that oral communication should do. But there are many times when we need to address people in person, either in a conversation or in a speech. Knowing *what* to say is important, but even more important is knowing *how* to say something. So what is the context for rhetorical public speaking? It includes the following characteristics:

- ▶ An issue that is forefront in the consciousness of a public or publics
- ▶ A speech situation that occurs within a larger dramatic context with a past and a future
- ▶ The necessity or desire to make a judgment in a timely fashion
- ▶ The lack of time to wait until further inquiry, which mandates drawing on the best available information
- ▶ The ability for members of an audience to gather in a shared space
- ▶ The need to establish common understanding and closer relationships among members of the audience

Rhetoric that takes the form of public speaking generally attempts to accomplish the following goals:

- ▶ Establish or reinforce relationships between members of the audience
- ▶ Encourage dialogue in the audience subsequent to the speech's conclusion, which contributes to shared understanding and solidarity
- ▶ Make listeners more attentive to the significance of their physical and social surroundings

- ▶ Provide a dramatic narrative that projects and clarifies long-term goals

- ▶ Highlight the importance of the most important available means to attain those goals

- ▶ Create a unified emotional response capable of moving and inspiring an audience

DISCUSSION

Think of a public speech you attended with friends or family. In that memory, what stands out about the experience as separate from the content of the speech itself? How did being there affect your interpersonal interaction before, during, and after the speech? Last, what was the most memorable moment of that experience: the speech itself or the situation surrounding the speech?

▶ COMMUNICATION AND MEDIA

The easiest way to conceptualize the relationships between these three media of communication is by considering how they actually function in multilayered persuasive campaigns in marketing, politics, and religion. All three types of campaigns make use of each medium, although in different ways and in different ratios. Marketing campaigns rely heaviest on electronic media, relying on humorous, seductive, or shocking spectacles to attract attention to a product or issue. Print media, usually in the form of take-home pamphlets, provide more detailed information to interested parties. Yet despite the millions spent on electronic and print advertising, the spoken word remains important both in "closing the deal" (particularly with big-ticket items such as cars and houses) as well as in sparking interest in products through various forms of guerrilla marketing, such as paying college students to wear products and talk about them to other students without disclosing the fact that they are being paid.

Campaigns for political candidates rely even more heavily on the spoken word. On the one hand, we often talk about candidates being "packaged" and "sold" like products precisely because they use the exact same strategies as marketing by paying for television and radio advertisements and disseminating print material to explain their platforms. However, any viable candidate knows that he or she must commit to hundreds of speaking engagements, often addressing only several dozen people at a time in local communities without significant press coverage, in order to solidify support from those communities. In addition, campaigns for higher offices such as Congress or the presidency require a significant staff of volunteers who "canvas" neighborhoods by knocking on doors and speaking individually to hundreds and thousands of people. This type of canvassing is worthwhile not because volunteers actually speak to everyone in a voting precinct but because each person they do persuade usually then speaks to his or her own family and friends about the candidate, thus creating a word-of-mouth network of supporters.

Last, religious campaigns rely heaviest on the spoken word precisely because they are long-term affairs that ask for a lifetime commitment from audience members. This is not to say they do not make use of print or electronic media. In fact, most religions feature an established sacred "text" that can be taken home and studied by adherents in their solitude, and excerpts from this text are almost always included in various pamphlets that can be widely disseminated. And there is a long tradition of various religious faiths using televangelists, billboard campaigns, and television advertisements to deliver their messages. Yet the basic medium of any religious community is the spoken word, delivered either in a sacred space to a whole congregation or in the home with members of an immediate family. This is because the spoken word is a powerful unifying medium that brings people together with a common message that forms emotional bonds not only between speaker and audience but between audience members themselves. It is hardly surprising, therefore, that orators like Emerson speak of eloquence in religious terms, such that "words" which are spoken with truth and passion become the way to realize the "Word" of some higher power.

One does not have to import any such religious understanding of public speaking to appreciate its unique capacity, amongst all forms of communication, to produce the type of shared experience capable of creating both commitment and community. Therefore, when I refer to rhetorical public speaking as "the art of the engaged citizen," I do so not because writing or electronic communication are of less significance to democracy; I do so because it is the most universal form of communication that has the greatest potential to make a change at the local level insofar as it speaks directly to an intimate audience about affairs that directly impact their lives and communities. In an age that requires significant resources to produce and disseminate messages through print or electronic media in a way that will actually reach a wide and influential audience, it is naïve to think that mere access to the Internet somehow equalizes the playing field against well-funded institutions, corporations, and government agencies that can easily overwhelm the national and international media with a well-planned agenda and multilayered yet concentrated message. The fact remains that although print and electronic communication are essential to sustain democratic movement of any kind, they nonetheless must be grounded in the power of the spoken word, which allows individual citizens to confront the power grounded in control of resources with the power of collective commitment grounded in shared experience that is constituted and made conscious by rhetorical public speech.

Of course, the value of public speech is not only found in the political sphere. Public speaking is also the art of the loving family member, the dedicated coach, the charismatic business leader, the persuasive salesperson, the inspirational teacher, the prophetic preacher, and the successful lawyer. Public speaking continues to justify its existence whenever people gather together in the same space to have a chance to hear what everyone else hears, to feel what everyone else feels, to consider what everyone else has considered, and to potentially act together in the knowledge that all present have heard, felt, and considered the same thing. There is no written or electronic substitute for a story told by a grandmother to her grandchildren in the living room, the halftime speech in the locker room, the confrontational challenge by the chief executive in the boardroom, the witty banter that goes on in an automobile showroom, the give-and-take that occurs in the classroom, or the pathos-written appeal delivered by a lawyer in the courtroom.

These are moments that demand the spoken word, and they are the moments for which this book has been written.

▶ DEALING WITH SPEECH ANXIETY

One of the side effects of the proliferation of electronic media, particularly anonymous social media, is an increase in the level of speech anxiety. The reason is obvious. The more we are given opportunities to avoid face-to-face contact with people and instead communicate primarily using text or images sent via computers, tablets, or smart phones, the more that standing physically in front of a group of people to give a speech makes us feel all the more vulnerable, nervous, and exposed by contrast. But people have always had a fear of public speaking. For decades it has ranked among the top three fears that people possess. The only difference today is that we have so many more opportunities to avoid public speaking when we can simply write an e-mail or post something on Facebook. But as explained in the previous section, we cannot avoid public speaking altogether. Any member of a family, social group, or organization has a need to gather together physically in one place in order to feel unified and intimately connected with others. Indeed, the rise in social media has led to an ever-increasing capacity to meet people in face-to-face settings, which has made public speaking more rather than less important.

The most important step in dealing with speech anxiety is simply recognizing that it is normal and then in identifying the factors that go into it. Michael Beatty identified eight factors of a speech situation that tend to increase **speech anxiety**: the novelty of the experience, the formality of the occasion, the subordinate status of the speaker, the degree of conspicuousness felt by the speaker, an unfamiliar environment, the dissimilarity and degree of attention from others, the degree to which one is being evaluated, and prior history.[11] Added to these situational factors is also the degree to which speech anxiety, for many people, is akin to an inborn, genetic predisposition.[12] Dealing with speech anxiety is thus a complex challenge, as each speaker's anxiety will be unique and derived from different sources. The following are some ways to approach speech anxiety that may be useful in preparing for a speech:[13]

1. *Nervousness is natural*: Being nervous is a biological manifestation of the "fight-or-flight" mechanism. It shows that your body is preparing you to deal with a challenging situation. The goal is not to get rid of nervousness but to harness that energy and use it to your advantage.

2. *Everyone experiences it*: Speech anxiety is universal. Even the greatest speakers get anxious because so much is riding on their words. But the feelings they experience are the same as those of a beginning student. The difference is that they have more tools to deal with that anxiety.

3. *You appear more relaxed than you feel*: Anxiety rarely manifests itself in overt signs of stress that can be seen by an audience. The most common expressions of stress are shaking hands and flushed faces, but usually they bother the speaker more than the audience.

4. *Have something important to say*: Nothing rattles a speaker more than standing up only to find that one's speech is boring even to oneself. Hastily written speeches made simply to "get it over with" are, more often than not, the causes of speech anxiety because one starts judging one's own speech as a failure. Taking the time to say something you want to say makes speaking a much more pleasurable experience.

5. *Visualize success*: Like almost any coach in competitive sports will tell you, if you focus on the little things, you will get so caught up in minutiae that you lose sight of the "big picture." As simplistic as it sounds, sometimes success comes from visualizing oneself succeeding.

6. *Release tension before speaking*: Purely on a physical note, clenching and then releasing muscles or exerting energy in some way loosens you up and often gets rid of nervousness that has been built up in your muscles.

7. *The audience is usually on your side*: With rare political exceptions, people do not attend speeches to watch people fail. They attend speeches to listen to people they find interesting. Hence, the audience will almost always wish for a speaker to do well. Despite the fact that they are ultimately "judging" your speech, they are a jury that hopes you succeed.

8. *Practice*: Nothing replaces simple practice. Simply knowing the words of a speech is not sufficient for a good performance. You need to feel "at one" with the speech so that your words and actions occur naturally together. Practice until you have memorized the speech and then practice again until you have completely internalized it. Usually, shoot for reading a speech out loud to yourself three times before delivering it to your audience. Reading it "in your head" *is not* the same as reading out loud. Actually verbalizing the words helps your mouth get used to saying the words and your ears get used to hearing them.

9. *Experience makes you more confident*: The more you speak in public, the easier it will become. We learn by habit, and public speaking can become a habit once you break through the initial fear. By the end of a public speaking class, one may even begin to find pleasure in this habit.

This series of "tips" addresses the basics of putting oneself in the right frame of mind for public speaking. However, not all speech anxiety can be dealt with by such simple attitude adjustments. A more systematic and clinical list of treatments includes the following:[14]

1. *Systemic desensitization*: This procedure attempts to change unconscious negative associations with speaking situations. First, it introduces students to methods of relaxation (e.g., meditation), and once relaxed, a trainer has them visualize a series of speech situations, beginning with the least stressful and progressively increasing in perceived anxiety. Through repetition, individuals become more familiar with public speaking situations, thus normalizing them.

2. *Cognitive modification*: This treatment deals with negative and irrational cognitions of public speaking that take the form of beliefs, such as "I can't do this" or "It's too frightening." With a trained therapist, individuals discuss specific fears about public speaking, including their self-evaluations, after which the therapist shows the irrationality of such self-evaluations and provides a coping statement (e.g., "I can handle this") that can be used while speaking.

3. *COM therapy*: Another method of treatment is to change an individual's orientation toward the function of public speaking. For those who hold a "performance-oriented" view, public speaking is like a trial by jury in which one is to perform and be judged. COM therapy attempts to change this orientation into a "communication-oriented" view in which public speaking is more like conversation in which each party is simply taking longer turns.

4. *Visualization*: Similar to systemic desensitization, visualization also begins with relaxation techniques, but instead of focusing simply on familiarizing oneself with the public speaking context, it focuses on visualizing success within that context. Visualization is thus a natural extension of cognitive modification.

5. *Skills training*: Skills training is another way of saying that practice, experience, and mastery will improve the confidence of public speakers.

6. *Performance feedback*: Another term for *constructive criticism*, performance feedback involves using nonverbal, oral, or written responses to a speaker's performance directed toward improving that performance. Notably, research shows that negative comments (when given in a constructive and honest spirit) are more helpful than positive ones, as they give speakers a sense that they know the problem and have the means to address it.

After years of research, studies have shown that no one method tends to work for all individuals. Each person faces his or her own particular type of anxiety and must develop a method tailored to individual needs. However, employing a variety of methods at different times, each overlapping the other, tends to have more benefit than adopting only one.

▶ A DEFINITION OF RHETORIC

Once we overcome speech anxiety, the question then turns to the specific goals or purposes that are served by public speaking. This book addresses this question by emphasizing the *rhetorical* qualities of public speaking. What does that term mean? "Rhetoric" is often used in public discourse or casual conversation to mean simply "empty words" (as opposed to action) or "false speech" (as opposed to truth). But in history, rhetoric refers to the art of public deliberation and persuasion that arose within the Greek democracies during the time of Pericles and the Persian Wars. As democracy spread through the Greek world, particularly in Athens, and expanded from the law courts into political and social forums, instruction in the art of rhetoric flourished and became progressively formalized, first by the development of a class of itinerant teachers called the Sophists and later by the more institutional education provided by the schools of Plato and Aristotle. This is not to say that rhetorical practice in Greece was an egalitarian enterprise. Access to education was restricted to those with financial resources, and the ability to even participate in politics was restricted to a relative minority of male citizens—women and slaves being two major groups excluded from public life. The birth of rhetoric thus did not lead to a "Golden Age" for everyone. Many of the powerless remained powerless, in part because they were denied both access to the political forum and the artful tools necessary to influence others.

Nonetheless, rhetoric and democracy contributed to each other's development because both were concerned with facilitating the process of collective judgment, even if for a relatively small—if expanding—group of free citizens. The more the burdens of advocacy and judgment were placed upon the shoulders of individual citizens, the more urgent that training in rhetoric became; the more citizens became skilled in rhetoric, the more they craved and demanded participation in the decision-making processes of governance. It was thus in Greece that rhetoric established its position as an *art*—not in the sense of being a form of creative self-expression, but in the sense of being a practical skill based on a body of knowledge, much as we think of engineering or architecture.

In the tradition of Greece and then Rome, the teaching of rhetoric was formalized into what they called the five "canons of rhetoric"—invention, arrangement, style, delivery, and memory. The canons of rhetoric provided a method for building a speech that produces such form. *Invention* provided categories that were helpful in focusing our attention on specific aspects of our environment to see what we could find there, including history, books, testimony, and experience. *Arrangement* then provided conventional templates or frameworks they could use to organize the things that they had found. It helped them rearrange material in new patterns to find the most appropriate and effective way to bring order out of a chaos of resources. *Style* then brought all of these elements together into a fluid whole by using tropes and figures to communicate complex facts and examples in a way more pleasing and with more comprehensible images and feelings. *Memory* provides the techniques for committing a speech to memory and making it feel like a natural expression of one's self rather than a written text. Last, *delivery* ensured that the brilliance of the composition was effectively transmitted to the audience through the actions and words of the speaker, including voice, gestures, and eye contact. Because these remain relevant to public speaking today, these canons will form the bases of the early chapters in this book.

But what exactly is rhetoric? The definition this book will use is the following: **rhetorical public speaking** *is the art of addressing pressing public concerns by employing deliberate persuasive strategies before a public audience at a specific occasion in order to transform some aspect of a problematic situation by encouraging new forms of thought and action.* In other words, rhetoric involves us in the social and political struggle over **meaning** and, hence, over power. It is about how people use language and symbols to transform the way a society or community thinks, feels, and behaves. Rhetoric is ultimately about how people act as agents of social change, using whatever symbolic power they can harness to move people from this place to that place.

This definition can be broken down into the following parts:

1. *The art*: Referring to rhetoric as an art distinguishes it from a mere instinctual or unreflective talent. *Art* thus does not mean an intuitive creativity or genius lacking in method. Quite the opposite, art requires the application of rational concepts and methods in the creative process of guiding situated judgment.

2. *of addressing pressing public concerns*: Except for matters of idle curiosity, the only reason we voluntarily expose ourselves to rhetorical discourse is because it speaks to a shared concern that is in the forefront of our consciousness. We listen to rhetoric with the hope that the person speaking might be able to suggest a path out of our current predicament or a solution to our current problem.

3. *by employing deliberate persuasive strategies*: Persuasion is often accidental or a product of sheer luck. This does not alter its *function* as a persuasive message, but it does change how we evaluate it in terms of *art*. In contradistinction to rhetorical criticism, which can evaluate anything that strikes us as persuasive, the productive art of rhetoric concerns itself with improving how something is produced, and one cannot improve accident or luck.

4. *before a public audience*: The *public* character of the audience means that it addresses an audience of relative strangers who come together to address areas of common concern. Persuading an audience of friends may still employ rhetoric, but that rhetoric generally appeals to the unique bonds of those friends rather than their shared characteristics as part of a larger public.

5. *at a specific occasion*: This aspect addresses the situated character of rhetoric *as a form of public speaking* and not simply a genre of persuasion. One can, of course, create rhetorical discourse in the form of a written or visual medium. The use of the Internet has certainly led to an explosion of attempts at long-distance persuasion. But rhetorical *public speech* more narrowly refers to rhetoric delivered in the physical presence of others.

6. *in order to transform some aspect of a problematic situation*: Rhetoric seeks to change some aspect of the natural or social environment that is *felt* to be problematic by members of a public. This shared experience of uncertainty, anxiety, and urgency focuses people's attention on a speech and thus gives it a unique power. Absent such a situation, the same speech might be experienced not as rhetoric, but as a form of poetry, news, or entertainment. It is not the speech itself that determines its character, but the total context in which it is spoken.

7. *by encouraging new forms of thought and action*: The means by which rhetoric transforms that environment is by symbolic persuasion—by the use of symbols which encourage other people to change their attitudes toward objective things in the world. Rhetoric is thus an indirect form of action. It makes changes by changing what people think and do with the hope that their behaviors might resolve some shared problem.

Because rhetoric becomes rhetoric only within urgent contexts of judgment, rhetorical public speech is a fundamentally *ethical* activity insofar as it forces one to take a stand about what "good" we should pursue and how we should pursue it. Paradoxically, however, the very problematic aspect of the rhetorical situation often throws into question the conventional ethical standards that had guided previous action. Thus, rhetorical public speakers must do more than seek mere tactical "success"; they must also determine what success would look like in such a situation

DISCUSSION

One of the most enduring rhetorical moments following the terror attacks of 9/11 was the image of President George W. Bush standing atop World Trade Center rubble, addressing an audience of workers with a bullhorn. How did this particular speech fit the definition of rhetoric? What aspect of the speech do you think was the most (and least) artistic?

and then justify that vision on the basis of a reflective ethical judgment. And to do that successfully means constructing an argument using the tools of reason (*logos*), credibility (*ethos*), emotion (*pathos*), and style (*lexis*) capable of challenging and transforming some aspect of public sentiment in the face of opposition.

▶ DIGITAL RHETORIC

When the Internet first became prevalent in modern culture, many people wondered if public speaking was going to be a lost art. In its original form, the Internet was primarily a platform for text and the occasional picture, thus making e-mail and html pages the dominant form of electronic communication. However, in today's digital age, the means by which high definition video can be recorded, uploaded, and distributed almost instantaneously has made the early days of the Internet appear like the Stone Age. Today, the online environment is dominated by video rather than text. Perhaps even more importantly, this video is often recorded on location by individuals with smart phones. Indeed, the capacity for ordinary citizens to record events as they occur and to simultaneously comment on what they are seeing has revolutionized the production and distribution of news. Now, news broadcasts often follow what citizens record on their own rather than vice versa.

All of these conditions have created the possibility for a new kind of **digital rhetoric**, by which I mean a type of public speaking in which individuals speak directly to the audience but do so not from a conventional public speaking context—an auditorium or rostrum—but from more intimate or on-site locations that imitate more traditional journalistic techniques. In these cases, digital rhetoric is not simply a long public speech recorded and rebroadcast online. Digital rhetoric is actually designed specifically for the video medium, and in this case makes use of film-style editing, broadcast-news style graphics and voiceovers, and a more direct and "close-up" style of delivery. Generally, this type of digital rhetoric is highly condensed and short enough to be viewed within a couple of minutes or less—perhaps while someone is standing in line for a coffee, waiting at a bus stop, or just having lunch.

All of the exercises at the end of each chapter will therefore contain one exercise that will provide an opportunity to make use of traditional public speaking strategies within the new context of digital rhetoric. The means by which these videos will be recorded, edited, and distributed will be left up to the student and the instructor based on the available technology—certainly by the time this book is published, any recommendations will have already been rendered obsolete. But with today's smart phone technology, any phone can record high quality video, edit it using an available movie-editing application, and either be forwarded as a video file to the instructor or uploaded onto a video-sharing site so that all students can view each other's videos. However, here are some general instructions for how to produce these videos:

1. *Record horizontally*: All video players use a horizontal screen to replay videos. Never use a vertical recording (that is, holding a phone upright rather than sideways) or it will appear narrow on playback with black empty space on either side.

2. *Keep it short*: An ideal artifact of digital rhetoric should be two minutes or less.

3. *Keep it quick*: Unlike public speeches, which can use pauses and patience to great effect, digital rhetoric relies on eliminating almost all pauses or empty time. Even if a speaker is directly addressing the audience for a minute, cut out long moments in which nothing is happening, in which "long" means one or two seconds.

4. *Avoid backlighting*: One simple way to improve your video quality is to avoid having a bright light behind your speaking subject. This puts your subject into shadow. Do not stand in front of a lamp or window or a bright sky. Instead, always have the light shining directly on you with a darker background.

5. *Use close-ups*: A video is a close-up medium. There is no reason to see your whole body or your whole room unless those things are an actual part of your speech. When you are speaking, try to include only your head and your torso and your hands.

6. *Use quick cuts*: Part of the fun of a video is the ability to turn the camera and capture other images before turning back to the speaker. For instance, if you are speaking of your messy apartment, you can start with a close-up on the individual and then do a quick cut in which the entire apartment is viewed before returning to a close-up.

7. *Alternative between direct speech and voiceover*: Similarly, try to alternate between addressing the camera directly and simply voicing over images that refer to the subject matter of your speech. Capturing a series of short images of litter on campus and stringing them together under a voiceover can be a powerful way to convey specific examples and give evidence.

8. *Use exaggeration*: Unlike in face-to-face interactions, video often rewards exaggerated gestures and facial expressions. Because of the close-up medium, one does not have to move around a great deal to make an impact. The close-up medium can often mean that subtle changes in facial expressions have a significant effect on a message.

9. *Change location*: Digital rhetoric is particularly effective in being able to immediately show the speaker in different environments. You might start speaking in your apartment and then immediately appear on the street or in a field or at a rally. During these times you might also capture other people's voices.

10. *Stay on message*: Digital rhetoric is not a medium to convey a complex and in-depth message. It is a medium to make a single point and to make it effectively and vividly. The beginning of your video must state exactly what it is doing, then it should do it, then it should remind the viewers what they just saw.

With the arrival of digital rhetoric, the techniques of public speaking have become ever more prominent in today's world. Indeed, as any individual can now capture on video any act of public speaking that previously would have only been confined to the people physically present, it becomes even more imperative to feel confident in one's speaking ability. Far from being obsolete, public speaking in a digital age has become perhaps the primary source of viral videos, political campaigns, social activism, and corporate social responsibility. Messages simply mean more when we connect them directly with the speaker and see them in action. That is an essential part of human nature and it will not soon change with technology. Indeed, technology only enhances what we instinctively desire.

▶ INTRODUCTION EXERCISES

1. **IMPROMPTU:** Recall the moment that you first gained access to portable electronic communication—namely some kind of smart phone (or, alternately, if you have never possessed one, think of the moment in which others possessed them while you did not). Tell a story about this moment and focus specifically on how your habits of communication changed with the people close to you, namely your friends and family. What kind of communication practices did you abandon, which stayed the same, and which changed? How was your life different before and after?

2. **DEBATE:** Consider the question of whether face-to-face communication is considered more "genuine" and "honest" than mediated forms of communication. For instance, it is a cultural maxim that genuine sincerity and trust can only be ensured when you "look a person in the eye." Do you think this is true? Alternately, do you think the prevalence of anonymous forms of communication in social media has made people more honest or more deceptive? Divide yourselves into two sides based on your beliefs and construct pro and con arguments for each position.

3. **GROUP:** Divide yourselves into groups and take a moment to share your own anxieties about public speaking, recalling in particular any past situation that you would generally consider a "public speaking failure." After sharing the stories, come up with what you believe to be the best approach to solving the problem and deliver a short "rhetorical" speech in which you advocate for your solution to the class as if you were selling a product.

4. **TAKE HOME:** Find a full-page print advertisement in a magazine that includes at least some text. To better understand the difference between print and orality, bring the advertisement into class and read the text out loud without, at first, showing the pictures. Then reveal the full advertisement and explain to the class why the picture corresponds with the text. What is the difference in how we experience the advertisement when it is delivered as a public speech as opposed to being encountered as a printed text?

5. **VIDEO:** To introduce yourself to the act of producing digital rhetoric, record a short introductory speech in which you simply talk about some of the interesting things in your dormitory, apartment, or room. Practice using quick editing so that you are able to cut together multiple scenes showcasing different objects without any transitions or gaps. The video should be short but packed with different images and objects in order to get a sense of what is interesting about your surroundings and which demonstrates something about yourself.

▶ NOTES

1. Ralph Waldo Emerson, "Eloquence," available at http://oll.libertyfund.org/?option=com_staticxt& staticfile=show.php%3Ftitle=86&chapter=104478&layout=html&Itemid=27 (accessed 15 December 2011).

2. Walter Ong, *Orality and Literacy* (New York: Routledge, 2002), 67.

3. Plato, *Phaedrus*, In *Plato: Complete Works*, trans. Alexander Nehamas and Paul Woodruff, ed. John M. Cooper (Indianapolis: Hackett Publishing, 1997), 275b.

4. Aristotle, *Rhetoric*, In *The Rhetoric and the Poetics of Aristotle*, trans. W. Rhys Roberts, ed. Edward P. J. Corbett (New York: The Modern Library, 1984), 1413b5.

5. Aristotle, *Rhetoric*, 1413b1020.

6. John Dewey, *The Public and Its Problems* (Athens: Ohio University Press, 1954), 218.

7. Marshall McLuhan, *Understanding Media: The Extensions of Man* (Boston: MIT Press, 1994), 79.

8. McLuhan, *Understanding Media*, 248.

9. McLuhan, *Understanding Media*, 77–79, 314.

10. McLuhan, *Understanding Media*, 50.

11. M. J. Beatty, "Situational and Predispositional Correlates of Public Speaking Anxiety," *Communication Education* 37 (1988), 28–39.

12. M. J. Beatty, J.C. McCroskey, and A.D. Heisel, "Communication Apprehension as Temperamental Expression: A Communibiological Paradigm," *Communication Monographs* 65 (1998), 197–219.

13. For more on speech anxiety, see Virginia P. Richmond and James C. McCroskey, *Communication: Apprehension, Avoidance, and Effectiveness*, 5th ed. (Boston: Allyn & Bacon, 1998); Peter Desberg, *No More Butterflies: Overcoming Stagefright, Shyness, Interview Anxiety, and Fear of Public Speaking* (Oakland, CA: New Harbinger, 1996).

14. The following list is a paraphrased summary of the conclusions presented in Graham D. Bodie, "A Racing Heart, Rattling Knees, and Ruminative Thoughts: Defining, Explaining, and Treating Public Speaking Anxiety," *Communication Education* 59, no. 1 (January 2010), 70–105.

1

Genres of Public Speaking

This chapter defines the appropriate contexts for public speaking and identifies the genres that are appropriate for distinct occasions. The notion of rhetorical "genre" refers to different arrangements of elements in a composition or discourse that are appropriate to certain occasions. Identifying what kind of genre is appropriate within a situation is perhaps the most important consideration any public speaker can make, for it provides the proper "form" in which claims can be made and ideas structured and expressed. Although the number of speech genres is, literally, countless, they generally can be divided into speeches of introduction, enrichment, advocacy, commemoration, encouragement, deliberation, solicitation, administration, and invective. The goal of this chapter is to provide a general method of organization and invention that enables a public speaker to achieve a level of decorum.

It may seem unusual to begin a book on public speaking by defining types of speeches rather than the "basics" of public speaking. For instance, it is not unusual for textbooks to begin with a chapter on "introductions" under the logic that one should begin at the "beginning." However, this is to misunderstand the actual logic and method of public speaking—particularly *rhetorical* public speaking. The problem is that it takes for granted not only on acquaintance with the over-all structure of a public speech, but assumes a desire and intention to give a public speech. But the fact is that people only engage in public speaking because there is a need and necessity to do so. We speak to others in public because the situation demands it—because some problem must be resolved or some goal attained. Without knowing the specific purpose of giving a speech or being aware of the general form in which a speech should take, there is hardly any use in pursuing a step-by-step method. The goal of this chapter, therefore, is to give an overall acquaintance with the different situations in which public speaking is called for and to distinguish them from one another. Its aim is to show the many different circumstances in which public speaking becomes a necessity in our everyday experiences. Public speaking is not some rare and unusual phenomena only pursued by celebrities and politicians. It is an activity that occurs in our homes, our workplaces, amongst friends, in the locker room, or in the boardroom.

All **public speeches** are interpreted by members of an audience as fitting a certain "genre." A rhetorical speech **genre** represents a coherent and recognized arrangement of elements in a composition or discourse that is appropriate to certain occasions and that creates audience expectations that constrain and guide a speech's content, style, and delivery. In rhetoric, genres are not properties of the speeches themselves in the way we think of, for example, color as a property of flowers; genres exist primarily in the mind. A genre is a method of interpreting a particular type of object, much in the way that a painting of flowers by Monet would be interpreted by the genre "Impressionism," whereas a painting of flowers by Picasso might be interpreted by the genre "Cubism." Genres are therefore practical tools that speakers can use to anticipate and control the reactions of an audience. Related to notions of appropriateness and occasion, speaking genres refer to what people *actually expect* (and prepare themselves to hear) when they attend a speech, much in the way that rooms in museums are given "generic" labels so that visitors will know what to expect on entering.[1]

The function of a genre is therefore to provide an audience with a framework of interpretation that situates any novelty within a stable and predictable structure that the audience can readily understand. Audiences attend and listen to public speeches at certain occasions with certain expectations of what they will hear and how they will hear it. Attendees of celebrity roasts, for example, *expect* that good friends of the "roastee" will all stand up to offer witty but biting remarks at his or her expense. To hear someone praise the host would be to violate the norms of appropriateness for the occasion—it would be to ignore the constraints of the speaking genre. The political stump speech also represents a certain genre, as does the religious sermon, the graduation speech, the parental lecture, the soapbox diatribe, the tearful public apology, the sales pitch, the friendly advice, the boss's reprimand, and the coach's inspirational rant. When we encounter these types of speeches, we can expect to hear certain things while knowing that other parts will be left out.

As with most things rhetorical, it was Aristotle who provided the first articulate categorization of the speech genres. When Aristotle defined the three dominant rhetorical genres, he based his definitions on what he saw in actual life. As the foremost scholar of Greek civilization, Aristotle could not ignore rhetoric precisely because it was so ingrained in almost every aspect of the Greek world. For a Greek philosopher to ignore rhetoric was to ignore what it meant to be a Greek in the Classical age. In his time, most public affairs were dealt with through the medium of face-to-face **public speaking**. Speeches in the courts (law), in the assembly (politics), and at ceremonial events (culture) structured and guided the collective life of the city-state. Aristotle's genres thus corresponded to these circumstances: **forensic speech** occurred in law courts, dealt with the past, and addressed matters of the just and unjust; **deliberative speech** occurred in the assembly, dealt with the future, and addressed matters of the expedient and the inexpedient; and **epideictic speech** occurred at ceremonial events, dealt with the present (or eternal), and addressed matters of praise and blame (including the playful praise and blame of animals and things).

Aristotle's crucial insight is his definition of a genre not by the qualities of the speech itself but by the expectations of the audience under the circumstances of the occasion. As he writes: "rhetoric falls into three divisions, determined by the three classes of listeners to speeches. For of the three elements in speechmaking—speaker, subject, and person addressed—it is the last one, the hearer, that determines the speech's end and object."[2] The rhetorical speech genres of deliberative, forensic, and epideictic should therefore be considered *ways of listening* before they should be considered *ways of speaking*. That is to say, we identify a speech as a certain type of genre less because of the inherent qualities in the speech itself and more because we interpret those qualities as being designed to satisfy certain expectations in an audience. When we visit a parliamentary body, we expect to hear deliberative debates about what to do about pending problems; when we enter a courtroom, we expect to hear forensic debates about the nature and quality of past actions; and when we gather for national holidays, we expect to hear epideictic addresses giving praise to the objects, events, and people we value as a nation. To fail to satisfy these expectations as a speaker is not to deliver one genre instead of another; it is simply not to deliver the goods at all.

The important lesson to be taken away from this discussion is that any successful speech must begin with a detailed consideration of the expectations of an audience before developing persuasive strategies to meet those expectations. Too often, speakers begin composing speeches by asking the question: "What do I want to say?" The actual question to begin with is: "What does my audience want to hear?" In other words, the outgoing act of listening by audience members always precedes successful expression by the speaker. After all, rhetorical public speaking as an oral performance is not delivered to a random group of people who simply happen to have found themselves at the same place at the same time. They have gathered there for a reason. They have a purpose for listening. For the speaker to take their interest for granted, and then to simply say whatever happens to be on his or her mind, reveals a speaker who is highly inconsiderate and overly self-involved. Thinking about your speech in terms of conforming to a genre is therefore an essential step in the act of composition, for it encourages thinking about the listener as an active agent rather than a passive target.

Although Aristotle's three categories remain useful in interpreting contemporary speeches, new speech genres are necessary to adapt to changing speech contexts. Unfortunately, the tradition of public speaking has long held to the rather unimaginative triad of informative, persuasive, and commemorative speaking, usually understood to mean speeches that convey accurate and relevant information, speeches that take a position pro or con on an issue, and speeches that praise something the speaker thinks is valuable. The problem with these categories is that they do not begin with the listener and the occasion, but instead imply that the nature of the speech is rooted in the intentions of the speaker and in the structure of the speech. Anyone who has taught public speaking for any length of time using such categories has encountered situations in which "The life of our Savior Jesus Christ" is submitted as an informative speech, in which "Why I think smoking is bad for you" is submitted as a persuasive speech, and in which "My loyal dog Max" is submitted as a commemorative speech. From the perspective of the speaker, these may seem to be valid speech topics. But from the perspective of the audience (in this case being a diverse group of two dozen university students), they are not. Clearly the "informative" speech will be interpreted by most people as being persuasive, the "persuasive" speech will be interpreted by most people as being redundant, and the "commemorative" speech will be largely frivolous. But these topics are difficult to reject using criteria that do not bring the audience into account.

Compounding this problem is the fact that the distinction between "informative" and "persuasive" speaking is largely erroneous. As Aristotle and every other Greek well understood, rhetoric is the art of **persuasion**. Consequently, there is no such thing as a rhetorical public speech that does not persuade in some way. The only question is what it is persuasive *about*. But that question cannot be understood apart from the perspective of the audience. On the one hand, the most dry and technical "informative" speech may be interpreted very persuasively by specific audiences. To use a very simple example, a speech about the history and origin of the myth of Santa Claus would be considered by most adults to be an informative speech. But for a 3-year-old child, it would be a highly persuasive speech intended to challenge one of his or her most core beliefs. On the other hand, the most passionately delivered "persuasive" speech may be completely boring to audience member who already believe everything that the speaker is trying to advocate. No child, after all, wastes her time trying to persuade her brothers and sisters that Santa Claus should bring them all as many gifts as possible. The child instead tries to persuade her siblings that Santa Claus favors her the most and hence will give her the most gifts—a most difficult, if not impossible, task.

This chapter will focus on defining the four primary speeches that will be taught in almost any classroom but will rename two of the speeches to conform to a more appropriate understanding of rhetorical persuasion. This book will retain the title for speeches of introduction and commemoration but will rename an "informative speech" as the more appropriate "speech of enrichment" while a "persuasive speech" will be called a "speech of advocacy." In order to better understand these four major genres, however, this chapter will also briefly define other common genres of speech, including speeches of encouragement, deliberation, solicitation, administration, and invective. The goal of these new categorizations is to focus attention on the occasion of the speech and the expectations of the listeners during those occasions in such a way that provides a general roadmap for how to structure a speech so as to satisfy those expectations. However, it is important to keep in mind that each term only points out the dominant *tendency* of certain speeches delivered at certain occasions. For just as all speeches persuade, most speeches, in some way, also *introduce, encourage, deliberate, solicit, commemorate, enrich, administer, advocate, and criticize.* Yet each individual speech will emphasize certain tendencies over others and may ignore some tendencies completely. One should think of each tendency of a speech as being one column on a music equalizer, therefore giving each speech its own unique equalization.

Selecting a speech genre is therefore much like selecting a preset equalization on a stereo as a starting point before making more detailed modifications based on the unique circumstance.

DISCUSSION

Consider Aristotle's three speech genres of forensic, deliberative, and epideictic and their respective emphasis on the past and justice/injustice, the future and expediency/inexpediency, and the present and praise/blame. Now consider the perspective of a parent in a household. In what context does a parent make these three types of speeches in a family context? In which room do they occur most of the time? What is the purpose of each type of speech, and what kinds of situations does each respond to?

▶ THE MAJOR SPEECH GENRES

This chapter will distinguish between "major" and "minor" speech genres. These are not categories intended to rank the level of importance of one genre over another. Any genre is equally important within the context of the situation. However, major speech genres are the ones that occur most frequently and have the widest applicability to different situations. Furthermore, they are typically the speech genres that will be assigned in any public speaking classroom, usually in the order that is discussed below. Speeches of introduction, enrichment, advocacy, and commemoration form the core of any knowledge of public speaking, and what methods are used in the four major speech genres are applied in different ways in the minor speech genres.

▶ SPEECHES OF INTRODUCTION

Introduction speeches seek to establish a relationship with an audience of strangers by using narratives to disclose central aspects of one's character that the speaker believes he or she shares with others. In many ways, an introductory speech fulfills the same function as a conversation or interview. However, the context is different. Whereas conversations or interviews happen among a few people, speeches of introduction are given before a larger group. Introductory speeches thus must be general enough to establish a broad relationship between speaker and audience that can include a number of different people.

There are two typical occasions for such speeches. First, introductory speeches are given by members of a group who wish to establish friendly and trustworthy relationships with one another. The speeches are either delivered by select individuals who have recently been assigned a role in a pre-established group (such as a new employee at work) or are delivered by each member of an impromptu group of strangers (such as a newly formed neighborhood book club) who have come together usually for more social than utilitarian goals. The overall goal of introductory speeches in this context is to create trust and a feeling of cooperation. Second, introductory speeches of a more rhetorical variety are given by individuals vying for support of an audience, for instance a candidate for office. In these cases, speeches of introduction are meant to solicit support and establish credibility.

The *listeners* for introductory speeches are people who expect to have some future interaction with the speaker in a cooperative environment, such as the workplace, the dormitory, the church, the classroom, the athletic team, or the community association. Consequently, they will want to gauge the overall attitudes and interests of the speaker in order to know what to expect of the speaker and to determine whether there are any qualities or experiences that they share that can form the basis of future conversations. The *speaker* in such occasions should usually present him- or herself as "one of the group" by speaking with good humor but also with humility, thereby avoiding the sense that one is simply putting on a show for the sake of applause. This does not mean having to dress and speak like everyone else, of course. One should preserve one's own unique personality in an introductory speech. The point is rather that one should not amplify such unique traits as a way of "impressing" an audience with one's charm and intellect, which usually simply serves to alienate one from the group. The *speaker* should strive to preserve individuality while at the same time putting him- or herself on the same level with others. The content of the *message* should largely be stories and anecdotes that are intrinsically interesting and that demonstrate some quality of the speaker's personality rather than those that are designed to prove a point. The message should be delivered casually and should strive to feel more like a conversation than a lecture delivered from the podium, which creates a sense of distance or authority.

Sarah Palin: "I Was Just Your Average Hockey Mom"

When Republican Senator John McCain ran for office in 2008 against Barack Obama, he surprised many political insiders by choosing as his running mate Alaska governor Sarah Palin, who previously had not been known on the national stage. During her address on September 3, 2008, at the Republican National Convention, Palin had to give an introductory speech to the nation:

> My mom and dad both worked at the elementary school in our small town. And among the many things I owe them is one simple lesson: that this is America, and every woman can walk through every door of opportunity. My parents are here tonight, and I am so proud to be the daughter of Chuck and Sally Heath. Long ago, a young farmer and haberdasher from Missouri followed an unlikely path to the vice presidency.

> A writer observed: "We grow good people in our small towns, with honesty, sincerity, and dignity." I know just the kind of people that writer had in mind when he praised Harry Truman. I grew up with those people. They are the ones who do some of the hardest work in America who grow our food, run our factories and fight our wars. They love their country, in good times

and bad, and they're always proud of America. I had the privilege of living most of my life in a small town.

I was just your average hockey mom and signed up for the PTA because I wanted to make my kids' public education better. When I ran for City Council, I didn't need focus groups and voter profiles because I knew those voters, and knew their families, too. Before I became governor of the great state of Alaska, I was mayor of my hometown.[3]

DISCUSSION

What are the ways in which Palin tries to establish a relationship to her audience? What is the type of "American" that Palin appears to be speaking to? What phrases particularly stand out that make her both an individual and also a member of a group? Think back on a time when you had to introduce yourself to a group of strangers. What aspect of shared experience did you try to emphasize?

▶ SPEECHES OF ENRICHMENT

Speeches of **enrichment** satisfy an audience's desire to successfully pursue preexisting interests by giving lively and engaging instruction about objects, events, processes, or concepts that promise to benefit the audience members' lives in some way. The term *enrichment* is meant to bridge the supposed division between information and entertainment. As noted earlier, there is no such thing as an "informative" speech; even if there was one, written forms of communication are better suited to disseminating detailed information anyway. Oral speech simply cannot even hope to mimic the logical complexity and efficiency of writing. Moreover, oral forms of communication, by their very nature, must satisfy more demands than simply the conveyance of data or else an audience will get restless. *Enrichment* thus closer approximates the *actual* function of so-called informative speaking, insofar as it does not seek so much to deliver "the facts" as it does to motivate an audience and to generate enthusiasm for things that the audience may have heard about but never took the time to investigate.

Speeches of enrichment are generally given in situations in which an audience has already acknowledged its lack of awareness about some problem or issue and has voluntarily attended an occasion to gain this knowledge in order to resolve a situation (such as learning how to get a job in a bad economy), to satisfy curiosity (such as learning about the latest discoveries of planets outside our solar system), or to enrich one's life (such as learning how to appreciate good wine). A good speaker in this genre will base whatever is said on the audience's **interests**, which are things that people enjoy doing, want to know about, or desire to attain. The speaker will present information in an entertaining but *noncontroversial* manner such that he or she is not advocating a particular position. For once audience members feel that they are not being informed, but being manipulated or pushed, they will no longer receive the information as a gift for enrichment, but as an active solicitation.

Speeches of enrichment (at least outside of the formal classroom) include such things as public lectures, such as the popular TED talks, usually by academics, activists, celebrities, or authors; paid seminars concerning methods of self-help or self-advancement; or what might be classified as "after-dinner speeches" to entertain a social gathering. But why seek enrichment from a speech rather than a book or video? First, with respect to written instruction, a speech promises to condense the main points of a subject and present them in a smooth, understandable, narrative form that speaks directly to an audience's everyday experience. Although it clearly leaves out a great deal of detail, a speech nonetheless makes a subject more immediately interesting and relevant to one's life. Second, with respect to multimedia or **online communication**, a speech of enrichment makes it a *community experience* of sharing knowledge rather than an isolated or detached event. Attending a speech of enrichment is itself an experience, and often it includes the discussion after the fact with other interested members of the audience. Not surprisingly, then, public lectures often serve an important community-building function, which is what makes their frequent setting in public libraries or public universities so appropriate.

The *listener* for speeches of enrichment has a clear and expressed interest to hear the subject matter presented as well as a desire to gather together with other like-minded people. Of these two motives, the second is often the most important. The reason people go to conventions, for instance, is usually to meet other people who share the same interests and to talk about the various enrichment speeches they have heard at those conventions (regardless of whether those speeches are about classic cars, Russian literature, chemical engineering, or *Star Trek*). Audiences listen not only to acquire information but also to establish camaraderie. Naturally, then, the dominant quality of the speaker of enrichment is goodwill toward the audience, displayed usually through interaction with audience members and constant attention to how the subject matter of the speech relates to the audience's everyday experiences. Demonstrating that one possesses sufficient knowledge to speak on the topic is important but should be done in an understated way and usually just in passing. An overemphasis on the "credentials" of the speaker as a means of establishing credibility often comes off as arrogant, which is why this task always falls to the one who introduces the speaker. The *message* should strike a balance between argument and anecdote, with clear claims and evidence supplemented by lively stories and examples. The message should challenge the intellect of the audience so that they feel they are learning, but not so much that it starts to sound like a written text; in fact, the result of a successful speech of enrichment in many circumstances will often be the purchase of a book.

Benazir Bhutto: "Today the Muslim World Boasts Three Women Prime Ministers"

Benazir Bhutto was the first woman democratically elected to lead a majority Muslim nation. She served as the 11th and 13th prime minister of Pakistan in 1988–1990 and 1993–1996. She was the eldest daughter of Zulfikar Ali Bhutto, a former prime minister who also founded the Pakistan People's party. The speech below she gave in 1995 during the fourth world conference on women organized by the United Nations. During this speech she addresses an audience concerned with advancing women's rights, but who may not quite understand the place of women in the Muslim world. Consequently, she uses her speech to enrich them as to the relationship between Islam and the role of women in such a way that they might organize more effectively on an international scale:

> As the first woman ever elected to head an Islamic nation, I feel a special responsibility towards women's issues and towards all women. And as a Muslim woman, I feel a special responsibility to counter the propaganda of a handful that Islam gives women a second class status. This is not true. Today the Muslim world boasts three women Prime Ministers, elected by male and female voters on our abilities as people, as persons, not as women. . . .
>
> Muslim women have a special responsibility to help distinguish between Islamic teachings and social taboos spun by the traditions of a patriarchal society. This is a distinction that obscurantists would not like to see. For obscurantists believe in discrimination. Discrimination is the first step to dictatorship and the usurpation of power.
>
> A month ago, Pakistan hosted the first ever conference of Women Parliamentarians of Muslim world. Never in the history of Islam had so many working women and elected representatives gathered together at one place to speak in one voice. . . . And, today, I feel that same sense of pride, that we women have gathered together at Beijing, at this ancient capital of an ancient civilization to declare: we are not alone in our search for empowerment, that women across continents are together in the search for self-esteem, self-worth, self-respect and respect in society itself. In distinguishing between Islamic teachings and social taboos, we must remember that Islam forbids injustice; injustice against people, against nations, against women. It shuns race, color, and gender as a basis of distinction amongst fellow men. It enshrines piety as the sole criteria for judging humankind.[4]

DISCUSSION

In the context of the conference, this speech was clearly an enrichment speech insofar as it attempted to give new information to an audience willing to embrace the idea of women's empowerment across the globe. In what situations, however, will this speech drift into a speech of advocacy? How does the relationship between speaker and audience determine the genre of the speech? Can you think of other subjects in which changing the audience for an otherwise mundane enrichment speech can become a source of controversy?

▶ SPEECHES OF ADVOCACY

Speeches of **advocacy** persuade an uncommitted audience to place certain beliefs and attitudes at the top of a hierarchy of needs (and others at the bottom) by showing how they are necessary to achieving ideal ends. The term "advocacy" is used in the sense that the speaker is an "advocate," which is literally defined as one who speaks on behalf of something or someone else, as when we might "advocate" for a friend by using our influence with others to help that friend. This means that speeches of advocacy always speak "on behalf" of some higher cause or ideal that transcends the self-interest of the speaker or even of the audience; it is in this way that an advocate might criticize members of an audience for being too concerned with their own immediate problems and not willing to sacrifice time and effort to strive for something greater than their own self-advancement. It therefore "advocates for" an idea by showing how it should hold a greater place in people's lives and thoughts than it currently does.

One of the puzzling things about speeches of advocacy is why people would voluntarily go to hear a speech that challenges them in this way. In almost every other speech genre, the audience has a clear reason for being there—to get to know someone (introduction), to feel part of a group (encouragement), to make an informed decision (deliberation), to pursue self-interest (solicitation), to pay homage to something important (commemoration), to make one's life more enjoyable (enrichment), or to fulfill one's professional responsibilities (administration). Why would an audience choose to attend a speech in which their beliefs and attitudes would be challenged and would demand of them a great deal of sacrifice? There is no easy answer to this question, but most attempts to answer it come down to one basic fact of human nature—the desire to overcome our immediate obstacles in search of becoming something higher than what we currently are. Richard Weaver says that rhetoric at its truest seeks to perfect men and women "by showing them better versions of themselves, links in that chain extending up toward the ideal, which only the intellect can apprehend and only the soul have affection for."[5] A lofty definition, to be sure! Yet it is an undeniable fact that when people are discontented with their current situation, they will willingly cast aside all conventional comforts and remake themselves according to a new ideal. Speeches of advocacy therefore rely on a basic level of discontent to make these transformations possible; when discontent is not present, sometimes it must be manufactured first. That is why the basic model of all such speeches is a combination of two sentiments: "this is intolerable" and "this is what must be done."

Making speeches of advocacy even more complicated is the fact that, very often, they speak to two audiences simultaneously. The first audience consists of *listeners* in attendance who usually already share some degree of the same discontent and aspirations, but who have attended the speech in order to solidify their commitment and more fully understand what is to be asked of them. With the exception of hecklers who attend primarily to disrupt the event, in speeches of advocacy the people gather in attendance to hear the speech because they already are in support of the speaker's overall position, as with protest rallies, religious revivals, or political campaign events. And even those who attend and who are uncommitted are nonetheless curious enough to listen attentively. The second audience consists of *spectators* who witness the spectacle of the gathering through the mass media, whether it is disseminated through conventional news sites or is reproduced through social networking sites or the blogosphere. This audience may have very little connection at all with the speaker or the issue, but may simply be interested to know what is going on that would attract so many people. In effect, then, speeches of advocacy gather like-minded people together to reinforce their beliefs and identify themselves as a group, and by doing so hope to produce a show of constituent support that justifies bringing their viewpoints to the attention and consideration of a larger public.

The context for speeches of advocacy thus occurs when a smaller public wishes to make its position heard by a larger public through the power of spectacle. Whereas speeches of encouragement and commemoration may help that smaller public form close bonds and establish long-term working relationships and attitudes, speeches of advocacy bring their perspective and arguments into the light of the public sphere. To contribute to a larger public discussion or advance a social movement, an effective speech of advocacy thus relies on having agencies of mass media to distribute news of the speech, which generates public attention and discussion about what was said and argued at the event. Thus, the effect of most public protest rallies is often determined by the level of press they generate after the fact. This is one reason why eloquent speaking that is quotable, and that generates a powerful but brief image, is crucial for producing the kind of media spectacle for which a speech of advocacy is intended. Speeches that may have actually been heard by but a few people have such power that they become reproduced and talked about in written or online communications, only to finally be discussed in oral speech between friends and within communities.

The ideal *listeners* for speeches of advocacy are people ready to commit themselves to a cause. This does not mean that listeners must be willing to throw themselves completely into a social movement. Sometimes it simply means that they must change their daily habits as a way of contributing to a long-term goal, such as when people start recycling, start voting in a certain way, or choose not to purchase certain products. Regardless of how much time and effort listeners are willing to expend, they nonetheless desire *some* kind of commitment in order to feel as if they are "doing their part" to help improve some aspect of the world and to be a part of something that expands their vision and horizon beyond the everyday. The *speaker* is somebody who has not only demonstrated his or her own level of commitment by having sacrificed for a higher ideal, but who also is something of a role model, and whose actions are capable of being successfully imitated by an audience. Unlike deliberative speakers, who may be called to speak because they possess a specific element of expertise that is beyond that of the ordinary person, successful advocacy speakers usually present themselves as "one of us" and tend to themselves be a part of the community they are addressing. The message is therefore delivered in a colloquial, vernacular style that typically mirrors the way that the audience members themselves speak. Whereas commemorative speeches tend to be highly poetic, deliberation speeches tend to be very logical, and solicitation speeches tend to be aggressively performative, advocacy speeches are written as if they are "speaking what is already on everyone's mind." The message should therefore be received with the expression, "That's exactly what I have been thinking!" In other words, the function of speeches of advocacy is to rally an audience around a common cause and give them a language with which they can speak to each other about that because that is consistent with their own perspectives.

George W. Bush: "The Debate over Immigration Reform Has Reached a Time of Decision"

During President George W. Bush's second term in office, one of his priorities was to push through comprehensive immigration reform on a bipartisan basis. On May 18, 2006, he made an address to the nation from the Oval Office in which he laid out his plan. Notable about this speech is how he attempted to bridge the significant political divide on immigration and create a sense of common ground that would allow his policy to move forward:

> The issue of immigration stirs intense emotions and in recent weeks, Americans have seen those emotions on display. On the streets of major cities, crowds have rallied in support of those in our country illegally. At our southern border, others have organized to stop illegal immigrants from coming in. Across the country, Americans are trying to reconcile these contrasting images. And in Washington, the debate over immigration reform has reached a time of decision. Tonight, I will make it clear where I stand, and where I want to lead our country on this vital issue.

> We must begin by recognizing the problems with our immigration system. For decades, the United States has not been in complete control of its borders. As a result, many who want to work in our economy have been able to sneak across our border and millions have stayed.

> Once here, illegal immigrants live in the shadows of our society. . . . Illegal immigration puts pressure on public schools and hospitals; it strains state and local budgets; and brings crime to our communities. These are real problems, yet we must remember that the vast majority of illegal immigrants are decent people who work hard, support their families, practice their faith, and lead responsible lives. They are a part of American life but they are beyond the reach and protection of American law.

> We are a nation of laws, and we must enforce our laws. We're also a nation of immigrants, and we must uphold that tradition, which has strengthened our country in so many ways. These are not contradictory goals. America

DISCUSSION

In the case of a televised address of this type, there is no direct audience for the president other than the television viewer. Consequently, it allows the speaker to bypass a direct appeal to an audience, which often gives a speech a greater capacity to include multiple viewpoints. How does President Bush attempt to incorporate both perspectives in order to create the possibility of compromise? Would he be more constrained if he had chosen to make these remarks directly to one or another political party or organization? What are the advantages and disadvantages of speaking directly to the American people from the Oval Office without a live audience immediately present?

can be a lawful society and a welcoming society at the same time. We will fix the problems created by illegal immigration, and we will deliver a system that is secure, orderly, and fair.[6]

▶ SPEECHES OF COMMEMORATION

Commemorative speeches establish or reinforce bonds between audience members by praising something or someone that the speaker believes reflects their shared values. Specifically, commemorative speeches make moral judgments about, and attribute values to, particular people, objects, or events important to the audience in a way that alters or reinforces their long-term attitudes toward those things. In other words, commemorative speaking is often directed toward things that have historical value. We commemorate something when we want to remember and preserve it. Most often in our lives, commemoration happens when we wish to remember loved ones who have died and to preserve in our memories the celebrations and triumphs of our lives. Cultures, too, memorialize certain people, events, or objects that have played an important role in their historical development. The purpose of the commemorative speech is thus to create a shared sense of reverence and memory for things of common value, thus reinforcing the close bonds of members of a group by celebrating that group's best qualities.

Contexts for commemorative speeches are either ritualistic, as with annual national holidays, or situational, as with weddings or graduations. Both, however, serve the same basic function. A commemorative speech brings people together to honor the values that unite them as a group and that are embodied in their members and their actions. Consequently, any group or institution that relies on the motivation of its members makes frequent use of commemorative speeches both to inspire excellence and to create a shared sense of commitment. Even commemorating loved ones at a funeral binds people together in a uniquely powerful way by using their stories to create a sense of reverence and legacy. Thus, although speeches of commemoration often do not usually argue specific points, they create and reinforce the values on which people often rely when called to make concrete judgments in practice. In speaking to the past and future, they endeavor to create a lasting impression in historical time.

The two central components of a commemorative speech are the *value,* which is an abstract and universal concept, and the *subject matter,* which is a specific and concrete thing. Either the value or the subject matter may be the starting point for a commemorative speech. A speaker before an audience such as the Veterans of Foreign Wars, for instance, may start with the values of honor and sacrifice and then seek to commemorate those soldiers who uphold those values. Or that speaker might begin with a particular person who has recently passed away and then seek to find appropriate values with which to praise that individual based on his or her own unique personality and contribution. One starts with a value and then finds subject matter to praise; the other starts with subject matter and finds values with which to praise it.

The *listener* for speeches of commemoration genuinely wishes to be inspired by something that represents the very best of life and that the listener believes should be valued and respected by all those present. Like audiences for speeches of identification, listeners for speeches of commemoration usually find pleasure in feeling common bonds with other audience members; however, they are different because the bond is established by common values rather than by explicit signs of group membership. Consequently, listeners for commemorative speeches are often very diverse, sometimes even bringing together people who otherwise may be competitive or antagonistic toward one another. This means that the *speaker* for speeches of commemoration is often very different than those for speeches of identification. A speaker seeking identification will often be very animated, charismatic, and vigorous in order to rally an audience around a common set of symbols, beliefs, or attitudes; a speaker seeking to commemorate is usually controlled, deferential, and eloquent, making sure that it is the object, event, or person being commemorated that is the focus of the audience rather than the cleverness of the speaker. The *message* for commemorative speeches relies heavily on **pathos** arguments that use highly stylistic narratives to generate emotional attachments and to show how the object commemorated possesses certain qualities worthy of praise. Commemorative speeches are not cluttered with facts and details; they select a few essential narratives and spend a great deal of time investing them with rich emotional nuance and power.

Barack Obama: "Selma Is Not Some Outlier in the American Experience"

On March 7, 2015, President Barack Obama delivered a commemorative speech honoring the 50th anniversary of "Bloody Sunday," a watershed moment of the civil rights movement. On March 7, 1965, a group of African-American men and women began marching from Selma, Alabama, to Montgomery to protest widespread voting discrimination but were met with police violence at Edmund Pettus Bridge. The violent scenes of police beating unarmed protesters, including women and children, simply because they wished to acquire the right to vote—at the time, African-Americans made up half the population of Selma but only 2 percent of registered voters—helped give momentum to passing the historic Voting Rights Act. Obama used this speech to clearly link Selma with the highest American values:

> As we commemorate their achievement, we are well-served to remember that at the time of the marches, many in power condemned rather than praised them. Back then, they were called Communists, or half-breeds, or outside agitators, sexual and moral degenerates, and worse—they were called everything but the name their parents gave them. Their faith was questioned. Their lives were threatened. Their patriotism challenged.

> And yet, what could be more American than what happened in this place? What could more profoundly vindicate the idea of America than plain and humble people—[the] unsung, the downtrodden, the dreamers not of high station, not born to wealth or privilege, not of one religious tradition but many, coming together to shape their country's course? What greater expression of faith in the American experiment than this, what greater form of patriotism is

there than the belief that America is not yet finished, that we are strong enough to be self-critical, that each successive generation can look upon our imperfections and decide that it is in our power to remake this nation to more closely align with our highest ideals?

That's why Selma is not some outlier in the American experience. That's why it's not a museum or a static monument to behold from a distance. It is instead the manifestation of a creed written into our founding documents: "We the People . . . in order to form a more perfect union." "We hold these truths to be self-evident, that all men are created equal." These are not just words. They're a living thing, a call to action, a roadmap for citizenship and an insistence in the capacity of free men and women to shape our own destiny. For founders like Franklin and Jefferson, for leaders like Lincoln and FDR, the success of our experiment in self-government rested on engaging all of our citizens in this work. And that's what we celebrate here in Selma. That's what this movement was all about, one leg in our long journey toward freedom.[7]

> ### DISCUSSION
>
> Obama uses the contrast between how the critics of 1965 viewed the march with how the Selma march is viewed today. How does his commemoration of Selma as the exemplar of American values also function as a critique? What type of emotions are evoked in this speech? And what does it say about our future? Can you think of other events often praised in United States history and determine which values or vices we associate with them?

▶ THE MINOR SPEECH GENRES

The minor speech genres are those speeches given in more narrow or constrained circumstances in which there are specific aims to be accomplished as well as specific limits on what can be said and how it can be said. The minor speech genres typically occur within more structured settings in which the speaker and the audience have a clear role to play.

Speeches of Encouragement   Speeches of **encouragement** focus on arousing a greater commitment and enthusiasm to a group identity already formed usually to meet some challenge or create excitement for being together. This kind of speech is frequently used in athletic contexts for rallying "team spirit," in business contexts for generating employee loyalty, in interpersonal contexts for creating group unity, or in political contexts for mobilizing members of political parties or movements. Thus, the core function of the speech of encouragement is to create a sense of group solidarity and passion. Whereas introductory speeches deal with the relationship between speaker and audience, speeches of encouragement deal primarily with the relationships among audience members, with the speaker being secondary. The occasion for such a speech is generally one in which a group of people, either strangers or a loosely knit group, feel it necessary to create a tighter bond in order to accomplish some task.

DISCUSSION

What was a group identity you tried to make with your childhood friends growing up? Did you give yourselves a group name? What were the qualities you attributed to your group identity? Did you develop any practices or rituals to express those qualities in public? Is this process fundamentally different than what occurs in a workplace or at a university? To what purposes are these group identifications put?

The *listeners* of a speech of identification wish to feel part of something that is larger than themselves and that provides a meaning and value for their actions that could not be accomplished on their own. The *speaker* must therefore portray him- or herself as a kind of representative of the group who speaks for the whole rather than from a particular perspective. Finally, the *message* should typically rely on highly emotional narratives loaded with value judgments and appeals to shared symbols and beliefs. In this way, speeches of encouragement are very similar to commemorative speeches, but differ in emphasizing the construction of an explicit "we" identity that carries with it explicit commitments to action and responsibilities to other members of the group.

Speeches of Deliberation   Speeches of **deliberation** occur when an audience wishes to hear a diverse group of speakers give different perspectives on how to address a common topic in order to come to an informed judgment about a matter of common concern. Contexts that call for deliberation speeches tend to occur when there exist clear divisions of opinion within a group or institution that cannot be resolved by further inquiry or polite conversation. Therefore, to be successful, deliberative speaking must not only provide a chance for the airing of different perspectives; it also must guarantee procedures of judgment based on a consideration of those arguments by an audience with respected authority, which may include the family, Congress, the jury, the board of directors, the stockholders, or the spectators.

DISCUSSION

Think of an experience you have had in which there were two or more people vigorously arguing two different sides of a position and were then interrupted by a third party who offered to moderate the argument—for instance a parent walking in on the argument of siblings or an employer or a teacher intervening in some dispute. How did the arguments change when they were directed not at one's opponent but at an objective third party? Did the issue get resolved to your satisfaction?

The *listener* for a deliberative speech is someone who is responsible for making a decision and wishes to hear two or more sides of an issue in order to consider every angle and alternative before coming to a judgment. Genuine deliberative listeners are therefore neither partisans nor merely disinterested observers; they are individuals whose primary concern is what to do about a specific issue. The *speaker* therefore presents him- or herself as someone with experience or knowledge who is worth listening to, who is equally concerned about the problem, who expresses goodwill toward the audience, and who tries to save the audience's time by getting to the point as quickly as possible. To accomplish this task, the *message* tends to be a highly compressed, logical affair that has no room for extraneous detours or lengthy personal narratives; it gets to the point quickly and defends positions articulately.

Speeches of Solicitation   Speeches of **solicitation** persuade an audience to adopt some policy, object, process, or attitude based on the perceived rightness or utility of the subject matter. Whereas deliberative speeches always face counter-argumentation, speeches of solicitation are typically made by a single speaker before an audience that may simply accept or reject the speaker's proposition rather than compare and contrast it with other points of view. In contradistinction, speakers who make solicitation speeches are often directly benefited by the audience's adoption of their judgment, as when a salesperson gets a commission, a fundraiser gets money for a cause, or a religious evangelist gains another faithful member. The explicit goal of speeches of solicitation is to thus argue before a reluctant and skeptical audience for the mutual benefit in buying some product, adopting some policy, or changing some behavior favored by the speaker. It can occur both in a traditional face-to-face setting, such as a car showroom, and in a more formal presentation in which an organized group invites a speaker to make a case for something that group members believe may actually benefit them.

The *listeners* for speeches of solicitation usually have almost no prior interest in establishing any sort of relationship with the speaker and are usually only interested in hearing how a speaker's proposal or product can benefit their own interests. The *speaker* is almost always a self-conscious performer who knows he or she is on stage and acts accordingly. The *message* therefore tends to be dominated by *if-then* causal arguments that show how *if* the audience chooses to adopt the advice of the speaker, *then* good consequences will be produced, with the desirability of consequences emphasized by entertaining narratives that dramatize ideal results and reinforce the importance of making the right decision.

DISCUSSION

Most of us have had some experience with fundraising to support some extracurricular activity or cause. When have you ever attempted to solicit money for such fundraising from people who are your friends or family? How does this differ from when you try to sell something to a stranger? Think about how your role as a speaker changes when you make an active solicitation. Did you find it liberating, or did you find it uncomfortable?

Speeches of Administration   Speeches of **administration** are delivered by officials of a group or institution to an audience whose presence is usually mandatory in order to justify policy decision and improve the procedures and communication structures of an organization. Although often presented as speeches of enrichment, introduction, or encouragement, administrative speeches are different because the audience was compelled to be present, and therefore such speeches do not have the power and influence characteristics that these other speeches hold. It is the difference between a politician giving an introductory speech to prospective voters and a new manager of the office introducing him- or herself as the boss, as well the difference between the speeches of identification given at pep rallies and the speeches by managers at early morning gatherings of employees at retail stores to get them enthusiastic about serving the customers. The difference between the speeches is that the latter are not designed to appeal to the preexisting, voluntary interests of the audience, but rather to implement decisions made by administrative authorities.

The *listener* for speeches of administration represents the most challenging audience for any speech, precisely because he or she may not want to be there but has been compelled to be present. The *speaker* for such speeches therefore has a considerable challenge. On the one hand, the speaker must present him- or herself as a credible and respected authority who is in charge of the situation and has a perspective of proven and recognized value. On the other hand, the speaker must also strive to adapt to the needs of the audience, not the least of which is the desire to be entertained and even, at times, flattered. The *message*, to be successful, should not consist of simply going over material that is better given in a pamphlet or handout. The message should go over the "high points" and should also strive to be as short as possible and conclude on a positive note, which leaves people in good spirit and with a short time to talk to each other casually before they return to their responsibilities.

> ## DISCUSSION
>
> Of all public speaking genres, speeches of administration are probably lowest on the bar of eloquence. What is the worst speech of administration you ever experienced? And was it even necessary? By contrast, have you ever experienced a good speech of administration? What do you think is the essential quality of making a good administrative speech as a "boss"?

Speeches of Invective   Last, it must be admitted that there are times when establishing a positive **ethos** within an audience is impossible or even undesirable. For people who stand outside some group, whether because they are considered an outsider or whether they are technically a member of the group but hold views diametrically opposed to many of them, are often unwilling to compromise their position when they have a chance to address this audience. In such cases, individual speakers do not seek the goodwill and respect of their audience by conforming to their ideas or values, but rather intentionally provoke a strong response by directly challenging them. This kind of speech is traditionally associated with the "prophetic voice" of those who would condemn the present actions, beliefs, or values of a particular audience by judging them by some higher virtue or principle.

Unlike typical rhetorical forms that seek to instigate social action through encouragement and persuasion, the speech of **invective** is a speech whose only function is to provoke an audience to self-reflection by directly attacking and ridiculing its most valorized conventions, values, attitudes, and beliefs by judging them in light of a higher ideal. In other words, the *listener* for such a speech is a group that is largely hostile to the interests or position of the speaker, while the *speaker* of an invective wishes to reveal to an audience its own hypocrisy, ignorance, and immorality. Consequently the *message* of an invective tends to focus heavily on giving examples that expose all the terrible things the audience does and how they are not living up to higher principles.

DISCUSSION

Most of the time we compose speeches of invective only in our imaginations, the kind of speech associated with the feelings of "I wish I had said that!" or "If only I had the chance to say this!" For obvious reasons, we are often never given the opportunity to directly confront a hostile audience. But can you think of any situation in your own past in which you were given the chance to deliver an invective? Did you take that opportunity or not? If you did, did any productive outcomes follow, or did it simply make the situation worse?

▶ SUMMARY

A speech genre represents a familiar, conventional, and appropriate way of responding to a particular and recognizable type of speech situation. As indicated by Aristotle's initial distinctions among forensic, deliberative, and epideictic speaking, which were based on the Greek experience in law courts, the assembly, and funeral orations, speech genres do not simply exist "on paper"; they exist in the habits and expectations of a particular culture whose members experience recurrent types of situations that demand predictable forms of rhetorical response. We can, of course, violate these expectations at any time if we so choose, either for the sake of humor or surprise or confrontation, but doing so always comes with a risk that must be calculated ahead of time. It is bad taste, for instance, to give a speech of solicitation when one is supposed to be commemorating the accomplishments of someone else, just as it makes you appear ridiculous to give a speech of administration to an audience with absolutely no obligation to listen to you. The easiest way to invite rhetorical failure is to misunderstand or to simply ignore which speech genre is appropriate to one's audience at a particular time and place.

Although each speech genre therefore performs a specific function in a specific type of situation, we can generally categorize speech genres into two distinct types: those whose primary function is to form the character of an audience and those whose primary function is to encourage an audience to come to a particular type of judgment. The first type of speech is what is represented by introduction, encouragement, enrichment, and commemoration speeches. We give speeches of *introduction* whenever we have to establish relationships with strangers in a situation that usually calls for some sort of cooperative activity. This type of activity might be practical, such as being part of a research team or a court jury, or social, such as having to live together in a dormitory or be part of a new neighborhood. Most often our speeches of introduction are not formal "stage" speeches but informal narratives that we deliver in the context of conversation. Speeches of *encouragement* thus follow naturally from those of introduction, for after we introduce our-selves to each other, there comes a demand to "identify" the nature of the group to which each of us belongs. Usually, such speeches are accompanied by symbols, such as team mascots, flags, squad colors, and the like, that embody some set of qualities and virtues that the group can rally around. Once a group is formed around common characteristics and goals, speeches of *enrich-ment* then provide more resources to educate an audience about the things that it finds interest-ing and holds valuable. A platoon of soldiers will thus be enriched about famous battle strategies, just as members of a political party will learn about the justification for their economic policies. Finally, *commemorative* speeches will praise exemplary people, objects, and actions that embody the values held dear by that particular group, thereby solidifying group identity by showing how representatives of that group are accomplishing great and worthwhile things.

By contrast, speech genres of deliberation, solicitation, advocacy, and invective focus more on specific matters of judgment than on questions of group identity. Speeches of deliberation, for instance, occur far more often *within* an identified group than between two contentious groups. This is because speeches of deliberation require shared commitment to certain procedures that allow deliberation to occur without breaking down into overly contentious polemics or even vio-lence. Therefore, speeches of deliberation are about debates over issues that members of a group have not come to a common decision about and therefore require the consideration of pro and con positions. That is why, perhaps, the ordinary large family is one of the most frequent sites for deliberative speeches. Speeches of solicitation, on the other hand, usually occur when represen-tatives of outside interests approach a specific group to market an idea or product that purports to serve their mutual interests. Whereas members of the family trying to decide where to take a vacation use deliberative speeches, travel agencies offering available trip packages to that family use solicitation speeches. Speeches of advocacy manage to cross all boundaries between audi-ences, speaking both to the committed and the noncommitted that it is in the interest of all to pursue a certain idea for the sake of some value higher than self-interest. That is why speeches of advocacy often are heard in the street, where anyone can come, and broadcast through the media so that everyone can hear. Speeches of advocacy break the conventional boundaries of group identifications in the name of some higher good or more prudent action. Finally, speeches of invective directly challenge group identities and often intentionally try to shatter them in order to perhaps generate radically new possibilities in the few people who might listen.

▶ CHAPTER 1 EXERCISES

1. **IMPROMPTU:** As a class, come up with a single general speech topic, such as "recycling" or "gun control" or "space exploration." Now assign every individual a speech genre and have them come up with a specific argument related to this topic that is delivered in that particular genre. Do not tell the class, however, which genre you have been assigned. Every-one delivers a speech of no more than 30 seconds and tries to guess which genre it is expressing.

2. **GROUP:** Divide the class into groups. Have each group come up with a "cause" and imagine that they are a group advocating for the cause. Have them identify five different situations in which they are speaking to five different audiences making use of five different speech genres. Have each group explain how they would adopt different strategies for different audiences to accomplish specific goals.

3. **DEBATE:** Divide yourselves into three groups: a pro group, a con group, and a jury. Select a topic of deliberation. Have the pro and con groups take affirmative and negative positions on this topic and present their cases before the members of the jury, who may interrupt and ask questions at any time. After arguments are completed, have the jury make an honest verdict based purely on the cases presented to it. What were some of the factors in the jury's decision?

4. **TAKE HOME:** Find a scene in a work of literature, a movie, or a television show that exemplifies one of the speech genres. Describe the character, the scene, and the plot, and describe how the speech of the characters conform to or violate the norms of a speech genre. Then identify the consequences of the speech in the story.

5. **VIDEO:** Find some object in your possession that you wish to "sell" to the class. Make a short "commercial" for this object featuring you as the spokesperson, no more than 30 seconds long. Make sure when you make this commercial that you not only talk about the object but somehow show it doing something that would be beneficial to those who purchase it.

▶ NOTES

1. The importance of expectation is emphasized by Karlyn Kohrs Campbell and Kathleen Hall Jamieson, who write that:

    > A genre is a group of acts unified by a constellation of forms that recurs in each of its members. . . . External factors, including human needs and exposure to antecedent rhetorical forms, create expectations which constrain rhetorical responses. But the internal dynamic of fused elements also creates expectations which testify to its constraining force. Generic exemplars have an internal consistency.

    Karlyn Kohrs Campbell and Kathleen Hall Jamieson, "Form and Genre in Rhetorical Criticism: An Introduction," in *Readings in Rhetorical Criticism*, ed. Carl R. Burgchardt (State College, PA: Strata Publishing Co., 1995), 403.

2. Aristotle, *Rhetoric*, 1358b1. In *The Rhetoric and the Poetics of Aristotle*, trans. W. Rhys Roberts, ed. Edward P. J. Corbett (New York: The Modern Library, 1984).

3. Sarah Palin, "Gov. Sarah Palin at the RNC," available at www.npr.org/templates/story/story.php?storyId=94258995 (accessed 17 August 2016).

4. Benazir Bhutto, "Address by Mohtarma Benazir Bhutto Prime Minister of Islamic Republic of Pakistan at the Fourth World Conference on Women," available at www.un.org/esa/gopher-data/conf/fwcw/conf/gov/950904202603.txt (accessed 8 August 2016).

5. Richard Weaver, *The Ethics of Rhetoric* (Davis, CA: Hermagoras Press, 1985), 25.

6. George W. Bush, "Speech on Immigration," available at www.nytimes.com/2006/05/15/washington/15text-bush.html (accessed 17 August 2016).

7. Barack Obama, "Remarks by the President at the 50th Anniversary of the Selma to Montgomery Marches," available at www.whitehouse.gov/the-press-office/2015/03/07/remarks-president-50th-anniversary-selma-montgomery-marches (accessed 17 August 2016).

2

Delivery and Memory

This chapter will outline the basics of the canons of delivery and memory in order to provide the foundations of public speaking as a performative act. The canon of memory outlines strategies of how to remember and recall one's speech without having recourse to notes or manuscripts. The canon of delivery will identify the basic components that go into a public speech. Delivery does not attend to what is said so much as the way it is spoken and performed. This includes not only the four ways of delivering a public speech, including from memory, extemporaneous notes, a manuscript, or impromptu, but also more specific aspects of verbal and physical performance including rate, pauses, volume, pitch, dialect, pronunciation, articulation, eye contact, position, gesture, and appearance. This chapter will also emphasize that despite not being considered "content," the way in which we deliver a speech actually conveys a great deal of information to an audience and can greatly affect how they interpret the words that we say.

Of the canons of rhetoric, those of delivery and memory characterize rhetoric as an art of public speaking. The canons of arrangement, invention, and style are equally applicable to written or even visual modes of expression, but only public speaking requires attention to a conscious art of delivery and of committing that delivery to memory. For that reason, despite being last in the original canon, this book will put them first in order to introduce you the foundations of what it means, from a purely performative standpoint, to talk in front of others. The canons of delivery and memory are highly personal and individual. No two individuals will have the same form of delivery or the same way of committing their speech to memory. Indeed, particularly in the case of delivery, having a unique and somewhat idiosyncratic delivery style can be highly effective—provided that the fundamentals have been mastered. But it is equally true that the canon of delivery also is responsible for public speech anxiety as it requires us to confront people in a face-to-face setting and put ourselves in a position to be judged. Yet this same anxiety also produces feelings of pleasure and accomplishment when we overcome them and hear the sound of applause.

Delivery deals with the manner in which a speaker physically performs the speech through the crafted use of the voice and gesture. Whereas the canon of style addresses the manner in which a speech is composed through words, the canon of delivery addresses the manner in which a speech is actually performed with the body. Although conceptually the simplest of the canons, it perhaps is the most difficult to master and requires a great deal of training and experience. It also is one of the most important. Emerson provides the following encomium to delivery in his essay "Eloquence," focusing specifically on the importance of voice:

> A good voice has a charm in speech as in song; sometimes of itself enchains attention, and indicates a rare sensibility, especially when trained to wield all its powers. The voice, like the face, betrays the nature and disposition, and soon indicates what is the range of the speaker's mind. . . . Every one of us has at some time been the victim of a well-toned and cunning voice, and perhaps been repelled once for all by a harsh, mechanical speaker. The voice, indeed, is a delicate index of the state of mind. I have heard an eminent preacher say that he learns from the first tones of his voice on a Sunday morning whether he is to have a successful day. A singer cares little for the words of the song; he will make any words glorious.[1]

For Emerson, not only can delivery undermine even the most carefully crafted composition, but it can also turn ordinary ideas into a glorious oration. Delivery has this power because of the unique capacity of the human voice to portray what Emerson refers to as the "nature and disposition" of the speaker. We are naturally drawn to people who speak with confidence and grace and power, trusting that the ideas contained within the language match the character and virtue conveyed through voice and stature.

In the classical order of the canons, the art of memory naturally followed style because once a speech was written, an orator in the Classical age had to memorize it before delivery. **Memory** as the fourth canon refers to the ability to memorize a text and to reproduce it in a manner that seems natural rather than artificial. The canon of memory, in short, is the act of absorbing the content and form of the speech so fully into oneself that the speech feels like an unforced expression of one's thoughts and feelings. Therefore, as a canon, memory remains a crucial component of a speech even when reading from a manuscript or from cue cards! Anyone who has attended an academic conference can tell you how excruciating it is to hear people reading from papers that they had never heard spoken out loud or had internalized to any degree. The canon of memory tells us that it is not enough to simply deliver words in the correct order—one has to feel what is being said and to deliver it with a sense of intimacy and passion. In a broad sense, then, memory should be considered essential to all forms of effective delivery.

DISCUSSION

One of the misunderstandings about memory is that it is assumed to simply be a reference to "storage," as if a memory is simply a closet full of things. But memory is, more importantly, also an art of "retrieval," of being able to know where something is and to find it and bring it forward. When have you thought that you knew something by heart, but when the time came to say it, you found yourself stumbling over words or feeling like your mind was a blank space—when, for instance, we try to impress someone to whom we are attracted? In retrospect, what could you have done to make retrieval easier for yourself in that situation?

▶ DELIVERY

When it comes to practicing delivery, there are no rigid rules or "scientific" laws about what makes effective delivery. There was a time during the "elocutionary" movement when people would write long books that matched specific ideas or emotions with specific hand gestures or facial expressions in the assumption that their meanings were stable and universal. Today, we know that almost every aspect of our physical performance is influenced by cultural assumptions and can be read very differently by different audiences and subcultures. Consequently, this book will simply define certain "factors" one should consider when making effective delivery. Oftentimes, improving our delivery is simply a matter of paying attention to certain parts of our performances that we had taken for granted or never actually noticed before. Considered in its specific parts, then, the components of delivery are as follows.

Appearance   When we address someone's appearance, we mean how a speaker dresses and physically presents him- or herself in terms of grooming, fashion, and posture. The function of **appearance** is not only to please the eye but also to identify oneself to an audience as a certain type of person who will deliver the message in a certain type of way. Our outward appearance can thus be considered a kind of "sign" of what is to come and a "promise" of what the audience should expect. It makes a big difference, for instance, whether one delivers a boardroom speech in a business suit or whether one delivers a speech in a swimsuit. In this case, one might deliver the same exact address, but in the first case be taken seriously and in the second case be interpreted as a source of comedy. But if one were giving a toast to a friend at a beach party, the exact opposite would be true, and the person with the business suit would be thrown into the ocean. In short, the important thing to consider with appearance is the setting of the speech and the audience who will be receiving it. Our appearance is a way of establishing a relationship with an audience and giving them a visible sign of what is to come before you even say a word.

Gesture   When we use gestures we mostly use our arms, hands, and face to convey nonverbal meanings. There are three primary functions of gesture. First, a gesture may have a meaning unto itself and condense complex meanings into simple and powerful movements. An upraised fist, hands placed in prayer, arms spread wide, fingers clasped together, all of these are typical gestures which in particular cultures have very specific meanings and can be used to take the place of words. Second, gestures provide a visual reinforcement of the words that are being said. For instance, in saying "let us all come together" it would be appropriate to move your hand slowly together until your fingers are intertwined. Gestures create a more visible performance akin to an actor on a stage that not only conveys a deeper and more artistic sense of meaning, but also makes the speaker more interesting to look at and concentrates attention not just on their voice but on their whole person. Last, gestures can literally demonstrate how something looked or happened, as when we might use gestures to show the size and shape and placement of objects, the way a room was laid out, the way a person behaved or acted, and the like. In this sense, gestures are kind of like a game of charades. This kind of effect can actually be very powerful on an audience, as it puts them at ease and gives them something specific to watch. In addition, specific attention to gestures can often relieve speech anxiety because it gives your body something to do.

Position   A speaker's **position** refers to how a speaker orients his or her body with respect to the audience, including the choice of whether to stand behind a podium, walk around, or sit down. The function of position is to develop a certain relationship to an audience and to the environment in which one is speaking. In general, one can distinguish between formal and informal positioning. A formal style will often be behind a podium or on a raised rostrum or in front of a long table, in which case one is expected to adopt a more direct lecture style of presentation in which one is in "command" of the room. Such position is intended to convey authority and focus attention on the speaker often at the expense of the audience. An informal style will usually be in a smaller setting with a more scattered or circular seating arrangement that offers room to move around and engage individuals directly in the audience. In this case, the speaker has a more relaxed posture and often engages in a give-and-take with the audience, sometimes directly approaching them in the manner as one would talk to a friend. The difference between formal and informal positioning can be seen in the difference between the president delivering the state of the union versus engaging in a town hall discussion, a priest delivering a sermon in a cathedral versus a youth minister talking with college students in a church basement, or an advertising agent giving a pitch before board meeting versus a car salesman engaging with customers in a showroom.

Eye Contact   One of the most important predictors of the impact of the speech is the degree to which a speaker actually looks at members of the audience while speaking. Merely glancing at the audience during moments of silence does not constitute eye contact. Ideally, one must "look" as if one is having a conversation with somebody. The function of **eye contact** is to create a relationship with the audience and make them feel as if the speaker is directly talking *with* them rather than simply talking *at* them. In addition, eye contact lets an audience know that the speaker is paying attention to them and is interested in their opinions and feedback. When a speaker does not look at the audience, an audience often drifts away and treats a speaker more as a recording than as an individual. Eye contact encourages an audience to treat the speaker as an individual. In turn, when the audience feels they are being directly engaged, they often generate more feedback that can help the speaker adapt to their nonverbal expressions and attitudes.

Articulation   One way public speaking differs from conversation is that there is far more attention paid to how distinctly words are pronounced, so that each stands out. The opposite of articulation is mumbling. The function of articulation is twofold. First, it serves the purpose of making each word distinct so that people are able to understand exactly what is being said. A missed word or a phrase that blends together often creates confusion and forces the audience to try to figure out what was said after the fact. This often leads to an audience being distracted. Second, articulating words conveys the impression that each word is meaningful and deserves attention. In this case, the effect is similar to how one might think of a staccato note in music that punctuates it and distinguishes it from other notes. Articulating one's words helps an audience remember them because they stand out in their memory.

Pronunciation   Although we often take this for granted, it is quite important to actually be able to pronounce words. The function of **pronunciation** is not only to accurately convey meaning but to show one's own credibility. It is relatively common, for instance, for candidates for public office to find themselves in an embarrassing news story because they could not pronounce the name of a country, a country's leader, or a word that has particularly significant meaning for a particular demographic. Mispronouncing words is a sign that one has not taken the time to actually figure out what the words mean and how they are used by the people who care about those words.

Dialect   A **dialect** is a local phrasing common in a particular group but not used universally. "Slang" can be considered a kind of dialect, although one person's slang is another person's cultural vocabulary. Dialect can have a positive and negative effect on a speech. The positive effect of dialect is to either emphasize the unique characteristic of one's heritage to an audience that does not speak in it or to create a sense of identification with an audience that does. The use of such dialect requires, of course, that one uses and pronounces it correctly. This leads to the negative effect of trying to use dialect, in which case it either alienates an audience to whom it is unfamiliar or, if misused, embarrasses oneself before an audience familiar with the dialect.

Pitch   The next four qualities of delivery have to do with the sound of one's voice. For individuals who have not had voice training, listening to one's own voice on a recording can be an uncomfortable experience. It is an interesting phenomenon of media that we do not mind looking at pictures of ourselves, but we cannot stand listening to recordings of ourselves. Nonetheless, actually recording oneself speaking and listening to it—without video accompaniment—can produce a great deal of improvement in our public speaking. The fact is that the sound of people's voices matter. We gain a lot of information from sound that is beyond the merely communicating information. Sound creates emphasis and conveys emotion as well as aids in memory and understanding. The first type of sound is **pitch**, a musical term that refers to the ability to speak each word as if it were a separate note in a melody, moving up and down the scale. When we turn up our voice at the end of the question, for instance, what we are doing is raising the pitch. Or when we make a declaration, we often go down at the end of our statement in order to convey that we have come to a rest. So the best way to think about the function of pitch is to create an alternation of tensions and resolutions which often accompanies specific emotional qualities such as excitement, warning, frustration, fear, happiness, or relief. Indeed, the same sentence spoken with different pitch can often connote a completely different meaning, as for instance the difference between being serious and sarcastic.

Volume   **Volume** is the dynamic between softly and stridently spoken parts of the speech. Of course, the essential part of volume is simply to speak loud enough so that you can be understood by the entire room. Oftentimes we overestimate the loudness of our voice. When we speak without microphones to an average-size room, we are often required to raise the volume of our voices beyond our normal speaking voice. However, one should avoid a volume so high that it appears that one is shouting at the audience. But volume can also be used for effects within the speech. A quieter voice communicates either suspense or caution or sympathy, whereas a louder voice communicates excitement or warning or confidence. An effective speech should always have softer and louder sections much as one would think of a symphony going through many acts. Last, one should think about volume in terms of how much participation you wish from your audience. The softer your voice is, the more an audience has to "lean in" to understand what is being said. The louder one's voice is, the more they sit back and simply listen to you without making any effort. Requiring too much effort might make them lose interest, whereas not requiring enough effort might make them seek to pay attention. Generally speaking, we can speak quieter when we know we have an audience's attention, whereas we speak loudly when we want to get their attention.

Pauses   Sometimes simply pausing in a speech, or adding a patient and conscious silence between words or thoughts, can generate a great deal of energy. A **pause** is important especially for creating tension or suspense as well as for giving the audience time to think or reflect for a few seconds. Particularly when one is making a grave or important point, pauses allow us to emphasize those key parts of the speech which you want the audience to pay special attention to. Generally, a speech should try to work in two or three distinct pauses for this reason.

Rate   The dynamic between rapidly and slowly spoken parts of the speech is **rate**. For the most part, we speak rapidly during parts of the speech that do not require a great deal of intellectual processing but are mainly to communicate simple ideas and generate enthusiasm in an audience.

The passages are also often spoken with a higher volume. Slower parts of the speech are meant to convey ideas that require either more intellectual reflection or a greater depth of emotional understanding. Sometimes these slower passages are spoken with a softer voice as well, as we wish the audience to participate in the moment in a thoughtful way. However, slow passages can also be spoken with great volume when they wish to hammer home a very specific point.

> ## DISCUSSION
>
> Think about your favorite speeches delivered by actors in movies. What is it about their delivery that made their speeches so perfect? Find an online clip of the speech and analyze the performance in detail. How did they dress and move around the room? How did they use gestures and expressions, pauses and volume, to engage their audience? And how do different settings make different styles appropriate and inappropriate?

▶ PREPARING FOR DELIVERY

Although it is important to consider each of these elements of delivery individually, when actually performing the speech, one should think of delivery as a coherent whole. An effective way to think of the overall strategy of delivery is simply to consider how different acting styles dramatically alter the way that an audience interprets the language of a character. Just as different actors bring different elements to the same character, different delivery styles alter the way the same speech text is received. Consequently, one should think of an oratorical rostrum as a kind of stage on which one steps into a certain "role" or "character." Rather than isolating each of the elements of delivery and building them up into a unity, one should simply think of certain familiar performance styles and imitate them as best one can. Not only does this method provide a coherent delivery style to imitate, but it also puts speakers into a performative frame of mind that relieves the anxiety of feeling as if they have to "be themselves." The fact is that when people are delivering public speeches, the last thing they should do is act like they always act in everyday life. A speech is a performance and should be treated as such. Indeed, it is not infrequent that people who are quiet or reserved in everyday conversation turn out to be the best public speakers. As Emerson says, "The most hard-fisted, disagreeably restless, thought-paralyzing companion sometimes turns out in a public assembly to be a fluent, various and effective orator."[2] The rostrum can be liberating for those who know it is a performance. Here are some general tips for preparing for delivery.

Put the Speech to Memory   All of the advice included in the canon of delivery will assist in producing a competent and persuasive delivery. Even the most charismatic individuals find it hard to look confident and composed when they forget their lines and must continually look down at their notecards. If the core elements of the speech are not adequately memorized, attempts at delivery often appear mechanical and forced.

Know Your Audience   Although this does not appear directly related to delivery, it is actually one of the most important elements. It is the difference between how we engage in conversations with our friends and how we speak to strangers. When we know our audience, we instinctively adapt our manner of speaking to their personalities and expectations, most notably in our level of formality but also in many other subtle aspects, including our rate of speaking, our volume, our level of animation, our use of humor, and our incorporation of slang terms or jargon. Knowing something about the audience ahead of time allows us to develop a presentation style adapted to their attitudes.

Know Yourself   Not only is good delivery contingent on knowing the audience, it is also contingent on knowing how one stands in relationship to that audience. In our everyday interactions with other people, we play many roles adapted to those situations—for example, father, sister, friend, boss, employee, classmate, customer, entertainer, and so on. "Knowing yourself" with respect to public speaking does not refer to a deep philosophical inquiry into the soul; it simply means know who you are for the people you are speaking to at that moment. Oftentimes, awkward speaking situations arise because speakers try to play a role that they are not suited for, most comically when older professionals try to speak to younger students as if they are "classmates" and adopt the students' mannerisms and ways of speaking. Adapting to an audience does not mean mimicking it; it simply means understanding the audience's needs and expectations and trying to fulfill them using the best of one's own resources.

Know the Speaking Environment   Whenever possible, a speaker should become familiar with the environment in which the speech is to occur, regardless of whether it is in a room, a park, a stadium, or an auditorium. The serves several purposes: (a) knowing the environment simply makes one feel more comfortable, much as walking into a gym familiarizes a visiting basketball team; (b) if the speech is to be amplified, testing equipment makes the speaker accustomed to the sound of his or her own voice; and (c) standing at the rostrum (or equivalent) allows a speaker to know where the audience will be sitting, where he or she can move while speaking, and what physical elements of the environment might be useful to incorporate into a speech in passing reference (e.g., the giant moose head hanging on the wall behind the podium as a resource for an opening joke).

Have Something to Say   It is very difficult to give an inspired delivery if the speech itself is boring and uninteresting for the speaker. Delivery is a natural outgrowth of enthusiasm, and enthusiasm is difficult to fake. Many people who are charismatic and charming in their everyday interactions are surprised to find themselves speaking awkwardly and timidly when they step up to the rostrum because of the mistaken impression that their charisma and charm will make lemonade out of lemons. The only thing that a speech made out of lemons will produce is a sour taste and considerable disappointment.

Break the Speech into Dramatic Acts   Think of a speech as a play. Determine the "feel" of each act and develop a performance style that makes the most of the material. Ideally, each act should demand a slightly different type of delivery. For instance, the introduction may require a storytelling delivery in which the speaker steps away from the rostrum and speaks directly to the audience in a lively and animated style. But the story may serve to introduce a serious thesis that demands a more formal delivery that sticks closer to the text that is read from the podium. And this action, in turn, might be followed by a commentary on a video presentation and then conclude with an informal question-and-answer session.

Rehearse Nonverbal Gestures in Front of a Mirror   Identify key moments in the speech that create opportunities for specific facial expressions or hand movements that can reinforce the points or themes in the speech. The importance of mastering these sorts of gestures can be seen in the act of stand-up comedians in particular, when the success or failure of jokes often is dependent on very subtle bodily movements and expressions. Rehearse these in front of a mirror until they become natural.

Vary Rate, Pitch, Volume, and Pauses   Public speaking requires us to speak in a manner that is much more animated and musical than our everyday speech. Experiment with different speech patterns as you would when trying to create different ways of singing song lyrics. Record yourself saying the same sentence multiple ways to hear the differences. Avoid the mundane speech pattern of simply speaking each word with the same volume and rate and then simply dropping the pitch at the end of the sentence.

Rehearse for Time   Do not time yourself by reading silently. Speaking out loud always takes more time than silent reading. Practice the speech from beginning to end, and time yourself to ensure that you stay within set limits. Failing to rehearse for time creates enormous speech anxiety once a speaker realizes he or she is approaching or is over the allotted time.

DISCUSSION

There is admittedly something comedic about the idea of practicing our social performance in front of our bathroom mirror. Moreover, the artificiality of performing for ourselves in order to seem "authentic" in a social setting sometimes seems hypocritical or fake—which accounts for the suspicion we sometimes have for people who may seem too rehearsed or who speak too well. Do you think that being "authentic" is the same thing as being "spontaneous"? Or do we become more authentic as we practice and rehearse and hear ourselves speaking until we feel we have gotten it right?

▶ DELIVERY FORM

One of the most basic elements of any speaking genre involves the expectations for how the speech is going to be delivered. The choice of how you will deliver your speech has important consequences for how it will be received by an audience. The choice also opens up and limits certain possibilities for how a speech will be written, how much information it will contain, and how long it will be. The following are considerations in delivery form.

Manuscript Manuscript speaking means writing out every word of a speech and delivering it as written. Except in cases with a teleprompter, the manuscript should be on a podium and the speaker should have practiced the speech to the extent that much of it has been partially memorized. This allows a speaker to look down briefly to keep his or her place but still maintain eye contact with an audience. In this regard, it is helpful to write marks on the speech for when to breathe (~), when to look up (↑), and when to look back down (↓) so that you can memorize particular sections that you think warrant a more significant delivery. Manuscript reading allows for a careful sculpting of stylistic language (in the cases of commemorative speaking) or complex arguments (in deliberative speaking) that would otherwise be difficult to convey. Manuscripts are most proper for formal occasions in which the audience expects and demands this kind of complexity and subtlety. However, a manuscript may provide a "crutch" that speakers rely on too much, which causes them to effectively ignore the audience and deliver the speech as if they were simply reading out loud.[3]

Impromptu Delivering impromptu speeches means to speak without preparation on a subject given to you at the moment. This form is the most natural and spontaneous and thus often the most interesting to hear. However, it also limits one's ability to sculpt a careful argument and also provides no safety net should one run out of ideas. The classic case of **impromptu speaking** is parliamentary debate, in which a subject is announced and debaters have just a few minutes to come up with opposing arguments. Exercises of this kind, also helpful in public speaking classes, allow you the freedom to be creative and to gain experience speaking before audiences without having anything "at stake." In public, impromptu speaking may be required during deliberative meetings, such as in the boardroom, the town hall, or the family kitchen, and also during celebratory occasions in which people are called upon to make a speech about themselves or others. And sometimes impromptu speaking is simply a way to entertain friends.

Extemporaneous The essential feature of this speech is the notecard, which includes key points, quotes, and transitions drawn from a larger outline but leaves the speaker to fill in the gaps during the actual delivery of the speech. This form provides structure but allows for adaptation in such a way that, ideally, the speaker will be able to connect with the audience on a personal level while still making a formal argument or presentation. A good notecard will thus be easy to read, will not be cluttered with information, and will support the speech by providing both information and delivery instructions, such as when to look up, when to make a gesture, when to speak loudly, and when to slow down. Extemporaneous speeches are ideal for people making "official" presentations in front of audience members who feel free to break in and ask questions at any time. The speaker is able to deal with such interruptions because he or she still has all the important information directly at hand, and he or she can flip backward and forward without completely disrupting the flow of the speech.

Memory   **Memory delivery** is to write a manuscript first and then rehearse it until one knows it by heart. At its best, it has all the advantages of manuscript style without the disadvantages, for it allows a speaker to engage an audience directly and to walk around a "stage" without being tied to a podium. However, speeches from memory also put one at great risk. If one forgets even the smallest part of a speech, there is the danger that one's mind might go blank like that of an actor in a play, at which point there is nothing to help the speaker find his or her place. In addition, relying on memory makes it almost impossible to adapt to an audience during the speech, such as when external interference occurs or when a speaker simply realizes that something isn't working. Speeches from memory are thus best when they are short and have only a few simple points, such as a wedding toast or an argument in a public meeting. They also are excellent for storytelling exercises, as stories are easier to remember and audiences enjoy hearing stories from people as if they simply sprung naturally from memory.

> ## DISCUSSION
>
> How does the manner in which we deliver a speech change how it is interpreted and received? Imagine, for instance, that the same exact speech with the same exact words was delivered to one audience as if it were spontaneous, to another as it was read directly from a manuscript, to another from notecards, and to another as if it had been memorized. If the audience knew ahead of time the manner in which the speech was to be delivered, how would they interpret the words and meanings differently? Would some things stand out in one form but not in another? Would certain aspects be impressive if delivered spontaneously but mundane if read from a manuscript?

▶ VISUAL AIDS

A **visual aid** supplements the verbal component of a speech with graphic displays intended to effectively condense complex material or to convey meanings that cannot be captured with language itself. Visual aids are different from visual rhetoric. In visual rhetoric, the image is the form of persuasion itself—as in a billboard, a political cartoon, or an iconic photograph. This textbook, focusing on the act of speaking, will not address the complexities of visual rhetoric. A visual aid, by contrast, is a part of figurative style, using an image to more effectively convey a specific idea or emotion. Such aids include the bar graphs and tables of administration speeches, the personal objects often used in introductory speeches, the graphic images and statistics used in advocacy speeches to dramatize problems, and the photographs or symbols useful in commemorative speeches in stimulating memory and emotion. Visual aids perform two major functions:

1. They simplify complex information that otherwise could not effectively be explained.

2. They graphically visualize an event, object, person, or process whose details are necessary for understanding a speech.

To be effective, visual aids should be large enough to see and colorful and interesting enough to capture an audience's attention. However, more is not necessarily better. We are often so inundated with visual images that we often assume that we should always try to use as many visual aids as possible. But as a general rule, visual aids should be kept to a minimum and should never be forced into a speech simply to "dress it up" if there is no reason for them to be there. If a good description can describe something with eloquence, then a picture of that event does not "add" to the speech. It replaces or competes with it. Visual aids should never be in competition with the speaker or the speech. Whenever a visual aid takes attention away from the speech itself, it has failed in its purpose as an *aid*. In other words, a visual aid should be used to supplement a speech by performing a task that only a visual aid can perform. For example:

1. A *bar graph* will easily compare the gross national products of 20 nations at a glance.

2. A *line graph* will show the growth and decline of a nation's economy over a decade.

3. A *pie chart* will demonstrate the economic wealth of ten different social classes.

4. A *map* will show where the highest concentrations of population are in a nation.

5. A *representation* will reveal the process of offshore oil drilling.

6. An *object* will best show the amount of butter people were allowed during World War II.

7. A *flowchart* will show the steps that it takes for grain to get to market.

8. A *photograph* will show how far glaciers have retreated in 20 years.

9. A *chalkboard* drawing will spell out what NAFTA stands for.

10. A *handout* will provide an audience with the specific language of a proposed law.

11. A *posterboard* will show different types of fabric manufactured in the 1900s.

It goes without saying, however, that most visual aids these days—no matter their specific representation—will occur using things like PowerPoint or Prezi software. In many situations, such as in academic conferences or boardroom presentations, speaking in front of a group using some sort of slideshow or visual media has become almost the norm. This is not necessarily a bad thing, but it can be done very badly. One of the biggest mistakes people make when using these sorts of presentation tools is that the person speaking makes themselves nearly supplementary to the actual presentation. This can occur when people actually put up virtually all of their information onto the screen so that the audience tends to simply read the screen rather than listen to or watch the speaker. This can happen when people basically translate their entire complex outline onto a PowerPoint presentation and add images. The effect of making oneself a mere "supplement" to the visual presentation is made worse when the person speaks in a dark room and stands off into a corner behind a podium reading from a manuscript without looking at an audience, thus creating the effect that they are just watching a movie. None of these things lead to an effective presentation. There are a few simple techniques which can aid the use of PowerPoint presentations and the like.

1. *Use position*: Concentrate on making yourself the center of the presentation by standing in such a way that it draws attention to yourself. Do not stand behind or off to the side of the screen, but stand between the screen and your audience.

2. *Use gestures*: Actively point to images on the screen as you would if using an old school chalkboard. The more hand or arm gestures and facial expressions you can use while interacting with the board increases your engagement with an audience.

3. *Use normal lighting*: Do not dim the lights to a degree where you put yourself into shadow. Most digital projectors these days can be easily seen in normal lighting.

4. *Use minimal text*: Writing text up on the screen always invites an audience to read it, even if it is not essential to your presentation. Always assume that what you put up on the screen people will take time to actually read. Never use it simply as background.

5. *Use photographs and/or charts*: Any visual image should be simple and striking. However, it should also require some interpretation that you will provide in your speech. Once the images are on the screen, actively interpret them for the audience.

6. *Use a clicker*: Use a hand-held clicker to advance the slides rather than standing behind a computer on a podium. Give yourself the ability to move around and not be tied to one specific place. Any clicker should also have a laser pointer to interact with the screen.

7. *Interact with your audience*: Last, do not sit back and allow the screen to be the source of interaction between your audience and the speech. Actively engage the audience by asking questions, walking around the audience, and maintaining eye contact.

▶ MEMORY

Often neglected, the canon of memory remains one of the most important facets of an effective speech for two reasons. For the speaker, memorizing and therefore internalizing a speech provides the level of confidence we normally feel in our casual conversations with others. One of the reasons we do not feel nervous speaking to people during most of the day is the fact that we know what we are going to say and have a reason to say it. When we fail to memorize a speech adequately, we often feel like we are speaking someone else's words and therefore feel awkward and self-conscious. For the audience, hearing a speech that feels like it comes "from the heart" and not from a manuscript or a teleprompter makes the message more powerful and more sincere and therefore creates a much greater feeling of community and participation.

Memorizing a speech has never become a science. After several thousand years of human beings giving orations and performing dramas, there are not that many more techniques for memorizing speeches than there were in classical times. However, certain general principles have largely been established that can be useful in developing one's own preferred technique for memorization. It is important to try out various combinations and strategies in order to find the one that best suits you.

Read the Speech Out Loud   When we read to ourselves silently, our minds and bodies are not preparing themselves to perform the text out loud. We read silently to absorb information and to process it, not to memorize it and reproduce it. An absolutely essential component of memorization is reading the speech out loud and in a strong voice that fills the room. Whispering to oneself on the bus will not produce a confident speech. One must find a private place in which one can hear one's own voice.

Practice with Your Whole Body   Do not practice a speech by sitting in a chair. Use your entire body. Walk around the room (ideally the room where you will be speaking) and use gestures as you speak to an imaginary audience. The more your body becomes engaged in the speech act, the more your mind becomes engaged as well. Treat your body as a partner in the speech and it will help you.

Record and Listen to Yourself   Listening to your own voice not only helps you improve delivery by hearing your own voice as an audience would hear it; it also improves memory by externalizing your voice and making you encounter it as you might encounter popular song lyrics.

Break the Speech into Parts   Think of a speech as you might think of rooms in a house. Each part of the speech should be a room with its own unique feel and purpose. Practice each part of the speech separately. Spend time in each room getting to know what it is like, including where you walk in and where you leave. Only after you know the atmosphere of each room should you put together the entire house tour.

Use Graphic Conceptualization   Diagram your speech on a piece of paper using creative images and drawings that represent your main points and forms of evidence. Feel free to be as ridiculous as possible, just so long as you remember the meanings of your icons. We may forget the specific words of a written manuscript, but we will not forget that we drew a picture of a person sunbathing next to an unhappy polar bear to remind us of the fact that global warming will melt the ice caps.

Identify Key Points   Try to summarize your speech out loud to yourself in as condensed a manner as possible, as if you were simply describing to somebody what your speech is "generally about" in casual conversation. This provides a general cognitive roadmap that allows you to always get back to the speech should you ever stumble or get lost.

Take Breaks Relying on one extended practice session is generally not sufficient to good memorization. Memory needs time to filter out what is important and then to solidify long-term memory by continually returning to the same thing. Taking breaks for a couple of hours, during which time you do nothing that is related to the speech, is often very helpful in retention. Memorization is a process and not a one-time event.

> ## DISCUSSION
>
> There is a venerable tradition in rhetoric to increase the power of memory by using the technique of breaking speeches into parts as if they were rooms in the house. Can you think of any other images, perhaps more related to contemporary experience, that might aid in speech memorization? What type of spatial metaphors are perhaps more salient than a Victorian house with many rooms to people in the twenty-first century?

▶ CHAPTER 2 EXERCISES

1. **IMPROMPTU:** Compose a short haiku poem about some general subject chosen by the class. A conventional haiku is structured by three lines that have a syllable structure of 5–7–5. The first two lines should concentrate on a graphic description of something simple, usually a phenomenon in nature, while the last line should comment more broadly on the meaning or emotional significance of this experience. Perform this haiku once, and then after making modifications based on the specific elements of delivery, perform it again.

2. **DEBATE:** When talking about delivery, Aristotle famously said that it was not a noble or respectable part of the art of rhetoric. Although he also acknowledged that delivery did have an impact that needed to be accounted for, he nonetheless insisting that in a court of law, for instance, one should only stick to the facts and not try to "warp" the judgment of the jury by trying to use delivery to arouse emotions of pity. Do you agree or disagree with Aristotle? That is to say, in a court trial which is attempting to determine one's guilt or innocence, is there any place for "delivery" in making a judgment or passing sentence on a defendant? Establish a case pro and con for this position.

3. **GROUP:** Organize yourself into different groups and have each group look at the same short poem provided by your instructor. Each group should then carefully analyze every word and phrase in the poem and decide as a group how it should be modified according to the parts of delivery such as rate, volume, gesture, etc. Assign one representative from each group to perform the poem and discuss how the different performances convey different meanings in the poem.

4. **TAKE HOME:** Search online for a scene in one of your favorite movies in which a character has a short monologue that you think is particularly powerful in terms of its delivery. Briefly interpret this scene according to the vocabulary of delivery and send an e-mail of this interpretation, along with the link to the scene, to your instructor.

5. **VIDEO:** Write a short "ode" to something located in a specific place that you frequently inhabit. For instance, and ode to your garden, your car, your kitchen, the tree you like to sit under, or the picture hanging in your apartment. Videotape yourself standing next to this object and perform your "ode" from memory in a way that emphasizes delivery.

▶ **NOTES**

1.   http://rwe.org/complete-works/viii-letters-and-social-aims/eloquence.html.

2.   http://rwe.org/complete-works/viii-letters-and-social-aims/eloquence.html.

3.   See James C. Humes, *Talk Your Way to the Top* (New York: McGraw-Hill, 1980).

3

Arrangement

This chapter will discuss the canon of arrangement, which deals with how to put material in order from beginning to end in a speech. It will outline how speeches can be organized by using specific strategies of introducing topics, ordering main points, and giving conclusions which support specific purposes. It will discuss how to construct a thesis that is clear and distinct which relates to the interest of a particular audience. By both analyzing the specific historical artifact of Patrick Henry's "Liberty or Death" speech, as well as discussing a hypothetical speech encouraging action on global warming, it will give examples of how to get attention and interest at the beginning of the speech, how to organize main points in a way consistent with the speech genre, and how to end a speech in order to leave a lasting impression on an audience.

Arrangement is the art of how to put things together effectively. We make use of the skill of arrangement in many parts of our lives. We arrange the space of our bedrooms and our places of residence to make us feel comfortable. We arrange our desks and our offices to be more productive. We arrange the schedule of our day so we can balance work and leisure. We make arrangements to go out socially in order to produce a certain type of experience. We arrange special dinners for family and friends during holidays and special events. In each case, whether we are arranging objects or time or people or events, we are placing things in a certain spatial and temporal order in order to bring about some desired effect. Similarly, we arrange how we express ourselves to others in words, actions, or images in order to communicate a desired meaning to other people and also to bring about certain experiences, feelings, ideas, or emotions. Public speaking is no different in this regard from any act of communication, but it differs in requiring a higher degree of arrangement in order to hold the attention of an audience and communicate meanings that are more complex or controversial than can be communicated in casual conversation or a social media posting.

Although **invention**, or the discovery of something to say, was the first in the order of the canon of rhetoric in classical times, it is more useful in the contemporary age to put the canon of arrangement ahead of invention. This is simply because it is hard to find something appropriate to say until one knows how it is going to be expressed—just as it would be difficult to prepare something appropriate to eat unless one understood the difference between a picnic and a Thanksgiving dinner. That is to say, it is more effective to understand the **form of communication**, meaning its overall structure and means of expression, before concentrating on what we might call the **content**, or the specific arguments, stories, or facts that it contains. Arrangement thus represents the step of giving order to a speech in anticipation of giving it "form." Consequently, resources for arrangement generally consist of templates that indicate where certain types of things should go and in what sequence, much as one would think of instructions of how to run a board meeting or how to throw a surprise party.

From the earliest history of rhetoric, arrangement has been a crucial part of public speaking. For instance, in Classical Roman oration, the arrangement was quite rigid and required a speaker to begin with an Introduction (*exordium*) to state the speech's purpose and establish credibility, then proceed through a Statement of Facts (*narratio*) to provide an overview of the situation, a Division (*partitio*) to outline what is to follow and specify the main point, a Proof (*confirmatio*) to present arguments and supporting facts, a Refutation (*refutatio*) to refute counterarguments, until ending up with the Conclusion (*peroratio*), which summed up claims and reinforced them with emotional appeal. Any speaker who wished to have an influence in the political sphere of the Roman Republic had to follow this arrangement or else violate the audience's expectations. Today we embrace a much looser and individualistic approach to arrangement, but almost any speech will nonetheless contain some if not all of these classical components in some form.

One should not, of course, simply look at arrangement as a set of rigid rules. Simply following mechanical instructions does not guarantee a successful persuasive speech any more than ensuring a successful meeting or an enjoyable party. Perhaps the most common misunderstanding about public speaking is that it is mostly concerned with conveying "information" that can be plugged into a mechanical template. From this perspective, one might think of public speaking much as one thinks of a standard news article, whose business is to convey the latest happenings of the world as truthfully and as sensationally as possible. The underlying set of assumptions behind this perspective is that the most powerful methods of maintaining interest are surprise and suspense, **surprise** meaning that which appears suddenly, unexpectedly, and shockingly (like a surprise party), and **suspense** meaning that which has been promised to appear but whose actual qualities have been kept secret (like a birthday gift). From this narrow perspective, rhetoric is about how to convey specific facts, details, events, or beliefs by packaging them correctly and delivering them at the right time.[1] In other words, it is simply about filling gaps with facts.

But arrangement is not about simply putting things in the correct order. It is about producing an experience of form in an audience by the careful arrangements of words. Following the ideas of Kenneth Burke, **form** is not an empty space waiting to be filled in with content, but rather an entire arc of temporal experience produced by symbols that first arouse and then fulfill desires and appetites in an audience. For him, not everything has form in this sense. Rather, a work has form insofar as one part of the work arouses interest in what follows and then provides gratification. Similarly, public speaking, too, requires a kind of *movement* from one place to another, a mental journey that begins at a familiar place and journeys toward somewhere new, and no amount of isolated facts, however surprising or suspenseful, ever really moves us anywhere.

In rhetoric, form is achieved when the end of the speech satisfies the desires that are aroused at its beginning, thereby generating a feeling of movement toward a powerful intellectual, motivational, and emotional satisfaction. For instance, when Martin Luther King Jr. announces that he has a dream, makes us desire to observe the meaning of that dream, and then places that dream before us in a way that brings about feelings of hope, belonging, and unity—that is form. By contrast, a speech that merely declares the content of a dream and then provides a list of supporting facts has only minimal form, as it relies instead on the audience's intrinsic interest in the facts themselves to capture and keep their attention. In other words, for a speech to have form, the audience must feel as if they are being carried forward on a wave while swimming toward a destination, meaning that the speech's words propel them forward (the wave) but also encourage them to participate in the movement itself (the swimming). Without this active participation by the audience to reach a destination with the speaker, persuasion is impossible because everybody stands still. Form is therefore not a quality of the speech itself in isolation; it is an accomplishment that occurs when a speech "works" with an audience to move them to a new place.

At all times, therefore, one must keep in mind that no specific technique or combination of techniques can ever amount to "form." Form is only attained when a speech conveys what John Dewey calls a "sense of qualitative unity" that comes about when one arranges "events and objects with reference to the demands of complete and unified perception."[2] By **qualitative unity**, Dewey means the feeling that one can sum up that entire arc of experience within a single term, as when one associates *exhilarating* with climbing a mountain, *tragic* with the death of a loved one, *joyous* with the family reunion on a holiday, or *inspiring* at the conclusion of a passionate speech. A speaker always wants someone to leave a speech feeling, "That was a ____ speech!" in which the blank is filled with some single dominating quality that lingers with the listener even after the specific facts may have been forgotten. Although mastering the individual techniques is essential to becoming an eloquent speaker, one should never allow attention to the parts (the "matter") to distract one from attending to the whole experience that is produced by the speech (the "form").

No amount of rhetorical templates can ensure that a speech achieves the level of "form" that arouses and satisfies an audience's appetites. More often than not, strict obedience to the rules of arrangement results in superficially competent but largely barren and uninspiring speeches that put an audience to sleep. The following techniques should therefore be considered more

DISCUSSION

Perhaps of all the social media platforms, that of Twitter has had the most recognizable impact on how we understand the relationship between arrangement and form. How does the combination of restricting a message to 140 characters and the incorporation of the hashtag alter the way we communicate on this platform? Also, do you think that our communication styles that we develop on social media has had an effect on the way we arrange our thoughts and expressions in face-to-face settings?

like experimental suggestions for getting started. The techniques of arrangement provide several different frameworks that can give an initial order to the chaos of material gathered together through invention. But the final arbiter of success is not how well the speech conforms to rigid rules and formulas; it is how effectively the arrangement captures the attention and interest of the audience and then moves them through the body of the speech until they reach a satisfying conclusion.

▶ MONROE'S MOTIVATED SEQUENCE

Perhaps one of the best efforts to condense rhetorical arrangement into a template for effective form is **Monroe's motivated sequence**. Alan Monroe was a professor of speech at Purdue University who developed a special sequence designed for policy speeches that encourage immediate action. Although its "method" is simply made up of basic public speaking strategies, Monroe's sequence incorporates the strategies into a form that is explicitly based on arousing the audiences' desires and then moving them, through the use of visual narrative, toward a promised satisfaction that results in concrete judgment and action. The five steps of attention, need, satisfaction, visualization, and action therefore follow neatly Burke's understanding of form and conclude with Dewey's understanding of qualitative unity.

1. *Attention*: Like any good introduction, get the attention and interest of your audience: "Little Margaret was an otherwise happy child. She liked television, she liked ice cream, and she liked to play with dolls. She also was six years old and weighed over one hundred pounds."

2. *Need*: Another word for "problem," *need* establishes the necessity to address some issue by graphically articulating why we "need" to act: "Childhood obesity is becoming a national epidemic. Over 30 percent of children under the age of eight are now considered obese. This leads to poorer school performance and chronic health problems."

3. *Satisfaction*: Another word for "solution," *satisfaction* lays out what is required to be done in order for audience members to feel that their needs have been satisfied: "We need to implement an aggressive health campaign in this nation that brings healthy lunches and active gym classes to the schools and also delivers a targeted marketing campaign to parents to encourage healthy eating and exercise."

4. *Visualization*: This step relies on heightening emotions by visualizing the wonderful state of affairs that will occur after satisfaction: "With such steps, Little Margaret could achieve a more active and energetic lifestyle in which she and other children leave the couch to play outside in the fresh air and sun."

5. *Action*: Now that the audience has been suitably inspired, this step tells them what they can do to help by laying out specific things to be done: "These changes must come from you. Become an active member in your school board and advocate changes at a local level while writing your congressional representative to support new health initiatives."

Because of the simplicity and clarity of the steps, there is almost no better method to start with than Monroe's motivated sequence to begin to understand the importance of form to rhetorical persuasion. It is a method that applies not only to politics and social action but also to our everyday interpersonal interactions in which we try to motivate our friends to choose a college major, our family to go on vacation to a certain place, or our colleagues to support a new office policy that will increase sales and morale.

DISCUSSION

Monroe's motivated sequence is perhaps most applicable to the setting of what used to be called the "hot sell." This was the context for a fast-talking salesperson of the type that one rarely sees anymore—an individual going door-to-door selling encyclopedias and vacuum cleaners—and who had only a few seconds to "hook" a potential buyer. Where do we today encounter this type of "hot sell" in which Monroe's motivated sequence would be put to use effectively? When discussing this, think not only in terms of selling products but also of selling politics, religion—or even oneself.

▶ PURPOSE

Public speaking is distinct from conversation or the more casual forms of mediated expression by being structured around a concrete goal—a **specific purpose**—that is expressed as a specific argument or position to be explained and defended—a **thesis**. A specific purpose is the answer to the question, "What is this speech trying to do?" whereas a thesis is the answer to the question, "What is this speech trying to say?" Especially for beginning speakers, the quality of a speech stands or falls with how well the thesis helps to achieve the specific purpose. The thesis is the center around which every aspect of a speech revolves. Conveying a thesis to the audience gives a speaker a concrete focus necessary to create a logical and coherent message and provides an audience reference point to understand the speech. All arrangement is grounded on having a specific purpose and clear thesis.

A specific purpose is an expression of an interest in a particular goal that the speaker finds interesting and that may have value for an audience. It involves four characteristics: (1) the *kind of speech* one is giving, (2) the *audience* to which this speech is delivered, (3) the *occasion* for the speech, and (4) the *effect* on the audience that the speech is supposed to have. Examples of specific purposes might include "to persuade my parents over dinner to buy me a car" or "to commemorate the Battle of Normandy during Memorial Day in front of a public audience to make them remember the sacrifices of veterans" or "to persuade the school board to support school uniforms during the monthly school board meeting." For a speech delivered in a public speaking class, the audience can be the actual class or some imagined situation, depending on the decision of the instructor. In general, however, speeches given to actual audiences (the class) generally have more value because one can gauge an actual rather than a hypothetical response.

A thesis is the specific argument that seeks to achieve the specific purpose. It is usually a single sentence that sums up what the entire speech is arguing, including a claim and reasons in support of that claim. Whereas a specific purpose is written for the speaker in order to help to *develop* a concrete idea during the writing process, a thesis is the *product* of that process. Thus, for the specific purpose "to persuade my parents over dinner to buy me a car," a thesis would be "You should purchase me a car because I have proved myself responsible, I require transportation to and from my job, and I need a car if I am ever to get a date." Let us imagine we are writing a thesis for the specific purpose "to persuade university students that they should support an international treaty to reduce greenhouse gases." A thesis in support of the specific purpose should do the following things:

Make a Specific Claim   A thesis should be specific. Vague and generic thesis statements always lead to speeches that are vague, confused, and lack impact. The more specific you can make a thesis, the more focused your speech will become and the greater impact it will have on an audience. A thesis that generally states that "we should tackle the problem of global warming" is less effective than one that tells us specifically, "We must support the 2016 Paris Climate Change Accord." A thesis should always seek to target a specific object, policy, or action that can be visualized more clearly than an abstract virtue or ideal.

Focus on a Single Topic   Avoid including too many topics in a speech. An audience can only follow a few lines of reasoning in a sitting, and a speech that attempts to go too many places will lose them. Too many topics also generally lead to superficial arguments that do not get to the "heart" of an issue. With a public speech, do not try to do too much or you will not accomplish anything. For instance, there may be many issues and reasons to support the 2016 Paris Climate Change Accord—economic, cultural, environmental, political, or militarily—but one should focus as much as possible on the topic that will make the most dramatic impact for those who are listening.

Be Audience-Centered   Consistent with the definition of rhetoric, therefore, any topic should be developed only with respect to the situated interests of an audience. How do we know which topic to focus on? Think about what the immediate audience may be most concerned about. For instance, a speech on global warming addressed to the business community would obviously focus on the long-term economic benefits. A speech directed at a younger audience of university students, by contrast, might be more idealistic and focus on issues of quality of life in 50 years or the devastating effects it might have on coastal communities and underdeveloped countries. So a thesis might be expanded to say, "We *university students have a responsibility* to support the 2016 Paris Climate Change Accord *in order to use our influence to protect fragile communities and ecosystems.*"

Present Reasons/Details   Following the claim should either be *reasons* in support of the claim or *details* about how it will be elaborated. The claim "We should build this bridge . . ." is generally followed by *reasons* like "because it will ease traffic, create a scenic walkway, and stop litter." But the claim "The universe is infinite . . ." should be followed by *details* like "and I will show how it expands in all directions, has no center, and possesses infinite possibility." A thesis might also have some combination of both reasons and details. In our thesis about the climate accords, let us combine one detail and one reason: "*As we witness dramatic increases in flooding, desertification, and devastating storms across the globe*, we university students have a responsibility to support the 2016 Paris Climate Change Accord *because unless we act now, we will see the widespread destruction of fragile communities and delicate ecosystems.*"

DISCUSSION

One way to think about the relationship between the specific purpose and the thesis is in terms of "sincerity" versus "manipulation." When we are sincere, our thesis is meant to explicitly achieve the specific purpose. In manipulation, however, our specific purpose may be different than what our thesis explicitly says—as when we imagine the Big Bad Wolf in Little Red Riding Hood expounding on the thesis of why he has such big teeth. Think about editorial news coverage of a speech by a politician by different news outlets. Each might quote the same thesis delivered in the speech but then attribute to it a completely opposite specific purposes. For a favorable news outlet, the politician is genuinely trying to accomplish a task consistent with the thesis. But for a news outlet critical of the politician, the specific purpose might be to undermine opponents, deceive the public, or distract attention to different issues. Can you think of any examples in which coverage of a political speech has attributed to that speech specific purposes which were not consistent with the stated thesis?

▶ INTRODUCTIONS

Once you construct a specific purpose and thesis, it is time to build the speech. An **introduction** should arouse some desire or appetite in the audience to hear the remainder of the speech. An introduction is therefore a kind of promise. It tells the audience what they are going to hear and promises that if they stick around, they will have an enriched experience. Introductions should thus be clear and interesting, ideally combining elements of argument and narrative that tell an audience that they will be hearing a well-informed argument as well as some interesting stories along the way. Broken down into specifics, the functions are as follows:

Capture an Audience's Attention   Making an audience interested in listening to what you have to say is *the* most important function of an introduction. If they are not interested, then nothing else you say will matter because they won't hear it. The following are some helpful techniques to "get attention and interest" before stating your thesis and moving to the body. Let us continue using the example of global warming:

1. *Use a quote*: Everyone enjoys hearing interesting quotes from famous people. Quotes should be relatively short and easy to understand and drawn from a person readily recognizable to and respected by the audience. These quotes should then be relevant to your own topic and preferably your argumentative claim as well. For instance, "In a recent interview, the President of the United States has said that every time he sees the latest projections of the influence of global warming, 'it literally terrifies me to see the consequences of our actions.'"

2. *Startling fact*: Stating some dramatic fact either reveals some problem in graphic form (like the fact that thousands of people die from some disease every day) or it demonstrates the relevance of your topic (like the fact that the amount of candy eaten in a year, when stacked on a pile, would reach to some spectacular height). Speakers then proceed from this startling fact to argue the less exciting details that are necessary to understand and give meaning to that fact. For instance, "Imagine, for a moment, standing on the coastline and looking out onto the Atlantic Ocean to see the skyscrapers of Manhattan jutting out from the water."

3. *Begin with a question*: To ask a question is to put your audience in the position of judgment. What would they do if such a thing occurred? What would they think about this or that idea? The intention of this strategy is to generate perplexity that your speech presumably would resolve. A poor question has an obvious answer, such as "If you had a choice, would you abolish cancer?" A good question actually raises some moral issue, such as, "If your family was hungry, would you steal bread?" For instance, "Imagine if the cost of driving our cars or operating our air-conditioning could be paid in islands. That is to say, every year we would choose an island in the ocean that would disappear from the face of the earth. Would you pay that cost?"

4. *Refer to a current event*: Usually drawn from news stories, current events demonstrate why your topic is relevant to everyday contemporary life. These events may be *shocking* (like a child imitating violent video games in real life), *inspiring* (like a person who struggled to overcome cancer), or simply *odd* (like a man who thinks he is the king of Canada). In either case, they are used to show how violent video games, cancer cures, or psychological disorders, for example, are relevant issues to talk about. For instance, "In August of 2016, a rain storm struck southern Louisiana and dumped so much rain that it flooded virtually the entire city of Baton Rouge. They called it a 500-year storm, but in the last year it turns out that there were 15 such 500-year storms across the United States."

5. *Tell a story*: A story in an introduction functions a lot like a fable. For instance, the "Boy Who Cried Wolf" conveys a lesson about trust. A story is a way of embodying some message by using plot and character as symbolic of a larger theme. Stories can come from personal experience, news, or history, or can be completely made up. However, completely fictional stories of the hypothetical variety are generally ineffective because the audience does not take them seriously. A good story relates some actual event, even if that event is your grandfather telling you a fictional story as a child. For instance, "In the Maldives islands, fisherman used to catch skipjack tuna with just a pole and line on the shore. But as the temperatures rise, the tuna are now swimming far offshore while the ocean itself is creeping up the beach and threatening to flood the coastal villages with every storm. The entire livelihood of the Maldives is now under threat."

6. *Perform a demonstration*: A technique with only very narrow applications, performing a demonstration involves actually doing some physical action to make a point. Anyone who has taken physics knows the typical kind of science demonstrations meant to demonstrate how Newton's laws function. A demonstration can also be *entertaining* (like doing a magic trick), or *controversial* (like showing how a condom works). In either case, it catches attention through actions rather than just words. For instance, to show how melting ice caps can increase sea level, one might actually bring in a snowball and during the course of the speech have it slowly melt into a container and cover a stone.

7. *Refer to literary material*: This strategy combines the strategy of quoting and telling a story. This is the one case in which fictional stories are effective because they derive from literature rather than just your imagination. The best source, of course, should be familiar to and appreciated by your audience, especially when it has acknowledged cultural significance for a larger community. For instance, one might quote a passage from Moby Dick in which Herman Melville says it is impossible to imagine humans being able to ever threaten whales with extinction. This would show how important it is for us to come to terms with the damage humans can do to the environment.

8. *Use humor*: As anybody who has ever attended a religious service knows, humor is not always reserved for "light" topics. Humor can be effectively used in any situation. It takes a very sensitive touch to use humor when the "tone" of the speech is not a humorous one, but when done well, it can be an effective way to "break the ice" with an audience.

9. *Create suspense*: Also a variation on telling a story, to create suspense you must set up conditions that may lead to some potential climax, thereby keeping your audience members on the edge of their seats. This suspense can be created through narrative or through demonstration. In many ways, suspense is a part of almost all of the examples already given above. Indeed, almost any introduction should involve some degree of suspense in order to keep the audience curious.

State Topic of the Speech and Purpose   Once you capture attention, you must retain it. You do so by making clear what your speech will be about so the audience will be prepared to sit through a more formal argument that may not be as "flashy" as your introduction. State your thesis as succinctly as you can which you should have already developed before the speech.

Relate the Topic to Your Audience   No topic is intrinsically interesting. Maintaining an audience's attention usually requires that they feel invested in what you have to say. Relating a topic to the interests and experiences of an audience creates this feeling of investment because what you say has value for *them*. Relating the topic to the audience should have already been incorporated to some degree in the thesis, but the introduction should make this connection stronger. For instance, "As university students, we often get wrapped up in our everyday concerns of going to classes and getting a job. But almost all of us dream of traveling to different locations, experiencing both nature and culture in new ways. Global warming threatens those dreams."

Set a Tone   Letting an audience know whether you intend to be serious, ironic, funny, critical, or deferential is what it means to "set a tone." Doing so puts your audience in a frame of mind so that they know what to expect, just as audiences prepare themselves for a different "tone" at a comedy club than at a graduation ceremony or a funeral. For instance, with issues like global warming, one could set an apocalyptic tone that dwelled on the notion of threat, or one might establish a more optimistic tone that emphasizes the positive actions we can take together to remediate this threat. The problem remains the same, but it makes a big difference if we seek to scare an audience or make them enthusiastic.

Preview Main Points   Although not always necessary, laying out the basic sequence of arguments can be helpful, especially when making a fairly complex or lengthy speech. Previews are generally inappropriate for commemorative or introductory speeches because they are too formal, but advocacy or enrichment speeches generally benefit from laying out the order of points so that an audience knows what to expect. For instance, "Today I am going to first diagnose the threat of global warming to fragile ecosystems and communities, second show how the climate accords offer an incomplete but yet necessary step to address this problem, and third to discuss the ways in which we can support these accords both politically and in our everyday actions."

Provide a Transition to the Body of the Speech   Always let your audiences know when the introduction is over and the actual body of the speech has begun. This encourages them to listen with a different set of expectations. Because they have committed themselves to listening to the speech, they no longer need speakers to "get their attention." They now want to hear the details. A transition lets them know when this shift has occurred. For instance, "Let me now turn to the crisis that we face as a global community."

Patrick Henry: "Suffer Not Yourselves to Be Betrayed with a Kiss"

In order to explore arrangement through an entire speech, this chapter will look at one of the most famous and also well-arranged speeches in American history—the "Liberty or Death" speech delivered by Patrick Henry. Following the Boston Tea Party of December 16, 1773, the British Parliament passed a series of acts intended to suppress the rebellion in Massachusetts. In May of 1774, General Thomas Gage arrived in Boston with four regiments of British troops. For the next two years, uncertainty spread as to whether Britain was preparing for a full-scale war on the colonies or whether tensions could be resolved through political petition and deliberation. When the Virginia Convention met in 1775, many delegates clung to the hope that the British government would rely on sensible reasoning instead of force. However, Patrick Henry firmly believed that war was imminent, and in his famous speech he laid out his arguments in a powerful but also logical arrangement that moved his audience to prepare for war. Here is his introduction:

> No man thinks more highly than I do of the patriotism, as well as abilities, of the very worthy gentlemen who have just addressed the house. But different men often see the same subject in different lights; and, therefore, I hope it will not be thought disrespectful to those gentlemen if, entertaining as I do opinions of a character very opposite to theirs, I shall speak forth my sentiments freely and without reserve. This is no time for ceremony. The question before the house is one of awful moment to this country. For my own part, I consider it as nothing less than a question of freedom or slavery; and in proportion to the magnitude of the subject ought to be the freedom of the debate. It is only in this way that we can hope to arrive at the truth, and fulfill the great responsibility which we hold to God and our country. Should I keep back my opinions at such a time, through fear of giving offense, I should consider myself as guilty of treason towards my country, and of an act of disloyalty toward the Majesty of Heaven, which I revere above all earthly kings.
>
> Mr. President, it is natural to man to indulge in the illusions of hope. We are apt to shut our eyes against a painful truth, and listen to the song of that siren till she transforms us into beasts. Is this the part of wise men, engaged in a great and arduous struggle for liberty? Are we disposed to be of the numbers of those who, having eyes, see not, and, having ears, hear not, the things which so nearly concern their temporal salvation? For my part, whatever anguish of spirit it may cost, I am willing to know the whole truth, to know the worst, and to provide for it.
>
> I have but one lamp by which my feet are guided, and that is the lamp of experience. I know of no way of judging of the future but by the past. And judging by the past, I wish to know what there has been in the conduct of the British ministry for the last ten years

DISCUSSION

Patrick Henry is clearly attempting to accomplish many different things in this introduction. He must establish goodwill with his audience, he must grab their attention without offending them, and yet he must establish his own position that clearly differs from their own. What are some of the strategies he uses in his introduction to accomplish the tasks? How do you think the speech would have been received differently if he had adopted alternative strategies?

to justify those hopes with which gentlemen have been pleased to solace themselves and the House. Is it that insidious smile with which our petition has been lately received? Trust it not, sir; it will prove a snare to your feet. Suffer not yourselves to be betrayed with a kiss.[3]

▶ BODY

If the primary function of the introduction is to arouse interest, the primary function of the body of the speech is to progressively move an audience toward satisfaction one step at a time. The **main points** are the most important claims made by the speech that are intended to support the main thesis. In fact, most of the time, the thesis itself indicates what the main points will be. Take, for example, this thesis: "We should establish more national parkland because it preserves wildlife, creates more opportunities for outdoor adventure, and connects people to the natural environment." The main purpose of the speech is to argue for the establishment of more national parks. The main points are then specific assertions, usually consisting of topic sentences at the beginning of each major section, that are intended to support this main purpose. For instance, these three main points might be written as follows:

- ▶ First, the survival of many species of large predators, such as wolves and mountain lions, depends on having free range in a wide expanse of undeveloped land.

- ▶ Second, national parks provide a destination for the many outdoor enthusiasts who desire to use the space for recreation.

- ▶ Third, national parks are the best means of creating a sense of stewardship with the environment, an attitude that is necessary for the health of the planet.

Main points can be thought of narratively like acts in a play or structurally like the rooms in a house. In both cases, each main point has its own separate purpose and character and yet only exists to support the construction of a whole work. Moreover, the house analogy should not be interpreted to mean that the rooms have only physical proximity to one another; a house is primarily made to live in, and rooms are constructed so that each room leads naturally to the next. A poor speech, like a badly designed house, will simply place things next to each other that shouldn't go together, like putting the main bathroom next to the kitchen and the dining room on the second floor. Likewise, a poor speech, like a badly written play, will introduce characters in the first act only to never mention them again and will jump from scene to scene without properly demonstrating their connection. In contrast, a good speech will feel like a guided house tour that reveals every aspect of the building's design and a dramatic three-act play in which all the major plot points are resolved in the final scenes. It will present the audience with a clear progression of ideas that they can easily follow so that they know what is coming. If a speech does not fit into any of these orders, then it is likely that the speech will be too disconnected to be effective. These are the basic ways of structuring main points, using as an example our global warming speech:

Chronological   Speeches that involve some process of time are suitable for chronological order that describes something from beginning to end. For example, chronological order is useful when doing biographies (the life of Martin Luther King Jr.), events (the Pamplona running of the bulls), or processes (how life may have developed on Mars). The essential character of chronological speeches is an emphasis on narrative storytelling, describing how events lead into one another and influence and are influenced by particular actors, whether they are individuals, groups, or nations. For instance, "The speech is going to discuss how the Paris Climate Change Accord has come about only after decades of scientific discovery, popular controversy, and political deliberation." This speech promises a story of how we got here. Commemorative, enrichment, and introduction speeches in particular make special use of chronological order.

Geographical   Whereas chronological order deals with differences across time, geographical order deals with differences across space. The classic geographical speech is a kind of "world tour" in which the speaker shows the different manifestations of something in different regions, whether the subject matter is language, culture, science, economics, history, war, or art. But geography can also be used in a more general sense of describing anything spatially, whether it is a microchip, a crime scene, a state capital, or the universe. What unifies a geographical orientation is how each "space" has a certain structure and quality that stand in relationship with other spaces so that they all add up to some sort of "whole," much as we might look at how individual states in the northeastern United States constitute a unity we call "New England." In the case of global warming, one might have the following structure: "The speech will show how global warming impacts each of the seven continents in radically different ways, producing minor benefits in some cases at the expense of large-scale disruptions." Geographical order is particularly suited to enrichment speeches.

Cause–effect   The cause-and-effect order almost always deals with speeches concerned with informing an audience about factual knowledge needed to address some problem. Consequently, such speeches almost always deal with issues of process (like the ways AIDS is transmitted or how smoking causes cancer) because a process is by definition something that causes change over time. What is important in cause–effect speeches is clearly identifying and diagnosing the cause and then tracing very clear arrows to specific effects that are not attributable to other causes. Often these types of speeches are most important when it or the effects of something are unknown or contested. For example, claiming that "it is the dramatic increase in carbon dioxide emissions by human sources which have brought about the devastating effects of climate change" is necessary only to an audience who questions whether humans are, in fact, responsible. This type of ordering is almost exclusively for enrichment speeches or advocacy speeches.

Pro–Con   The pro–con order is the counterpart of the cause–effect order in that it deals with the analysis of solutions that respond to problems. A pro–con order examines a particular solution to some problem and articulates its positive and negative qualities in order to provide an audience with sufficient objective knowledge to make a decision (like the potential environmental benefits of regulating carbon dioxide emissions compared with its economic downsides). A version of the pro–con order is the *comparative advantage* order, which in effect simply looks at comparative "pros" while leaving aside the drawbacks. In either case, these orders typically rely on a combination of competing narratives tied up with competing causal arguments. For instance, "There are two competing proposals to deal with the threat of global warming. The first simply accepts the fact of global warming and tries its best to make accommodations to it; the second denies that global warming is inevitable and seeks to eliminate the effects before they happen." This type or ordering can be present in enrichment, advocacy, or deliberative speeches.

Topical   The most general organizational structure is "topical," which simply means a series of related qualities or characteristics of your subject matter. Examples are "The four unique aspects of Louisiana cooking," "The hierarchies of English feudalism," and "Varieties of world religions." These do not fit into any of the previously described orders but still are speeches with thematic connections. A topic order can be thought of as a kind of prism by which we analyze a single topic (the "white light") by separating it into its different qualities (the different "color spectrums"). The idea is that by looking at each specific aspects of a topic, we will then be able to put it back together to create a sense of a whole. For instance, "Global warming will have dramatic effects on human migration, on the production of energy, on the production of food, on the ecological balance, and on cultural traditions." Topical order can be used effectively for virtually any speech genre, although it is particularly useful for commemorative speaking in order to understand the noble qualities of a particular subject.

Problem–Solution   Quite simply, this speech lays out the problem and then addresses that problem by presenting a clear solution. It can also incorporate the pro–con format within its structure. It is a very simple and straightforward speech structure very common in political deliberations. For instance, "To confront the challenge of global warming, we must institute the 2016 Paris Climate Change Accord immediately." This type of speech is common in advocacy, deliberative, and enrichment speeches.

As stated earlier, these methods of arrangement should be thought of as different ways of putting the same material together to produce different effects. Although there are exceptions, for the most part almost any general topic can be arranged using any of these methods. For instance, let us say you are interested in giving an enrichment speech about Martin Luther King Jr.'s civil rights rhetoric. By examining the topic through each of these lenses of arrangement, a speaker can experiment with different ways of presenting the speech.

1. *Chronological*: How King's oratory changed over time

2. *Geographical*: Speeches given in the rural South versus the urban North

3. *Cause–effect*: The impacts that his speeches had on civil rights legislation

4. *Pro–con*: The benefits and detriments of using nonviolent resistance methods

5. *Topical*: Racism, poverty, and war as three dominant themes in his speeches

6. *Problem–solution*: How nonviolent resistance helped overcome segregation

7. *Comparative advantage*: The comparison between nonviolence and violence

Testing out these different perspectives can be very useful in generating new ideas on a topic that may not have been obvious to a speaker at first. They force us to look at a familiar object in different ways and therefore make us ask new questions to arouse new interests.

Transitions   Once you have sufficiently articulated a main point and concluded a section, it is necessary to provide a "bridge" to move your audience from one idea to another. A **transition** provides this bridge by showing the connection between the two ideas and the need to proceed from one to the other. For example, a transition between points 1 and 2 in the preceding parkland example could be accomplished by the following transition: "This space can be used not only by animals, however, but by humans who wish to 'get away from it all.' " This passage shifts our attention from one object (wildlife) to another (park visitors) that are nonetheless connected by the idea of how the park can be "used" in a practical sense.

Internal Previews   An **internal preview** is a sentence within the speech that lets an audience know what they are about to hear—for example, "I shall show through a series of testimonials how experience with natural parks changes the way that individuals see themselves as connected with nature." Previews of this kind are helpful with a long speech that contains complex details. For shorter, less complex speeches, internal previews are often unnecessary.

Internal Summaries   An **internal summary** is the opposite of a preview. Instead of telling people what to expect, a summary reminds them what they have heard so as to reaffirm some important point. For example, at the end of the first section you could write, "All of these animal species I have described would find it hard to survive without continuous land preserved for their habitat." A summary should restate the idea of the main point but do so in a way that refers to the specific forms of evidence presented in the section.

Signposts   A **signpost** is a way of saying to your audience "You are here." It marks a path along the way and lets them know your location. In the earlier articulation of the main points, these took the form of "First," "Second," and "Third." Other signposts include "To begin," "In conclusion," "Next," and so forth. These very simple tools make a big difference in the way an audience follows along.

Patrick Henry: "There Is No Retreat but in Submission and Slavery"

Let us return to the speech by Patrick Henry. After gaining the attention of his audience and articulating his position, Patrick Henry then had to clearly arrange his points in order to defend his own position and counter opposing arguments. To do so, he adopted the style of asking hypothetical questions and answering them in sequence, step by step, knocking down the opposition and establishing his own argument as the only one left standing:

Ask yourselves how this gracious reception of our petition comports with those warlike preparations which cover our waters and darken our land. Are fleets and armies necessary to a work of love and reconciliation? Have we shown ourselves so unwilling to be reconciled that force must be called in to win back our love? Let us not deceive ourselves, sir. These are the implements of war and subjugation; the last arguments to which kings resort. I ask gentlemen, sir, what means this martial array, if its purpose be not to force us to submission? Can gentlemen assign any other possible motive for it? Has Great Britain any enemy, in this quarter of the world, to call for all this accumulation of navies and armies? No, sir, she has none. They are meant for us: they can be meant for no other. They are sent over to bind and rivet upon us those chains which the British ministry have been so long forging.

And what have we to oppose to them? Shall we try argument? Sir, we have been trying that for the last ten years. Have we anything new to offer upon the subject? Nothing. We have held the subject up in every light of which it is capable; but it has been all in vain. Shall we resort to entreaty and humble supplication? What terms shall we find which have not been already exhausted? Let us not, I beseech you, sir, deceive ourselves. Sir, we have done everything that could be done to avert the storm which is now coming on. We have petitioned; we have remonstrated; we have supplicated; we have prostrated ourselves before the throne, and have implored its interposition to arrest the tyrannical hands of the ministry and Parliament. Our petitions have been slighted; our remonstrances have produced additional violence and insult; our supplications have been disregarded; and we have been spurned, with contempt, from the foot of the throne! In vain, after these things, may we indulge the fond hope of peace and reconciliation.

There is no longer any room for hope. If we wish to be free—if we mean to preserve inviolate those inestimable privileges for which we have been so long contending—if we mean not basely to abandon the noble struggle in which we have been so long engaged, and which we have pledged ourselves never to abandon until the glorious object of our contest shall be obtained—we must fight! I repeat it, sir, we must fight! An appeal to arms and to the God of hosts is all that is left us!

They tell us, sir, that we are weak; unable to cope with so formidable an adversary. But when shall we be stronger? Will it be the next week, or the next year? Will it be when we are totally disarmed, and when a British guard shall be stationed in every house? Shall we gather strength but irresolution and inaction? Shall we acquire the means of effectual resistance by lying supinely on our backs and hugging the delusive phantom of hope, until our enemies shall have bound us hand and foot? Sir, we are not weak if we make a proper use of those means which the God of nature hath placed in our power. The millions of people, armed in the holy cause of liberty, and in such a country as that which we possess, are invincible by any force which our enemy can send against us. Besides, sir, we shall not fight our battles alone. There is a just God who presides over the destinies of nations, and who will raise up friends to fight our battles for us. The battle, sir, is not to the strong alone; it is to the vigilant, the active, the brave. Besides, sir, we have no election. If we were base enough to desire it, it is now too late to retire

> **DISCUSSION**
>
> What is clear from Henry's speech is that a complex and effective arrangement does not rely on only a single type of organizational method. Henry actually combines multiple forms of arrangement within his speech. What are some of the different strategies of arrangement he employs? How do they serve different functions? Which arrangement is dominant—meaning which one organizes all of the main points—and which ones are subordinate—meaning which are used to structure the points in a paragraph rather than the entire speech?

from the contest. There is no retreat but in submission and slavery! Our chains are forged! Their clanking may be heard on the plains of Boston! The war is inevitable—and let it come! I repeat it, sir, let it come.[4]

► CONCLUSIONS

Whereas the purpose of the introduction is to get attention and interest, the purpose of the **conclusion** is to satisfy an audience's desires and make them feel as if the speech has come together as a whole and therefore achieved qualitative unity in form. Specifically, the conclusion should always perform two essential functions irrespective of persuasive strategy. First, it should *help the audience remember the speech.* Audiences need to be left with something concrete in their imagination that helps them recall what was said. Sometimes this can be achieved by calling attention to the physical environment so that your speech is linked to some memorable object or event that is present. Other times you recall something important or imaginative in the earlier part of the speech and emphasize it again so as to leave the audience with a lasting "impression." Second, it should *clearly end your speech.* Let people know when you are nearing the end of your speech. Letting an audience know that you are about to end gives them a sense of "closure" and encourages concentration and attention even if they might have drifted off during the body. Otherwise, a conclusion can end with a variety of different strategies:

Leave with a Call to Action   Oftentimes, persuasion requires a lengthy detour through factual accounts, narratives, reasons, and explanations. A conclusion should show how all of these things lead to a specific action that is within reach of the audience. This helps it end on *a positive note.* Even with speeches that articulate the most graphic and devastating conditions, audiences want to know that there is some hope in making the world a better place. It is important to give audiences this hope at the end of a speech so that they leave believing they can make some small difference. For example, "We can meet this challenge of global warming! But first we must convince those around us that it is a serious problem. Talk to someone close to you today to start changing minds one at a time."

Startle Your Audience   After a long speech, sometimes audiences get too relaxed or even bored. A conclusion that makes some startling claim or demonstration can "wake them up" and make them pay closer attention to your concluding arguments. For example, "Look out the window at campus and imagine that all you see is water. That is the fate that is faced by millions of people today in island and coastal communities."

Challenge Your Audience   Similar to startling the audience, a speaker can also take the risky move to challenge them. This usually involves a combination of critique and imagination. To challenge an audience means to suggest that they are not living up to their potential, and that a better future may be ahead of them if they rise to new heights. For example, "We all might care about this global problem, but we will soon be absorbed in our own daily routines. Take a moment every day to step out of those routines and change one habit, however small, in your life, if only to remind yourself of the collective habits we must change as a nation."

Come Full Circle   A very effective way of concluding a speech is to refer back to the introduction and pick up where it left off. If it asked a question, then answer it. If it began a story, give the ending. If it quoted a famous philosopher, quote that philosopher again. This does not mean simply repeating what is already said, but continuing a line of thought and bringing it to a proper conclusion. For example, "In 50 years, the grandchildren of the fishermen in the Maldives will have been born. Let us all work so that they might fish on those same shores rather than having them exist only in faded photographs or memories."

Visualize a Positive Future   One way of ending on a positive note is to dramatize the great future that will come about through the committed actions of the audience. This is the basic strategy of much advertising that features before-and-after sequences. Thus, you not only want to tell people that their future is going to be better; you want to visualize that future for them in order to develop an emotional attachment. For instance, "If we only have the commitment, in only a few decades we can have virtually every automobile produced in the country run on electric energy. We can invest in technology to remove carbon dioxide from the atmosphere. We can restore the coastlines which have already been eroded. This we can do together."

Visualize a Negative Future   The opposite strategy is to visualize the negative future that would come about from inaction or choosing a different action. In the advertising analogy, this would be the future of choosing the competitor's product. Instead of a popular person wearing a colorful line of new clothes, for example, one would show a sad and lonely person wearing his or her old wardrobe. For instance, "If we do nothing, millions of people will be condemned to living in squalid refugee camps. All of our great coastal cities will be underwater. And the cultural richness which has grown up over millennia in harmony with the environment will be lost."

Ask a Question   Unlike the introduction, which poses a question that will then be answered, this question should leave the audience with something to ponder. For instance, "Will you do nothing?"

Employ Quotations   This strategy is identical to using a quotation in an introduction, except that the quotation should sum up the points that have come before and leave us with some kind of eloquent maxim to remember. For instance, one might quote Henry David Thoreau on the importance of nature to civilization or quote Genesis on how humans were commanded to tend the garden.

Tell a Story   Often used effectively to give "moral lessons," a story at the conclusion of a speech sums up in narrative what was already explained using logic. A story can also be used simply to encourage the audience to laugh or to cry or to feel some kind of emotional response. For instance, returning to another story about an island community to generate concern, or telling a satirical story of a climate change denier to generate laugher.

Patrick Henry: "Give Me Liberty or Give Me Death!"

Having knocked down all of his opponents' arguments and left his own alternative as the only alternative, Henry now attempts to clinch his argument in the conclusion by creating one of the most memorable phrases in American oratory:

It is in vain, sir, to extenuate the matter. Gentlemen may cry, Peace, Peace—but there is no peace. The war is actually begun! The next gale that sweeps from the north will bring to our ears the clash of resounding arms! Our brethren are already in the field! Why stand we here idle? What is it that gentlemen wish? What would they have? Is life so dear, or peace so sweet, as to be purchased at the price of chains and slavery? Forbid it, Almighty God! I know not what course others may take; but as for me, give me liberty or give me death![5]

> **DISCUSSION**
>
> What do you think it is about this phrase that stands out as original? Certainly the sentiment he expressed is by no means unique. The willingness to die for one's country or one's freedom or one's family is certainly universal. But something in the way that Patrick Henry expressed this idea cemented it into the memory of the nation. Why was this phrase so powerful and how would its absence have changed the speech?

▶ SUMMARY

Delivering a rhetorical speech is the consummation of a long process that begins not with an "idea" but with a response to a situation. Rhetoric draws its energy from its surroundings and puts it into a form capable of mobilizing public audiences to act in such a way that corrects that situation, in either the long- or the short-term. By "form," then, we do not simply mean a pre-given shape, like a template or shell. Form means the ability to rouse the interests, energies, and appetites of an audience, to carry them through a logical and narrative structure from one place to another, and to bring together elements in such a way that satisfies these interests and leaves a lasting impression on the mind, imagination, and emotions. A good rhetorical speech therefore constructs a message that produces "form" in the psychology of the audience by giving form to a previously unformed situation, an act that produces both pleasure and learning.

▶ CHAPTER 3 EXERCISES

1. **IMPROMPTU:** Come up with a speech topic as a class and assign everyone a different strategy of getting attention and interest. Have everyone give this speech and determine what were the most effective strategies appropriate to the topic.

2. **DEBATE:** Divide the class into four or more groups and assign each a different perspective on a local issue that does not require extensive research (for instance, that university dining commons should serve only low-fat food). Have each group organize a speech that advocates for their position using a pro–con structure that shows its own position to be better than those of the opposing groups and deliver these speeches in a debate format.

3. **GROUP:** Select a specific purpose for the whole class. After dividing the class into groups, assign a different strategy of introduction, organizing main points, and conclusion for each group. Have them compose a brief speech according to their assigned arrangement. Compare and contrast the speeches and discuss how the different forms of arrangement influenced the type of speech that was given.

4. **TAKE HOME:** Find an editorial in a major newspaper and analyze its arrangement structure. Write down whether it had clear strategies of introduction, organizing main points, and conclusion. Suggest also how the editorial might have improved by adopting a different strategy in any one part.

5. **VIDEO:** Find a specific location that you typically use, whether it is where you live, where you work, where you eat, or where you play. Record a minute-long video in which you present a "geographically" organized speech that introduces your class to this particular space.

Make sure you explore at least three different parts of the space and discuss how they add up to a "whole."

▶ NOTES

1. See Kenneth Burke, *Counter-Statement* (Chicago: University of Chicago Press, 1931), 33.

2. John Dewey, *Art as Experience* (New York: Perigree Books, 1934), 142.

3. Patrick Henry, "Liberty or Death," available at www.law.ou.edu/ushistory/henry.shtml (accessed 17 August 2016).

4. Patrick Henry, "Liberty or Death," available at www.law.ou.edu/ushistory/henry.shtml (accessed 17 August 2016).

5. Patrick Henry, "Liberty or Death."

Invention

This chapter reviews the canon of invention, which is the method by which we discover specific things to say within our speech that defends our claim, elaborates our beliefs, and narrates our values. Although all of us possess an innate sense of invention every time we try to find something interesting to talk about, we often pursue this aim intuitively rather than methodologically. This chapter seeks to establish the specific paths and processes a speaker can use to find original and creative content. First, it explores what resources are readily available in the public memory of one's culture, including such resources as maxims, myths, and social knowledge. Second, it provides guidance on how to find reliable sources and to cite them effectively in one speech. Third, it outlines specific resources for invention in terms of specific content, including facts, statistics, testimony, examples, and narratives. Fourth, it defines four different perspectives, called topics, that one can use to find a new approach to a subject matter. Last, this chapter discusses how to outline a speech in a way that both serves a creative and a documentary function.

Once we are familiar with how a speech is structured and put together through arrangement, the next task is to find the appropriate matter/substance/content with which to produce the most effective form. This search is no different in kind than our ongoing effort to find interesting things to say in our everyday casual conversations. When we run into our co-workers we might mention something we saw on the news or encountered on the way to work. When we see old friends we might recollect familiar stories about things that happened to us years before. When we get together with family we might fill them in on the important events in our lives. When we have casual interactions with strangers at the store, the bus stop, or the elevator, we might talk about the weather or the traffic. In each encounter we have every day, our mind goes through the process of invention in order to find something to say that is appropriate for the situation and for the audience to whom we are speaking. The more books we read, the more news we listen to, the more conversations we have with different people, the more experiences we have, the more we explore the science, art, and history of our world, the more resources for invention we possess.

When Aristotle defined rhetoric as the capacity for discovering the available means of persuasion in each case, he defined rhetoric as an *inventional* art. Derived from the Latin word *invenire*, "to find," **invention** refers to the act of finding something to say that lends support to the speaker's position. It is not surprising that the scientific-minded Aristotle would place such emphasis on invention, for it is precisely invention that provides a public speaker with the resources and knowledge that gives a speech its substance and value. Without invention, a speaker is left simply repeating the same statement over and over again. Consequently, it was taken for granted in the literature on classical rhetoric that invention was the most important and most difficult of the five tasks of the speaker. The reason it is difficult is because invention requires us to exert a great deal of time and effort not only trying to think of the *type* of resources that might be helpful to defend a claim but also trying to *find* them. One of the most common reasons for a speech's failure is neglect of invention, usually in the assumption on the part of the rhetor that his or her claim is so obviously true and persuasive that it needs no further backing by extensive research and creative argumentation. But facts on their own do not generate persuasion. Facts must be delivered within a form that is persuasive and adapted to one's audience.

With respect to rhetorical form, however, the materials of invention should not be considered the "core" of a speech that are only later conveyed to an audience through "style" any more than tubes of paint are the "core" of a painting only later given "style" by the hand of the painter. The "core" of the speech, as for a painting, is the qualitative unity in thought and in feeling that is produced in an audience after having experienced it. The materials of invention are merely resources to be used by the speaker to construct a message capable of producing that effect. The act of invention, therefore, should be thought of as the act of gathering things together and spreading them out on a table. As the creative work of composition ensues, some of that material finds a central place in the speech, while other material is made peripheral or not used at all. What is important is not what percentage of possible material is used in a speech, but that the speaker feels confident that what has been selected is the best choice of all available options. In other words, the best speakers leave many potential resources on the "cutting room floor" as evidence that they have selected only the most fitting material.

Last, it is important to point out that the vast quantity of resources now available at our disposal through the Internet and social media, easily accessed through smart phones wherever we go, has created both great potentials and even greater threats to the art of invention. On the one hand, being able to locate interesting facts, quotations, stories, primary resources, statistics, and scientific explanations has never been easier than at the present moment. Even just a few decades ago, many libraries still used card catalogs in order to locate books or magazines that were often well out of date. Today, a virtually infinite amount of data is immediately accessible through a simple search. On the other hand, it is also true that what is also ready to hand

are prepackaged arguments, ideologies, diatribes, explanations,
conspiracy theories, and entire
speeches that any individual can
find and pass off as their own.
This has not only led to an obvious increase in the temptation for
plagiarism, but perhaps more per-
vasively has encouraged imitation
rather than creativity. Rather than
putting together a variety of different material into a speech that
is uniquely one's own, the temptation is simply to take material that
is already been prepared and simply rearrange it so that it looks slightly different but is really
the words and ideas of someone else. It is contingent upon an ethical public speaker, and also
one who wishes to make a genuine expression of individuality, to resist this temptation for mere
imitation and to endeavor to make a public speech that is a unique and creative contribution to
the art of rhetoric.

DISCUSSION

The challenge to find new material for expression is
most prominent in the various fields of art. Think
of different genres of creative expression, such as
comedy, jazz, dance, painting, or sculpture. Where
do artists find material for invention? When you have
engaged in any creative project, where have you gone
to find new material? And do you think that these
strategies are at all applicable to the art of public
speaking?

▶ PUBLIC MEMORY

One of the best resources to draw from when beginning a speech is that collective resource
known as public memory. **Public memory** represents the storehouse of social knowledge, conventions, public opinions, values, and shared experiences that a speaker can appeal to within a
speech and feel confident that they will resonate meaningfully with that audience. For example,
William West says of memory:

> The study of memory encompasses not just ideas of memory at a particular historical
> moment, but entire regimes of memory, ways of privileging certain types of knowledge,
> certain values, certain ideas, beliefs, symbols—in short, an entire cultural ethnography
> coalesces around the apparently innocuous ability to remember the past. Memory serves as
> the locus of personal history and individual identity.[1]

Public memory represents those memories that are handed down from generation to generation,
usually through stories and maxims and rituals that attempt to preserve the past in the present.
In a political environment that moves at such a rapid pace as ours, creating such a lasting object
in the public memory is a rare and significant accomplishment. In this way, public memories
of this type can act as a reservoir of feelings, images, and stories from which a rhetor can draw.
Especially if a rhetor shares common memories with his or her audience, the appeal to collective
memory can be very powerful in gaining interest and focusing attention.

Rhetorically, public memory is a resource for what is called social knowledge. **Social knowledge** signifies a culture's conventional wisdom and practical judgment as expressed in maxims, generally held beliefs, and value judgments.[2] In other words, social knowledge represents what we might call "common sense." Social knowledge tells us what is better and worse, what the acknowledged facts of the world are, and thereby represents something of a cultural "second nature." Social knowledge thus signifies an attitude that is almost universally held by a wide number of people and has been passed down through generations and reaffirmed throughout history. Consequently, social knowledge is the most durable and most hard to change of any of the qualities of the public. It represents the collective judgments of a social group that are the result of past experience and that guide beliefs and behaviors in future situations. Consequently, social knowledge and public memory are vast storehouses of resources that a rhetor can select from when beginning to compose a speech.

The social knowledge stored up in public memory provides public speakers two primary resources—maxims and myths. A **maxim** is a short, pithy statement expressing a general truth or rule of conduct that is commonly accepted by culture and used to justify a variety of beliefs and actions. We often encounter maxims in the form of proverbs ("A tree is known by its fruit") and clichés ("The early bird catches the worm"). All cultures at all times have made use of maxims to bind together a community through shared principles and rules. The key for the speaker is to know which maxims speak to the unique culture of the audience while also being fitting to the situation and the argument. The best type of maxims not only convey generally accepted ideas, but also might be given a creative expression by particular individuals in history (Benjamin Franklin: "We must all hang together or we shall all hang separately"). Maxims of this type are readily understood and clearly state the position and motive of the speaker.

A **myth** is an emblematic story from the past that captures and expresses both a moral lesson and an understanding of historical origins and destiny of a particular group or nation. Calling something a myth does not necessarily mean that it is false or untrue. But it does mean that what factual truth it does contain has been transformed in such a way to convey a meaning that is above and beyond its historical veracity. For instance, the myth of the first Thanksgiving, in which English settlers to America and the native tribes who already lived there shared a dinner celebrating the fall harvest, may have actually taken place, but its meaning *as a myth* is supposed to represent the founding of America in cooperation and sharing between different peoples rather than, as with the myth of Columbus, a celebration of European expansion and colonization. Myths may be attached to *individual* people, such as Rosa Parks refusing to give up her seat on a bus, or to *groups* of people, such as the uprising by gay patrons of the Stonewall Inn. But almost always a myth deals with the celebration and memorial of specifically human actors to whom we look for exemplary actions whether positive, such as George Washington telling the truth about cutting down the cherry tree, or negative, such as Benedict Arnold betraying the colonial army. Consequently, we make use of myth even when we simply label someone as a "George Washington" or a "Benedict Arnold." We do not have to actually retell the myth to make it useful. A speaker simply has to make reference to it as long as everyone is familiar with the story.

Susan B. Anthony: "Resistance to Tyranny Is Obedience to God"

The use of public memory as a resource for invention is demonstrated in the testimony of Susan B. Anthony before a court of law. Anthony still appears on the face of some dollar coins, but it is not as well known that she also was convicted of a crime—the crime of casting a ballot in the 1872 presidential election, which happened during a time when women could not vote. On June 19, 1873, after having been denied the opportunity to say a word in her defense, she stood before Judge Ward Hunt after her lawyer appealed the guilty verdict. This excerpt from her interaction with the judge shows how a person can still make effective arguments without appealing to any specific facts or details as long as they draw from available social knowledge and maxims to make their case:

JUDGE HUNT   (Ordering the defendant to stand up) Has the prisoner anything to say why sentence shall not be pronounced?

MISS ANTHONY   Yes, your honor, I have many things to say; for in your ordered verdict of guilty, you have trampled under foot every vital principle of our government. My natural rights, my civil rights, my political rights, my judicial rights, are all alike ignored. Robbed of the fundamental privilege of citizenship, I am degraded from the status of a citizen to that of a subject; and not only myself individually, but all of my sex, are, by your honor's verdict, doomed to political subjection under this, so-called, form of government.

JUDGE HUNT   The Court cannot listen to a rehearsal of arguments the prisoner's counsel has already consumed three hours in presenting.

MISS ANTHONY   May it please your honor, I am not arguing the question, but simply stating the reasons why sentence cannot, in justice, be pronounced against me. Your denial of my citizen's right to vote, is the denial of my right of consent as one of the governed, the denial of my right of representation as one of the taxed, the denial of my right to a trial by a jury of my peers as an offender against law, therefore, the denial of my sacred rights to life, liberty, property and . . .

JUDGE HUNT   The Court cannot allow the prisoner to go on. . . . The Court must insist the prisoner has been tried according to the established forms of law.

MISS ANTHONY   Yes, your honor, but by forms of law all made by men, interpreted by men, administered by men, in favor of men, and against women; and hence, your honor's ordered verdict of guilty, against a United States citizen for the exercise of *"that citizen's right to vote,"* simply because that citizen was a woman and not a man. As then, the slaves who got their freedom must take it over, or under, or through the unjust forms of law, precisely so, now, must women, to get their right to a voice in this government, take it; and I have taken mine, and mean to take it at every possible opportunity.

JUDGE HUNT   The Court orders the prisoner to sit down. It will not allow another word. . . . (Here the prisoner sat down.) The prisoner will stand up. (Here Miss Anthony arose again.) The sentence of the Court is that you pay a fine of one hundred dollars and the costs of the prosecution.

> ## DISCUSSION
>
> Clearly the most powerful rhetorical strategy is the maxim she uses at the end. How does this "clinch" her argument? How would the argument have been different if she had used another related maxim? However, this is not the only rhetorical resource she uses. She appeals to both public memory and social knowledge in order to link her cause to the principles and values of America as well as to specific historical movements. What are some of these other resources she uses in this speech?

MISS ANTHONY   May it please your honor, I shall never pay a dollar of your unjust penalty. All the stock in trade I possess is a $10,000 debt, incurred by publishing my paper— The Revolution—four years ago, the sole object of which was to educate all women to do precisely as I have done, rebel against your man-made, unjust, unconstitutional forms of law, that tax, fine, imprison and hang women, while they deny them the right of representation in the government; and I shall work on with might and main to pay every dollar of that honest debt, but not a penny shall go to this unjust claim. And I shall earnestly and persistently continue to urge all women to the practical recognition of the old revolutionary maxim, that "Resistance to tyranny is obedience to God."[3]

▶ FINDING SOURCES

Although tapping into public memory is a good place to start with a public speech, the majority of your inventional resources should be drawn from active research that helps you discover something new that is persuasive, reliable, and novel. The power of invention in this respect often derives from the integrity and breadth of one's **sources**. Finding sources that are respected by your audience is paramount to persuading them that you are both informed of the situation and sympathetic to their attitudes and concerns. Except in special circumstances, most people generally tend to respect the same sources—usually those coming from representatives of some established public or private institution such as a university, a news organization, or research bureau.

However, it is important also to keep in mind that how people have come to understand what a "reliable" resource is has changed with the rise of Internet searches and now with social media. In the age of "mass media," or the time in which there were only a few major sources of news or information on which most people relied upon, there was a shared understanding of what constituted a trustworthy source. However, the sources of news and information have proliferated exponentially. Not only have their quantity increased, but their ability to target specific audiences has led to what is commonly called the "echo chamber" effect in which people are only exposed to opinions and facts that already support their judgments. Consequently, it is very easy to find a host of sources on the Internet supporting any number of positions and claiming to be reliable and objective—including the wildest conspiracy theories. Once again, with the vast increase in material available to us at our fingertips, it becomes even more contingent upon us to evaluate our resources carefully and avoid simply quoting a source simply because it agrees with our position.

Here are some general considerations about how to go about finding sources:

1. *Websites*: As a general rule, independent websites that are not affiliated with a professional institution such as a university, newspaper, or government agency are notoriously poor sources for information, particularly those websites that sell themselves as being dedicated to a specific issue. More often than not, these websites are themselves acting as forms of rhetorical advocacy in some way or another. Consequently, they are usually only valuable when they are themselves examples of rhetoric, for instance as one might do a paper on an ongoing debate in the public sphere using competing advocacy sites as examples. By contrast, sites like Wikipedia can offer a good overview of a topic and provide a basic framework of understanding that allows you to narrow your focus on more particular aspects of the subject. For general knowledge that does not need citation, Wikipedia can be valuable. However, it should only be considered a means of familiarizing yourself with a topic before delving into more detailed research. Whenever possible, speakers should get in the habit of looking elsewhere than the Internet for material for invention, for even when the material found is not invalid, it more often than not is commonplace and overused.

2. *Newspapers, magazines, or other journalistic sources*: These serve four purposes. First, they are excellent sources for getting first-person quotations from ordinary people about events of public interest. Nothing livens up a speech better than hearing what everyday people have to say about things that happened to them directly. Second, they provide quotations from various "experts" in a highly condensed and lively form that saves a speaker from having to delve through densely written academic material. Third, they usually provide the necessary facts to understand any issue, thus orienting a speaker to the situation. Fourth, journalistic writing is especially helpful in finding examples to use in introductions and conclusions, as newspaper articles are written with a similar incentive to "get attention and interest." A note of caution is in order, however. Like websites, newspapers and magazines are notoriously "slanted" toward specific audiences and therefore tend to pick and choose certain facts, certain experts, and certain stories in order to appeal to the stereotypes of their audiences. A reliable speaker will cross-reference numerous articles from respected news sources in order to determine which facts are accepted and which matters are in dispute.

3. *Books written about your subject by respected authors*: These generally provide a wealth of primary material as well as interpretative resources to help back up your claims. Books by university presses are generally more respected than books by popular presses, although they can be more dense and time consuming to search through. For books that appear only in print, a good strategy is to first go to the index to see whether your particular interest is represented by a category entry. Often, a quick index search in a biography or history book will give you a wealth of details that could give your speech character. However, many books are now available online through Google Books. It is generally a good idea to first do a search on Google Books in order to see if there is any quotable material easily accessible online before having to spend hours flipping through pages in the library.

4. *Academic journal articles*: The best electronic database for essays from communication and rhetorical scholars is the Communication Source database, accessed via the EBSCO search engine. The database includes all the essays from journals such as *Quarterly Journal of Speech* and *Philosophy and Rhetoric*. These usually present a very specific argument about an aspect of your case studies from either a scientific or a theoretical perspective. Even if they may not be directly relevant to your argument, they often provide good models for how to critically analyze objects for the purposes of drawing meaningful conclusions.

5. *Government documents*: Documents prepared and distributed by government agencies are often very useful when looking for data or analysis on general social conditions that can be measured by some objective standard. In general, the value of government documents is found in statistics.

Doing Proper Searches   When using electronic database searches, particularly newspaper and magazine databases, you need to try many different strategies. First, you should always avoid relying on general terms alone, such as "global warming" or "civil rights." You should always try to pair general terms with specific terms to narrow the search. Try adding specific names, places, dates, or "catchwords" that will call up more relevant searches—for instance, "Global warming Gore documentary controversy," or "intelligent design Dover 2006 debate," or "Malcolm X violence social change." Second, once you find one source, you should also scan it for more keywords that might be unique and helpful. Last, always check the bibliographies of articles and books to find new sources. Even if they are not immediately helpful, these new sources might, in turn, cite other articles and books in their own bibliographies that are helpful.

Documenting Sources   Through the invention process, make sure you keep a careful document of your sources. A simple model is the Modern Language Association (MLA) citation style. Use this in recording your sources in an outline, making sure also to retain the page numbers.

1. *Journal or magazine article*: Paroske, Marcus. "Deliberating International Science Policy Controversies: Uncertainty and AIDS in South Africa." *Quarterly Journal of Speech* 95.2 (2009): 148–170.

2. *Newspaper article*: Mitchell, Gordon. "Scarecrow Missile Defense." *Pittsburgh Post-Gazette*, 8 July 2001: E-1.

3. *Book*: Danisch, Robert. *Pragmatism, Democracy and the Necessity of Rhetoric*. Columbia: University of South Carolina Press, 2007. Print.

4. *Book article or chapter*: Keränen, Lisa Belicka. "Girls Who Come to Pieces: Shifting Ideologies of Beauty and Cosmetics Consumption in the *Ladies' Home Journal*, 1900–1920." In *Turning the Century: Essays in Media and Cultural Studies*. Ed. Carol A. Stabile. Boulder, CO: Westview Press, 2000. 142–165. Print.

5. *Website*: Furness, Zack. "My Dad Kicked Ass for a Living." *BadSubjects.com*. October 2001. Web.

When citing a source in a written paper or outline, you should put the last name of the author and the page number in parentheses at the end of the sentence where the material was cited. This allows you to avoid accusations of plagiarism and also shows your paper to be well researched and documented.

Spoken Citation Style   Especially for informative speeches, it is vital not only to acquire but to cite and quote accurate sources to give yourself credibility. Here are some guidelines for how to smoothly incorporate citations into your speech:

1. *Well-known and uncontroversial facts*: There is no citation needed for the obvious. Do not clutter a speech by citing things an audience takes for granted.

    a.   GOOD. "Over 2,000,000 people were killed in the Civil War."

    b.   BAD. "According to *Encyclopedia Online* . . ."

2. *Unknown or controversial facts released by people and institutions in press releases*: When your information comes directly from the source and you have access to that source, just cite that original source by name. Do not cite any subsequent news publication that may have repeated this information.

    a.   GOOD. "The Economy Institute released a report in June that claimed environmental restrictions hurt economic growth."

    b.   BAD. "*The Times* reported in July that a report by the Brookings Institute in June said . . ."

3. *Unknown or controversial facts published secondhand by news publications*: When a newspaper has cited some startling fact, make sure to cite *both* the source and the news publication that first reported it. The fact is that sometimes news reports will "spin" facts in certain ways, so it is important to acknowledge that you are getting it secondhand.

    a.   GOOD. "Hodgedale Industries recently was reported in the *New York Times* as saying that its medical screening technologies have saved over 2,000 women's lives in the year 2001."

    b.   BAD. "*The New York Times* claims that Hodgedale Industries has saved . . ."

    c.   BAD. "Hodgedale Industries has saved . . ."

    d.   BAD. "Hodgedale Industries claims to have saved . . ."

4. *Quoting famous people*: Generally, important quotes by famous people only need a citation by the name of the person, not the time, place, or manner in which the passage was written or spoken.

    a.   GOOD. "Socrates once said that "the unexamined life is not worth living."

    b.   BAD. "In 430 B.C.E., Socrates was once quoted in Plato's *Critias* that . . ."

5. *Quoting professionals or experts*: For all other quotes, cite the name, status or position, and the forum in which the quote appeared.

    a.   GOOD. "In the *New York Times*, September 3, 2012, Gail Hansen, an epidemiologist who works for Pew Charitable Trusts, said 'at some point the available science can be used in making policy decisions.' "

b.   GOOD. "In today's *New York Times*, a notable epidemiologist said . . ."

c.   BAD. "Gail Hansen said . . ."

d.   BAD. "The *New York Times* reported that 'at some point . . .' "

6.   *Citing bare, uncontroversial facts reported in newspapers*: For isolated facts that do not merit a lot of attention, just cite the publication in which that fact appeared.

a.   GOOD. "The *New York Times* reported in 2010 that 34 percent of the population is obese."

b.   BAD. "Thirty-four percent of the population is obese."

c.   BAD. "A study based on national surveys that record heights and weights of a representative sample of Americans, in which people are considered obese if their body mass index—a ratio of height to weight—is thirty or greater, noted that 34 percent of the population is obese."

7.   *Using stories or anecdotes found in magazines or websites*: When you use examples, it is important to make them sound like stories. The temptation is to ignore the need for citation. However, it is very important to cite the source and its author to give examples credibility. You simply need to find a discrete way to fit it in without ruining the flow of the narrative.

a.   GOOD. "Anna had just arrived from Russia when she was arrested by police, who accused her of spying. She was put in a cell for two months and was not able to see anyone. Her story, finally told last August in *The New Republic*, raises serious questions about our civil liberties."

b.   BAD. "Anna had just arrived from Russia when she was arrested by police, who accused her of spying. She was put in a cell for two months and was not able to see anyone. Can we let this happen in the United States?"

c.   BAD. "In a recent issue of *The New Republic*, a story appeared about a girl . . ."

DISCUSSION

Sociologist Bruno Latour had a way of talking about the use of evidence and sources that captured their rhetorical character quite well. He said that quoting someone, pointing to a particular fact, or citing some historical event was a way of generating "allies" for one's position. For instance, quoting Gandhi or Mother Teresa in a speech supporting one position was akin to inviting them into the room to speak on your behalf and defend you. Similarly, pointing to physical evidence, such as a fingerprint, was a way of making an ally with the natural world. How does this metaphor of "allies" change the way we think about our sources? If we could create hologram images of our sources and have them stand behind us as we speak, would that make us more or less reluctant to cite them?

▶ RESOURCES FOR INVENTION

What do we look for when we find a good source? Any good speech will draw from five basic categories available to the public speaker to persuade an audience—**facts**, **statistics**, **testimony**, **examples**, and **narratives**. Gathering together material from each of these categories will provide a wealth of resources from which to draw upon to construct a speech that is complex and powerful.

Facts   A fact is a condensed empirical claim that tells us about some facet of the world that we can rely upon to be true. Most of the facts that we know come from everyday experience, such as "heavy objects fall" or "the sun sets at night." Other facts are derived from scientific research and are based on our trust in expertise, such as "objects are weightless in space" or "the earth goes around the sun." A speaker can use both types of facts to support claims, drawing on everyday facts to make a claim seem supported by common sense while also appealing to the facts of scientific research to make the case for more specific and controversial claims that might challenge common sense. In summary, facts should be considered the "building blocks" of any speech insofar as they are solid, particular, concrete elements that we can rely upon to support our case. The most powerful fact should be easily comprehended, succinctly spoken, and should call up a very specific image in people's minds that guarantees that when they encounter something, they will know exactly what it is and what to expect from it.

Statistics   Statistics are different from facts because they do not deal with specific assertions about concrete objects but are mathematical generalizations that help us make predictions about certain types of objects or events. They do not tell us what something *is* but rather what we can probably *expect* of it. For instance, direct use of numeric facts and statistics is helpful to either show the magnitude of something ("Over 90 percent of the colonists now support a revolution") or the probability of something ("Given the number of British warships in Boston Harbor, it is likely that war shall come"). In other words, statistics let us know that if we were to encounter an American colonist, there is a good chance that he or she would support a revolution, just as if we were to see British warships in Boston Harbor, then it is likely that we will see a war. Particularly when we are concerned with the outcomes of our potential judgments, statistics that tell us the likelihood of certain outcomes are very persuasive, provided that the statistics come from respected sources and are not distorted by partisan influences. In summary, facts and statistics often work closely together. For instance, one can say the fact that nicotine is addictive because of the nature of this chemical compound and how it reacts to the body. However, because everyone reacts to nicotine differently, the level of addiction varies widely according to a person's biology and habits. Consequently, when it comes to describing how nicotine actually influences a population, one must rely on statistics in terms of what percentage of cigarette users become addicted. A fact then tells me something that is always the case. A statistic tells me only the likelihood that something will be the case for a certain specific population of things or events.

Testimony   Testimony consists of direct quotations from individuals who can speak with some authority on a certain state of affairs. Testimony can come in various forms. **Lay testimony** derives from ordinary people who have had relevant experience with some issue. Such testimony can prove that something exists or has happened by drawing on the personal experience ("I have seen warships in Boston Harbor") or it can give a "human touch" to a story by using vivid and striking quotes to exemplify some point ("I saw the young man bleeding to death in my arms"). **Expert testimony** comes from individuals who may not have directly experienced something but who know a considerable amount about the subject matter due to extensive research. Such testimony is used to challenge or override competing explanations by appealing to the author-ity of knowledge ("According to General Nash, 'There is no conceivable reason other than war for so many ships to be in Boston Harbor'"). Last, **prestige testimony** comes from famous and well-respected individuals who may have nothing directly to do with an issue but whose words provide inspiration and insight. ("So I say we should pursue revolution against the King of Eng-land, for as John Locke wrote, 'In transgressing the law of nature, the offender declares himself to live by another rule than that of reason and common equity'")

Examples   These include descriptions of actual or hypothetical events, people, objects, or processes that can embody an idea or argument in a concrete form so that audiences can "see" what it means ("If one wants to know the nature of tyranny, go to Boston. There, the streets are filled with armed men, the courts have been abolished, and young men are killed in the streets"), and/or that can act as evidence to prove the existence or define the nature of something ("War is upon us, as evidenced by the battle of Concord and the presence of British troops marching through our countryside"). Examples can be drawn from newspapers, history, biographies, sci-ence, or personal experience. They are crucial in embodying abstract claims within concrete visual images that bring to life the causes and consequences of certain actions and beliefs.[4]

There are two main kinds of examples: actual examples and fictional examples. **Actual examples** are descriptions of real things that exist or have existed, that happen or have happened. The main sources of actual examples are history, the news, personal experience, or science. Thus, one could use the Salem witch trials to exemplify intolerance, a feature story about a New Orleans family to exemplify the struggles after Hurricane Katrina, a personal story about one's immigrant grand-father to exemplify personal courage, or a scientific discovery of an Egyptian tomb to exem-plify ancient wisdom. Actual examples are important for making speeches appear thoroughly researched and backed by evidence rather than simply being expressions of personal opinion. Actual examples thus function both to *prove* one's point as well as to demonstrate it.

Fictional examples are descriptions of events that are only imagined to have happened in the past, present, or future. There are two kinds of fictional examples: third-person examples (refer-ring to "he" or "she") and second-person examples (referring to "you"). **Third-person fictional examples** describe the actions of other people as if they actually happened until usually reveal-ing at the end that it is just a story. For example, one might say, "Joe was an aspiring actor until he started doing drugs and then had an overdose and died. Joe is not a real person, but there are thousands of people like Joe every day." The most effective third-person examples come from stories taken from literature or other popular forms of art that are commonly known by an audience. The other kind of example is a **second-person fictional example**, which places the audience in a hypothetical situation that asks them to envision doing something. For example, one might say, "Imagine you were walking down the street and saw a homeless man being beaten. Would you rush to save him or walk away?" Second-person examples usually offer the audience some choice in order to get them thinking about the problem that the speech then proceeds to address. Fictional examples can be helpful in demonstrating the meaning of a speech, but being pure fabrications, they generally lack the authenticity and power of actual examples. As a general rule, a speaker should choose actual examples over fictional examples whenever possible.

Narratives   A narrative is a dramatic story that is more complex than an example, and that captures and holds the attention of an audience by promising that, through the unfolding of the plot and character, something new and satisfying will be produced at the end. Narratives are excellent ways of conveying complex states of affairs in ways that are meaningful and memorable for an audience. It is important to note that stories are not "irrational" components of speeches that are to be opposed with facts and statistics. Quite the opposite: when faced with competing narratives, an audience must decide which narrative is more "rational" to follow. According to Walter Fisher:

> Rationality is determined by the nature of persons as narrative beings—their inherent awareness of *narrative probability*, what constitutes a coherent story, and their constant habit of testing *narrative fidelity*, whether the stories they experience ring true with the stories they know to be true in their lives."[5]

In other words, **narrative fidelity** refers to how accurately a narrative represents accepted facts, such as newspaper reports of Paul Revere's ride printed days after the event. **Narrative probability** refers to the coherence of the narrative as a story apart from the actual facts, such as the poem "The Midnight Ride of Paul Revere" written by Henry Wadsworth Longfellow in 1860, almost a century later. The most effective narrative from a rhetorical standpoint should have both high narrative probability *and* high narrative fidelity. By presenting an argument in a form of a story that accurately represents reality in a coherent, engaging, and powerful manner, a speaker invites an audience to vicariously participate in a new vision of reality. Especially when narratives are broad in scope, they can completely alter an audience's basic worldview. The narratives we tell of our common histories have particular power in structuring our social organizations, our self-conceptions, and our relationships with other groups.

Eugene Debs: "Gold Is God Today and Rules with Pitiless Sway in the Affairs of Men"

One of the most prominent places in which a variety of different conventional resources are needed is the court of law. One of the most famous addresses to the court was made on

September 18, 1918, by American labor leader Eugene Debs. He had been arrested under the Espionage Act of 1917 for an anti-war speech on June 16, 1918, in Canton, Ohio, protesting how the war was hurting working men and women. By demanding such things as a 40-hour work week, safety standards, and minimum age requirements for employment, he was prosecuted for interfering with the operation or success of the armed forces of the United States. His speech to the court was not intended to emancipate him—he had already been convicted—but to narrate what he saw as the tragic divide between rich and poor that was established on the basis of a skewed value system:

> Your Honor, years ago I recognized my kinship with all living beings, and I made up my mind that I was not one bit better than the meanest on earth. I said then, and I say now, that while there is a lower class, I am in it, and while there is a criminal element, I am of it, and while there is a soul in prison, I am not free.

> I listened to all that was said in this court in support and justification of this prosecution, but my mind remains unchanged. I look upon the Espionage Law as a despotic enactment in flagrant conflict with democratic principles and with the spirit of free institutions. . . . Your Honor, I have stated in this court that I am opposed to the social system in which we live; that I believe in a fundamental change—but if possible by peaceable and orderly means. . . .

> Standing here this morning, I recall my boyhood. At fourteen I went to work in a railroad shop; at sixteen I was firing a freight engine on a railroad. I remember all the hardships and privations of that earlier day, and from that time until now my heart has been with the working class. I could have been in Congress long ago. I have preferred to go to prison. . . .

> I am thinking this morning of the men in the mills and the factories; of the men in the mines and on the railroads. I am thinking of the women who for a paltry wage are compelled to work out their barren lives; of the little children who in this system are robbed of their childhood and in their tender years are seized in the remorseless grasp of Mammon and forced into the industrial dungeons, there to feed the monster machines while they themselves are being starved and stunted, body and soul. I see them dwarfed and diseased and their little lives broken and blasted because in this high noon of Christian civilization money is still so much more important than the flesh and blood of childhood. In very truth gold is god today and rules with pitiless sway in the affairs of men.

> In this country—the most favored beneath the bending skies—we have vast areas of the richest and most fertile soil, material resources in inexhaustible abundance, the most marvelous productive machinery on earth, and millions of eager workers ready to apply their labor to that machinery to produce in abundance for every man, woman, and child—and if there are still vast numbers of our people who are the victims of poverty and whose lives are an unceasing struggle all the way from youth to old age, until at last death comes to their rescue and lulls these hapless victims to dreamless sleep, it is not the fault of the Almighty: it

cannot be charged to nature, but it is due entirely to the outgrown social system in which we live that ought to be abolished not only in the interest of the toiling masses but in the higher interest of all humanity. . . .

I believe, Your Honor, in common with all Socialists, that this nation ought to own and control its own industries. I believe, as all Socialists do, that all things that are jointly needed and used ought to be jointly owned—that industry, the basis of our social life, instead of being the private property of a few and operated for their enrichment, ought to be the common property of all, democratically administered in the interest of all. . . .

I am opposing a social order in which it is possible for one man who does absolutely nothing that is useful to amass a fortune of hundreds of millions of dollars, while millions of men and women who work all the days of their lives secure barely enough for a wretched existence. This order of things cannot always endure. I have registered my protest against it. I recognize the feebleness of my effort, but, fortunately, I am not alone. There are multiplied thousands of others who, like myself, have come to realize that before we may truly enjoy the blessings of civilized life, we must reorganize society upon a mutual and cooperative basis; and to this end we have organized a great economic and political movement that spreads over the face of all the earth.

There are today upwards of sixty millions of Socialists, loyal, devoted adherents to this cause, regardless of nationality, race, creed, color, or sex. They are all making common cause. They are spreading with tireless energy the propaganda of the new social order. They are waiting, watching, and working hopefully through all the hours of the day and the night. They are still in a minority. But they have learned how to be patient and to bide their time. They feel—they know, indeed—that the time is coming, in spite of all opposition, all persecution, when this emancipating gospel will spread among all the peoples, and when this minority will become the triumphant majority and, sweeping into power, inaugurate the greatest social and economic change in history. In that day we shall have the universal commonwealth—the harmonious cooperation of every nation with every other nation on earth. . . .

Your Honor, I ask no mercy and I plead for no immunity. I realize that finally the right must prevail. I never so clearly comprehended as now the great struggle between the powers of greed and exploitation on the one hand and upon the other the rising hosts of industrial freedom and social justice. I can see the dawn of the better day for humanity. The people are awakening. In due time they will and must come to their own.

When the mariner, sailing over tropic seas, looks for relief from his weary watch, he turns his eyes toward the southern cross, burning luridly above the tempest-vexed ocean. As the midnight approaches, the southern cross begins to bend, the whirling worlds change their places, and with starry fingerpoints the Almighty marks the passage of time upon the dial of the universe, and though no bell may beat the glad tidings, the lookout knows that the midnight is passing and that relief and rest are close at hand. Let the people everywhere take heart of hope, for the cross is bending, the midnight is passing, and joy cometh with the morning.

I am now prepared to receive your sentence.[6]

DISCUSSION

Although the speech clearly lacks the detailed statistics or cited facts that would be required of most public speeches, it nonetheless contains every resource for invention in some way. In particular, Debs makes use of examples and narratives that are particularly powerful (as well as containing many elements of style—which makes it worth returning to after reading that chapter). What are some of the narratives he uses? Keeping in mind the speech was given in 1918 when the term "socialist" had a much broader meaning than it does today, which narratives have, in your opinion, more or less narrative probability and fidelity given the time period?

 TOPICS

The last resource for invention is not a particular "thing" but rather a way of relating things together. These are called "topics of invention" (in Greek, *topoi,* which means "places"). **Topics of invention** therefore represent specific ways of placing material into relationships that ideally bring about new questions and new insights. If one imagines all of the previous material for invention spread out on a table, topics represent certain places on the table that make the material look different when placed within their circle, much as placing objects under different microscopes or lenses makes them disclose new characteristics. Topics therefore serve the function of invention by encouraging a rhetor to experiment with different ways of asking questions about the subject matter to find out if anything interesting is produced by the different lenses. Here are four such topics:

Definition   The topic of **definition** simply asks something to define itself properly. Often, a speaker persuades simply by providing a more correct and precise definition of a situation, object, person, or action. For instance, the Founding Fathers often distinguished between a "democracy" (which was direct majority rule by the people) and a "republic" (which was indirect representative government by elected leaders). Demanding proper definitions often can challenge unspoken preconceptions about things and invite people to inquire about their real natures.

Division   **Division** either takes something that seems to be a "whole" and breaks it into its constituent parts ("A republic requires fair elections, a parliamentary body, separation of powers, and the rule of law") or combines disparate parts into a whole ("I may be a New Yorker, and you might be a Virginian, but we are all Americans"). Division tells us either what something is made of (by breaking it up) or how to make something (by putting it together).

Comparison   **Comparison** takes two different things and puts them side by side to show their similarities and differences. Sometimes comparison can be used to make something seem more valuable ("Those who died in the Boston Massacre are akin to the Greeks who died at Thermopylae, sacrificing themselves for the sake of freedom"), to make it seem less valuable ("The British soldiers are merely well-dressed thieves"), or simply to identify it properly ("I call it a massacre because like other massacres in history it featured an armed force killing unarmed innocents").

Relationship   A **relationship** puts two or more things in causal relationship to one another in order to understand how something was produced. Unlike comparison, which simply shows how two things are similar or different, relationship asks how one thing influenced another thing. Relationships can either be described in terms of physical cause and effect ("Oppressive taxation of the colonies has led to revolt") or in terms of historical lineage ("The colonists are the children of the English king").

Sojourner Truth: "Ain't I a Woman?"

One of the most fascinating orators in American history is civil rights champion and former slave Sojourner Truth. Born Isabella Van Wagenen (a Dutch name given by her Dutch slave owners) in about 1797, Truth achieved her freedom in 1827 and changed her name in 1843. Despite growing up illiterate, she was a woman of remarkable intelligence and presence. Her most famous extemporaneous address, "Ain't I a Woman?" was delivered at the Women's Convention in Akron, Ohio, on May 29, 1851. This type of convention was a major component of the early women's rights movement, which involved the organization of women's conferences to bring together feminists to discuss goals and strategies. However, many of these conferences attracted men (including several ministers) who came largely to heckle the speakers and to argue that women's proper place was one of being both subservient to and cared for by men. It was the heckling of one of these ministers that inspired Truth to speak. Reacting to a black-robed minister who argued for male superiority based on "superior intellect" and "manhood in Christ," Truth argued that women were in fact more powerful than men and also that black women had been denied even the limited rights given to white women. To make her case, she uses a variety of topics to challenge conventional understandings of race and gender:

> Well, children, where there is so much racket there must be something out of kilter. I think that 'twixt the negroes of the South and the women at the North, all talking about rights, the white men will be in a fix pretty soon. But what's all this here talking about?

That man over there says that women need to be helped into carriages, and lifted over ditches, and to have the best place everywhere. Nobody ever helps me into carriages, or over mud-puddles, or gives me any best place! And ain't I a woman? Look at me! Look at my arm! I have ploughed and planted, and gathered into barns, and no man could head me! And ain't I a woman? I could work as much and eat as much as a man—when I could get it—and bear the lash as well! And ain't I a woman? I have borne thirteen children, and seen most all sold off to slavery, and when I cried out with my mother's grief, none but Jesus heard me! And ain't I a woman?

Then they talk about this thing in the head; what's this they call it? [member of audience whispers, "intellect"] That's it, honey. What's that got to do with women's rights or negroes' rights? If my cup won't hold but a pint, and yours holds a quart, wouldn't you be mean not to let me have my little half measure full?

Then that little man in black there, he says women can't have as much rights as men, 'cause Christ wasn't a woman! Where did your Christ come from? Where did your Christ come from? From God and a woman! Man had nothing to do with Him.

If the first woman God ever made was strong enough to turn the world upside down all alone, these women together ought to be able to turn it back, and get it right side up again! And now they is asking to do it, the men better let them.[7]

> ## DISCUSSION
>
> Although it might not be clear at first, Truth actually makes use of all four topics. She starts by questioning a conventional definition of woman as relatively passive and helpless and needing the care of a man, and then proceeds in subsequent paragraphs to approach the subject using division, then comparison, then relationship. Indeed, her use of the topic of relationship borders on a revolutionary re-understanding of the definition of "woman." How do each of these strategies operate in her speech?

▶ OUTLINING

The outline is one of the primarily tools for helping to arrange all of your "discoveries" into a concrete form guided by the canon of arrangement. **Outlining** allows you to organize the "highlights" of a speech into sections and put them into a linear progression of beginning, middle, and end. A **working outline** is a tentative plan for the speech that allows a speaker to experiment with different arrangements before exerting the time and energy required to finalize the speech. In a classroom setting, a working outline also provides a medium of communication between instructor and student during the composition process. As a collaborative medium, outlines are often more valuable when they are incomplete, because they help identify the gaps that need to be filled. In the *creative stage*, a working outline should function as both a rough draft and a brainstorming session. The rough draft aspect records the basic arguments, facts, quotes, and strategies that the writer confidently feels are useful. The brainstorming aspect puts them together with ideas and possibilities that may not yet have any clear structure or backing. Both students and instructors should thus use outlines *as a tool for collaborative communication* during the process of invention and development. The **final outline** then represents the last stage of your speech preparations that precede the actual writing or delivery of a speech and is useful both for evaluation purposes (for the instructor) and to allow the speech to be performed again (for the speaker). The author should be careful to accurately record all quotations in full, as well as dutifully record all facts as faithfully as possible.

To be effective as a tool for creative composition, an outline should identify not only the content of what is going to be said but also the composition methods being used to organize the material. This includes not only methods outlined in this chapter but also the more specific strategies in subsequent chapters. As students become more familiar with the specific techniques, working outlines should become more complex. Each specific entry should therefore include not only examples, arguments, and proofs, but also labels (in parentheses) attached to those examples, arguments, and proofs that tell both the instructor and the speaker what persuasive strategy is being employed. The outline should also include a bibliography with sources cited according to MLA style (or the instructor's preferred style), discussed in the previous section on invention.

Here is an example of a full manuscript speech written to support state funding of the arts in the 2010 Louisiana budget. In an old Louisiana tradition, it is intended to be spoken at a "jazz funeral" for the arts, in which a fake coffin would be carried in front of the state capital accompanied by a jazz band:

> Thank you all for joining together in our solemn remembrance for the loss of a dear friend. It is fitting that jazz accompanies our gathering here today, and not just because we lie upriver from the birthplace of America's classical music. Louis Armstrong said of jazz: "The memory of things gone is important to a jazz musician. Things like old folks singing in the moonlight in the back yard on a hot night or something said long ago" (Collier, 32). So when we hear jazz, we think both of what was and what might be again, even as we face up to the reality of what is before us in the moment. We think of the sacrifice and courage of those who struggled not only to forge a life along this sultry stretch of land, but who put their blood in the soil to bring forth something called beauty. We think of the lives stretching ahead of our children, who may, too, discover that a difficult life of creation is more rewarding than an easy life of consumption. And we think of the friend who lies prostrate before us in the knowledge that someone we cared about has passed into memory.
>
> But we are also here for a specific reason. Today we hold a jazz funeral for the arts in order to accomplish a political task as well. We wish to protest the dramatic cuts in arts funding in

Louisiana that will not only harm the state's vibrant cultural life but also diminish its economic growth, and by protesting these cuts we hope to give the arts a second life despite the financial challenges ahead.

But first, let us be clear about whom we eulogize. We do not mourn the passing of art itself. Art, like all great human inventions, is born out of struggle. There is no accident that jazz was invented in New Orleans. Art becomes great in proportion to the obstacles it must overcome. Violence cannot kill it. Poverty cannot starve it. Waves cannot drown it. And government irresponsibility cannot suffocate it. Indeed, though the small-minded and the thin-willed may occasionally place their bony thumb upon the pulse of invention as a display of power, they have more to fear from art than art from them.

Neither do we mourn the passing of artists. Those joining us today already prove them to be alive among us. But that is hardly a surprise. The artistic spirit has proven time and again that it does not give way easily, even to force. If it could survive in the harshest of times, who would expect it to acquiesce before a combination of stupidity and neglect? No, we do not mourn the death of artists. In fact, artists have joined us today in this funeral to honor what is lost.

But although art and artists will always endure, the Louisiana Decentralized Arts Fund will not. The estimated 83 percent cut in its relatively small $3-million budget effectively dismembers an organization that is not only a national model for local arts funding but that economically produces a major return on every dollar invested. Gerd Wuestemann, the executive director of the Acadiana Center for the Arts, a regional grant-distribution agency, says he anticipates two things as a result of the cuts: "Some of the smaller organizations that do good work, especially in the more rural areas, may have to close doors," he says. "And I think it will result in fewer projects and less income to the communities and less vibrancy in our lifestyle, and I think that's a shame" (Pierce). But such reasoning runs too far ahead for those who have their heads screwed on backwards. As our governor remarked recently to Larry King about federal investment in the arts: "Fundamentally, I don't think . . . $50 million for the National Endowment for the Arts is going to get the economy moving again as quickly as allowing the private sector to create jobs" (Knight). With the nonprofit arts sector bringing in millions of visitors each year to this state and creating jobs, one might have reason to object to the logic that kills the jobs in the village to save them. But we are not here for an argument, but a eulogy. And the death of the arts fund is more properly reserved for the memorial for the impending massacre of public agencies not only across the state but nationwide. The body of the arts fund will thus be thrown on the pyre with those of health care, education, environmental protection, and all the other extensions of the social body that have been sacrificed on the altar of rampant greed and high-sounding idiocy.

But there is yet another body to mourn as well in a larger sense. For without support of the arts, we eventually will mourn the passing of the community. Without democratic organizations that enable local communities to integrate the arts into their cultural fabric, the effects of art are broken into a thousand isolated threads that one encounters only sporadically and accidentally. Without collective investments in the arts, a community spirit withers, and citizens retreat into their private spheres. Like we see here today, the arts bring people together into the open to share in their *common* world and to make it a *better* world.

There is, of course, no physical body here to mourn over. The community is not something one can witness. The community exists between us, and art not only forges those bonds that produce a sense of belonging and happiness, but also provides a vehicle for creative invention that is always produced when democratic citizens invest their collective energies in improving their common world. A great American philosopher, John Dewey, once wrote that: "Creation, not acquisition, is the measure of a nation's rank; it is the only road to an enduring place in the admiring memory of mankind" (Dewey, 255–256).

In summary, Louisiana, despite its natural wealth, has never been ranked high on the measure of acquisition. But it has achieved a standing in the memory of humankind as one of the greatest sources of creation ever seen. Jazz has been one of its grandest achievements, but we miss its power if we use it only to reflect on the greatness of what was. Its potential comes from memory, but its power comes from its second line. So although the body of the community may lie prostrate before us at the moment, once that Second Line starts, you watch it get up and dance. Strike it up!

That is the complete text of the speech. However, let us back up and imagine how you might structure this speech as a final outline that you would turn in to the instructor prior to its completion. First, you would turn in a summary of the speech which includes the title, the topic, the specific purpose, and the thesis:

Title: Eulogy for the Jazz Funeral for the Arts

Topic: Budget cuts to arts funding in Louisiana

Specific Purpose: To advocate that funding to the Louisiana Decentralized Arts Fund should be restored.

Thesis: We wish to protest the dramatic cuts in arts funding in Louisiana that will not only harm the state's vibrant cultural life but also diminish its economic growth, and by protesting these cuts, we hope to give the arts a second life despite the financial challenges ahead.

Then you would generate an outline form that indicates the main points you will be using, the resources for invention you will be including, as well as the persuasive strategies you will be employing (marked in *italics*). This last part is particularly important as it indicates to the instructor that you are consciously employing rhetorical strategies rather than simply placing material in a speech without understanding its rhetorical function. Many of the strategies used here will appear throughout the rest of the book. Finally, the outline should be easily transferable to note cards if you are making an extemporaneous speech.

Introduction   (**Material to arouse interest**—*Tell a Story/Use Quote/Utopia/Virtue*): Thank you all for coming. It is fitting to be in birthplace of America's classical music. Louis Armstrong said of jazz that: "The memory of things gone is important to a jazz musician. Things like old folks singing in the moonlight in the back yard on a hot night or something said long ago" (Collier, 32). Jazz reminds of sacrifice/courage/beauty of people long past. Think of children choosing creation over consumption. And we think of the friend prostrate before us.

(**Thesis**): But here for political task as well. We wish to protest the dramatic cuts in arts funding in Louisiana that will not only harm the state's vibrant cultural life but also diminish its economic growth, and by protesting these cuts we hope to give the arts a second life despite the financial challenges ahead.

Body (Topical Order)

I.   (**First main point**—*Identification*): People in Louisiana love the arts and the arts will endure despite budget cuts.

   A.   (**Subpoint 1**—*Idol*): New Orleans jazz is a symbol of art that arises out of suffering and challenge.

      1.   (**Sub-Subpoint 1**—*Example*): Violence/racism of past.

      2.   (**Sub-Subpoint 2**—*Example*): Poverty.

      3.   (**Sub-Subpoint 3**—*Example*): Hurricanes Katrina and Rita.

   B.   (**Subpoint 2**): Artists will continue to work in Louisiana as well.

   (**Transition**: But although art and artists will always endure, the Louisiana Decentralized Arts Fund will not.)

II.   (**Second main point**—*Causal Argument*): The budget cuts are unwise because they will result in the destruction of the agency and damage Louisiana culture and economy.

   A.   (**Subpoint 1**): The 83 percent cut in $3-million budget effectively dismembers an organization that is a national model.

      1.   (**Sub-Subpoint 1**—*Quotation/Wasteland*): Gerd Wuestemann, the executive director of the Acadiana Center for the Arts, a regional grant-distribution agency, says he anticipates two things as a result of the cuts: "Some of the smaller organizations that do good work, especially in the more rural areas, may have to close doors," he says. "And I think it will result in fewer projects and less income to the communities and less vibrancy in our lifestyle, and I think that's a shame" (Pierce).

2. (**Sub-Subpoint 2**—*Quotation/Sinner*): Governor of Louisiana on Larry King speaking of arts in general: "Fundamentally, I don't think . . . $50 million for the National Endowment for the Arts is going to get the economy moving again as quickly as allowing the private sector to create jobs" (Knight).

3. (**Sub-Subpoint 3**): Tourism is important to Louisiana economy.

B. (**Subpoint 2**): The reduction of support for the arts damages the community of Louisiana and destroys its cultural richness.

1. (**Sub-Subpoint 1**—*Causal*): Without state support art and artists are not able to bring a community together.

2. (**Sub-Subpoint 2**—*Wasteland*): Louisiana's culture thrives in nonprofit festivals and without them it will lose what makes it great.

3. (**Sub-Subpoint 3**—*Quotation/Virtue*): A great American philosopher, John Dewey, once wrote that: "Creation, not acquisition, is the measure of a nation's rank; it is the only road to an enduring place in the admiring memory of mankind" (Dewey).

(**Transition**: In summary, Louisiana, despite its natural wealth, has never been ranked high on the measure of acquisition.)

Conclusion   (**Concluding Remarks**—*Visualize a Positive Future*): But it has achieved a standing in the memory of humankind as a source of creation. Jazz is its grandest achievement. But we miss its power if only thought of as a past accomplishment. Its potential comes from Second Line. So although the body of the community may lie prostrate before us at the moment, once that Second Line starts, you watch it get up and dance. Strike it up!

Works Cited

Collier, James Lincoln. *Louis Armstrong: An American Genius*. Oxford: Oxford University Press, 1985. Print.

Dewey, John. "Art as Our Heritage." *John Dewey: The Later Works*, vol. 14. Ed. Jo Ann Boydston. Carbondale: Southern Illinois UP, 1988. 255–257. Print.

Knight, Christopher. "Gov. Jindal Exorcizes Arts Funds from Louisiana Budget." *Los Angeles Times*. 30 March, 2009. Web.

Pierce, Walter. "Short-Sighted Solons Gut Arts Funding." TheInd.com. 4 June 2012. Web.

Notecards   **Notecards** are used for extemporaneous speaking as a means of reminding the speaker of the order and content of material to be presented. Although based on the substance of the outline, they should not simply consist of the entire outline cut into small pieces of paper. Notecards act primarily as reminders rather than a manuscript. Only quotes, transitions, theses, and introductory and concluding remarks can be written out, although speakers should strive to reduce

DISCUSSION

One of the drawbacks of our reliance on computers for composition is that they tend to put us in the mind frame that we are always generating a finished product. Computers have turned outlines into exercises that we do after the fact rather than what they are intended for—as means of creative arrangement. How do you think it changes the experience of outlining when it is done on a pencil and paper rather than on a computer screen? What do you think is the best medium for generating new ideas and thoughts of one's own?

even this material to a minimum. Although it is tempting to add more "just in case," the fact is that the more one writes on a notecard, the more a speaker is tempted simply to read out loud, thereby ruining the purpose of extemporaneous speaking. Notecards should not be too "packed" with information, but should be written in clear, bold letters with a lot of "white space" so that one can easily see what comes next without having to hunt within a clutter of words.

▶ CHAPTER 4 EXERCISES

1. **IMPROMPTU:** Choose a fictional character we often associate with holidays or special occasions—such as Santa Claus, the Easter Bunny, the Tooth Fairy, leprechauns, and the like. Create an impromptu speech using at least three resources for invention available to the average child, including maxims, myths, social knowledge, testimony, examples, facts, narratives, or statistics, to prove the existence of these fictional characters.

2. **DEBATE:** One of the ongoing debates in the past two decades has been the effect of open source media online on our understanding of what makes a "legitimate" source or a "reliable" fact. Before the computer, it was generally understood that quotes from any major newspaper, library book, or encyclopedia counted as at least somewhat authoritative. But with the proliferation of online sources, it is often difficult to tell fact from fiction. Do you think that our reliance on readily available sources accessed from our smart phones have made us more informed or less informed? Debate this question citing specific examples and drawing on all available resources for invention.

3. **GROUP:** Decide as a class on a speech topic that is simple and focused enough that everyone should have at least some knowledge about the subject matter. In your groups, create a brief speech in which you defend a claim about that subject using one maxim, two facts, one example, one narrative, and one testimonial quote. Assign an individual to deliver the speech and compare and contrast the speeches to determine whose was the most persuasive.

4. **TAKE HOME:** Locate a recent news story from a news outlet that you often use. Print out the story and circle and identify each of the resources for invention used by the journalist. After identifying all of its parts, do you feel that the story was more or less factual and reliable than you felt on first reading it? How does specifying the specific parts of invention change the way you interpreted the story? Write down your reaction on the bottom of the printout.

5. **VIDEO:** Recall a true story that your parents once told to you that was supposed to convey a specific lesson. Retell the story on video in a way that emphasizes both its narrative probability and its narrative fidelity. At the end, give us the moral lesson you were supposed to learn and remark about why this story stuck with you all these years.

▶ NOTES

1. William West, "Memory," in *Encyclopedia of Rhetoric*, ed. Thomas Sloan (Oxford, UK: Oxford University Press, 2001), 483.

2. Thomas Farrell, "Knowledge, Consensus, and Rhetorical Theory," in *Contemporary Rhetorical Theory: A Reader*, ed. John Louis Lucaites, Celeste Michelle Condit, and Sally Caudill (New York: The Guilford Press, 1999), 147.

3. Susan B. Anthony, available at http://law2.umkc.edu/faculty/projects/ftrials/anthony/sbaaccount.html (accessed 6 September 2012).

4. For more on the persuasive use of examples, see Scott Consigny, "The Rhetorical Example," *Southern Speech Communication Journal* 41 (1976), 121–134.

5. Walter Fisher, "Narration as a Human Communication Paradigm: The Case of Public Moral Argument," in *Contemporary Rhetorical Theory: A Reader*, ed. John Louis Lucaites, Celeste Michelle Condit, and Sally Caudill (New York: The Guilford Press, 1999), 247. See also Walter Fisher, *Human Communication as Narration: Toward a Philosophy of Reason, Value, and Action* (Columbia: University of South Carolina Press, 1987).

6. Eugene Debs, "Statement to the Court," available at www.americanrhetoric.com/speeches/eugenedebspleatocourt1918.htm (accessed 18 August 2016).

7. Sojourner Truth, "Ain't I a Woman?" available at http://voicesofdemocracy.umd.edu/truth-address-at-the-womans-rights-convention-speech-text/ (accessed 20 March 2017).

5
Style

This chapter examines the techniques for giving a speech "style," meaning a sense of aesthetic wholeness that carries with it a clear and powerful meaning. It approaches style not as a series of superficial decorations that one can add to a speech, but as one category of artistic form that gives body to otherwise disconnected parts. Style is described by using familiar terms—meaning, concrete words, examples, metaphor, simile, rhythm, alliteration, repetition, parallelism, and antithesis. The goal is to provide a perspective on these techniques of style that give them greater significance (cognitively, emotionally, and practically) that is more than just external bedecking. Style is to be taken seriously.

Style is the complement of invention; whereas invention provides material to work with, style is the art of putting that material together in such a way that it adds up to an attractive and meaningful unity. To appreciate the importance of style, however, one must overcome certain presumptions about style that tend to think of it in terms of "mere decoration." For instance, the proverb that one should not "judge a book by its cover" or that one cannot "put lipstick on a pig" implies that style is mere artifice, an external and artificial covering that one puts upon a core substance that has a meaning of its own, whether it is a good book or an ugly pig (although owners of pigs will then tell you that one should not judge a book by its cover). The assumption here is that the content of a speech is self-contained and that style is simply something added from outside. However, if we look at our choices that we make in our everyday life, we realize that style matters a great deal. On a superficial level, for instance, we often purchase products primarily by how they are packaged. But style is more substantial than this when it comes to how we understand ourselves and our relationships with others. We invest a great deal of energy in how we choose to dress, eventually accumulating a wardrobe in which we will have a style for every occasion that matters to us. This is because we understand that style has a significant impact on the impression that we make on others and how this impression informs our subsequent relationships with them. We also know that our style actually impacts how we feel about ourselves. In other words, our style of dress actually changes the "substance" of our speech and behavior and directly affects the way others respond to us. The same is true with public speaking. When we attend to style, we often find that our choices of metaphors or speech patterns actually begin to have a direct impact on the very arguments we are making. Not only does attention to style make a speech more attractive to an audience, but it literally changes the content of the speech itself.

In short, although style is often thought of simply as "ornamentation," the Latin term *ornare* is substantive and means "to equip, fit out, or supply." A soldier was thus "ornamented" with the weapons of war, meaning that a soldier without style was not, in fact, prepared to fight as a soldier. Similarly, rhetorical **style** is not the frivolous decoration of ideas; it is the filling out and forming of ideas in order to allow them to stand on their own and organize themselves as a coherent whole. With respect to the notion of form as the arousing and satisfying of the appetites of the audience, style represents the unique manner in which a speaker guides an audience through a speech and makes transitions between different items gathered through invention and then structured through arrangement.

There are two kinds of style, each serving an important function. **Formal style** is effectively synonymous with what I have called "form," which is the overall tone and feel of a speech in its totality. Formal style is connected with the notion of genre, such that we might think of a speech as fitting a certain type that carries with it a certain feeling, like a "somber eulogy" or an "impassioned defense" or a "soapbox oration" or an "old-time revival." It is the complete impression left upon us by a speech that allows us to reflect upon it as a whole experience and that gives it its unique "character." **Figurative style** represents specific elements of the speech designed to capture the attention and seduce the ear of the audience, thereby making it engaged with what is being said and creating more of a feeling of continuity and unity. Figurative style focuses on providing short, refined, effective parts of a speech that give clarity and power to specific ideas. In sum, *style as* **figure** *is associated with particularly eloquent turns of phrase, examples, or visualizations.* To draw an analogy with fashion, style as figure is the dress shoe, the sharp tie, or the

> ## DISCUSSION
>
> What are the ways in which style matters as something more than a superficial appearance? Consider further the metaphor of "fashion" in terms of the clothes that we wear. What are the everyday judgments we make about others when we see their style? How often are our judgments about other people either validated or contradicted? Conversely, what are other ways in which we have found ourselves changing our behavior because we have adopted a new style? Has the choice to adopt a new style or discard an old one made a difference in your life? Now think in terms of a style of speaking. When did you pick up a new phrase or way of speaking, and did it make a change, for good or ill, in your relationships with others?

well-worn hat. *Style as* **form** *is associated with the entire feel of the speech experienced as a unified work of art.* Continuing with the fashion analogy, style as form is how everything fits together so that someone might say, "Wow, that person has style." This chapter will focus on figurative style. The rest of the book will concentrate on mastering formal style.

▶ THE MEANING OF SIGNS

Understanding the basis not only of style but also of substance requires a brief excursion into **semiotics**, or the study of signs. Whenever we ask why a word (a "sign") means what it does, we are discussing semiotics. This discussion is important for rhetoric for the simple fact that the success of speeches often is contingent on the very careful choice of words. Oftentimes, speakers will carelessly use familiar words without realizing that words can have multiple meanings for multiple audiences, and that often what we think is a very clear expression of a concrete idea becomes, when expressed in a speech, a vague expression of a muddled thought that results in misunderstanding. Correcting this state of affairs is what led the logician, scientist, and philosopher Charles Peirce to study the logic of signs. For him, "to know what we think, to be masters of our own meaning, will make a solid foundation for great and weighty thought."[1] Similarly, to know how to speak well and to be masters of our own meaning will make a solid foundation for great and weighty rhetoric.

For the goal of making our ideas and language clear, Peirce designed a triadic theory of the meaning of a sign that consists of a *sign*, an *object*, and its *interpretant*. A **sign** is that which addresses somebody, in some respect or capacity, for something else (for instance, a sign that says "beware of dog" addresses a visitor to a house and "stands in" for the presence of the dog itself). The **object** is what is represented by the sign (in this case, the thing which the child perceives to "be" the doggy out in the world). The **interpretant** is a more developed sign that mediates between the sign and its object that explains why they should go together (for instance, that "doggy" highlights the cute, furry, and friendly qualities of a domestic canine which makes the object more meaningful to a child). If one uses the metaphor of a dictionary, the sign is the word, the interpretant is the definition, and the object is the picture which is beside the word and the definition. This relationship would be represented graphically in this way:

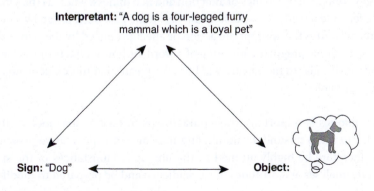

FIGURE 5.1 An example of a triadic sign.

The arrows go in both directions because the relationship can begin with any one of the three elements. For instance, a toddler might see a picture (the *object*) of a dog and ask, "What is it?" The response is the *sign*: "A dog." The child then asks, "But what is a dog?" The answer is the *interpretant*: "A dog is a four-legged furry mammal which is a loyal pet." Or one might know both the *object* and the *interpretant* but forget the sign. For instance, an adult might ask, "What is that brown and black dog with pointed ears that police usually use?" The answer is a *sign*: "German Shepherd." Or one might know the *sign* and *interpretant* but actively seek its "real" object. For instance, a child wishes to find "my dog" (sign) at the animal shelter. Although there existed an image of the object in the child's imagination, only after seeing many dogs does she point to one and say, "That one!" The sign has now found its "real" object which corresponds to the "idea" of the object previously in the child's mind. Consequently, one can see that it is important to keep in mind that the "object" of the sign is not necessarily an actual, concrete thing; it is merely the "thing" that is called forth in the mind by the sign. Sometimes it is real; other times it is a mere wish or a hallucination or figment of our imagination.

What Peirce wished to stress, however, was that it was the meaning of interpretants which was the most determining factor in our ability to generate shared understanding. Just think in terms of the act of translating one language into another. The only way we are able to know that "bonjour" and "hola" and "hello" mean the same thing is that they share the same interpretant—a way of greeting another person in a friendly way. Or think in terms of synonyms. We often choose one word over another, despite sharing almost the same object, because they differ in terms of how they are interpreted. It makes a big difference, for instance, whether one uses the sign "dog," "canine," or "doggy" when speaking to a child, even if all three technically "refer" to the same object. This is because the interpretants differ both in content and form. Peirce points out that interpretants come in three forms: emotional, energetic, and logical. The **logical interpretant** is analogous to the dictionary definition and corresponds to what is conventionally called the denotative meaning of a word, or what "thing" it objectively refers to. For instance, the term "dog" used in a veterinary classroom will mostly have a logical interpretant that emphasizes its biological characteristics as a type of mammal with certain health and nutritional needs. The **emotional interpretant** represents the feeling produced by the sign and comes closest to what is conventionally called the connotative meaning, or what qualities we associate with the object. The term "doggy" thus evokes feelings of affection and playfulness, whereas the same term would likely produce fear and anxiety for a person who has in the past been bitten by a dog. Finally, the **energetic interpretant** is the appropriate action or effect produced by the sign and corresponds to what we might call the pragmatic meaning of a word, or how it affects our behavior. The term "dog!" shouted by a burglar to his partner will literally "mean" that this object is something to flee from as soon as possible.

Rhetorically, semiotics is important in encouraging us to take a close look at the words that we use in order to avoid misunderstanding and maximize our persuasive power. A rhetorical speaker must therefore be highly attuned to the unique circumstances of the speech act and the idiosyncratic qualities and attitudes of the audience and be prepared to modify a speech on the spot when it becomes apparent that words that were intended to do one thing start doing another. Here is a brief list of things to consider when trying to choose the right sign (or "word") for the right occasion:

1. *For certain audiences, some signs may not refer to any objects*: This simple fact is readily apparent any time we visit a foreign country in which we do not know the language and the signs simply do not call forth any object whatsoever. We also have this experience when we encounter unfamiliar slang or technical jargon. Simply because a sign may be meaningful to certain audiences does not mean it is meaningful to any audience. It is the responsibility of the speaker to speak in meaningful signs.

2. *Simply labeling an object with a sign does not produce an interpretant*: Oftentimes, people are content simply with pointing at something and giving it a name and thinking that is sufficient for the production of meaning. For instance, one might walk into a garden and find lots of Latin names stuck in front of plants. But this does not convey much in the way of meaning to those unfamiliar with botanical terminology. It does not tell us what characteristics the plant has, what emotions we should attach to the plant, or what we should do when encountering the plant. When introducing new signs for objects, the burden falls on the speaker to suggest to the audience the proper interpretants, as when the Latin name suggests a species of poison ivy that we should avoid direct contact with and then tear up from the root using gloves.

3. *A single sign may refer to multiple objects*: For instance, the sign "table" can be both a noun and a verb. As a noun, it can call forth the image of ▨ or of ▦ As a verb, its object is the act of putting off an item of business until a later time. Only the context of its use determines which object is called forth by the sign.

4. *Members of an audience may each have different interpretants for the same object*: For instance, the sign "the American dream" for most people may call forth the same basic image of a person aspiring to a better life. However, for some people, the logical interpretant will be "the guiding principle of American political economy" (with its corresponding emotional interpretant of pride), whereas for others it will be "a myth propagated to mask economic inequality" (with its corresponding emotional interpretant of disgust). Still others will call forth an energetic interpretant to take out a loan and start a business.

5. *Some signs have only emotional interpretants*: For instance, Peirce writes that "the performance of a piece of concert music is a sign" whose meanings "usually consist merely in a series of feelings."[2] Consequently, often when we talk about music, our reactions usually deal with our emotional responses of like and dislike. Most of our interactions with the signs of art or nature call forth objects that primarily have emotional interpretants.

6. *Some signs have only energetic interpretants*: For instance, imperative signs such as "Go!" or "Fire!" or "Hey!" are primarily intended to bring about immediate actions rather than any particular "idea" that can be stated as a proposition.

7. *Some signs have only logical interpretants*: Many technical terms bring forth neither emotional nor energetic reactions because they refer to objects that are not connected with our everyday

lives. Few people feel passion or the need to act when they encounter the signs "hexide" and "blastocyst." However, it is not infrequent that signs normally confined to technical jargon become terms loaded with emotional and energetic interpretants when they cause potential health concerns, as with the signs "asbestos" and "dioxin."

8. *Referring to the same object with different signs produces different interpretants*: The interpretant is not tied to the object. It is produced by the interaction between the sign and the object. For instance, the signs "water" and "H2O" technically both refer to the same object. However, the sign "water" produces stronger emotional and energetic interpretants than H2O because water is something we drink and swim in, whereas H2O refers simply to the atomic composition of a molecule. Similarly, the words "dog," "doggie," "mutt," "pooch," and "canine" all arguably refer to pretty much the same object; however, each one has very different potential logical, emotional, and energetic interpretants. A master rhetorician will select the precise sign for each audience that produces the desired interpretants of specific objects.

Susan Cain: "Solitude Is a Crucial Ingredient Often to Creativity"

What does "solitude" mean? Is it the same as loneliness? Does it have a positive or negative connotation? This is the issue that Susan Cain, a former corporate lawyer and negotiations consultant, addressed in her 2012 TED talk. She argued that our culture undervalues introverts and neglects their contributions. Part of her speech reinterpreted "solitude" to give it a positive rather than a negative connotation. In doing so, she altered the object to which solitude points—the creative artist rather than the lonely hermit—while enriching the meaning of its interpretant to focus more on its constructive and positive aspects:

> Solitude is a crucial ingredient often to creativity. So Darwin, he took long walks alone in the woods and emphatically turned down dinner-party invitations. Theodor Geisel, better known as Dr. Seuss, he dreamed up many of his amazing creations in a lonely bell tower office that he had in the back of his house in La Jolla, California. And he was actually afraid to meet the young children who read his books for fear that they were expecting him [to be] this kind of jolly Santa Claus-like figure and would be disappointed with his more reserved persona. Steve Wozniak invented the first Apple computer sitting alone in his cubicle in Hewlett-Packard where he was working at the time. And he says that he never would have become such an expert in the first place had he not been too introverted to leave the house when he was growing up.[3]

> **DISCUSSION**
>
> Think about how you defined "solitude" or "introvert" previous to reading this excerpt. How has the meaning of these terms changed? Has reconsidering their meaning brought forth new "objects" in your imagination? How might you treat yourself and others differently if you accepted her redefinition?

▶ CONCRETE WORDS

We begin to see the practical utility of semiotics when we begin applying it to matters of style. For instance, most public speaking textbooks advise speakers to use concrete words in their speeches. A **concrete word** has a meaningful reference to specific and readily identifiable qualities or actions in order to give an audience a more vivid experience of some thing or event. From a semiotic perspective, a concrete word is a familiar sign that immediately calls forth clear and distinct objects that have explicit logical interpretants and powerful emotional interpretants. Peirce defines something that is "clear" as being "so apprehended that it will be recognized wherever it is met with, and so that no other will be mistaken for it. If it fails of this clearness, it is said to be obscure."[4] Too often, we use relatively obscure words like "good" and "people" and "virtuous" because they come to mind easily, usually avoid risk, and are vague enough not to be wrong. When we are not sure what we are talking about and do not want to offend anyone, speaking obscurely is a way of playing it safe. However, obscure language never persuaded anyone of anything. Only language that calls forth vivid images in the mind that carry with them strong emotional and energetic responses can carry the day with rhetoric.

The advice to use concrete words therefore is simply to use clear and powerful words whenever possible. Usually when people think of concrete words, they think of nouns. For instance, the noun *the red table* is preferable to the pronoun *it*, the word *Brazil* is preferable to *country*, and the word *fire ants* is more concrete than *insects*. However, it is important to point out that a concrete word does not refer only to nouns. Concrete words also apply to verbs and adjectives. In terms of verbs, the weakest way of writing is the use of the "passive voice," which makes the subject a target of an action rather than the initiator of one. Consider, for example, "The book *was read* today" or "He *is being* punished." Notice how much more "concrete" it sounds to write, instead, "Janet *read* the book" or "His father *punished* him." Also, overuse of the verb *to be* tends to make a speech repetitive. A sentence like "I am mad" can be turned into "My blood boils," and "Rain is good" can be turned into "Rain gives life." Finally, adjectives can also be made more concrete. Rather than sticking to generic adjectives such as *good, bad, happy, sad, helpful, harmful,* and the like, try to pick out the specific aspects of a thing that make it those things. For example, "That's a pretty car" can be made into "The red color on the hood made a striking contrast with the bright white roof." In other words, the more specifically you can describe something, the more vivid the image will be in the mind of the audience and the more they will enjoy your speech.

Chimamanda Ngozi Adichie: "All of These Stories Make Me Who I Am"

Nigerian novelist Chimamanda Ngozi Adichie has written books that have captured the unique perspectives and stories of many different characters, whether poor, middle class, or rich, all of whom expose in some way the scars that colonialism in Africa has left on the landscape. In her 2009 TED talk, "The Danger of a Single Story," Adichie challenges our habit of relying on single stories to stereotype whole cultures or regions. In this particular passage, note where she uses concrete words to express her own story growing up in Nigeria:

> When I learned, some years ago, that writers were expected to have had really unhappy childhoods to be successful, I began to think about how I could invent horrible things my parents had done to me. But the truth is that I had a very happy childhood, full of laughter and love, in a very close-knit family.
>
> But I also had grandfathers who died in refugee camps. My cousin Polle died because he could not get adequate healthcare. One of my closest friends, Okoloma, died in a plane crash because our fire trucks did not have water. I grew up under repressive military governments that devalued education, so that sometimes, my parents were not paid their salaries. And so, as a child, I saw jam disappear from the breakfast table, then margarine disappeared, then bread became too expensive, then milk became rationed. And most of all, a kind of normalized political fear invaded our lives. All of these stories make me who I am. But to insist on only these negative stories is to flatten my experience and to overlook the many other stories that formed me.[5]

DISCUSSION

Not all of Adichie's narrative uses concrete words. In fact, some of her description here uses abstract terms to communicate her experience. Which sentences stand out for their concreteness, while others use language that is far more general? How do the two different types of description affect the rhetorical power of her narrative?

▶ FIGURES

Whereas concrete words attempt to use clear language that conveys ideas that cannot be mistaken for any others, figures and tropes exploit the capacity for signs to take on multiple meanings and to convey multiple feelings. A **figure** is a series of signs designed to produce emotional interpretants based on an appeal to the ear (e.g., alliteration: "The day dawned with delight"). A figure uses language that departs from its conventional structure for the purpose of integrating poetic style and a musical sense of rhythm, which usually produces feelings of pleasure and harmony that we associate with beautiful works of art. By contrast, a **trope** is a series of signs designed to produce complex logical interpretants based on appeal to the mind (e.g., metaphor: "The year began with a sigh"). Whereas a figure seduces and calms the ear, a trope stimulates and challenges the mind to discern the logical meaning within a play of signs. In this case, the mind knows that a year cannot literally begin by exhaling a great deal of air once; it therefore uses the emotional interpretant of "sigh" (being a state of sadness, exhaustion, and resignation) as the proper sign to interpret the beginning of the year.

Figures are valuable to speeches because they provide a sort of "musical accompaniment" to the speech, thereby setting the tone for the occasion as well as placing the audience in a certain frame of mind to receive the message. It is a commonly known fact that messages tend to be recalled with greater clarity and emotional weight when they have a sense of rhythm and rhyme. The fact that complex song lyrics are easier to remember than clear but abstract definitions indicates the power of figures to leave a lasting impression. The same message conveyed without figures has a far greater chance of being forgotten than the one that was composed by a speaker who took the time to listen carefully to the sound of language with a musical ear. Following are listed some of the most important figures that appear in rhetoric:

Rhythm

Whether we think we have musical talent or not, it is true that our thoughts tend to move in rhythm. Rhythm in public speaking is how words "flow" through time. When we think of our natural environment, we might think of the rhythm of ripples on a lake or even the rhythm of a mountain range as one looks across the horizon. Replace ripples and mountain peaks with words and syllables, and you have an understanding of how rhythm functions in public speaking. To use **rhythm** in rhetoric is to compose words that, when spoken and heard, follow some kind of musical pattern that is recognizable and predictable and helps an audience move along with the words. For example, take the sentence "This place is, reflecting on it, a very pretty place with a view." This can be described as a "clunky" sentence with many starts and stops. It is like riding over potholes in a car. By contrast, the sentence "We gaze from the mountaintops over the verdant hills of green" has rhythm. It has a "flow" that carries an audience along and deposits them at the end.

Rhythm can be distinguished, like style, as something inherent in a *figure* and in the larger *form*. As a figure, a powerful rhythmic tempo is created particularly when emphases fall regularly on concrete words and important phrases. This can be graphically represented by underlining the intended emphases: "We *gaze* from the *mountain*tops over the *verd*ant *hills* of *green.*" Rhythm as a figure is important for that same mystical reason that we sometimes find certain songs or lyrics stuck in our head. Rhythm acts like a thread that holds words together in a certain sequence which makes them easier to store in the filing cabinets of our memory. As form, rhythm represents the tempo, the rising and falling, the climax and conclusion, the tensions and resolutions, of an entire speech. If rhythm as figure is a riff, then rhythm as form is a whole composition. A speech with rhythm thus generally starts on a tension, rises to a climax, and comes to some resolution, carrying the audience along the whole time on a continuous flow. A speech without rhythm, no matter how powerful the proof or the principles, will inevitably be forgotten; without the binding force of rhythm, words and meanings fall apart over time.

Donovan Livingston: "We Were Born to Be Comets"

When Donovan Livingston, a master's graduate at Harvard University, was chosen by a committee of faculty, staff, and students to speak at the School of Education's convocation, he opted to deliver a spoken word poem rather than a traditional speech. He used his poem to address not only the racial inequalities in the educational system, but more importantly to use their education degrees to help others tap into their own inner potentials. The use of rhythm in the poem thus generates a kind of momentum toward "lift off" as individuals discover their own unique powers and creativity:

> At the core, none of us were meant to be common.
> We were born to be comets,
> Darting across space and time—
> Leaving our mark as we crash into everything.
> A crater is a reminder that something amazing happened here—
> An indelible impact that shook up the world.
> Are we not astronomers—looking for the next shooting star?
> I teach in hopes of turning content, into rocket ships—
> Tribulations into telescopes,
> So a child can see their potential from right where they stand.
> An injustice is telling them they are stars
> Without acknowledging night that surrounds them.
> Injustice is telling them education is the key
> While you continue to change the locks.[6]

DISCUSSION

Part of having rhythm is creating tensions and resolutions. Which passages in this poem generate tension that remains unresolved at the end of the line? And which passages come to a "rest" as the rhythm naturally brings one to a conclusion? Now think of all the famous quotations from public speeches that you know off the top of your head. How many of them have rhythm? What are the differences in the type of rhythm they express? Do the different rhythms convey different meanings?

Alliteration

If rhythm is a connecting thread, alliteration is like a hammered nail. **Alliteration** is the use of words that begin with the same consonant sound. By punctuating the same consonant sound, alliteration "hammers" individual words into our memories. For example, the sentence "We *d*elved into the *d*ark *d*ungeon of the night" has more oral impact than "We walked into the dark of the evening." It should also be noted that alliteration is only effective when it is used with words that are worth remembering and emphasizing. The sentence "Tim's tie is too tight" has alliteration, but because the words are somewhat trivial, it sounds more comedic than profound. By contrast, a good speaker will alliterate words of importance that also fall on rhythmic "downbeats." For instance, "Let us strive not for power but for peace and prosperity" emphasizes all of the key terms in the speech that are important and memorable. Keep in mind also that alliteration is more effective at the concluding and climactic parts of a speech that warrant emphasis. One should use alliteration during those parts of the speech that one wishes to truly emphasize one's point.

Jesse Williams: "The Hereafter Is a Hustle"

In June of 2016, actor Jesse Williams accepted the Humanitarian Award at the BET awards ceremony. Mr. Williams played the role of Dr. Jackson Avery on *Grey's Anatomy*, but the award was in recognition of his commitment to championing causes related to civil rights, including producing a documentary, *Stay Woke: The Black Lives Matter Movement*. On accepting his award, he used his stage to address the recent shootings of black men by police offers and the subsequent controversy that arose afterwards concerning the effectiveness of the protests that resulted. In his speech he use alliteration twice to highlight different points:

Now, freedom is always coming in the hereafter. But, you know what though? The hereafter is a hustle. We want it now. And let's get a couple of things straight, just a little side note: The burden of the brutalized is not to comfort the bystander. . . . If you have no interest in equal rights for black people then do not make suggestions to those who do. Sit down.[7]

> ### DISCUSSION
>
> Williams uses two alliterations, "the hereafter is a hustle" and "the burden of the brutalized," to emphasize his point. First, what does each phrase signify? Second, how does using alliteration call attention to these phrases and encourage us to figure out their meanings? Think about how alliteration is a kind of "signal" that calls attention to certain words and makes them stand out in your memory. How do they function differently than, for instance, the final sentence, which does not use alliteration?

Repetition

Ever since the birth of modern advertising, people have recognized the power of repetition. There is a reason that advertising tends to say the same thing over and over again—it trains the mind to associate certain meanings with certain objects, events, or people. As a figure, however, repetition is not simply repeating the same idea or claim; **repetition** is the repeated use of a key phrase to begin a series of sentences whose endings vary. For example: "*Our people strive* for independence. *Our people strive* for freedom. *Our people strive* for justice. *Our people strive* for nationhood." As with alliteration, effective use of repetition will emphasize key ideas and terms that also contain a certain rhythm. The phrase "Our people strive" not only establishes the character of the people as desiring something better, but it also fits into a sentence structure that has a rhythm that builds up to a conclusion. Like the climactic finale of a symphony, the phrases are structured so that *nationhood* is the final consummation of their struggles for independence, freedom, and justice.

Note how less effective this example is despite its use of repetition: "*It would seem* that we are lost. *It would seem* that we are hopeful. *It would seem* that we need a map. *It would seem* that we are thirsty." This example uses repetition, but the repeated phrase lacks any visual impact, and the sequence of sentences has no clear connection or climax. Rhetorical use of repetition should only be used when the statement being repeated represents one of the key ideas of a speech. Nobody wants to remember the fact that something "seems" to be the case, but we do find it important to remember that a people strive for something. In other words, the repeated phrase should itself have a meaning unto itself that makes it worth remembering.

Leymah Gbowee: "Refuse to Stay in the Shadow"

In 2011, Liberian peace activist, social worker, and women's rights advocate Leymah Gbowee was awarded the Nobel Peace Prize. The Founder and President of the Gbowee Peace Foundation Africa, based in Monrovia, Gbowee is best known for leading a nonviolent movement that brought together Christian and Muslim women to play a pivotal role in ending Liberia's devastating 14-year civil war in 2003. During her commencement address to Barnard College graduates in 2013, Gbowee uses repetition to call on her audience to refuse to stay in the shadows and tolerate abuse and injustice:

> Don't stay in the shadows. Refuse to stay in the shadow. Break out about your dreams. Break out about your passion that you have for changing the world. Break out about how you feel about things. Never hold back. Refuse to be in the shadows as you step out into this life. Don't be shy no matter how crazy it seems to you. That crazy idea may just be the solution for some crazy global or local problem.

> From 1989 until 2003, the women of Liberia were also in the shadows. However, in 2003, tired of being used, and misused by over-drugged militias, we stepped out to confront the demons of militarism and violence. We refused to allow our bodies to be used anymore. We knew we would die, but we refused to allow our legacies to be "they died without trying." We stepped out of the darkness of victimization, and into the light of activism and peace.[8]

DISCUSSION

There are actually numerous overlapping instances of repetition in this speech. What are they, and how is each case of repetition connected to a certain set of attitudes and ideas? And how does alternating between different phrases increase the effect by generating tension? Think about Martin Luther King Jr.'s famous repetition "I have a dream." What makes this particular kind of repetition so powerful? What does it invite the audience to do?

Parallelism

The figure of parallelism is more complicated than the earlier figures because it involves putting a longer string of words into a coherent structure that also conveys a balanced meaning. In this way, the figure seems to take on qualities of a trope. **Parallelism** is the repeated pairing of different, usually opposing, ideas in a rhythmic "couplet" within the same sentence. A rhythmic "couplet" is simply two ideas expressed in the same rhythm connected by an "and" or an "or." For example, "my blood or my tears" is a couplet, as is "the greatest of fears and the weakest of hopes," as is "the life of glory or the death of shame," as is "good and evil." Parallelism simply strings several of these couplets together in a single sentence. For example, "I see before us a choice between *the hopes of millions* and *the fears of a few*, *the poverty of the many* and *the wealth of the one*, and the *progress of humanity* and *the debasement of mankind*." By pairing opposite ideas or outcomes, it graphically presents the audience with a stark choice. However, it can equally be used to *bridge* opposites, as in the statement, "Whether you were born within its borders or arrived on its shores, you are all Americans." In either case, parallelism operates most effectively when there are two distinct ideas or images which are being compared or contrasted.

Margaret Mead: "A New Quality of Life, Based on Conservation Not Waste"

Parallelism plays an important role in a speech by Margaret Mead, former curator of the American Museum of Natural History in New York and an anthropology professor at Columbia University, as she addressed the challenge of a new technological era. Mead was an advocate for reforming how human beings use the resources of their environment so as to achieve sustainable development that benefits both people and nature. In her speech "The Planetary Crisis and the Challenge to Scientists," given at the American Museum of Natural History on December 6, 1973, Mead presents the choices we face in stark terms by using parallelism to sum up her argument:

During the inevitable disorganization of everyday life, business, industry, and education, we will be taking stands, making decisions, learning new habits and new ways of looking at things, and initiating new research into alternative technologies in transportation, agriculture, architecture, and town planning. It is vital that these activities move us forward into a new era, in which the entire nation

DISCUSSION

It is in the final sentence where Mead uses parallelism to contrast the positive and negative virtues that stand before us as a choice. This is a fairly typical structure for parallelism, competing terms divided by a "not" or an "or." Can you think of a different way in which she might have structured the oppositions using a parallel arrangement—particularly in the final couplet—that may have been more rhythmic or stylistic?

is involved in a search for a new standard of living, a new quality of life, based on conservation not waste, on protection not destruction, on human values rather than built-in obsolescence.[9]

Antithesis

An even more complex form of parallelism is antithesis. **Antithesis** is when two similarly phrased, but contradictory, ideas are consecutively expressed in order to favor one over the other. This is a complicated definition that is more easily expressed through an example: "We live in a nation where laws are the rulers of men, not where men are the abusers of law." Antithesis is a form of parallelism in that it employs a rhythmic couplet, but it is more difficult to construct because the words have to be carefully chosen so that they can be manipulated for the opposite effect.

Putting together an antithesis is a lot like creating a puzzle, and its effectiveness is explained in the pleasure an audience gets from "solving" it. Ideas expressed in an antithesis should carry great weight, for otherwise an antithesis will sound more like a pun than a principle. To create an antithesis, simply take any phrase and try to find a similar wording that conveys the opposite idea or tendency that, when combined, creates a whole thought. Keep in mind, too, that opposites need not be competitive. For instance, the Golden Rule is also an antithesis: "Do unto others as you would have them do unto you." In this case, the opposition is simply directional. The antithesis thus creates a sense of cooperation where before there were two forces going in different directions. Like other forms of style, antithesis often works best when "punctuating" a thought at the end of an argument.

Martin Sheen: "We're Not Asked to Do Great Things"

Actor Martin Sheen, perhaps now most well known for playing President Bartlett on *The West Wing*, is also known for his social and political activism, particularly his campaign against nuclear weapons and for workers' rights. It was his activism that earned him an invitation to speak at "We Day" in 2015, a youth empowerment event organized by international activists that involved over 12,000 students and teachers in London. In his speech he used antithesis to capture the essence of his message to individuals who wished to make a difference in the world:

Whether we choose to acknowledge it or not we are all responsible for each other and the world which is exactly the way it is because, consciously or unconsciously, we have made it

> ### DISCUSSION
>
> Put Sheen's use of antithesis against perhaps the most famous antithesis by John F. Kennedy: "Ask not what your country can do for you, but what you can do for your country." What does each form have in common in terms of structure? How does antithesis help emphasize a certain type of argument but not others? Inspect both phrases closely. What are the limitations to antithesis when it endures logical inspection?

so. And while none of us made any of the rules that govern the universe, we do make all the rules that govern our own hearts, and we are all beneficiaries of those many heroic strangers who've gone before us over the centuries who assure us that the world is still a wonderful and safe place despite our fears and we're not asked to do great things, we're asked to do all things with great care.[10]

▶ TROPES

Tropes differ from figures insofar as they appeal more directly to the rational imagination than they do to the musical ear or rhythmic body. Tropes are useful because they encourage an audience to discern the meaning behind signs, thus generating a pleasure in participation very similar to the effects of a good puzzle or a riddle. The basis behind tropes can be understood through the previous discussion of semiotics. As described previously, not only can a single sign refer to multiple objects, but multiple signs can refer to the same object and therefore produce multiple interpretants. For instance, the statement "the man is a lion" is meaningful to us even though we know that the man is not literally a lion. The mind realizes that the two objects cannot be synonymous, so it starts sifting through other possible interpretants of those objects that then can be translated into appropriate meanings. The harder and more difficult the trope, the harder the mind has to work to discern its meaning. This can increase the pleasure and level of participation in an audience when it reaches the correct level of difficulty, but beyond that, it becomes too much labor and thereby acts as a repellent to the audience members, who will turn their attention to other things. Writing tropes that convey the correct meaning and challenge the audience at the ideal level is a most difficult art.[11]

One can get a sense of the difference between figures and tropes by looking at some of the simpler tropes that are usually most effective in single sentences or phrases. **Personification**, for instance, describes abstract or nonhuman objects as if they possessed human qualities ("The waves leapt forward and pulled me back into the ocean"). **Hyperbole** uses extreme exaggeration to highlight a specific quality or idea ("When my boss started yelling at me, I could feel the whole office building shaking"). **Oxymoron** places two terms together that seem contradictory in order to highlight their tension ("There is no such thing as a smart bomb. They are all equally mindless"). And **paradox** is a statement of an apparent contradiction that nevertheless contains a measure of truth ("How strange it is that getting cancer saved my life. Only now have I come to value what is important in the world"). In each of these, the rhetorical influence comes not from how it sounds or feels but how the words bring up ideas in the minds that are counterintuitive, surprising, distorted, exaggerated, amusing, or puzzling. The rest of the section will look at five of the more significant tropes, that of metaphor, simile, synecdoche, metonymy, and irony.

Metaphor

The use of metaphor is to give an audience a unique and creative perspective on some object, person, idea, or event in order to highlight and make salient specific qualities or properties that might otherwise go unnoticed. A **metaphor** describes one thing by using language that is normally used to describe something seemingly unrelated in order to imply that they share some essential underlying quality. The simplest type of metaphor is a definition or comparison. Metaphors rely on comparing two terms with different denotative meanings but which share similar connotative or associative meanings. For example, to say "That man is a lion" is not to literally call him a lion but to say that he shares the qualities of ferocity and courage that we associate with lions. *Metaphor* is different than *analogy*, however, because the comparison is not to be taken literally but symbolically. To argue that American democracy is similar to Greek democracy is an analogy because it implies we can learn practical lessons about governance by looking to Greek history. By contrast, arguing that a politician is a snake is not to imply we will learn about him or her by studying snake behavior; it is simply to associate a politician with acts of deceit and manipulation.

One major source of confusion about metaphors, therefore, is that their meaning comes from the relationship between the object and its comparison—between the "man" (object) and "lion" (comparison). But this ignores the persuasive intent that is the whole purpose of metaphorical argument. As I. A. Richards explains, the meaning of a metaphor grows out of the interaction between the *tenor* and the *vehicle*. The **vehicle** is how the tenor is embodied and expressed in a specific figure (the use of the term "lion" to describe the man rather than, for instance, a "bear" or a "fox"). The **tenor** is the underlying quality or property that is intended to be highlighted (in this case, "courage"). However, the **meaning** of the metaphor is *not* simply its tenor. The meaning is the interaction between the tenor and the vehicle. Each of those vehicles *alters* how the tenor is interpreted for an audience, and it is in that "alteration" that occurs within the experience of an audience where meaning lies.[12] In other words, the meaning is the specific images that appear in the imagination of *being courageous as only a lion can be courageous*, rather than courageous as some other type of animal. For instance, it is actually more appropriate to say that "the man is a lioness" to imply courage, as in nature it is a lioness who hunts and defends her young with courage. However, even if the intended tenor remains the same, the meaning of comparing a man with a lioness is very different than comparing him with a lion.

It must be stressed, however, that comparison is not the only way to understand metaphor. Metaphor occurs any time we replace conventional description with words traditionally used for a different type of object. For instance, much of our metaphorical language comes from our creative use of verbs rather than any explicit comparison. To continue with the previous metaphor, take the phrase "I am woman, hear me roar!" This uses the metaphor of the lion without actually making explicit comparison, choosing instead to simply describe a woman using terms typically reserved for lions. Metaphors are often more effective in this way because they are less explicit and appeal more subtly to the imagination. In addition, to use Aristotelian terms, they put image "before the eyes" and make them "move." It is more visual to imagine a woman roaring like a lion than simply a man "being" a lion. When we use metaphors, it is better to make these images come alive by using active verbs and adjectives rather than simply comparing two objects using the verb "to be."

Kathy Jetnil Kijiner: "That Lagoon Will Devour You"

On September 23, 2014, Kathy Kijiner, a teacher, poet, and activist from the Marshall Islands, addressed the Opening Ceremony of the UN Secretary-General's Climate Summit, performing a poem entitled "Dear Matafele Peinem" written to her daughter. The poem was meant to highlight the threat of climate change, specifically that of rising sea waters which threatened to place many island communities underwater. The poem makes use of metaphor in order to create a jarring perspective that encourages her daughter to look at the peaceful, beautiful lagoon she currently knows as if it were a creature coming to devour her village and her land:

> dear matafele peinem,
> i want to tell you about that lagoon
> that lazy, lounging lagoon lounging against the sunrise
> men say that one day
> that lagoon will devour you
> they say it will gnaw at the shoreline
> chew at the roots of your breadfruit trees
> gulp down rows of seawalls
> and crunch through your island's shattered bones[13]

DISCUSSION

If Kijiner had followed the traditional structure of metaphor, she would have included a line that said "the lagoon is a monster," or something similar. How would using this traditional structure have diminished the power of the metaphor? Indeed, Kijiner never actually compares the lagoon to anything, but only describes it in terms of its threatening actions. As Aristotle said, she makes the lagoon come alive and appear as a threat. What are the metaphorical terms that she uses here to make the lagoon appear "before the eyes"?

Simile

Similes are similar to metaphors but they are more explicit in their comparison and often explain the reason why this comparison is being made. We often think of the defining quality of a simile as a comparison that uses the words "like" or "as." For instance, "terrorism is a cancer" is considered a metaphor while "terrorism *spreads like* a cancer" is considered a simile. This is generally true, but focusing exclusively on these minor grammatical differences misses the more important difference. Unlike metaphors, **similes** highlight a specific quality of a thing by explicitly comparing it to a like quality in something unrelated. For example, the second example specifically indicates that terrorism is a cancer because it possesses the same quality of "spreading." It does not leave it simply up to the imagination but indicates why, explicitly, the comparison is being made. In other words, metaphors often leave it up to the audience to make the connection between the two things being compared, while similes do the job for them. Put in the terminology of metaphor, the vehicle of a simile explicitly makes reference to the tenor in order to narrow and specify its meaning. Thus, instead of saying the vehicle "She is a whip" to express the tenor "She is very smart," one uses the simile "She is as *smart* as a whip."

Similes limit the range of possible interpretations in order to reduce miscommunication. They are therefore helpful in settings of instruction, where a clear message needs to be conveyed by using simple examples. Parents thus often employ similes with children ("The moon shines because it reflects like a mirror"), whereas they employ metaphors with their adult friends in casual conversation ("My old car was a lemon"). The drawback is that they also tend to have less impact because the audience isn't as involved in the creative process. A good metaphor is like a good joke—the audience should be able to "get it" without too much explanation. Similes are like offering explanations to your jokes so that people understand them. They convey the right message, but they also aren't as enjoyable to hear. Metaphors, by contrast, are very difficult to create, but effective ones can often make an ordinary speech extraordinary.

Monica Lewinsky: "It Feels Like a Punch in the Gut"

Today, Monica Lewinsky is an American activist, television personality, and fashion designer—but she remains nonetheless identified primarily as the White House intern with whom President Bill Clinton admitted to having had what he called an "inappropriate relationship" while she worked at the White House in 1995 and 1996. But whereas for most Americans this event is long past, for Lewinsky it remains sometimes oppressively present. In her address at Forbes "30 Under 30 Summit" at Philadelphia, Lewinsky addressed an audience of a thousand young entrepreneurs about the dangers of cyberbullying, using the simile of a "punch in the gut" to describe what it feels like to be attacked online:

DISCUSSION

Compare the way Lewinsky uses the simile of a "punch in the gut" to how Kijiner uses metaphor to describe the lagoon. How does it represent a different emotional and cognitive experience when one uses a simile to make a difficult or foreign experience understandable and relatable to an audience? What does this say about the different types of situations in which similes or metaphors are called for?

What does it really feel like to watch yourself—or your name and likeness—to be ripped apart online? Some of you may know this yourself. It feels like a punch in the gut. As if a stranger walked up to you on the street and punched you hard and sharp in the gut.

For me, that was every day in 1998. There was a rotation of worsening name calling and descriptions of me. I would go online, read in a paper or see on TV people referring to me as: tramp, slut, whore, tart, bimbo, floozy, even spy. The New York Post's Page Six took to calling me, almost daily, the Portly Pepperpot. I was shattered.

Thankfully, people aren't punched every day on the street. But it happens all the time on the internet. Even as I'm talking to you now, this is happening to someone online. And depending on what you guys are tweeting, this may be happening to me later. The experience of shame and humiliation online is different than offline. There is no way to wrap your mind around where the humiliation ends—there are no borders. It honestly feels like the whole world is laughing at you. I know. I lived it.[14]

Synecdoche

Whereas a metaphor is a way of gaining perspective on something by looking at it in a unique and different way, a **synecdoche** is a way of representing a larger complete whole by describing it only in terms of a smaller part or microcosm. In its most traditional form, a synecdoche simply describes an object by using a term for its most recognizable "part." For instance, before the invention of the steamship, people would use the term "sail" to stand for ships, as in "the merchant possesses 30 sail." Today, phrases like "we need more *boots* on the ground" (the boot being just a part of a soldier) or "I would like another pair of *hands* over here" (meaning a person who can help do something physically with their hands) or "that's a nice set of *wheels!*" (to indicate a car or motorcycle) are all common uses of synecdoche. In the traditional sense, the important part of synecdoche is finding the *essential* and most *representative* part of the object being described in order to best convey what is significant about it.

However, a synecdoche also refers to anything which "stands in" for a whole. In other words, sometimes the "part" can be an individual amidst a group, as for instance a congressional representative is a synecdoche for his or her district or the testimony of a Holocaust survivor represents in general form the experiences of all Holocaust survivors. Similarly, any graphic representation of a complex environment that simplifies it using a "key" is also a synecdoche. Think, for instance, of stereotypical treasure maps in which only specific key features of an environment are highlighted in order to guide someone to a buried chest. All of these aspects are simplified representations, or parts, of the whole. In these cases, one must choose the essential features of an object that genuinely capture its essential and most prominent qualities.

Ronald Reagan: "It's All Part of the Process of Exploration and Discovery"

On the morning of January 28, 1986, schoolchildren across the country watched as the Space Shuttle Challenger was launched with seven persons aboard, including Christa McAuliffe, a 37-year-old teacher from New Hampshire—the first ordinary citizen in space. Just over a minute later, the shuttle exploded in midair, killing all seven crewmembers. That evening, President

Ronald Reagan addressed the nation from the Oval Office in order to make sense of this national tragedy. The speech is today most known for its closing metaphor, drawn from a poem by a World War II pilot, in which Reagan described how "they prepared for the journey and waved goodbye and 'slipped the surly bonds of earth' to 'touch the face of God.'" But equally important was how he made sense of this tragedy by using it as a synecdoche for the entire process of exploration that he defined, in turn, as representative of the virtues of openness and discovery that characterized democracy:

> And I want to say something to the schoolchildren of America who were watching the live coverage of the shuttle's take-off. I know it's hard to understand, but sometimes painful things like this happen. It's all part of the process of exploration and discovery. It's all part of taking a chance and expanding man's horizons. The future doesn't belong to the fainthearted; it belongs to the brave. The Challenger crew was pulling us into the future, and we'll continue to follow them.

> I've always had great faith in and respect for our space program. And what happened today does nothing to diminish it. We don't hide our space program. We don't keep secrets and cover things up. We do it all up front and in public. That's the way freedom is, and we wouldn't change it for a minute.

> We'll continue our quest in space. There will be more shuttle flights and more shuttle crews and, yes, more volunteers, more civilians, more teachers in space. Nothing ends here; our hopes and our journeys continue.[15]

DISCUSSION

One of the aspects which distinguish synecdoche from metonymy or metaphor is that, as a representation of the whole through a part, one can understand important aspects of the whole by closely examining the part—much as one would study a map to learn the terrain. In this case, what is it that we learn by examining closely the space program of which the shuttle mission is itself but one of many? How does Reagan's use of synecdoche transform the shuttle disaster into a kind of civics lesson and defense of democratic life?

Metonymy

Conventionally understood, a metonymy is when something is not called by his own name, but by some object associated with it. For instance, a traditional example of a metonymy might be a "badge" to stand in for a police officer, or a "tiara" to stand in for a princess. However, this leads to confusion, because one can also understand this in terms of synecdoche insofar as a badge is a part of an officer's uniform or a tiara a part of a princess. The difference is subtle but important. Strictly speaking, a metonymy using a badge or a tiara would actually be standing in for the *idea* of "law and order" or of "monarchy," not a specific person. To understand this difference, let us turn to the definition of metonymy. If a metaphor is a *perspective* on something by using language usually reserved for something else, and a *synecdoche* is a representation of a whole of something through a part of it, then a metonymy is *reduction* of an idea by naming it as if it were an object. Specifically, **metonymy** is a way we represent a purely abstract idea, a notion, or concept by treating it as if it has a purely physical existence. The function of metonymy, therefore, is to help us tangibly grasp and visually represent something which would otherwise be very difficult to communicate. For instance, one of the most frequent expressions of metonymy is the picture of a red heart to symbolize "love." To return to the example of the badge, therefore, it is a synecdoche if the badge is being used to stand in for the physical person to whom it belongs—as one might see a badge on the ground as evidence that a police officer had been there. The key difference with metonymy is that the badge is not being used to represent a specific individual or even a group of police officers, but the *abstract idea of law and order in general*. For instance, a more explicit and common use of metonymy is the notion of balanced scales to represent "justice." The essential quality of metonymy, therefore, is that the object being represented has no other physical existence beyond its representation. It exists only as an "idea" or "abstraction."

One must be careful about using metonymy. On the one hand, it is risky to represent the idea of specific groups of people as it tends to "objectify" a group, often in an insulting or derogatory way. For instance, it is a synecdoche to communicate that there were a lot of well-dressed people at a meeting when one says, "There were a lot of suits there!" However, it is something of an insult to represent the entirety of one's personality using a metonymy by saying, "You are just a suit!" (thereby reducing the meaning of their existence to being a cog in a corporate machine). On the other hand, many of our most powerful symbols are those that represent the abstract ideals of the nation (such as a flag) or the virtues of a religion (such as the cross, star, or crescent), and so therefore must be treated with particular care.

Abraham Lincoln: "We Are Met on a Great Battle-Field of That War"

We use metonymy when we wish to have some tangible artifact to help us grasp the intangible. It was to accomplish exactly this task that President Abraham wrote and delivered the "Gettysburg Address." The address was delivered on the afternoon of November 19, 1863, during a dedication of the Soldiers' National Cemetery in Gettysburg, Pennsylvania, four and a half months after the defeat of Confederate forces at the Battle of Gettysburg. Although Lincoln's speech was just a few minutes long, dwarfed by the two-hour harangue delivered by the speaker who preceded him, the Gettysburg Address became famous because it used the battlefield as a metonymic symbol to show to the American people why the battle was being fought. The physical space of the battlefield, which itself is but earth and grass and rock, comes to embody not only the courage of the soldiers but the virtues and the promise of the nation since its origin. That is why Lincoln begins the speech with the famous words that recall the founding of the nation:

> Four score and seven years ago our fathers brought forth on this continent a new nation, conceived in liberty, and dedicated to the proposition that all men are created equal.

DISCUSSION

The power of metonymy is that it allows one to invest a physical object with the highest principles and most abstract ideas. How would the address have been different, for instance, if Lincoln had used a strategy of synecdoche instead—perhaps by honoring a specific soldier or a specific regiment for their particular courage and dedication that might stand in for the entire Union Army? Note, for instance, that Lincoln does not specifically mention winners or losers or even acknowledge that there were two sides. What does honoring the physical space of the battlefield give him the freedom to do that honoring a living person might not?

Now we are engaged in a great civil war, testing whether that nation, or any nation, so conceived and so dedicated, can long endure. We are met on a great battle-field of that war. We have come to dedicate a portion of that field, as a final resting place for those who here gave their lives that that nation might live. It is altogether fitting and proper that we should do this.

But, in a larger sense, we can not dedicate, we can not consecrate, we can not hallow this ground. The brave men, living and dead, who struggled here, have consecrated it, far above our poor power to add or detract. The world will little note, nor long remember what we say here, but it can never forget what they did here. It is for us the living, rather, to be dedicated here to the unfinished work which they who fought here have thus far so nobly advanced. It is rather for us to be here dedicated to the great task remaining before us—that from these honored dead we take increased devotion to that cause for which they gave the last full measure of devotion—that we here highly resolve that these dead shall not have died in vain—that this nation, under God, shall have a new birth of freedom—and that government of the people, by the people, for the people, shall not perish from the earth.[16]

Irony

The last and perhaps most complex of the major tropes is irony. **Irony** occurs when the apparent or expected meaning is the opposite of its actual or consequent meaning. At its most primitive level, irony can be communicated with simple sarcasm. If someone trips and falls, and another person says, "Well, that was graceful!" the apparent (or literal) meaning of the words is clearly the opposite of its actual meaning. However, Kenneth Burke said that the essence of irony is what he called "dialectic," which for him meant simply the relationship between two competing statements. In the case of this example of sarcasm, the apparent meaning "that was graceful" is put in conversation with its implied actual meaning of "that was clumsy."[17] The resulting meaning is the interaction between these two competing statements. As with metaphor, therefore, the meaning is the result between something akin to the tenor in the vehicle. For instance, if one used the vehicle "acrobatic" instead of "graceful," the tenor might remain the same, but the meaning would be slightly different insofar as images of being acrobatic are different than being grateful. What

Burke reminds us is that one must keep in mind *both* statements when trying to find out the meaning of an ironic statement.

Irony is most persuasive when one reveals an unexpected meaning, contradiction, or outcome. There are three types of irony one can employ in public speaking. The most common type is **verbal irony**, which is a variant of sarcasm in which case one says the opposite of what one actually means. More often than not, this is most effective when used to produce laughter by indirectly referencing a fact which is common knowledge. Sometimes it is used to criticize an opponent or another person's position, and other times it is used to make light of oneself. A more complex type of irony to use is **situation irony**, in which someone's actions produced the very opposite effect than what they had intended. In this case, the speaker has to narrate a particular situation and show how certain choices that had been made to bring about a certain goal had in fact made the opposite thing occur. More often than not, this type of irony is used as a criticism of the choices of others. For instance, if someone had initiated a policy to bring peace and save money, and that policy had in fact initiated war and sent a nation into debt, then someone could use situation irony to reveal either bad luck or bad judgment. Last, **dramatic irony** *occurs when an audience is aware that something is going to happen but the characters in a narrative do not.* For instance, viewers of a horror movie might know that a monster is in the closet and thus can see what a terrible decision it would be for the characters to hide from that same monster in that same closet. One can see, therefore, how in rhetoric, dramatic irony and situation irony often turn out to be the same thing. Using dramatic irony, one can narrate the past as if it is a type of movie and show how people in the past made decisions that we now know to have turned out in a certain way. Replaying the past can thus be a way of creating that sense of dramatic irony in which we wish we could go back in time and tell people to make the right decisions.

Emma Goldman: "They Turned Our Office into a Battlefield"

One of the most devastating effects of irony is ridicule, which the early twentieth-century labor activist Emma Goldman was a master at producing. During the buildup to the U.S. entry into World War I, the government wished to portray anyone who attempted to obstruct the draft or to in any way undermine the war effort as traitors to be prosecuted. Pacifists and anarchists like Emma Goldman and Alexander Berkman, who founded the No-Conscription League and distributed 100,000 copies of a manifesto declaring military conscription to be a violation of liberty, were thus predictably arrested under the Espionage Act and put on trial. However, even more predictably, Goldman used her address to the jury on July 9, 1917, in a New York City court, as a forum to condemn the government's actions instead. But rather than simply offer general criticisms, she made use of irony—verbal and situational—within a narrative that demonstrated how absurd and futile was the government crackdown on her activities:

> On the day after our arrest it was given out by the U.S. Marshal and the District Attorney's office that the "big fish" of the No-Conscription activities had been caught, and that there would be no more trouble-makers and disturbers to interfere with the highly democratic

> ### DISCUSSION
>
> Goldman uses situation irony to first show how the intentions of Marshal McCarthy to catch a "big fish" turned out to have the opposite effect. How does this narration of situation irony then make the final statement of verbal irony have that much more impact? Also, Goldman makes explicit use of different metaphors throughout her defense. How does the creative use of metaphor actually increase the effect of irony?

effort of the Government to conscript its young manhood for the European slaughter. What a pity that the faithful servants of the Government, personified in the U.S. Marshal and the District Attorney, should have used such a weak and flimsy net for their big catch. The moment the anglers pulled their heavily laden net ashore, it broke, and all the labor was so much wasted energy.

The methods employed by Marshal McCarthy and his hosts of heroic warriors were sensational enough to satisfy the famous circus men, Barnum & Bailey. A dozen or more heroes dashing up two flights of stairs, prepared to stake their lives for their country, only to discover the two dangerous disturbers and trouble-makers Alexander Berkman and Emma Goldman, in their separate offices, quietly at work at their desks, wielding not a sword, nor a gun or a bomb, but merely their pens! Verily, it required courage to catch such big fish. . . . They turned our office into a battlefield, so that when they were through with it, it looked like invaded Belgium, with the only difference that the invaders were not Prussian barbarians but good American patriots bent on making New York safe for democracy.[18]

▶ CHAPTER 5 EXERCISES

1. **IMPROMPTU:** Pretend you are a reporter whose job it is sometimes to transform rather ordinary events into things which seem extraordinary and interesting to read. As a class, think of a common event that everyone has experienced or witnessed at some point. Now pretend you are writing the first few lines of a sensational story that uses metaphor to make this rather common event into something that will grab a reader's attention. Make sure that no one uses the standard structure "X is Y" but rather replaces verbs, adjectives, or nouns to make the event appear "before the eyes."

2. **DEBATE:** Divide the class into two or more groups, assigning each group a position on a specific policy proposal that deals with something simple but that directly impacts every-one in the class—for instance, that everyone should ride bikes to campus. Now develop your arguments using *only* the resources of synecdoche, irony, and metonymy, such that you isolate specific parts to represent whole subjects, demonstrate how our intentions

often produce the opposite effects, and how we can represent certain ideals or abstractions through specific concrete objects. Present your arguments in competition with each other.

3. **GROUP:** Divide the class into groups and assign each group to write a commemorative speech about some object that one of the members in the groups have in their possession. This speech should use every single type of figure defined in this chapter but only one of the tropes. Present the speeches as a group and see if the class can identify the specific strategies being used.

4. **TAKE HOME:** Find one of your favorite poems that is 20 lines or shorter that makes use of some of the stylistic strategies defined in the chapter. Prepare this poem to present before the class and then define what you think was the most important figure or trope that made it stand out for you.

5. **VIDEO:** Find a particularly interesting object in your immediate natural environment—a tree, an ant hill, a bird's nest, a squirrel, a sunset—and write a short poem in praise of this object using at least five stylistic techniques. Record a video of this object and recite your poem without actually appearing in the video yourself.

▶ NOTES

1. Charles Peirce, "How to Make Our Ideas Clear," in *The Philosophy of Peirce*, ed. Justus Buchler (New York: Harcourt, Brace, and Co., 1950), 25.

2. Charles Peirce, "Pragmatism in Retrospect: A Last Formulation," in *The Philosophy of Peirce*, ed. Justus Buchler (New York: Harcourt, Brace, and Co., 1950), 277.

3. Susan Cain, "The Power of Introverts," available at www.ted.com/talks/susan_cain_the_power_of_introverts/transcript?language=en (accessed 18 August 2016).

4. Charles Peirce, "How to Make Our Ideas Clear," 23.

5. Chimamanda Ngozi Adichie, "The Power of a Single Story," available at www.ted.com/talks/chimamanda_adichie_the_danger_of_a_single_story/transcript?language=en (accessed 18 August 2016).

6. Donovan Livingston, "Lift Off," available at www.gse.harvard.edu/news/16/05/lift (accessed 18 August 2016).

7. Jesse Williams, "BET Speech," available at http://time.com/4383516/jesse-williams-bet-speech-transcript/ (accessed 18 August 2016).

8. http://barnard.edu/news/transcript-speech-nobel-peace-prize-winner-leymah-gbowee

9. Margaret Mead, "A New Quality of Life, Based on Conservation Not Waste," in *Great American Speeches*, ed. Gregory R. Suriano (New York: Gramercy, 1993), 275.

10. Martin Sheen, "Find Something Worth Fighting For," available at http://apewiki.pbworks.com/w/file/fetch/70983722/Something%20Worth%20Fighting%20For.pdf (accessed 18 August 2016).

11. See I. A. Richards, *The Philosophy of Rhetoric* (Oxford, UK: Oxford University Press, 1936).

12. See Richards, *The Philosophy of Rhetoric*.

13. https://kathyjetnilkijiner.com/2014/09/24/united-nations-climate-summit-opening-ceremony-my-poem-to-my-daughter/

14. www.forbes.com/sites/clareoconnor/2014/10/20/full-transcript-monica-lewinsky-speaks-out-on-ending-online-abuse/#180dd5367d13

15. Ronald Reagan, "Space Shuttle Challenger Tragedy Address," available at www.americanrhetoric.com/speeches/ronaldreaganchallenger.htm (accessed 19 August 2016).

16. Abraham Lincoln, "The Gettysburg Address," http://myloc.gov/Exhibitions/gettysburgaddress/Pages/default.aspx (accessed 15 July 2012).

17. Kenneth Burke, "Four Master Tropes," *The Kenyon Review* 3 (4) 1941: 421–438.

18. Emma Goldman, "Address to the Jury," http://americanrhetoric.com/speeches/emmagoldmanjuryaddress.htm (accessed 12 November 2012).

6

The Rhetorical Situation

This chapter introduces rhetoric as a situated discursive act within a larger public context of deliberation about controversial and pressing issues. It expands the notion of "public speaking" beyond the walls of the classroom to encompass one's larger social and historical environment. The rhetorical situation is divided into rhetorical background, which provides the broader historical and social context of the speech and its audience, and rhetorical foreground, which represents those aspects that stand out significantly to specific audiences in the immediate present. The rhetorical background includes components such as the public, public opinion, public memory, social knowledge, counterpublics, and the state, while the rhetorical foreground includes the components of exigence, audience, constraints, motive, practical judgment, and occasion. The most important of these concepts for rhetorical public speaking is attention to exigence, which focuses rhetorical public speaking on the shared problems that an audience wishes will be addressed in a timely manner.

In much of our daily lives, we take most of the aspects of our environment for granted. Like fish in water, we are rarely aware of the medium through which we are moving—and rightly so. If a fish was always dwelling on the water, it would undoubtedly have little energy left for eating and finding shelter. Our "critical" spirit usually arises whenever some **contingency**—some unexpected obstacle, perplexity, or problem—arises out of that environment, stands out concretely before us, and threatens to disrupt our lives in some way. The appearance of contingency makes us look critically at our previous choices in the assumption that the path we had earlier chosen may not, in fact, be the best way forward. According to John Dewey, this process of reflection, judgment, and valuation

> takes place only when there is something the matter; when there is some trouble to be done away with, some need, lack, or privation to be made good, some conflict of tendencies to be resolved by means of changing conditions.[1]

Rhetoric is the creature of shared contingency. Thus, a **rhetorical situation** is one that occurs when public contingencies generate concern and uncertainty within a public audience and give force and effectiveness to persuasive discourse that encourages collective action.[2] In rhetorical situations, contingencies are problematic aspects of a situation shared by a group of people who must collectively deliberate about which actions to take to resolve their common problem. Contingencies are experienced this way whenever people encounter shared obstacles without knowing for sure the nature of the problem or the way to proceed effectively. Aristotle summed this up best:

> The duty of rhetoric is to deal with such matters as we deliberate upon without arts or systems to guide us. . . . The subjects of our deliberation are such as seem to present us with alternative possibilities: about things that could not have been, and cannot now or in the future be, other than they are, nobody who takes them to be of this nature wastes his time in deliberation.[3]

Of course, not all contingencies require rhetorical resolution. Many contingencies already have pre-established means of resolution that are generally accepted as effective. In such cases, we have a **technical situation**, which exists when we confront problems with a proven discourse and method to guide us. A technical situation does not guarantee a positive result, but it does resolve the uncertainty about how to proceed. For example, a person diagnosed with cancer faces a contingency—his or her health might go this way or that way. But most people treat cancer by following the advice of established medical authorities and pursue some combination of chemotherapy or radiation treatment. Although they do not know their fate, they know the course to pursue. Yet the same applies for one who might choose alternative methods of healing, such as prayer or herbal medicine. What makes a situation "technical" is not the prudence of the response, but the assurance that one knows the way forward. A situation only becomes "rhetorical" when the way forward is in doubt and multiple parties engage in symbolic persuasion to motivate cooperative action.

There are two major structural or "scenic" components to the rhetorical situation. The first is the **rhetorical background**, which represents the larger environment that defines the historical and social context for any particular rhetorical event. Knowing the rhetorical background provides a speaker with a broader perspective to more efficiently identify resources from which to draw when creating the speech and to better anticipate the possible long-term consequences after speaking. In Chapter 4, we have already encountered certain aspects of the rhetorical background in the discussion of **public memory**, **social knowledge**, and **maxims**. These are the basic build-ing blocks of what holds any public together. This "public," then, forms the rhetorical background for any rhetorical speech act. In common interpretation, the public is thought to represent the total population of any national culture. However, a "public" is more than just a "mass." A **public** is a complex interaction of individuals that constitutes a political culture. Defined in a functional way, a public is a group of citizens who recognize each other's interests and have developed hab-its of settling disputes, coordinating actions, and addressing shared concerns through common communication media. Therefore, what ultimately characterizes the American public in general is common participation within a political process. A public, then, comes about when a group of strangers comes together for a common purpose that affects them all directly or indirectly. The **state** is thus distinct from the public insofar as it represents the instrument that the public uses to address consequences that it deems important enough to manage. In this sense, democracy is defined in terms of a state developed as a means for the public to regulate itself.[4]

However, if a state (in the name of one clearly defined public) formally excludes other publics, then **counterpublics** develop outside of and counter to the established mechanisms of the state. As Michael Warner writes, the discourse that constitutes a counterpublic "is not merely a differ-ent or alternative idiom, but one that in other contexts would be regarded with hostility, or with a sense of indecorousness."[5] Consequently, their rhetoric tends to be directed internally, toward group cohesion, rather than externally, at social persuasion. Yet the goal of a counterpublic is usually to form a genuine public able to express its will through legitimate public institutions and governing bodies. They exist as counterpublics only when this access is denied and they are forced to organize through alternative channels of communication. Once democratic reforms are initiated, they reclaim their status as one public among many.

This functional idea of the public influences rhetorical invention in three ways. First, rhetorical persuasion can produce visible and concrete changes in reality only if there is an audience capa-ble of acting on its beliefs through organized channels. Speaking to people who have opted out of collective social life may produce persuasion, but those persuaded people will have few means of acting upon that new belief in collaboration with others—unless they have been persuaded to participate in the public. Second, a functional definition of the public encourages a speaker to think of people as something other than a stereotyped group of generic individuals who all think and feel the same thing. A functional definition of the public helps us realize that what binds people together is common interests in regulating social affairs and resolving common problems for the benefit of everyone *despite* their obvious differences. Third, it reminds a speaker that there is almost always a plurality of "publics" that exists within any more generic "public." It is a relatively straightforward matter to adapt to the specific group of people who might be arranged in a room. It is quite another to interpret that specific group as an amalgam of overlapping pub-lics joined together in a common space.

What is most important in constructing a speech with respect to knowledge of the public is the current state of public opinion. **Public opinion** thus represents the percentage of people who hold certain views to be true about public affairs. Often we see this portrayed in "opinion polls" that represent public opinion with a series of bar graphs and pie charts. Although there are many flaws to such polls, not the least of which is the assumption that opinions are discrete entities that can be discerned by narrow questioning, they are nonetheless valuable to the extent that they show general trends of opinion.[6] Walter Lippmann defines public opinion this way:

> Those features of the world outside which have to do with the behavior of other human beings, insofar as that behavior crosses ours, is dependent upon us, or is interesting to us, we call roughly *public affairs*. The pictures inside the heads of these human beings, the pictures of themselves, of others, of their needs, purposes, and relationship, are their public opinions. Those pictures which are acted upon by groups of people, or by individuals acting in the name of groups, are Public Opinion with capital letters.[7]

The important thing about public opinion from a rhetorical perspective is the fact that it represents the collective *opinions* of a public audience. An **opinion** is a conscious personal belief expressed as a commitment to a certain matter of fact or value. An opinion might be that coffee makes me nervous, cats are better than dogs, or that one should drink wine before every meal. However, a public opinion is something that deals with our views on matters of shared concern. We might have public opinions that television is a wasteland, that our neighbor's yard is a mess, that America's foreign policy is too isolationist, or that global warming is an urgent crisis. Public opinion is thus valuable for rhetoric in that it provides a starting point to approach an audience. It lets rhetors know what truths they can take for granted, which ones they need to challenge, and which ones they need to promote.

The rhetorical background, as represented by the current state of the public and of public opinion, is important to consider, in order to provide a broader perspective on how to understand a specific speech act. One encounters extensive explanations of a speaker's rhetorical background in any biographical account of famous orators. Here, for instance, is biographer Douglas L. Wilson providing a bit of the rhetorical background to Abraham Lincoln's Gettysburg Address:

> Lincoln had a theory about public opinion. He told a meeting of his fellow Republicans in 1856 that public opinion "always has a *'central idea'* from which all its minor thoughts radiate. That central idea in our political public opinion, at the beginning was, and until very recently has continued to be, 'the equality of all men.' And although it has always submitted patiently to whatever of inequality there seemed to be as a matter of actual necessity, its constant working has been a steady progress toward the practical equality of all men." What had changed by 1856 was that the defenders of slavery had begun either to deny that this assertion from the Declaration of Independence was meant to apply to blacks, as Stephen A. Douglas would do in his debates with Lincoln, or to disparage it as a "self-evident lie." Lincoln had discovered in his campaigning in the 1850s, if not previously, that the Declaration's theme of the equality of all men had an especially powerful effect on ordinary

citizens, appealing, it would seem, to something deeper than parties or policies, something, perhaps, having to do with ordinary people's sense of themselves.[8]

As this account demonstrates, considering the rhetorical background of any particular rhetorical situation provides a speaker added resources from which to draw upon, namely, the general values, maxims, conventions, memories, attitudes, and aspirations that hold together publics over time and provide good reasons for particular judgments, in this case embodied in the language of the Declaration of Independence. Without acknowledging the rhetorical background, a speaker will have tunnel vision that risks either ignoring or even offending the core beliefs of an audience, thereby making even the most well-defended position fall flat.

By contrast, the **rhetorical foreground** represents the specific and salient aspects of a common situation as it affects or interests some audience at a particular moment in time, including the motives of the audience itself. The rhetorical foreground represents those aspects of a situation that "stand out" from the background. These aspects include not only the problem or contingency at hand, but also the components of the specific speech situation in its relative immediacy. Expanding on the model initially posed by Lloyd Bitzer, these include exigence, audience, constraints, motive, practical judgment, and occasion. Although each of these aspects emerges out of the rhetorical background, the nature of the contingency gives each a distinct individuality that demands our focused attention. Importantly, every rhetorical speech begins with an understanding of the rhetorical situation; it does not begin with the desires or ideas of the speaker. What the speaker initially wants to say is merely a stimulus to learn about a specific rhetorical situation. But it is knowledge and acquaintance with the situation that is the ground on which any worthwhile speech is constructed.

> ## DISCUSSION
>
> Consider the relationships between publics, public opinion, and the state in a democracy. In theory, the actions of a democratic state are guided by the dominant public opinion expressed by various publics about matters of public concern. In this system, rhetoric becomes the way that public opinion is formed during large-scale rhetorical situations. In your experience, do you feel that how the state actually governs is influenced directly by public opinion? If it is not, what are the constraints that limit the ability of public opinion to guide the policies of the state?

▶ EXIGENCE

What dominates the foreground of any rhetorical situation is the presence of an exigence that requires an act of persuasion to resolve. An **exigence**, in a general sense, is any outstanding aspect of our environment that makes us feel a combination of *concern*, *uncertainty*, and *urgency*.

Not all exigencies are rhetorical. During our everyday lives, we encounter numerous exigencies, both large and small, that require an exertion of energy to deal with and possibly overcome, but these may not call out for any particular rhetorical response. For instance, you may have woken up too late to get to work on time, you might have forgotten your anniversary, you may be at risk of losing your home to foreclosure, or you may be anxious about an oncoming hurricane. In each of these situations, you are concerned because they each have the possibility of impacting your life negatively or positively, you are uncertain because you are not sure what to do about it, and you feel a sense of urgency because you must act soon if you are to change the outcome. But you may be able to deal with these situations by non-rhetorical action, such as not taking a shower and running red lights to get work on time, buying an extra-special gift for your spouse and pretending it is a surprise, taking out a loan to cover a mortgage payment to avoid foreclosure, or packing things in a car and driving north out of the hurricane's path.

A specifically *rhetorical* exigence is more than just the existence of a pressing problem; a **rhetorical exigence** must be an issue that generates concern and uncertainty for some organized or semi-organized group that can be resolved, in whole or in part, by persuading an audience to act in a way that is actually capable of addressing the situation. For instance, each of the four examples just given can become rhetorical under certain circumstances. If you discover that lateness to work is a constant problem in the office due to more structural problems such as pervasive road construction or cuts to public transportation, you can make a case to management of the need for flex time. If you decide that you forgot the anniversary because both you and your spouse have been working too many hours and not seeing each other enough, you can persuade your spouse that you should both quit your jobs and hitchhike around Europe for year. If your home foreclosure is a result of what you think to be a systematic policy of unethical loan practices, you can form a network with other homeowners to petition Congress to alter financial policy. And if you have no resources to use to escape the hurricane, you can make public demands that the state provide adequate shelter for you and your family. In each of these cases, what makes the situation rhetorical is a practical problem, or contingency, experienced by a large number of people, a shared desire to address that problem, and a realization that certain significant parties need to be persuaded to act in a certain way in order to solve it.

The concept of a rhetorical exigence can be difficult to grasp because there is often no agreement about the nature or even the existence of a particular problem. Indeed, convincing people that there *is* an exigence is often one of the most significant challenges to any speaker. Consequently, it is helpful to distinguish between two kinds of rhetorical exigence relative to the different nature of consensus and uncertainty. With a **contested exigence**, not everyone agrees that a problem exists. Sometimes people disagree whether certain things exist or not, such as whether or not Saddam Hussein of Iraq actually possessed weapons of mass destruction that threatened the United States. Others acknowledge the existence of things but question whether we should consider them a problem, such as those who might argue that even if Hussein did possess such weapons, he would never use them. In these cases, speakers have to work to persuade people of the nature of the exigence itself before ever getting to proposing a solution. By contrast, an **uncontested exigence** is one that everyone acknowledges to be a pressing problem that demands to be addressed; the issue is not to acknowledge the problem but to come up with an adequate solution. In such cases, a speaker concentrates on advocating some solutions over others, such as the preference for sanctions over war or for war instead of appeasement. For instance, most scientists agree that global warming is an uncontested exigence, but it remains a contested exigence for the public.

Bryan Stevenson: "The United States Now Has the Highest Rate of Incarceration in the World"

An important part of establishing an exigence is making visible and tangible what might have been hidden or abstract. The crisis of the level of incarceration in the United States is difficult to express precisely because this population, once incarcerated, is out of the public view. Bryan Stevenson, a public-interest lawyer and founder of the Equal Justice Initiative who has dedicated his career to helping the poor, the incarcerated, and the condemned, has tried to bring this exigence to public attention. In his 2012 TED talk, "We Need to Talk About an Injustice," he attempts to make a contested exigence into an uncontested exigence and force the American public to come to terms with a systemic problem:

> Well I've been trying to say something about our criminal justice system. This country is very different today than it was 40 years ago. In 1972, there were 300,000 people in jails and prisons. Today, there are 2.3 million. The United States now has the highest rate of incarceration in the world. We have seven million people on probation and parole. And mass incarceration, in my judgment, has fundamentally changed our world. In poor communities, in communities of color there is this despair, there is this hopelessness, that is being shaped by these outcomes. One out of three black men between the ages of 18 and 30 is in jail, in prison, on probation or parole. In urban communities across this country—Los Angeles, Philadelphia, Baltimore, Washington—50 to 60 percent of all young men of color are in jail or prison or on probation or parole.
>
> Our system isn't just being shaped in these ways that seem to be distorting around race, they're also distorted by poverty. We have a system of justice in this country that treats you much better if you're rich

DISCUSSION

How does Stevenson use facts and statistics to make his case that the incarceration rates in the United States are at crisis proportions? Why do you think he chose that strategy rather than a more graphic, narrative strategy? Think about other problems which have difficulty attracting public attention and compare them to the kinds of issues that are often featured in the news. Why does one type of problem that may seem trivial tend to attract news coverage over other types of problems that may in fact need immediate attention?

and guilty than if you're poor and innocent. Wealth, not culpability, shapes outcomes. And yet, we seem to be very comfortable. The politics of fear and anger have made us believe that these are problems that are not our problems. We've been disconnected.[9]

▶ AUDIENCE

In its most general sense, an **audience** represents any person, or group of people, who hears, reads, or witnesses any communicative event. However, there are always multiple audiences to consider in any speech act, some existing in other places, some existing at other times. In an age of reality television, for instance, navigating multiple audiences simultaneously has become something of an art form. One contestant, for instance, might conspire with a second with the pretense of knocking a third out of the game. Yet the first one does this with the knowledge that the second contestant will tell a fourth contestant (at a later time) about their conversation, and therefore influence the actions of the fourth contestant from a distance. Meanwhile, all of the contestants are well aware of the television audience, with individuals watching simultaneously (in different places) all across the country. And many of them hope that their performance will be so engaging that it will persuade other television producers (in a different place at a later time) to cast them for exciting roles once their current show has ended. Only those unfamiliar with the genre interpret the on-screen characters to be the "real" audience; similarly, only those unfamiliar with rhetoric believe that an audience consists only of those immediately listening to a speech at a particular place and time.

We can break down audience into three categories: the primary audience, secondary audience, and the target audience. The **primary audience** for rhetorical public speaking consists of those people actually assembled together to hear the speech as it is delivered in person by the speaker—for instance, the delegates at the Virginia convention for Patrick Henry. **Secondary audiences** represent all those people who encounter the speech either through some other media or secondhand through the spoken word of another person; in the case of Henry's speech, this would include not only the King of England and the American colonists but also readers of this textbook. Finally, **target audiences** are those individuals or groups in either the primary or secondary audiences who are able to be persuaded and are capable of acting in such a way to help resolve the exigence. For Henry, the target audiences included not only the Virginia delegates but also the opinion leaders throughout the colonies who would read his words as they were reprinted and distributed through the printing press. For he understood that even if the Virginia delegation voted to support a war policy, actually raising an army would require the full support of the majority of the property-owning class, those who held all the resources necessary for an extended campaign.

As indicated by the discussion on speeches of advocacy, the relationship between the primary and secondary audiences is actually very significant. Even though secondary audiences may only receive transcripts of the speech (as we do with Henry), knowing that his actual speech brought the entire delegation to its feet chanting "give me liberty or give me death!" has a direct impact on how we receive and interpret his words. We are naturally drawn to read speeches that we know had a very powerful effect on the primary audience, for we interpret its reaction as we do the reviews of a movie critic. Its excitement is a sign to us that the speech contains something significant, particularly when the crowd in attendance is of a significant size. Bringing thousands of people to their feet, as Martin Luther King Jr. did on the Washington Mall with his "I Have a Dream" speech, draws the attention of the news media and these days becomes a candidate for a viral video or social media distribution campaign. Consequently, even if the primary audience has only minimal significance as a target audience (as many audiences do during presidential campaigns in which candidates deliver major policy addresses in front of select organizations), they cannot be ignored. With only rare exceptions (and those usually for unflattering reasons), nobody wants to read a speech that was a complete dud during its actual delivery. Almost any successful public speech must therefore satisfy the expectations and desires of the primary audience even if the target audience is a secondary audience watching from a distance.

Michelle Obama: "Show Them the Path That You Took"

An important part of speaking to an audience is making clear what collective capacity they possess to make a difference in a situation. Often it is not enough simply to make a general appeal to action—one has two show clear "paths" that one can take. In her address to Dillard University, a historically black university founded in New Orleans in 1869, Michelle Obama spent a great deal of time retracing the history of its founders to show the difficult struggles that many of its early faculty and students endured in order to earn a higher education after the long history of slavery and its legacy in segregation. She used this history to remind her audience of the responsibilities and powers they have to continue to make the world a better place:

> You all have opportunities and skills and education that so many folks who came before you never could have dreamed of. So just imagine the kind of impact that you're going to make. Imagine how you can inspire those around you to reach higher and complete their own education.

> And you can start small. Start by volunteering at an after-school program, or helping some high school kids fill out their college applications. Show them the path that you took. Or you can think a little bigger—you can get your entire congregation or your community to start a mentoring program; maybe convince your new employer to sponsor scholarships for underprivileged kids. Or maybe you could think a little higher—maybe you could run for school board or Congress, or, yes, even President of the United States.

> And then maybe you could build preschools for every single one of our kids. Maybe you could help turn that pipeline to prison into a highway to college; help give every child in America an education that is truly worth of their promise. Those are the kind of big dreams that folks who founded this university reached for. That is how high they set their bar.[10]

DISCUSSION

Two questions often linger after people hear a rhetorical speech: first, "Is that speaker talking to me?" and second, "What can I do about this issue, if anything?" It is the duty of the speaker to answer these questions for the audience. Although it might seem to make sense to be as inclusive as possible when one is speaking to an audience, in fact it is often more effective to target a specific audience and make them feel as if they have a unique responsibility to do something that others may not have. How does Obama's specific suggestions for action impact an audience's sense of responsibility over a more generic call to action? What are the potential drawbacks of "calling out" specific members of the audience?

▶ CONSTRAINTS

Almost nothing that we do in life happens without resistance. Only in the realm of fantasy or dream does a wish become a reality by a word and a snap of the fingers. And even our most simple tasks often require an exertion of physical and mental effort, as we have all experienced on mornings when we simply cannot get out of bed for one reason or another. Every single reason why we cannot accomplish a task is a **constraint**, which represents any counterforce that stands between us and the attainment of our interests. Sometimes these constraints are physical things, such as when the car doesn't start or when we hit traffic on the road. Sometimes they are emotional things, such as when we dislike our job so much that it is hard to perform up to our potential. And sometimes they are other people, such as when our co-workers resist our suggestions about how to streamline an office's business practices. Anything that restrains or inhibits movement toward a desired end functions as a constraint.

In rhetoric, constraints are defined in relationship to interests or ends that require rhetorical persuasion to achieve. **Rhetorical constraints** are those obstacles that must be overcome in order to facilitate both the persuasive and practical effects desired by the speaker. By "persuasive" effects, we mean those effects that make people think and act differently than they did before the speech. Constraints relating to persuasive effects are thus called **internal constraints**, referring to the beliefs, attitudes, and values of an audience that must be changed if persuasion is to occur. For example, convincing a population to support a tax on junk foods to cut down on child obesity may require challenging the **belief** that obesity is not a social problem, changing the pervading attitude of resisting higher taxes, and dissociating the eating of junk food from the value of personal choice and freedom. Unless these internal constraints can be modified, they will lead to the rejection of the proposal. However, a public speaker who actually desires to make a lasting change in actual conditions must also consider **external constraints**, which are the people, objects, processes, and events that may physically obstruct any productive action even if persuasion of an audience has occurred. A *person* acting as a constraint is someone who cannot be persuaded and who possesses the power to obstruct your goal, such as the governor who threatens a veto of your bill. An *object* is defined here as any tangible and enduring thing that tends to resist change while having constant influence on an environment, such as the presence of vending machines in schools (a "physical" object) or the laws that give schools financial incentives to place them in schools (a "legal" object). An *event* that is a constraint is a tangible but ephemeral thing that occurs at a specific point and time and has a distinct beginning and end, such as a sudden downturn in the economy that makes new taxes unpopular. Last, a *process* represents a sequence of events that must be followed in order to bring something to conclusion. As a constraint, such a process might be a lengthy and burdensome petition process by which any changes in tax laws require years of persistent effort.

Any of these external constraints may impede successful social action even *after* an audience has been persuaded to act. Consequently, public speakers who fail to account for external constraints may recommend a course of action, only to find it to be impossible to implement later, thereby wasting everyone's time and energy. Successful speakers should always consider all possible constraints before creating and delivering rhetorical discourse. Ignoring constraints often ruins any possibility of instigating effective social action. On the one hand, if external constraints are ignored, a speaker risks appearing ignorant about the "realities" of the situation. On the other hand, ignoring internal constraints is the common flaw of all "technical" discourse, believing that the only things needed for persuasion are accurate facts and reasonable solutions. The most effective speaker combines elements of both types of discourse by adapting his or her language to both types of constraints.

Yang Jisheng: "Ask for Nothing and Fear Nothing"

Part of overcoming constraints is not only having the power to resist external forces but also having the courage to make the effort. One profession that requires tenacity and courage is that of an investigative journalist. Although popular media is often easy to criticize, throughout the world there are thousands of committed writers who risk their lives every day to investigate and report the truth. Yang Jisheng is a Chinese journalist and author of *Tombstone*, a comprehensive account of the Great Chinese Famine during the Great Leap Forward. Although Yang joined the Communist Party in 1964 and worked for the Xinhua News Agency, the 1989 Tiananmen Square massacre made him a critic of the Chinese government. In 2016 he was selected by the Nieman Foundation to receive the Louis M. Lyons Award for Conscience and Integrity in Journalism, but had to have someone else read his remarks because he was prevented from traveling to Cambridge to receive the award:

> Insisting on being a journalist with conscience and integrity carries risks. When giving a lecture to a class of journalism students, I passed along a tip for avoiding danger: "Ask for nothing and fear nothing, and position yourself between heaven and earth." By asking for nothing I mean not hoping for promotion or wealth; by fearing nothing I mean examining

> ## DISCUSSION
>
> What do you think Yang meant when he said that aspiring journalists should not expose a "pigtail"? Notice that Yang also gives advice about avoiding external constraints by focusing specifically on regulating one's own internal emotional states and personal behavior. What does this say about the relationship between internal constraints and external constraints when it comes to the profession of journalism?

one's own behavior and not exposing a "pigtail" for anyone to grab. Don't rely on the powerful, but rather on your own character and professional independence. . . .

Since China embarked on Reform and Opening, many journalists of conscience and integrity have emerged. In the face of enormous impediments they've reported the truth, chastised evil and moved Chinese society forward.[11]

▶ MOTIVE

As indicated by the discussion of internal constraints, the psychological state of the audience is a crucial component of a rhetorical situation. Following Kenneth Burke, we can describe this psychological state as a structure of motives. A **motive** refers to any conscious psychological or physiological incitement to action within a particular situation.[12] A motive is not to be confused with a mere "wish," however. Wishes merely exist in the abstract realm of fantasy and need not relate to anything actual; a motive only exists within a situation in which successful attainment of a goal is possible. For instance, a child may wish to fly to Mars and take great pleasure in imagining a fantastic voyage; this wish only becomes a motive when it stimulates the child to earn a degree in astrophysics while training to be a pilot. In other words, the number of wishes we might have at any one time is nearly infinite, which of course means they are all equally powerless to alter our actual behavior at any one time. By contrast, motives only occur in particular situations when a single desire or goal moves us to action and judgment.

The study of rhetoric in many ways is equivalent to the study of how to influence human motivation through conscious symbolic appeals. For Aristotle, audiences were motivated by respect for the speaker (**ethos**), by emotional affection or dislike (**pathos**), and by the strength of reason and evidence (**logos**). This study of motivation then took a "scientific" leap during the Age of Enlightenment when the new study of psychology was used to explain the phenomenon of persuasion. Rhetorician George Campbell, for example, wrote that the function of rhetoric is "to enlighten the Understanding, to please the Imagination, to move the Passions, or to influence the Will."[13] The novelty behind this definition was the application of the recently discovered mental "faculties" to the study of rhetoric. Much like different departments within a modern corporation, these faculties were explained as existing in our minds as discrete units, each with its own unique process and function. So when we wanted to think about ideas, we called on the understanding (sometimes called thought or reason); when we felt like stimulating our bodies, we sought out the passions (sometimes called Emotions or feelings); when we pondered the unknown, we appealed to the imagination; and when we wanted to act, we rallied the will. The most successful rhetoric engaged all the faculties at once. We argued logic to the understanding, aroused the passions through visual examples, used fantastic possibilities to excite the Imagination, and moved the will through imperatives to action.

Today, we tend not to think in terms of discrete "faculties" that exist as separate entities in our minds. We simply talk about having beliefs, feelings, emotions, habits, desires, and values. However, the basic model of crafting language that is imaginative, thoughtful, and passionate in order to redirect human motivation remains effectively the same. The specific concern for rhetoric is those motives that arise in the context of the exigence as a means of resolving the situation in accordance with the needs and desires of an audience. The following concepts are therefore useful in understanding the structure of motivation of an audience. Each of these components represent one of three things for the speaker: (a) *a preexisting resource* to draw upon in support of judgments, (b) *a constraint* to overcome because its presence in the audience obstructs a course of action, or (c) *a possibility* to create as a means to encourage people to think, feel, or act a certain way as a means to resolve a situation.

1. **Belief**: A belief is a statement of fact on which a person is prepared to act. Beliefs can be stated as propositions, such as "the earth goes around the sun" or "all men are created equal" or "cutting taxes increases economic growth" or "people shouldn't smoke." Each of these beliefs only acts *as* a belief for a person if he or she actually acts in accordance with its content. When someone says one thing but does another, we do not attribute belief but accuse that person of hypocrisy. Rhetorically, beliefs are the building blocks of judgments, for they provide a concrete place to stand so that we know we are acting on a firm basis of understanding of reality (e.g., "Clean water is an essential component of a healthy nation").

2. **Value**: A value is an abstract ideal quality that guides our behavior across a variety of situations. Whereas beliefs are propositions, values are usually stated as single virtue terms, such as "love" or "justice" or "liberty" or "equality." A value is a "quality" because it is something that we feel to be present in certain situations and that we treasure and wish to preserve for as long as possible. Usually values are things that almost everybody agrees are valuable; contention arises only in the clash between two competing values and their relative importance. "Love" and "justice" are in competition when a parent must decide whether to turn in a child who has committed a crime, and "liberty" and "equality" are in competition in economic debates that weigh the balance between the unregulated pursuit of individual wealth and the regulated distribution of resources to all. Rhetorically, values guide the speaker by investing the speech with an overall quality that resonates with the treasured values of the audience (e.g., "When we cannot drink clean water or breathe clean air, we cease to have freedom").

3. **Feeling**: A feeling is a sensory response to some environmental stimulation or physical state. Feelings make up the substance of our perceptual world and represent the basic elements that physically connect us with the world around us. However, each audience comes to a situation being acquainted with a unique set of feelings based on that audience's particular experiences in an environment. For instance, people who live in a busy metropolis know the feelings associated with traffic, crowds, skyscrapers, construction, and city parks, whereas those who live in a rural farming community know the feelings associated with quiet landscapes, isolation, farmhouses, animals, and swaying fields of grain. Rhetorically, the familiar feelings (both negative and positive) of an audience can be effectively re-activated through language by calling forth familiar senses and by incorporating them into metaphor (e.g., "Many of us here remember the first time we walked with our bare feet through the cool, rocky streams during a sultry August day").

4. **Emotion**: An emotion is a dramatized feeling that attracts or repels us to certain objects because of their specific character and qualities. An emotion is a kind of "feeling" because it is usually a reaction to sense perception and also is attached to feelings of pleasure or pain; but it is a "dramatized" feeling because emotions carry with them narrative elements in which we play out scenarios in our minds of what will happen. It is the difference between simply perceiving the color red (as in feeling) and seeing a blinking red warning light on a console (as in emotion). Our emotional response to the red light is based on our narrative sense of whether the light signifies a danger that brings about a state of fear and urgency. Consequently, emotions are always related in some form or another to the "things" that surround us and are never simply "in our heads." Rhetorically, emotions are powerful tools to direct people toward or away from certain actions or judgments by connecting them to the people, objects, and events that bring about powerful emotions (e.g., "The month after a chemical spill in a nearby town, a thousand dead, stinking fish washed ashore, and the water was covered with a frothy yellow scum").

Despite their incredible variety, all emotions can be characterized by two things—orientation and salience. An **orientation** represents how we stand in relationship to a thing, whether we are attracted to (+) or repulsed by (−) it. A *neutral* orientation, in which we have no stance, thus represents the absence of emotion. For instance, I might have a positive orientation toward my family, a negative orientation to the fire ants in my back yard, and a neutral orientation to my neighbor's mailbox. **Salience** represents how strongly this emotion is felt within a particular situation. When I go on a long business trip I might miss my family terribly (high salience), whereas I like to look at the picture of my family during my lunch break at work (low salience).[14] Chapter 9, on pathos, will explore how rhetoric attempts to encourage orientations and heighten or reduce salience in order to encourage certain beliefs or actions.

5. **Habit**: A habit is a learned sequence of behavior in which mental and physical energies work relatively effortlessly together to accomplish a familiar task. Habits are what Aristotle called "second nature" because once acquired they take almost the same form as instinct, guiding our thoughts and actions in familiar groups without the requirement of deliberative choice or reflective thought. Habits therefore include more than simply ordinary tasks such as tying shoes or waking up early or cleaning up after oneself; they also include complex tasks such as writing depositions and painting landscapes and fly fishing. Any type of group, no matter how large or

small, has common goals and common activities and shares a core group of habits. There are habits of being a carpenter, an engineer, a bachelor, or a U.S. citizen. Rhetorically, habits can be problems ("We are careless with our waterways"), resources ("Let us apply the habits of housekeeping to our rivers"), or goals ("We need good habits of water conservation").

6. **Desire**: A desire is a concrete energetic ideal that propels people to action in pursuit of some value or pleasure. Desires are products of either *imagination* or *memory*—imagination when they are products of novel creations of the mind and memory when they are recollections of the past that a person aspires to re-experience. Like a motive, a desire is not simply a "wish" that exists in an ideal and impossible realm of fantasy; it is something that we invest energy in seeking and that guides our decisions in actual situations of choice. Our desires are based on how clearly we can envision a future state of affairs and how powerful the subsequently produced emotions are. Rhetorically, similar to habits, desires can be problems ("We dream too much of big houses and fast cars"), resources ("Don't you all want to bring your kids to the same clean streams?"), or created products ("Let us imagine a whole nation of clean waterways where humans and nature care for one another").

The motives of the audience are thus a product of how all of these components interact. An audience enters into a situation holding to a specific set of beliefs; treasuring certain values over others; being acquainted with a general sphere of feelings; associating specific emotions with types of events, objects, and people; having developed a nexus of habits that helps them deal with their environment; and harboring certain desires for which they will sacrifice time and energy to attain. A speaker must then decide which of these things to draw from in support of the position, which represent problems that prevent an audience from attaining their goals, and which need to be created in an audience in order for them to accomplish something new.

Aung San Suu Kyi: "It Was Also the Humiliation of a Way of Life"

One of the most challenging events to understand in terms of motive are the revolutionary periods in which established powers are overturned by movements of the people. Aung San Suu Kyi witnessed such an event. Born in Yangon, Myanmar, in 1945 to one of the founding fathers of Myanmar, Aung San returned to her native country after living and studying abroad in order to support the uprising in 1988 against the brutal rule of dictator U Ne Win. After the newly formed party National League for Democracy won control of the government, the military overturned the results and placed her under house arrest where she would spend the next 15 of 21 years in custody until returning to power in the 2015 elections. In 1990, she composed the address "Freedom from Fear," which spoke in part to the causes of the 1988 uprising in terms of the complexity of motives, explaining that although economic hardships were a cause of the movement for democracy in Burma, there were deeper reasons as well:

> It was more than the difficulties of eking out a barely acceptable standard of living that had eroded the patience of a traditionally good-natured, quiescent people—it was also the humiliation of a way of life disfigured by corruption and fear. The students were protesting

> ## DISCUSSION
>
> In reading her account, what are the primary agents or groups whose motives she spends time on trying to discern? Can you identify specific beliefs, values, feelings, emotions, habits, or desires that distinguish the motives of one group from another? Also, she clearly implies that people watching these events from a distance might attribute only certain motives as the primary ones while neglecting others. How does it help make sense of the social and political changes to map out a more complex network of motives?

not just against the death of their comrades but against the denial of their right to life by a totalitarian regime which deprived the present of meaningfulness and held out no hope for the future. . . . Some of its keenest supporters were businessmen who had developed the skills and the contacts necessary not only to survive but to prosper within the system. But their affluence offered them no genuine sense of security or fulfilment. . . . The people of Burma had wearied of a precarious state of passive apprehension where they were "as in the cupped hands" of the powers that be.[15]

▶ PRACTICAL JUDGMENT

Once an exigence becomes universally recognized, the immediate question becomes, "What do we do?" The answer to this question always involves a **practical judgment**, which is the act of defining a particular person, object, or event for the purposes of making a practical decision. In other words, practical judgment tells us both *what things are* and *what we should do about them*. The mere giving of commands—such as "Go!" or "Halt!—is therefore *not* a practical judgment because it does not satisfy the first criterion of the definition. A practical judgment demands action but only after an act of cognition that explains to our minds the relationship among a *thing*, an *idea*, and an *action*. For example, I wake up at night and hear a tapping sound (thing). Fearful that it is a burglar (hypothetical idea), I get up and discover it is just the rattling of the air conditioner (conclusive idea). I then decide to go back to sleep (action). As indicated by this example, usually our practical judgments are absorbed into the habits and **conventions** (or shared, normative habits) of our everyday lives. We do not need to think consciously about whether we should respond to a stop sign (thing), by associating it with the command to stop (idea), and then stopping (action). We just stop. But when we are learning to drive, all of these practical judgments must be consciously taught and enforced through instruction.

As indicated by the discussion of exigence, practical judgment takes on rhetorical qualities when we are unsure about what *to do* because we are unsure about what things *are*. Are British soldiers in Boston "peacekeepers" or "oppressors"? Should we view the violence in Darfur as "genocide" or "civil war"? In each case, rhetorical conflict involves the struggle to properly name things in such a way as to advance one judgment over another and thereby encourage forms of action on the basis of that judgment. The question of practical judgment thus centers around the matter of naming and therefore of meaning. We must be very careful of the words we use to describe our environment, because every word is loaded with particular denotations and connotations and associations that inevitably lead people to act in certain ways instead of other ways. One of the central challenges of any rhetorical public speaker is to promote his or her version of practical judgment and thereby provide the correct "names" for any contingency that will make an audience prefer certain options over others.

Lady Gaga: "Doesn't It Seem to Be That 'Don't Ask, Don't Tell' Is Backwards?"

"Don't ask, don't tell" was the official U.S. policy on military service by gays, bisexuals, and lesbians that was instituted by the Clinton Administration on February 28, 1994 (and finally ended by the Obama administration in 2011). It stated that the military would continue to ban these groups from military service when their sexual orientation became known, but that it would cease to actively determine the orientation of service members while at the same time requesting that they keep that orientation to themselves. At a 2010 rally in Portland, Maine, organized by the Servicemembers Legal Defense Network, musician Lady Gaga urged Senators Susan Collins and Olympia Snowe to vote to repeal the policy. Her argument was grounded in the logic of practical judgment—that is to say, the logic of how we apply a specific principle to determine how we should treat a specific case:

> Doesn't it seem to be that "don't ask, don't tell" is backwards? . . . Doesn't it seem to you that we should send home the prejudiced, the straight soldier who hates the gay soldier, the straight soldier whose performance in the military is affected because he is homophobic. . . .
>
> I am here today because I would like to propose a new law; a law that sends home the soldier that has the problem. Our new law is called "if you don't like it, go home." A law that discharges the soldier with the issue, the law that discharges the soldier with the *real* problem, the homophobic soldier that has the real negative effect on unit cohesion. . . . A law that doesn't prosecute the gay soldier who fights for equality with no problem, but prosecutes the straight soldier who fights against it.[16]

DISCUSSION

Lady Gaga used the confrontational strategy of actually arguing that our practical judgments have been completely upside down. Instead of saying one individual is a problem, we should have been saying the completely opposite individual is the problem. Note, too, how she developed a new law in correspondence with our newfound practical judgment. Given the changes in how American culture has treated sexual orientation over the past few decades, how do you account for this radical shift in practical judgment? What does that say about where we get our principles and how we apply them to specific cases?

▶ OCCASION

Rhetoric as a form of public speaking specifically refers to rhetoric that occurs at a specific time and place shared by both speaker and audience. In other words, occasion represents all of those elements that characterize a particular rhetorical act as a distinctly *oral* performance. The **occasion** is the specific setting shared by speaker and audience whose circumstances determine the genre, the purpose, and the standards of appropriateness of what is said. Examples of different types of occasions include a wedding ceremony, a political rally in front of City Hall, a Thanksgiving dinner, a graduation ceremony, or a murder prosecution at a law court. The power of occasion is its tendency to focus attention and interest on a single subject, a tendency that on the one hand significantly constrains the freedom of a speaker but on the other hand allows him or her to more powerfully use language to unify the audience's emotional, intellectual, creative, and physical capacities around a single theme. Consequently, it is not unusual for speakers to provide two rhetorical responses to any rhetorical situation, one using the spoken word to address people at a specific occasion, and the other using writing or electronic media to communicate to secondary audiences without the constraints of occasion.

The most important function of occasion is to establish a common purpose for bringing speaker and audience together in the same place. The **purpose** for rhetorical public speech represents the reason for and circumstances under which an occasion occurs. To be clear, the purpose is not the purpose of the *speaker*; it is the purpose for the *event*. Purpose establishes common expectations among members of a diverse public that help direct their attention and focus. This is obvious for most conventional occasions. The occasion of the wedding establishes the purpose of the best man's speech, regardless of who is chosen for that role, just as the purpose of a defense attorney's speech is not up to the whim of the lawyer. In these cases, the occasion came first, and the speaker was selected based on his or her ability to fill its purpose. However, many times the speaker's intent and the occasion's purpose coincide. These are situations in which an individual creates an occasion explicitly for the purpose of speaking his or her mind and generates an audience on that basis alone. These types of speeches are usually given by well-known celebrities or political figures capable of attracting an audience based on the strength of their *ethos* alone, although one cannot rule out the proverbial "soapbox" oratory of the anonymous citizen standing up on a street corner. However, once these speeches begin, they nonetheless take on a purpose of their own that still constrains what can be said.

In addition to purpose, the occasion determines the genre and standards of appropriateness of the speech. A selection of genres has already been defined in Chapter 1, but these should not be taken as comprehensive. Speech genres are literally infinite. Speeches of commemoration alone can be broken down into endless subgenres, such as wedding speeches, graduation speeches, award ceremony speeches, Veterans Day speeches, coronation speeches, and so on. The important thing is simply to keep in mind that any occasion creates generic expectations in an audience for what they will hear and how they will hear it based on tradition and on past experiences. Finally, occasion determines **appropriateness**, or how "fitting" the speech is to all of the particular elements and unique circumstances of the speech.[17] An appropriate speaker considers the audience's needs and desires before composing the speech, whereas an inappropriate speaker thinks first of his or her own self-interest and only afterward makes minor accommodations to the audience. For instance, the speech by a best man at a bachelor party has norms of appropriateness vastly different from a speech given in front of grandparents and grandchildren. More than one movie has used a best man's ignorance of standards of appropriateness as a source of comedy.

It is important to note, however, that the constraints of appropriateness are not fixed rules or absolute responsibilities. They are norms of behavior usually established through cultural tradition and social habit. In everyday life, following the dictates of appropriateness as determined by the purposes of the occasion is the easiest way to get our voices heard. Anyone preparing for a job interview quickly realizes the importance of saying the right thing in the right way in order to get what one wants. Yet sometimes norms of appropriateness are so narrow as to be oppressive. What is considered appropriate might not equate with what we consider ethical or moral. It is simply what is expected. It is up to rhetors to judge whether their conformity to or violation of these constraints helps enable the productive resolution of some larger problem.

Nadezhda Tolokonnikova: "Taking Part Is the Very Spice of Human Life"

During the summer of 2012, members of the Russian punk band "Pussy Riot," Maria Alyokhina, Yekaterina Samutsevich, and Nadezhda Tolokonnikova, were put on trial by the Russian government for "hooliganism motivated by religious hatred" after lip-syncing to a punk song in an Orthodox church for 40 seconds. During their incarceration for the first half of the year, they were deemed "prisoners of conscience" by Amnesty International, and many Western musicians and celebrities express their support. During her closing statement of her trial, Nadezhda Tolokonnikova used the occasion to express her solidarity with earlier Russian dissidents persecuted under Stalinist rule. The three were convicted and sentenced to two years in a prison camp—only later commuted to probation:

> Katya, Masha and I are in jail but I don't consider that we've been defeated. Just as the dissidents weren't defeated. When they disappeared into psychiatric hospitals and prisons, they passed judgement on the country. The era's art of creating an image knew no winners or losers. The Oberiu poets remained artists to the very end, something impossible to explain or understand since they were purged in 1937. Vvedensky wrote: "We like what can't be understood, What can't be explained is our friend." According to the official report, Aleksandr Vvedensky died on 20 December 1941. We don't know the cause, whether it was dysentery in the train after his arrest or a bullet from a guard. It was somewhere on the railway line between Voronezh and Kazan. Pussy Riot are Vvedensky's disciples and his heirs. His principle of "bad rhythm" is our own. He wrote: "It happens that two rhythms will come into your head, a good one and a bad one and I choose the bad one. It will be the right one." What can't be explained is our friend. The elitist, sophisticated occupations of the

DISCUSSION

Later in the speech, Tolokonnikova also aligned herself with Dostoevsky and Socrates, both also imprisoned for their beliefs. How does the fact that she was actually in prison at the time change the meaning of her protest? How would it have been different if the occasion were different—perhaps if she had fled the country and was speaking from the safety of a foreign embassy? What other examples can you think of in which the occasion for the speech had as much importance as what was said?

Oberiu poets, their search for meaning on the edge of sense was ultimately realized at the cost of their lives, swept away in the senseless Great Terror that's impossible to explain. At the cost of their own lives, the Oberiu poets unintentionally demonstrated that the feeling of meaninglessness and analogy, like a pain in the backside, was correct, but at the same time led art into the realm of history. The cost of taking part in creating history is always staggeringly high for people. But that taking part is the very spice of human life.[18]

▶ SUMMARY

Considering the rhetorical background that frames any rhetorical public speech provides a speaker with the broader perspective that is necessary for any sustained effort at persuasion. This perspective not only expands the spatial horizon beyond the immediate physical context, but it also extends the temporal horizon so that it speaks to the past and looks toward the future. For example, simply thinking in terms of a larger "public" makes even one's immediate audience representatives of a larger social group with a shared history. One must simply remember that the qualities of the rhetorical background should never be taken to represent anything more than convenient and pragmatic shorthand that ultimately proves the worth of those qualities within the successful act of rhetorical persuasion. In the end, all groups and individuals are unique and exceed the capacity for such broad generalizations. But these generalizations are necessary starting points nonetheless, for they help us look beyond the immediate moment and give us perspective. As Roman orator Cicero observed long ago, audience adaptation requires a great deal of labor beyond just adapting to what the members of an audience might be thinking, feeling, and saying in the present:

> We must also read the poets, acquaint ourselves with histories, study and peruse the masters and authors in every excellent art, and by way of practice praise, expound, emend, criticize, and confute them; we must argue every question on both sides, and bring out on every topic whatever points can be deemed plausible; besides this we must become learned in the common law and familiar with the statutes, and must contemplate all the olden time, and investigate the ways of the senate, political philosophy, the rights of allies, the treaties and conventions, and the policy of empire; and last we have to cull, from all the forms of

pleasantry, a certain charm of humor, with which to give a sprinkle of salt, as it were, to all of our discourse.[19]

Although we are far from ancient Rome, the same principles apply. The best public speakers always think beyond the scope of their immediate situation and audience, thinking not only in terms of the past and the future but also the larger publics that might encounter their speeches in various mediated contexts. The more one knows about the complexities of history and culture, the richer and more durable one's speech becomes.

However, no speech is successful without first and foremost being able to address the *unique* and *pressing* characteristics of the problem in the *present*. The considerations of the rhetorical foreground thus link us to the concrete characteristics of our present surroundings that help balance the more universal characteristics of our larger social and historical environment. Attention to exigence, practical judgment, audience, constraints, speaker, and occasion gives a speech its energy and life. Whereas the rhetorical background helps to identify the general aspects of a somewhat generic national audience, the rhetorical foreground puts us in a specific place and time. It tells us what stands out from a background environment and strikes us as being something urgent and important.

Each of the concepts within the rhetorical foreground distinguishes different parts of a rhetorical situation to help focus attention on specific aspects before addressing the whole situation. The *exigence* defines the immediate problem at hand rather than some vague moral abstraction or political maxim. The *constraints* represent the known obstacles to resolving this problem, whether they be physical constraints in a situation or emotional and psychological constraints within an audience. The *audience*, in turn, identifies that particular group, often a subset of some public, whose members are capable of resolving that problem if they act in a specific way. The *motives* represent all of those characteristics of an audience (actual or potential) that influence their decision in that particular moment. *Practical judgment* represents the specific action they are called upon to make by the speaker, in this case a judgment upon a certain event, person, or object that affects the course of future events. Finally, the *occasion* stands for the actual context of the speech situation, including the place and time of the event, the purpose for the occasion, and the expectations of the audience in attendance.

▶ CHAPTER 6 EXERCISES

1. **IMPROMPTU:** Practice trying to turn a contested exigence into an uncontested exigence. Do this by starting a speech with the phrase: "Most people say that X is a good thing to do/ think, but I say that this is a problem." To make this challenging and entertaining, choose an ordinary belief or practice which is completely mundane, such as wearing shoes or brushing my teeth or telling the truth. Generate a short counterpoint that turns this belief or practice into a serious crisis.

2. DEBATE: Identify an exigence that has recently gotten a lot of attention in the news—ideally something that has not gotten previous media attention. Divide the class physically in terms of those who believe that this is a serious problem and those who believe that it is not, with students taking seats on each side, depending on their initial attitude. Discuss as a class your reasoning, focusing particularly on the qualities of urgency and uncertainty in the evidence for your beliefs. After your discussion, see if anyone changes their opinion by shifting sides of the room.

3. GROUP: Divide into groups and have each student briefly describe a personal example of when he or she actually experienced a rhetorical exigence and made an effort to resolve it through persuasion. (This includes rhetorical situations isolated to friends or family.) From these stories, choose which story is the best and then as a group analyze the situation according to all of the components of a rhetorical situation and present the results to the class.

4. TAKE HOME: Send each student home with a copy of a whole speech provided by the instructor. On each copy of each speech, circle the exact passages or phrases that refer to the components of the rhetorical situation and label them. On a separate paper, write a brief paragraph that summarizes how the speaker defined his or her rhetorical situation based on your findings.

5. VIDEO: Explore the importance of "occasion" by having yourself filmed giving a short speech on location in a public space. Your speech should concern some aspect of your immediate environment. You have two options. First, you can call our attention to a problem (i.e., the lack of a stop sign on a street corner). Second, you can commemorate something positive (like the installation of a stop sign on a street corner that had previously not had one).

▶ NOTES

1. John Dewey, "Theory of Valuation," in *John Dewey: The Later Works*, vol. 13, ed. Jo Ann Boydston (Carbondale: Southern Illinois UP, 1988), 34.

2. The literature on the rhetorical situation includes Lloyd Bitzer, "The Rhetorical Situation," *Philosophy and Rhetoric* 1 (1969), 13–14; Richard E. Vatz, "The Myth of the Rhetorical Situation," *Philosophy and Rhetoric* 6 (1973), 154–161; Barbara A. Biesecker, "Rethinking the Rhetorical Situation from Within the Thematic of Difference," *Philosophy and Rhetoric* 22 (1989), 110–130; Alan Brinton, "Situation in the Theory of Rhetoric," *Philosophy and Rhetoric* 14 (1981), 234–248; Scott Consigny, "Rhetoric and Its Situations," *Philosophy and Rhetoric* 7 (1974), 175–186; Kathleen Hall Jamieson, "Generic Constraints and the Rhetorical Situation," *Philosophy and Rhetoric* 6 (1968), 162–170; John H. Patton, "Causation and Creativity in Rhetorical Situations: Distinctions and Implications," *Quarterly Journal of Speech* 65 (1979), 36–55.

3. Aristotle, *Rhetoric*. In *The Rhetoric and the Poetics of Aristotle*, trans. W. Rhys Roberts, ed. Edward P. J. Corbett (New York: The Modern Library, 1984) 1357a.

4. This notion of the public comes from John Dewey, *The Public and Its Problems* (Athens: Ohio University Press, 1927).

5. Michael Warner, "Publics and Counterpublics," *Public Culture* 14, no. 1 (2002), 49–90 (86).

6. For an exploration of public opinion, see Carroll J. Glynn, Susan Herbst, Garrett O'Keefe, and Robert Shapiro, *Public Opinion* (Boulder, CO: Westview Press, 1999).

7. Walter Lippmann, *Public Opinion* (New York: Simon & Schuster, 1922), 18.

8. Douglas L. Wilson, *Lincoln's Sword: The Presidency and the Power of Words* (New York: Alfred A. Knopf, 2007), 202.

9. Bryan Stevenson, "We Need to Talk About an Injustice," available at www.ted.com/talks/bryan_stevenson_we_need_to_talk_about_an_injustice/transcript?language=en (accessed 19 August 2016).

10. Michelle Obama, "Commencement Address at Dillard University," available at www.whitehouse.gov/the-press-office/2014/05/10/remarks-first-lady-commencement-address-dillard-university   (accessed 19 August 2016).

11. Yang Jisheng, "Remarks in Acceptance of the Louis Lyons Award," http://nieman.harvard.edu/awards/louis-lyons-award/yang-jisheng-speech-transcript/ (accessed 19 August 2016).

12. For an explanation of Burke's theory of motive, see Andrew King, "Motive," *American Communication Journal* 1, no. 3 (1998).

13. George Campbell, quoted in *The Philosophy of Rhetoric*, in *The Rhetorical Tradition: Readings from Classical Times to the Present*, ed. Patricia Bizzell and Bruce Herzberg (Boston: Bedford Books of St. Martin's Press, 1990), 749–750.

14. For an exploration of the situational characteristic of emotional response, see Phoebe C. Ellsworth, "Some Reasons to Expect Universal Antecedents of Emotion," *The Nature of Emotion: Fundamental Questions*, ed. Paul Ekman and Richard J. Davidson (Oxford, UK: Oxford University Press, 1994), 150–154.

15. Aung San Suu Kyi, "Freedom from Fear," available at www.thirdworldtraveler.com/Burma/FreedomFromFearSpeech.html (accessed 19 August 2016).

16. Lady Gaga, "Don't Ask, Don't Tell Speech," available at www.mtv.com/news/1648304/lady-gagas-dont-ask-dont-tell-speech-the-full-transcript/ (accessed 19 August 2016).

17. For the Sophistical view of appropriateness, see John Poulakos, "Toward a Sophistic Definition of Rhetoric," in *Contemporary Rhetorical Theory: A Reader*, ed. John Louis Lucaites, Celeste Michelle Condit, and Sally Caudill (New York: The Guilford Press, 1999), 38–48.

18. Nadezhda Tolokonnikova, "Statement to the Court," available at www.businessinsider.com/pussy-riot-trial-nadezhda-tolokonnikovas-closing-statement-2012-8 (accessed 19 August 2016).

19. Cicero, quoted in *The Philosophy of Rhetoric*, in *The Rhetorical Tradition: Readings from Classical Times to the Present*, ed. Patricia Bizzell and Bruce Herzberg (Boston: Bedford Books of St. Martin's Press, 1990), 221.

7

Ethos

This chapter discusses how a rhetorical public speaker develops a relationship with an audience. A "relationship" means more than simply letting an audience know a speaker's identity and his or her qualifications. A relationship is something personal that involves an emotional attitude toward another person or group and negotiates their reciprocal identities. This chapter explores the strategies that can be used to develop a relationship between speaker and audience that is most conducive to persuasion. Starting with the classical definition of ethos as a combination of goodwill, practical wisdom, and virtue that make us think a speaker is credible and trustworthy, this chapter moves into more specific concepts that help define ethos, including persona, evoked audience, identification, distinction, and polarization.

Perhaps what most distinguishes public speaking from any other form of persuasion is the fact that its effectiveness relies heavily on the character of the speaker. As an oral performer, a public speaker steps before the members of an audience and effectively asks them a favor—to listen attentively as the speaker rewards their time and energy with a speech that is tailored specifically to their interests. An advertisement or a YouTube clip or an e-mail has no analogous constraint. Because of their reproducibility, these media can be watched or read at any time that is convenient to an audience and can be turned off or ignored just as easily without offending anyone. Yet when members of an audience ignore the speaker entirely or walk out of the room, we think of it as highly rude or antagonistic. That is why the choice to actually attend a public speech is usually a more personal and important decision than simply clicking on a video link. When we decide to be a member of an audience, we do so because we want to listen to the *speaker*, and we have done so because we have put trust in that speaker to reward our time commitment. Any successful public speech must therefore begin with the existence of mutual trust that forms a temporary relationship between speaker and audience. Without a sense of this "bond," a speaker's words fall on deaf ears.

For the purposes of rhetorical public speech, **ethos** represents this sense of public character that is recognized by an audience and influences their reception of the speaker's arguments. Ethos is thus the capacity to influence an audience based on the audience's perceptions of the credibility and character of the speaker in relationship to the audience's own interests and values. Importantly, even though the Greek word for ethos is "character," this does not have the modern connotation of being something private and inside of us that others cannot see. That is why it is perhaps more appropriate to call it *public* character. Ethos in the rhetorical sense is not something absolute and stable that one carries around wherever one goes; it is determined by the relationship one has with an audience. The president of a country may possess great ethos with respect to his or her own constituency and yet be despised by a foreign population. This is because any act can be interpreted differently by different groups. A presidential declaration of war may be seen as a courageous defense of freedom by one side and a brutal act of imperialism by the other. To understand the possible effects of one's rhetoric, then, a person must understand how an audience perceives his or her character.[1] For the Greeks, people with ethos were those people who earned respect, admiration, and allegiance rather than those who simply possessed a good "soul" that went unseen by others.[2]

The concept of ethos has distinctly rhetorical implications because it deals with aspects of credibility and authority that influence our choice of whom to trust when faced with important decisions.[3] In other words, because we often do not have the time or resources to be able to make crucial judgments on our own, we look to those who possess strength of character, or ethos, to help guide our actions. For this reason, Aristotle believed that among the three forms of rhetorical proof (ethos, pathos, and logos), ethos was often the most powerful. He writes:

> This kind of persuasion, like the others, should be achieved by what the speaker says, not by what people think of this character before he begins to speak. It is not true, as some writers assume in their treatises on rhetoric, that the personal goodness revealed by the speaker contributes nothing to his power of persuasion; on the contrary, his character may almost be called the most effective means of persuasion he possesses.[4]

The reason that ethos is the most authoritative form of persuasion is simply because we tend to accept the opinions of those people who we feel are more like us and who have our best interests at heart. Particularly when hundreds of different messages surround us every day, demanding our attention for this thing or that, ethos provides us an efficient and often (if not always) reliable way of selecting those few that we think are tailored specifically to our lives and our concerns. This is why public speaking, as an oral performance, still remains a powerful medium of persuasion in a digital age. It is the only medium that establishes a meaningful bond between speaker and audience and distills from the cacophony of popular and political culture a single message that creates a sense of shared experience between both speaker and audience and between audience members themselves.

Because it is so central to the act of public speaking, establishing ethos is a complex process that involves more than simply offering an audience a list of accomplishments and admirable characteristics. Developing ethos in a public speech is not the same as presenting a written resume for a job application. The goal of developing ethos is to establish a relationship, not to document facts. Aristotle explains the difficulty of establishing ethos and its three components:

> There are three reasons why speakers themselves are persuasive; for there are three things we trust other than logical demonstration. These are practical wisdom (*phronesis*), and virtue (*arête*), and goodwill (*eunoia*): for speakers make mistakes in what they say through failure to exhibit either, all, or one of these; for either through lack of practical sense they do not form opinions rightly; or through forming opinions they do not say what they think because of the bad character; or they are prudent and fair-minded but lack goodwill, so that it is possible for people not to give the best advice although they know what it is. These are the only possibilities.[5]

Understanding the subtleties of Aristotle's argument requires a clear distinction between these three components of ethos. By **practical wisdom**, he means a proven ability to size up problematic situations and make judgments that show prudence and forethought. It is a capacity to make the right decisions given many alternatives. For instance, at a job interview you might prove practical wisdom by talking about the many "tough choices" you had to make in times of high stress that proved to be the right move. By **virtue**, he means an established habit of doing good, of performing particular activities that are held in high regard and embody the best cultural values. Virtue in the Greek did not refer to some inner goodness, however, invisible to others. It meant "excellence," like we would refer to the virtues of an athlete, a musician, a parent, a leader, or a solider. Thus, in an interview, one might refer to one's habits of performance, the fact that one works hard, shows up on time, and tells the truth. Last, by **goodwill**, he means the presence of conscious and thoughtful consideration of the audience's well-being, as we would expect from a good friend. Goodwill does not guarantee good advice or even good judgment. But it does ensure that a person has our best interests at heart. We might prove goodwill in an interview by how much volunteer work we do, our loyalty to our former employers, or our love of our profession.

In summary, we prove practical wisdom by boasting of our track record of past decisions, we prove virtue by showing how we have committed ourselves to certain noble habits of action, and we prove goodwill by addressing the concerns and interests of our audience and by revealing our willingness to sacrifice our own self-interest in service of their prosperity. As Aristotle remarks, however, it is difficult to show all three in a speech. For instance, a criminal may have demonstrated practical wisdom in his ability to rob banks but lack virtue and goodwill. A reclusive monk might be well esteemed in virtue but have little practical wisdom for everyday situations

DISCUSSION

As indicated by many of the speeches included in this textbook, many times celebrities whose ethos comes from their acting ability try to also establish ethos in the political sphere. Which celebrity activist do you think has successfully established goodwill, practical wisdom, and virtue with respect to some political issue? And who do you think has done the opposite?

and perhaps might not care. And an old high school friend might have all the goodwill in the world toward you, but lack good sense and most components of virtue. In each case, we might have interesting conversations with each of these individuals, but rhetorically we would not necessarily look to them for counsel in times of crisis or uncertainty. It is during these times that ethos becomes a powerful persuasive tool because it focuses an audience's attention on the message that comes from one respected individual. Developing this rhetorical ethos will be the subject of the rest of this chapter.

▶ PERSONA

Most people step into any familiar social situation with an **inherited ethos,** which is the actual reputation that rhetors "carry with them" because of an audience's acquaintance with past behavior. When an inherited ethos is strong, such as the ethos of a mother for her child or that which close friends have with each other, the rhetor rarely has to spend any time establishing his or her reputation or credibility. It certainly would be strange for a mother to say to her child, "Because I have worked hard these many years learning how to cook healthy meals (good sense), because I care deeply for your future (goodwill), and because I am a just and honorable soul (virtue), please listen to my recommendation to eat your spinach." Having already established her ethos, she simply says, "Eat your spinach." Inherited ethos is this kind of unspoken credibility that needs no mention to function. In Aristotle's language, it is "inartistic," meaning something that one can just "point to," rather than craft through language, as in "artistic" proofs.

Ethos becomes a uniquely rhetorical concern of *art* only when rhetors, in some form, create or modify the perception of an audience about them. **Persona** is this rhetorical creation; it represents the constructed ethos that a rhetor creates within the confines of a particular rhetorical context. Persona, in other words, is more a creation of language rather than an inheritance of history. Like the costume that transforms an actor into a new personality on stage, rhetoric can create a "public face" that best suits the immediate needs of a rhetor. Unlike inherited ethos, which is the product of cumulative interactions or exposure over time with an audience, one's persona is always tied to a specific discourse and is completely contained within that discourse. For example, a convict before a parole board enters the hearing with an inherited ethos as a liar and a thief, and he attempts to counter that reputation by describing himself as a "changed man" who has seen the error of his ways. The decision of the board rests on whether the convict's persona of a "changed man" is more convincing than the inherited ethos of a liar and a thief.

Deciding when to construct a persona and when to rely on the strength of one's inherited ethos depends upon the presence and quality of one's reputation within an audience. On the one hand, when a speaker is unknown to an audience, creating a persona is necessary in order to present a favorable "first impression."[6] We are all familiar with our first job interviews when we had to define ourselves as an ideal employee. On the other hand, when a speaker enters a situation as a respected leader, there is no need for such self-promotion; indeed, it would be seen as being in bad taste. Rarely do we enjoy listening to famous and powerful people talking about their fame and power. But most speaking situations usually fall somewhere in between these two extremes. In these cases, one must construct a persona that somehow addresses, modifies, and transcends the limits of one's inherited ethos.[7]

Because the construction of personae deals not just with possession of knowledge or skills, but with notions of character, it relies heavily on personal stories and the form of delivery. **Personal stories** are narrations of one's life experience that provide insight into the speaker's practical wisdom, virtue, or goodwill. Phrases like "The time I was behind enemy lines . . ." or "When I saved my sister's life . . ." or "Growing up in a tough neighborhood . . ." signify to an audience that a person is relating a story that offers a window into his or her deeper self. The **form of delivery** reveals character by using phrases, words, accents, or gestures commonly associated with certain character types. Hence, a president often vacillates between acting "presidential" by speaking in firm, calm, and authoritative terms in formal settings and behaving as an "ordinary American" by doing volunteer work with rolled-up sleeves and telling jokes around a barbeque. Form of delivery is important because we trust those who speak like us, not just because it is familiar, but because it shows a mastery of the type of language that can only be acquired through life experience. It is thus an expression of goodwill.

The personae available for a rhetor are literally infinite. However, there are general types of personae that are always familiar and that conform to our social conventions. Take, for instance, just a few popular personae: the country lawyer, the wise sage, the teenage rebel, the religious prophet, the CEO, the father/mother figure, the loyal friend, the iconoclast, the president, the confidant, the drill sergeant, or the door-to-door salesperson. Any person attempting to create his or her own persona, of course, will always individualize his or her character such that no two personae will ever be alike. But these models provide general guides for action.

In their review of the research on the roles typically played by rhetors in rhetorical situations, Roderick Hart and Susanne Daughton identify four recurring personae: the apologist, the agent, the partisan, and the hero.[8] These roles represent fitting responses to situations that also take into account the personality and intentions of the speaker.

1.   The role of **apologist** is employed when speakers wish to rebuff attack, including both attacks on one's personal character and more often on one's position. The essential characteristic of the apologist is *righteous indignation*. The apologist does not actually "apologize." Like Socrates in front of the jury, the apologist instead corrects the mistaken impression of the audience and seeks to clarify the essential rightness of his or her position. The most powerful

way to do this is by employing one of three strategies: *bolstering*, which supports one's case by "correcting" the erroneous facts and narratives held by the audience ("My accusers have been deceived by liars and are in turn distorting the truth about my position"); *differentiation*, which clarifies misunderstanding by more clearly separating, or differentiating, two issues that have been carelessly conflated ("My critics do not understand the difference between making policy statements and telling jokes"); and *transcendence*, which resolves tensions by invoking a higher principle that clarifies apparent contradictions ("I am accused of inciting violence, and yet the only thing I want is peace. But sometimes peace must be achieved through war"). Successful apologists appear noble because they're willing to suffer for their cause while seeking to clarify the truth.

2. The **agent** speaks on behalf of some institution as a spokesperson of legitimate authority, thereby standing as a "representative" of a recognized institution (such as church body, a government, or a corporation) or social group (such as the leaders of social movements). The essential characteristic of the agent is *enthusiastic loyalty*. Typical people who fit the role of agent in society are public relations specialists, priests, presidents, CEOs, chancellors, community leaders, social movement activists, and ambassadors of all kinds. What makes a successful agent is the fact that he or she charismatically can "stand in" for a larger institution, thereby putting a personal face on a sometimes abstract entity. It is difficult to have affection for the Catholic Church or the United States or Microsoft simply as institutions, but we can generate great enthusiasm at the prospect of meeting the Pope or the president or Bill Gates. At the same time, our enthusiasm at meeting these individuals is only because they "stand for" a form of organized authority that is greater than them as individuals. In other words, a successful agent conveys personal charisma while at the same time being an effective representative of a larger and more powerful group that asks our allegiance.

3. The **partisan** is one who represents not a group or institution but an idea or ideal. This individual tends to thrive in heated debates during times of turmoil and upheaval, when people are looking for new directions based on new ideas. The essential characteristic of the partisan is *critical idealism*. Partisans are idealists because they are advocating a vision of society or politics or religion that is not yet real but that might be possible with faith and effort, and they are critical because in order to make this possibility a reality, they must remove many obstacles in the path, obstacles that are usually tied to tradition, law, or institutional inertia. Partisans are most influential, therefore, on the margins of politics, often as social movement leaders or public intellectuals or iconoclastic artists, musicians, and poets. The biggest difference, therefore, between the partisan and the agent is that the partisan can hypothetically stand alone, whereas the agent is always a representative of an established institution; ironically, then, when partisans actually succeed in promoting their ideas, they become agents.

4. Finally, the **hero** is defined as an individual who is willing to actively confront power in the name of helping others, even if it means that great suffering might come upon him or her. The essential characteristic of the hero is therefore *romantic courage*. Heroes are "romantic" because, unlike the partisan, they do not have a coherent political vision they are promoting, but instead boldly stride into the unknown against all obstacles with the optimistic faith that things will

work out for them in the end. And unlike agents, they do not have to speak "on behalf" of the group they defend. They do so simply because they need defending. And they are courageous because they do not simply "talk the talk" but also "walk the walk." Without a commitment to action, particularly the type of action that directly and physically confronts a more powerful foe, the hero is merely a big talker. It is for this reason that heroes are often spontaneously found or discovered in moments of crisis, because the hero reacts spontaneously to defend the weak and challenge the strong in the name of an abstract value that is shared by the community the hero fights for. Finally, what makes heroes capable of making such self-sacrifices is their confidence that even if they die in the struggle, their legacy will live on as martyrs.

It is important to also keep in mind that these roles are not mutually exclusive. Some of the greatest orations combined many or even all of these roles, with the speaker taking on new personae during different phases of the speech. For instance, an American president might assume the role of the apologist in defense of the wisdom of some military policy ("Those who question the wisdom of toppling this dictator do not properly understand the nature of evil"), then might take on the role of agent ("As the commander-in-chief of this nation, I will not allow its foreign policy to be determined by petty tyrants"), only to then transition to being a partisan ("Furthermore, this campaign is not simply about our national self-interest. I advocate this policy not simply because I am president, but because I believe that the true task of humanity is to spread freedom and democracy around the globe"), and then end on a heroic note ("Finally, I can no longer stand to see children suffer and mothers weep; when evil shows its face, it must be confronted at all costs if we are to live with ourselves"). A role is not something that locks us permanently into any type of performance; it is a type of script we perform to accomplish a specific rhetorical task.

Russell Means: *"Hau Mitakuyepi, Miye Malakota"*

Actor and activist Russell Means, born an Oglala/Lakota Sioux Indian, knew what it meant to adopt a persona. As an actor, he appeared in the *Last of the Mohicans* and *Natural Born Killers*. But as an activist, he was the first national director of the American Indian Movement (AIM) and played a prominent role during the 1973 standoff with the U.S. government at Wounded Knee. Means was comfortable both in front of a crowd and in front of a camera and used his charismatic persona to advance American Indian (he preferred this to "Native American") causes throughout his life. In 1989 he testified before the Senate Special Committee on Investigations in order to criticize government complicity in the corrupt tribal leadership imposed by the federal government. In the opening to his testimony, he clearly established his persona by speaking in the language of his tribe:

> Hau mitakuyepi, miye malakota. Maje tahan ki ne zi tiyospaye ki le hesa woke lila wakan. Mitakuye ate tasunka witko tiyospaye. Mitakuye ina wanbli zuya tiyospaye.

> This is the traditional greeting of my people that I am bound to give; albeit, it's a short version. What I said in my own language translated into English thusly:

Hello my relatives, I am an *Oglala Lakota* and I come from a very sacred holy land, the Black Hills where Yellow Thunder Village is. My mother is from the War Eagle clan and my father's family is from the Crazy Horse clan.

This greeting is, to this day, the way all Indians throughout the nation still greet one another, those that still know their culture. This is the only way we present ourselves to one another that is acceptable. We tell you who we are, where we are from, who we are from, our clans, and we do this without ever saying our name. Anything less would be an insult to you and to my people.

Senators, my morning prayers to the great mystery always include you and your colleagues in Congress, as well as leaders in all governments. It is an honor to come before you as a spokesman for my people, the American Indians of the United States of America. In these United States of America, this great country of ours, we American Indians, we can be anything we want to be except American Indians; and that is created by the laws of this nation and condoned by its subsidiaries, the so-called Tribal Government, and designed for the Indian to fail, to be expendable, to be eliminated.[9]

> **DISCUSSION**
>
> Means clearly rejects the "apologist" role in his speech, but what other roles does he adopt here in his speech? Which do you think is his primary role in the context of his congressional testimony? Also, how does he establish his individual persona using a distinct form of delivery that separates him from any other individual that appeared before Congress? How does this persona leverage influence over his audience?

▶ EVOKED AUDIENCE

If the persona is the image that the rhetor constructs of him- or herself as a speaker, the **evoked audience** is the attractive image that the rhetor constructs of and for the audience. If the speaker's constructed self-image can be considered as the "first" persona (in which the speaker tells the audience who "I" am), then the evoked audience can be considered as the "second" persona (in which the speaker tells the audience who "you" are). The concept of the second persona was advanced by Edwin Black. For him, an astute rhetorical critic can thus see "in the auditor implied by a discourse a model of what the rhetor would have his real auditor become."[10] The function of the evoked audience, or this "second persona," is to create an attractive image of unity that makes members of an audience desire to be a part of a common group rather than an aggregate of separate individuals.

In its most general form, we find politicians using evoked audiences whenever they speak of the *American people* as a collective body of people who love liberty, freedom, and democracy. By creating a category of identity that can unify a group of separate individuals, an evoked audience creates the possibility of cooperative action because it contributes to the creation of a sense of unity that may not have existed before the speech. For example, we often take for granted that everyone who is born within the geographic boundaries of the United States is an "American," but prior to the revolution, people identified themselves more with their local city or region. For revolutionaries to start using the term *American* thus helped make possible a national identity that stood apart from the British Empire.[11] So a revolutionary speaker trying to "evoke" an audience at this time might use an argument like "You lovers of liberty! You fighters for Freedom! You are not members of states and cities. You are Americans!" This would invite the audience to embrace a common identity they did not previously accept.

Like the concept of persona, the evoked audience is a partly fictional identity that usually overstates the unified character of the people listening to a speech (who in reality are far more diverse). Like persona, the evoked audience often is what a rhetor *wants* an audience to be rather than what it literally *is*. Yet this ideal often brings a new reality into existence. For instance, a collection of teenagers may all be talented at a certain sport, but they do not think of themselves as a "team" until the coach starts telling them to act like one ("Go Tigers!"). The coach's rhetoric creates a sense of commonality by evoking the team spirit within the individual players that may not have been fully present before. The most typical sign that such a team spirit is being attempted by a speaker is the repetitive use of "we" or "you," such that an audience feels it is being grouped together under a single category. One can imagine a parent telling his or her children, "If we are a family, then we will eat together at the dinner table." The implicit choice now placed upon the audience is whether or not to accept that group membership.

Therefore, although there is a fictional quality about an evoked audience, this does not mean that it is an illusion. Clearly, a speaker who speaks to an audience of schoolchildren as if they were all members of Congress is not literally accurate. However, motivational teachers *can* speak to them as "future leaders of America" and anticipate an energetic response. In other words, the evoked audience should always select and amplify shared qualities that are already present (or at least potentially present) within an audience. The average audience of college students, for instance, can be referred to as "university students," or "citizens," or "eager young people," or "future leaders," or "party-goers." Each of these designations may be partly true, but each of them only speaks to one portion of that group's identity. Consequently, deciding what identity to evoke in an audience has different consequences for rhetorical persuasion.

Despite what has been said, however, one should not think that the evoked audience is something that the speaker always *does* to the audience. Many times, an audience goes to a speech, as with a "rally," precisely to feel a part of a common identity. In this case, the evoked audience is merely the vehicle through which this desire is actualized. In other words, the audience must be *active*, not *passive*, in generating its sense of common identity. It is this constitution of a common emotional bond between members of an audience that makes public speaking, as an oral performance, so powerful.

David McCullough Jr.: "None of You Are Special"

Before he delivered a commencement address to the 2012 graduating class at Wellesley High School, David McCullough Jr. was nothing "special" himself. Although distinguished as the son of a Pulitzer Prize-winning writer, McCullough was just one of thousands of high school English teachers. However, once his speech went viral online and received over two million views, he suddenly found himself a celebrity. Nonetheless, his message remained the same. What he meant to accomplish in his speech was not to diminish the uniqueness of his students, but to challenge their sense of each being somehow "exceptional" that made them something radically different than every other graduating senior across the country. In short, he wanted to challenge their assumed identifications as "special" kids and to evoke a new self-understanding that made them work hard and appreciate the small things in life without the need for constant validation through meaningless awards, prizes, and titles:

> Contrary to what your U-9 soccer trophy suggests, your glowing seventh grade report card, despite every assurance of a certain corpulent purple dinosaur, that nice Mister Rogers and your batty aunt Sylvia, no matter how often your maternal caped crusader has swooped in to save you . . . you're nothing special.

> Yes, you've been pampered, cosseted, doted upon, helmeted, bubble-wrapped. Yes, capable adults with other things to do have held you, kissed you, fed you, wiped your mouth, wiped your bottom, trained you, taught you, tutored you, coached you, listened to you, counseled you, encouraged you, consoled you and encouraged you again. You've been nudged, cajoled, wheedled and implored. You've been feted and fawned over and called sweetie pie. Yes, you have. And, certainly, we've been to your games, your plays, your recitals, your science fairs. Absolutely, smiles ignite when you walk into a room, and hundreds gasp with delight at your every tweet. . . . But do not get the idea that you're anything special. Because you're not.[12]

DISCUSSION

Of course, the speech does not end there. After challenging his audience to cast off the notion that they are each "special" (that is, different and unique and disconnected from others), he tries to create a new unified identify based on commonality. He starts rebuilding an identity in which everyday hard work, passion, and enjoyment take the place of striving for social validation or financial reward. However, it is in this early part of the speech where he accomplishes the most important task of evoking in his audience a sense in which they are just one of millions of young people throughout the world going through a similar ceremony with similar hopes and dreams. Given the reaction to the speech, how do you think its effect would have been different if he had avoided this kind of confrontational strategy and instead focused only on the positive rather than the negative?

▶ IDENTIFICATION

When we "identify" with someone, we see ourselves as sharing some quality or experience with another person or group. Usually this feeling comes after the revelation of a life experience that we see as similar to our own. The process of making friends with people often begins with this step of identification in which two strangers find themselves sharing some common interest, habit, belief, or feeling. In this sense, the process of identification is how two or more people come to form a bond that generates commonality out of what might seem, at first, to be different perspectives. What we "identify," then, is some quality in another person that he or she shares with us. Identification is not merely labeling something; it is identifying the qualities in others that we find in ourselves as well.

In rhetoric, **identification** is the strategy of creating a common bond with an audience by drawing parallels between the characteristics of speaker, audience, and the subject matter of the speech. For Kenneth Burke, *identification* is a broad term that ranges from the simple schoolyard attempt to make friends by asserting a common quality or interest (e.g., "We are all baseball lovers") to religious or nationalistic attempts to create a unified group with common goals and characteristics.[13] What each of these examples has in common is a sense that two or more distinct and unique individuals share in some "essence" or "quality" that transcends their individuality (love of farming, class identity, and divine origin). This sense of commonality thus leads to people uniting in a common purpose. For instance, when Sojourner Truth argues that she also possesses "masculine" qualities, she creates a commonality between men and women that had not previously been present. In short, identification represents the persuasive attempt on the part of the rhetorical agent to say "I am one of you" in order to create a sense of "we." The justification for such a strategy is that we tend to prefer listening to people who feel and think like we do—particularly as it relates to how we think and feel about the subject matter we are talking about.[14]

Identification is perhaps the most important tool in building ethos in a speech. It is through methods of identification that the speaker and audience feel connected throughout the speech. What is important to keep in mind is that this strategy is not simply something to use in the introduction, in which we might formally introduce ourselves to an audience. For instance, "It is good to be here talking with you young voters. I remember when I was in high school before I ran for Congress," and so on. Identification is more powerful when it is more subtly sprinkled throughout the speech any time there is an opportunity to indicate a commonality not only between *speaker* and audience but also between *subject* and audience. For instance, if you are making a speech criticizing the horrible conditions of sweatshop labor to an audience that has never experienced any such condition and has no familiarity with the countries in which such labor occurs, you have to find a way to make them care about the subject and feel some sort of common interest in preventing exploitation. To do so, one can point to the clothes that people are wearing that might have come from such factories; one can portray the workers as if they are not strangers but individuals very much like people brothers or sisters; one can draw from more familiar experiences the audience have with labor to try to make them feel what it is like to work in one of these factories. By doing so, this creates a margin of overlap between subject and audience, which in turn then create a sense of identification with you, the speaker, insofar as all of you now share a common interest in regulating sweatshop labor. In other words, you create identification not simply by saying "you and I are alike" but rather by saying "you and I care about the same subject because it all touches us in some way." This is a far more subtle but lasting strategy to create identification.

Lana Wachowski: "I'm Just Trying to Fit In"

Almost everyone has memories—some happy, some painful—of the struggle to "fit in" to some group while growing up. These experiences and memories are all the more powerful for those whose identifications don't line up with culturally accepted categories. As an adult, Lana Wachowski is a successful screenwriter, producer, and director, most famous for bringing the *Matrix* trilogy to life with her sister Lilly. But before 2012, the Wachowski Sisters were known as the Wachowski Brothers, Larry and Andy. Both announced during this time that they had taken on identities as transgender women, the first Hollywood directors to have ever done so. As a result of speaking out about her experience as a transgender woman, Lana was awarded the Human Rights Campaign's Visibility Award, at which she talked about her experience growing up. This excerpt captures the essential character of the nature of "identification," being that experience of feeling as if one shares some essential quality or character with another individual or group:

I remember the third grade. I remember recently moving and transferring from a public school to a Catholic school. In public school I played mostly with girls. I have long hair and everyone wears jeans and t-shirts. In Catholic school, the girls wore skirts, the boys wear pants. I am told I have to cut my hair. I want to play foursquare with the girls but now I'm one of them, I'm one of the boys. Early on I am told to get in line after a morning bell, girls in one line, boys in another. I walk past the girls feeling this strange, powerful gravity of association. Yet some part of me knows I have to keep walking. As soon as I look towards the other line, though,

DISCUSSION

Wachowski's memory exemplifies how our experiences of identification are more than simply verbal affairs. When we identify with something (or don't), we often feel it as a very intimate and deeply felt experience. When you read her account, where do you find yourself identifying with any individual in her story, including the other kids or teachers? Now consider more broadly your own experience growing up. How does crisis of identification as a young person manifest in practical action and judgments? What are some of the things you did to identify yourself with some social group that you wished, back then, to be a part of that you now look back on with some sense of embarrassment or humor?

I feel a feeling of differentiation that confuses me. I don't belong there, either. I stop between them. The nun I realize is staring at me, she's shouting at me. I don't know what to do. She grabs me, she's yelling at me. I'm not trying to disobey, I'm just trying to fit in.[15]

▶ DISTINCTION

Identification is a mainstay of rhetorical persuasion, but it is not always sufficient. Especially in times of uncertainty in which we seek good advice rather than loyal friendship, we often look to those people who are very *unlike* us because they possess uncharacteristic excellence in character or special expertise in a very specific subject. In other words, we often want speakers not to "fit in" but to "stand out." In this case, we look not for identification but for **distinction**, which is the attempt to establish credibility by the possession of special knowledge and/or unique experience that are superior to those of the audience. **Special knowledge** refers to the kind of knowledge one receives by learning technical discourses and procedures, such as the knowledge one receives from attending a university. Whether experts are scientists, theologians, ethicists, economists, or movie critics, they all base their arguments on knowledge not accessible to the general public. **Unique experience** refers to the kind of expertise one acquires by having "been there" or "gone through that." For example, it is a common dramatic technique used in all war movies that the highly educated new officer always defers to the practical experience of the veteran soldier once combat begins. The officer might be more capable to discuss broader military strategy (thus having special knowledge), but the enlisted soldier usually knows better what to do in the heat of battle (thus possessing unique experience). The ideal, of course, is a fusion of both qualities within a single person.

In cases of *distinction*, the persona of the rhetor stands apart from the evoked audience; in cases of *identification*, it is aligned with it. Both represent forms of credibility, but distinction is credibility from *difference* (even if it is just difference in degree), whereas identification is credibility from *likeness*. Frequently, some combination of the two is most useful.[16] To continue the military metaphor, a four-star general cites the possession of superior knowledge and broader experience in order to justify leading a campaign, but he or she usually makes an effort to also establish how he or she is still a common soldier "at heart" in order to command loyalty. Presidential candidates, too, often spend a great deal of time touting their expertise while simultaneously spending most of their days eating hot dogs, going bowling, or kissing babies. They want to appear as ordinary citizens and extraordinary leaders simultaneously.

Ken Burns: "I Am in the Business of Memorializing"

Filmmaker Ken Burns is most well known for his popular documentaries of America—including *The Civil War*, *Baseball*, *Mark Twain*, and *Jazz*. Although his documentaries have always been made to appeal to a wide audience, avoiding overt political messages beyond a celebration of democratic values, in his commencement address to Stanford University he acknowledges that history always has a political significance. Particularly given the charged political atmosphere of the 2016 election, Burns used his address to discuss the importance of learning history in order to perceive and evaluate controversial and often dangerous political speech. In doing so, he also sought to define what makes the historian distinct from other speakers when it comes to his or her credibility and authority:

> I am in the business of memorializing—of history. It is not always a popular subject on college campuses today, particularly when, at times, it may seem to some an anachronistic and irrelevant pursuit, particularly with the ferocious urgency *this* moment seems to exert on us. It is my job, however, to remind people—with story, memory, anecdote and feeling—of the power our past also exerts, to help us better understand what's going on now. It is my job to try to discern patterns and themes from history to enable us to interpret our dizzying, and sometimes dismaying, present. For nearly 40 years now, I have diligently practiced and rigorously maintained a conscious neutrality in my work, avoiding the advocacy of many of my colleagues, trying to speak to *all* of my fellow citizens.[17]

> ### DISCUSSION
>
> The way Burns speaks about the historian is reminiscent of the old adage, "Those who do not know history are doomed to repeat it." Do you think this adage is true? What lies behind the idea that learning history can inform present judgments? When have you turned to "history"—even if it is personal or family history—to help make a decision? To whom did you turn when you did so? What experiences or knowledge or skills did this person possess that made them worthy of distinction?

▶ POLARIZATION

An understanding of the complex ethics behind strategies of ethos would not be complete without a consideration of polarization (or "division"). Just as any action has a reaction, any attempt to establish unity inevitably also creates a division between "in" groups and "out" groups that results in inevitable polarization. For something to be "polarized" is to have two objects that repel each other from a distance. For instance, the North Pole and the South Pole represent two sides of the earth, but they are not antagonistic toward one another. They are simply far apart. Two magnets of the same polarity, however, will literally repulse each other when brought together. Similarly, two friends separated by thousands of miles are not polarized, but simply distant; two enemies in the same room, however, will create a palpable tension. Polarization thus represents a division based on antagonism. For example, we are often forced to choose between aligning ourselves with one group or another with little room for compromise. Either we are "with them or against them." And those who seek compromise in this situation are thus usually attacked from both sides for being wishy-washy. In a polarized environment, the decision not to choose is also a choice that puts us at risk of being abandoned, rejected, or ignored.

By its nature as an art that thrives in conflict and uncertainty, rhetorical discourse often magnifies these choices and uses the contrast to force a decision. In rhetoric, **polarization** is the strategy of dividing an audience into a positive "us" and a negative "them" in order to create unity through difference. The "them" in this case is usually a **criticized audience** that represents a group antagonistic to the rhetor's interests, such as another political party, or simply a demonized audience that is used as a convenient foil, such as a group of "traitors" or "evil-doers." The strategy is then to argue that if one does not follow the path preferred by the rhetor (a path that ends in belonging to an evoked audience), then this person will align him- or herself with a group of people who lack ethical or practical judgment. Most children become acquainted with this strategy early on in their lives when they are encouraged to behave during the year so that Santa Claus includes them on his "nice" list rather than his "naughty" list. This same model can be applied effectively in the analysis of contemporary partisan politics.[18] In summary, if the first persona presents the "I" who is speaking and the second persona defines the "you" who is being spoken to, polarization defines a "third" persona representing the undesirable "they" who are not present but who are used to define who the "I" and "you" are not.[19]

Including "polarization" within a public speaking textbook may appear to border on the unethical. After all, are we not usually advised to invite as many people as possible to hear our speech? Is it not completely inappropriate in a tolerant age to pick out a group of people (or a type of person) to criticize or condemn? The work of Kenneth Burke is instructive here. Throughout his writings, Burke lamented the tendency for **scapegoating** in public rhetoric, in which all of a public's "sins" are placed upon a largely defenseless group that is then run out of town. At the same time, however, Burke also recognized that division is a natural state of human nature, and that rhetoric arises whenever individuals and groups are in conflict with one another. Moreover, rhetorical action cannot avoid the effects of polarization. For instance, even the statement "we should all love one another" can be used to divide those who love from those who hate. Burke's point is that we must be aware of the implicit acts of polarization that occur in all our identifications, make them explicit, and do our best to make our criticisms of others intelligent, precise, just, and sympathetic.

One common strategy to make polarization less ethically problematic is to base it more on hypothetical values or attitudes than on actual characteristics of specific social groups. Certainly, parents who ask their children whether they want to be a "doctor" or a "couch potato" are using polarization primarily to inspire them to do their best. In this case, the negative audience is not real but hypothetical—it represents a "type" of behavior we find distasteful. This still involves ethical responsibility, but it often can be used for purposes of genuine encouragement. The responsibility of speakers is thus to identify all possible divisions and to avoid unnecessary or unintentional castigation of other groups, even in the name of the most noble and respectable goal or virtue. As history has shown, many of the greatest atrocities were committed by those who truly believed they were fighting in the name of truth and freedom and goodness. As important as it is to be motivated by noble values and inspiring identifications, it is also important to analyze who is being excluded or condemned.

Indira Gandhi: "Even People Who Do Science Are Quite Unscientific in Their Thinking"

Ancient cultures such as India always struggle to negotiate between preserving tradition and adapting to modern technology and techniques. In her address at the golden jubilee celebrations of the Indraprastha College for Women in Delhi, India, in 1974, then Prime Minister Indira Priyadarshini Gandhi—to date the only female Prime Minister of India—addressed this challenge by using polarization to distinguish scientific from unscientific ways of thinking. For her, one could work professionally as a "scientist" but still act and think unscientifically—that is, fail to critique and evaluate all beliefs and traditions and resources without bias or blindness. Consequently, she praised valued traditions while nonetheless making a contrast between genuinely scientific and unscientific forms of education and of living:

> Sometimes, I am very sad that even people who do science are quite unscientific in their thinking and in their other actions—not what they are doing in the laboratories but how they live at home or their attitudes towards other people. Now, for India to become what we want it to become with a modern, rational society and firmly based on what is good in our ancient tradition and in our soil, for this we have to have a thinking public, thinking young women who are not content to accept what comes from any part of the world but are willing to listen to it, to analyse it and to decide whether it is to be accepted or whether it is to be thrown out and this is the sort of education which we want, which enables our young people to adjust to this changing world and to be able to contribute to it.[20]

DISCUSSION

How do you understand the distinction between "scientific" and "unscientific" that she uses here? In reflecting on this strategy of persuasion, when do you think polarization is ethically warranted? We often do not think that it is ever right to speak in terms of "us" versus "them," and yet nothing is more common in political and moral discourse. How can you tell between an ethical and unethical use of polarization?

▶ SUMMARY

Ethos is something given to a speaker by an audience based on how a speaker displays himself or herself within a particular rhetorical situation. We should therefore not confuse ethos, as a rhetorical concept, with personal concepts such as affection or trust or reputation. Each of these things is certainly relevant to considerations of ethos, but they are not determining conditions. Indeed, sometimes we grant ethos to people we hate, distrust, and think are of low repute. These situations occur, for example, when these individuals testify against their own best interests about something that they have specialized knowledge about, as when an executive convicted of insider trading testifies at a congressional committee about the need to regulate insider trading. As Anthony Pratkanis and Elliot Aronson observe, "a communicator can be an immoral person and still be effective, as long as it seems clear that the communicator is not acting in her or his self-interest by attempting to persuade us."[21] Although this particular strategy is only relevant to a small class of people in extraordinary circumstances, it nonetheless shows that we should consider *ethos* not as a quality of a person's character but as a criterion for judgment in a specific speech situation.

In most of our everyday interactions, the Aristotelian categories of goodwill, practical wisdom, and virtue are usually sufficient for acquiring ethos. Goodwill represents an emotional attitude of the speaker toward the audience such that he or she appears to wish the very best for the person or people to whom the rhetor is speaking. We tend to think people have goodwill toward us when they make sacrifices on our behalf, sometimes in the moment but usually over a longer course of a relationship. Practical wisdom represents an intellectual capacity to make decisions in complicated situations that make those situations turn out for the better far more often than they turn out for the worse. Those with practical wisdom are people with much experience and knowledge to whom we look for specific advice. Whereas our close friends might give us the emotional support of goodwill, oftentimes we look to professionals or even strangers for counsel about complicated judgments. Finally, virtue represents a condition of character that embodies multiple values, such as courage, temperance, generosity, humility, and the like. We look to people with character because they seem to be "well rounded" and thoughtful, thus assuring that their counsel will not be based on narrow criteria but broader considerations. It is no accident that we often associate virtue with age, as it takes a great deal of time and diverse life experience to accumulate multiple virtues in a coherent and stable character.

Developing a message that also supports one's ethos requires further conceptual strategies, however. Persona provides a way of developing a specific presentation style that can balance the needs of a specific situation with the imperative to maintain consistency in character. *Persona* should not be considered a way of simply "acting," and thereby putting on a mask, for narrow purposes of persuasion; rather, it should be considered a method of amplifying or diminishing certain characteristics in one's own personality in order to best respond to a situation and an audience. Similarly, the evoked audience is not a purely fictional creation that is offered to an audience as in a fantasy role-play exercise. An *evoked audience*, like persona, is rather a selective amplification of certain qualities that are already shared by members of an audience and then given a concrete name and identity that serves as an appropriate response to a rhetorical situation. Turning a group of teenagers interested in basketball into the "Fighting Tigers" does not invent their interest in being a part of an athletic team out of the blue; it simply solidifies this interest and gives it a concrete manifestation. Identification is thus a natural bridge between persona and the evoked audience, as it represents a way of creating a common "we" out of an "I" and "you," even while retaining certain differences. A general may still be a general and a platoon a platoon, but they are all soldiers fighting for their nation and for "freedom."

The categories of distinction and polarization, being categories of difference, are usually only effective once such a common identification has been made. Distinction takes for granted the assumption of identification but seeks to add extra qualities to make the speaker stand out from the group. For instance, once the "Fighting Tigers" have been identified and their emotional bond solidified through various practices and rituals, it comes time to select a team captain. This is the time for speeches of distinction, in which each member of the team justifies why he or she stands apart from others (while still retaining the members' common unity). Distinction is thus a delicate balancing act of sameness and difference.

Last, polarization occurs when a speaker attempts to further solidify the identification of a group by comparing its members with an outsider group that represents the opposite in values and goals. Polarization presents an unsavory "other" (real or fictional) that usually serves to increase competitive motives. Of all the strategies, therefore, polarization has the most potential for ethical abuse, as speakers all too easily descend into vicious caricatures of competing groups. As with all strategies of ethos, one must be careful of exaggerating one's own virtue while condemning the vice of others for narrowly selfish ends. Some degree of polarization is virtually inevitable in any speech, but one must at all times be careful to reduce its possible negative impacts to a minimum. We can have goodwill, after all, even toward those who disagree with us or are unlike us.

▶ CHAPTER 7 EXERCISES

1. **IMPROMPTU:** Find some object currently in your possession. Create an impromptu speech in which you attempt to "sell" this commodity to the class primarily by creating a sense of identification not only between you and the audience but also between the commodity and the audience. In other words, try to create a sense in which possessing this object is a necessary and natural extension of their own identity.

2. **DEBATE:** Consider the ethical question of whether or not it is ever morally justified to explicitly use polarization against an actual (and not merely hypothetical) "out group" for any persuasive purpose. Divide the class into three groups, one who supports the strategy, one who rejects it, and a third who are undecided. Have each pro and con group present their argument, and at the end have the undecided group make a decision and make a yes or no vote, justifying their decision.

3. **GROUP:** As a class, come up with a topic of advocacy that directly concerns your interest as students (for instance, advocating for free tuition). Divide the class into four groups and assign

a different persona to each group—agent, partisan, hero, or apologist. Each group should be supporting the cause of the students, but should advocate for this cause adopting a different "fictional" persona as if the group were an individual (who may or may not be a student). For the apologist group, one must imagine an external audience who are criticizing students for various failings and to which one must respond in order to make the case for advocacy. Start with the apologist group, and then proceed through the agent, the partisan, and the hero.

4. **TAKE HOME:** Look through some of your favorite "memes" that take the form of a popular photo or image to which people add their own funny caption. Find one that makes use of some kind of identification or polarization. Print out the meme and bring it to class and interpret its message according to the categories of this chapter to account for its popularity.

5. **VIDEO:** Practice using a combination of identification and distinction to define yourself. Identify some particular activity that you both like to do and consider yourself somewhat good at—for instance, cooking, playing an instrument, drawing, etc. Create a very short video in which you talk about why you like this activity (identification) and then briefly demonstrate or give proof that you are particularly good at it (distinction). Ultimately, try to encourage your audience that this activity is something that they should do as well, trusting in your expertise.

▶ NOTES

1. For more on speaker credibility, see chapter 5 of Gary C. Woodward and Robert E. Denton, Jr., *Persuasion and Influence in American Life*, 5th ed. (Long Grove, IL: Waveland, 2004).

2. For more on the Greek notion of public life, see chapter 2 of Hannah Arendt, *The Human Condition*, 2nd ed. (Chicago: University of Chicago Press, 1958).

3. For excellent essays exploring the concept of *ethos*, see Michael J. Hyde, ed., *The Ethos of Rhetoric* (Columbia: University of South Carolina Press, 2004).

4. Aristotle, *Rhetoric*. In *The Rhetoric and the Poetics of Aristotle*, trans. W. Rhys Roberts, ed. Edward P. J. Corbett (New York: The Modern Library, 1984), 1356a.

5. Aristotle, *Rhetoric*, 1358a.

6. An interesting account of an actual scholarly persona is found in James Darsey, "Edwin Black and the First Persona," *Rhetoric & Public Affairs* 10, no. 3 (2007), 501–507.

7. The relationship between rhetor and audience can be described in terms of the ratio between the level of credibility and the level of agreement. These considerations are explained in detail in chapter 7 of Woodward and Denton, *Persuasion and Influence in American Life*.

8. Roderick Hart and Susanne Daughton, *Modern Rhetorical Criticism*, 3rd ed. (Boston: Pearson, 2005), 220–221.

9. Russell Means, "Statement to the Senate Special Committee on Investigations," available at www.americanrhetoric.com/speeches/russellmeanssenatetestimony.htm (accessed 21 March 2017).

10. Edwin Black, "The Second Persona," in *Readings in Rhetorical Criticism*, ed. Carl R. Burgchardt (State College, PA: Strata Publishing Co., 1995), 90.

11. For more on the "public" as an evoked audience, see Michael McGee, "In Search of the People," *Quarterly Journal of Speech* 71 (1975), 235–249.

12. David McCullough Jr, "Address to the 2012 Wellesley High School Class," available at http://time.com/4116019/david-mccullough-jr-graduation-speech-wellesley-high/ (accessed 19 August 2016).

13. For more on identification, see Kenneth Burke, *A Rhetoric of Motives* (Berkeley: University of California Press, 1969), xiv.

14. For more on identification, see Gary C. Woodward, *The Idea of Identification* (Albany: State University of New York Press, 2003).

15. Lana Wachowski, "Acceptance Speech for the Human Rights Campaign's Visibility Award," available at www.hollywoodreporter.com/news/lana-wachowskis-hrc-visibility-award-382177 (accessed 19 August 2016).

16. The desirability of a mixture of both qualities is exemplified by the notion of "source credibility" as explained by Jack Whitehead in "Factors of Source Credibility," *Quarterly Journal of Speech* 54 (1968), 59–63.

17. Ken Burns, "Commencement Address at Stanford University," available at http://news.stanford.edu/2016/06/12/prepared-text-2016-stanford-commencement-address-ken-burns/ (accessed 20 August 2016).

18. Some examples discussing the rhetoric of polarization include Andrew King and Floyd Douglas Anderson, "Nixon, Agnew, and the 'Silent Majority': A Case Study in the Rhetoric of Polarization," *Western Speech* 35, no. 4 (1971), 243–255; William D. Harpine, "Bryan's 'A Cross of Gold': The Rhetoric of Polarization at the 1896 Democratic Convention," *Quarterly Journal of Speech* 87, no. 3 (2001), 291–304; and David E. Foster, "Bush's Use of the Terrorism and 'Moral Values' Issues in His 2004 Presidential Campaign Rhetoric: An Instance of the Rhetorical Strategy of Polarization," *Ohio Communication Journal* 44 (2006), 33–60.

19. See Philip Wander, "The Third Persona: An Ideological Turn in Rhetorical Theory," *Central States Speech Journal* 35 (1984), 197–216.

20. Indira Gandhi, "What Educated Women Can Do," available at http://gos.sbc.edu/g/gandhi3.html (accessed 20 August 2016).

21. Anthony Pratkanis and Elliot Aronson, *Age of Propaganda: The Everyday Use and Abuse of Persuasion* (New York: Henry Holt, 2001), 134.

8

Logos

This chapter addresses the forms of reasoning that can be used to persuade an audience based on factual evidence. Of all forms of proof, those from reasoning are the most cognitive (as opposed to "affective" or "emotional"). In rhetoric, reasoning is the capacity to interpret and organize elements of a problematic situation in order to prove certain practical judgments to be more prudent than others. The relevant concepts for logical reasoning are the relationships among claims, grounds, and warrants; the list of most common warrants (generalization, sign, causal, principle, and analogy); and the list of common fallacies. The goal of this chapter is to show how to develop rational arguments, based on the best available evidence, that are also clear and persuasive by being related to audience beliefs and attitudes.

When citizens of Classical Greece used the word *logos*, they usually used it to mean words, arguments, or reason. For example, the term *dissoi logoi* (meaning "double arguments") was a common phrase that referred to the Greek belief that there were always two or more arguments opposed on every issue. The Greeks acquired this belief largely because of their reliance on courts of law to decide almost any dispute. Any time two people came into conflict, their instinct was to bring this conflict into court in order to hear both sides and come to a practical judgment. In these sorts of rhetorical contexts, **logos** refers to the use of rational arguments and evidence to persuade an audience of the reasonableness of one's position. It is based on the belief that human beings are rational beings with the potential to make decisions based on logic, principles, and evidence.[1] John Dewey offers the following narrative of how logic, as the conscious study of the structure of logos, originated as a conscious art:

> The conditions under which logical theory originated are indicated by the two words still generally used to designate its subject matter—logic and dialectic. Both of these words have

to do with speech, not of course with speech in the form of mere words but with language as the storehouse of the ideas and beliefs which form the culture of a people. Greek life was peculiarly characterized by the importance attached to discussion. Debate and discussion were marked by freedom from restrictions imposed by priestly power and were emphasized with the growth of democratic political institutions. In the Homeric poems the man skilled in words which were fit for counsel stands side by side with the man skilled in martial deeds. In Athens not merely political but legal issues were settled in the public forum. Political advancement and civic honor depended more upon the power of persuasion than upon military achievement. As general intellectual curiosity developed among the learned men, power to interpret and explain was connected with the ability to set forth a consecutive story. To give an account of something, a logos, was also to account for it. The logos, the ordered account, was the reason and the measure of the things set forth. Here was the background out of which developed a formulated theory of logic as the structure of knowledge and truth.[2]

The study of rhetoric corresponded with the study of logic. It was simply considered a "practical" logic of law or politics, a logic directed toward providing "ordered accounts" of contingent situations in order to suggest rational courses of action to resolve them. In other words, rhetoric no less than logic is grounded in the faith that human beings are rational creatures who seek reasons for their actions. Without the faith that people make better practical judgments when presented with more comprehensive and accurate facts, we would be forced to rely purely on either habit, passion, or luck. However, this faith in human rationality should not be interpreted to be somehow in competition with the other rhetorical appeals of ethos and pathos. Reason plays a vital role in human decision-making, but it is rarely, if ever, sufficient for making good decisions. Often, our emotions are necessary to judge right from wrong, effective from ineffective, and pleasure from pain. Likewise, our ability to discern who is a more reliable advisor during times of crisis can rarely be made by logic alone. In fact, our need to trust other people usually arises precisely when logic reaches its practical limit. The very idea of the rhetorical situation supports this conclusion—for if we had all the facts that we needed to make a decision, we would hardly need to be persuaded of anything. Only when we lack sufficient reason do we usually seek out a path based on a more intuitive form of judgment.

The difference between rhetoric and logic is that whereas logic examines the validity and coherence of argumentative propositions apart from situated context of action, rhetoric is concerned with how arguments affect specific audiences in specific times and places. This distinction comes from Charles Peirce, one of the founders of the study of logic in the United States. He defines logic as "the science of the conditions which enable symbols in general to refer to objects," and rhetoric as "the science of the formal conditions of intelligibility of symbols."[3] The distinction is not as complicated as it sounds. Peirce defines logic in terms of the formal relationship between symbols and objects, such as the difference between how a photograph and a name refer to the same thing. However, he defines rhetoric in terms of the "intelligibility" of symbols, meaning the intelligibility to specific people in specific situations. A young student, for instance, might look at a periodic table of the elements for the first time and have no idea what it refers to, and the job of the chemistry teacher is to make the logic of the periodic table "intelligible" to that particular student by adapting the message to his or her particular experiences, interests, and expectations. By using color coated charts, analogies, images, and examples, the teacher in effect uses "rhetoric" to make what is confusing and opaque into something comprehensible and clear.

What the study of logic brings to rhetoric is, in Peirce's words, the increased capacity to make our ideas clear, both to ourselves and to our audience. Unfortunately, it is a bad habit of virtually all human beings to assume that we make more sense than we actually do, which is only made worse by the accompanying assumption that other people's thoughts are more muddled than our own. Peirce wryly observes that

> few persons care to study logic, because everybody conceives himself to be proficient enough in the art of reasoning already. But I observe that this satisfaction is limited to one's own ratiocination [rationality], and does not extend to that of other men.[4]

Yet the fact is that we are all in the same boat: "We come to the full possession of our power of drawing inferences, the last of all our faculties; for it is not so much a natural gift as a long and difficult art."[5] Although effective public speaking is not the same thing as mastery of logic, understanding the basic process of logical inference and recognizing that logic is not an innate faculty but a long and difficult art makes us more careful in the research, composition, and performance of our speeches. This chapter hopes to provide the rudiments of logical reasoning in order to improve the clarity of our public speeches.

In rhetoric, **logical reasoning** comes into play any time we use inferences and proofs to establish relationships among propositions that warrant specific conclusions. Whenever we debate with ourselves or with others about why one thing or action is better than another, and use evidence and proof to defend or arrive at our conclusion, we engage in the process of logical reasoning. Put more simply, logical reasoning occurs any time we give a "reason why." A bare assertion ("It is sunny today"), request ("Let's get going"), or definition ("The best beach is one with the best waves") does not engage us in logical reasoning. Only when we provide a reason for these utterances do we start the process of making **inferences**, which is the act or process of deriving conclusions from premises known or assumed to be true. For instance, let us say I wake up and say, "It is sunny today, because I see light coming through the window shades," or "Let's get going, because we don't want to get caught in traffic," or "The best beach is the one with the best waves, so let's go to the North Shore." Each of these arguments seems to make sense without further need for elaboration, but in fact we are drawing inferences to make these comprehensible. Consider, for instance, the following possible conditions that show our inferences to be false: that the light is from the neighbor's car, that the cottage is within walking distance of the beach, and that you are talking to someone who can't swim.

One way to explain this process is through the Aristotelian-inspired model developed by Stephen Toulmin.[6] For him, logical arguments consist of the relationship between three things: the claim, the grounds, and the warrant. A **claim** is the primary position or conclusion being advanced by a speaker that represents the "payoff" of the reasoning ("We should drink more red wine"). The **grounds** are the supporting evidence for the claim that represents the "proof" for the conclusion ("Because we want to savor the good life"). The **warrant** is the inferential leap that connects the claim with the ground, usually embodied in a principle, provision, or chain of reasoning ("Wine is a necessary condition for bringing about the good life"). What makes this relationship subtle is the fact that the warrant is often (but not always) left unstated because, more often than not, it is taken for granted. Except in very complex chains of reasoning, we usually assume that audience members will "fill in" warrants for themselves by drawing from their own resources of common sense, experience, and education. For instance, if we say, "You should drink some water, because you are probably thirsty," we leave out the warrant "Water quenches thirst" because it is obvious. But invoke an absurd or false warrant, and it immediately becomes obvious to us. If I said, "You should drink some whiskey, because you are probably thirsty," we would probably laugh because nobody drinks whiskey for quenching thirst. That is what makes it funny.

One way to think about the function of a "warrant" is as a bridge. A warrant simply connects the claim to the ground. A warrant does not make a new argument or provide new evidence. It simply is the connecting link that makes an argument "make sense" and instructs us how we get from one place to another. Think of a warrant, therefore, as one would think of a bridge between two places that would otherwise be kept apart. How do I get from the claim "We should get married" to the grounds "because we love each other"? And how is this path different than the one between the same claim "We should get married" and the different grounds "in order to appear respectable"? In the first case, the warrant is "You should marry the one you love." In the second case, the warrant is "Marriage provides cultural respectability." Both of these are reasonable paths and are logically coherent and socially acceptable (as opposed to the path that connects the claim "We should get married" with the grounds "because we need a good laugh"). Rhetorically, however, certain paths, no matter how logically coherent, nonetheless appeal to certain types of people more than others. A young couple unconcerned with material success and who fall in love while hitchhiking through Europe would find the first path more agreeable, whereas two successful adults with great political ambition might find the second warrant very persuasive. The art of crafting a rhetorical argument, therefore, includes creating attractive bridges between claims and grounds that are constructed for a particular audience to generate movement in thought and action.

Let us go back to Aristotle for a moment to clarify one important distinction. For Aristotle, the difference between logic and rhetoric represents the difference between two forms of reasoning, the **syllogism** and the enthymeme. The syllogism represents a complete form of reasoning with all parts clearly defined and explicit. The most common example of a syllogism is as follows:

All men are mortal (warrant)

Socrates is a man (grounds)

Socrates is mortal (claim)

But in rhetoric, the goal is not simply to make clear and explicit all of the premises of the argument. The goal is to please an audience, to arouse emotions, to create tensions and resolutions, suspense and satisfactions. Consequently, he defined the **enthymeme** as a "rhetorical syllogism." Its essential component was that it left out one or more premises that the speaker could rely upon the audience to "fill in" or "supply" on their own. Consequently, one might say: "Socrates is a man. He can't live forever" (thereby leaving out the warrant), or "Socrates too will die, as all men are mortal" (leaving out the grounds), or "I am afraid that I am a man as well, and all men are mortal" (leaving out the claim). In each case, the basic logic is the same, but what is left out changes the way the audience "participates" in the construction of the argument. One could imagine, for instance, the first argument being made by someone who wishes Socrates ill, while the last might be said by a father to a son.

The next step in understanding how logic functions is to look at it as a kind of algebraic formula. In logic, it is common to use "S" and "P," such as in the formula "All S's are P." An "S" stands for "Subject," which is either an individual or a class of specific objects that can be labeled with a name (Socrates) or a noun (men). A "P" stands for a "Property" of that object, which represents a quality, condition, character, or effect that we associate with a subject, for instance "mortal" or "male." And sometimes there might be more than one subject or property, in which case one can speak of two individuals like "Socrates" and "Athena" as S_1 and S_2 and opposing qualities such as "mortal" and "immortal" as P_1 and P_2. So if I say "Socrates is mortal, but Athena is immortal," that would be "S_1 is P_1 but S_2 is P_2." But if I simply say that "all Greeks are philosophers" that would be "All S's are P." One possible source of confusion is that a "philosopher" appears itself to be a subject, and hence an "S" rather than a "P." But this is simply due to a colloquial way of speaking. In fact, whenever we make such a claim, what we are really saying is that all Greeks have certain properties, that of being philosophical, that make them suitable to be included under a specific category. It is important not to get hung up on this distinction. What is important is that any "P" functions to alter the way we look at, understand, react to, or anticipate the effects of some individual or category of things, objects, or people. For instance, if I say, "That liquid is poison" ("That S is P"), I am saying that it has poisonous characteristics that should make us careful not to drink it or expose ourselves to it in any way. An "S" represents the name we give to something. A "P" modifies the way we understand that thing.

Finally, to understand the process of reasoning we must distinguish the five types of warrants that are used in logical argumentation: *principle, causal, sign, analogy,* and *generalization.* The easiest way to distinguish these types of warrants is by imagining each of them as a type of algebraic formula. A principle warrant defines an entire class of things by associating them with a specific property ("All S's are P." For instance, "All candy is sweet"). A causal warrant explains that the presence of a class of objects/activities/events will bring about a specific effect ("All S's bring about effect P." For instance, "Eating a lot of candy will make you gain weight"). A sign warrant declares that certain sensible properties are indicative of the presence of a certain class of objects ("The experience of P is indicative of the presence or state of S." For instance, "A funny aftertaste means that something is sugar-free candy"). An analogy warrant suggests that a less familiar object or class of objects can be treated the same way as a more familiar object or class of objects ("We can treat S₁ as we treat S₂". For instance, "We can treat chocolate mousse like we treat chocolate pudding"). A generalization warrant licenses us to treat an entire class of objects in the same way that we treat a specific individual case or selection of individual cases (All S's are P because S_1 and S_2 was P. For instance, "All candy from this bag is sweet because these two pieces of candy from the bag were sweet"). All warrants thus follow these general patterns. If a warrant cannot be rephrased in one of these ways, it is probably not a warrant but a claim or a ground. Here are some examples stated as syllogisms (to make them enthymemes, simply remove one of the claims and rearrange the order or presentation):

Principle	Warrant: "All intentional killing is murder."
	Grounds: "Capital punishment is an intentional killing."
	Claim: "Capital punishment is murder."
Causal	Warrant: "Smoking causes cancer."
	Grounds: "You smoke."
	Claim: "You are going to get cancer."
Sign	Warrant: "A high fever is indicative of the flu."
	Grounds: "You have a high fever."
	Claim: "You have the flu."
Analogy	Warrant: "We can treat the Iraq War like the Vietnam War."
	Grounds: "The Vietnam War was a disaster."
	Claim: "The Iraq War will be a disaster."
Generalization	Warrant: "One cat is representative of the behavior of all cats."
	Grounds: "My cat always woke me up at 3 am."
	Claim: "All cats wake you up at 3 am."

In each of these cases, the warrant acts as (a) a "bridge" between the claim and the grounds that explains why the two should appear together, and/or (b) a "guide" that tells an audience that if you have one thing, another thing will naturally follow as a consequence. In short, all forms of reasoning help go beyond what is immediately present before our eyes or our mind in order to make connections that expand our horizons of understanding.

When a speaker wishes to construct an enthymeme, the first step is to understand what the full syllogism looks like. For instance: "Only wars of self-defense are just. This war is not initiated in self-defense. This war is not just." (Principle: Only S's are P. This is not an S. This is not P). The second step is to determine which parts of the syllogism can be left out and which are the most important to emphasize given the audience in the situation. The easiest way to determine this is to figure out (a) which part of the syllogism is already obvious to an audience and would be redundant to make explicit, and (b) which part of the syllogism is the part you wish to stress because you think it will change their opinion. For instance, if a speaker is addressing an audience favorable to pacifism, then one can effectively leave out the warrant. The point of contention might simply be whether or not the war is legitimately one of self-defense or not. Consequently, that is the part of the argument to stress: "Despite the claims of the warmongers in Congress, this is not an enemy that could ever threaten us in any way. Initiating a war in this context is not justified." However, if one is speaking to an audience which does not hold that warrant to be true, then stressing the truth and significance of the warrant is actually the most important persuasive strategy, as the rest would naturally follow. So one might say: "Although it is noble to want to eradicate an enemy we perceive to be evil, the fact is that war is never justified except as an act of self-defense. And I'm afraid that means that this war is not justified." In this case, the speaker would leave out the grounds if it is largely accepted that the enemy could not pose a serious threat to the nation. However, if both the warrant and the grounds were at issue, one must emphasize both of them and leave the claim to be logically deduced: "Although it is noble to want to eradicate an enemy we perceive to be evil, the fact is that war is never justified except as an act of self-defense. And this enemy is halfway across the globe and has no capacity to injure us directly." Once again, the basic syllogistic structure of each remains identical, but the style changes dramatically depending on the nature of the audience and the desired effect of one's argument.

A good public speaker should make argumentation look and feel "easy" to an audience. But this effect only is produced through a great deal of conscious labor beforehand. The art of the well-crafted argument is in identifying the parts of an argument that a particular audience already believes and is ready and willing to draw upon in filling out the logical assertion. As Aristotle emphasized, the most successful arguments are those in which the speaker gives the audience just enough for them to complete the argument on their own. Too much information makes a speech tiring and pedantic; too little information makes a speech obscure and confusing. But if the speaker can craft an argument that invites warrants that the audience is ready and willing to contribute to the completion of the logical proposition, then audience members become active participants in the construction of meaning, which brings about a pleasurable feeling of learning without even realizing they are doing so.

When inventing arguments, then, *first* think about the perspective of your audience and consider what types of beliefs, attitudes, values, and shared experiences they possess. *Second*, think about which of these resources can be phrased as a logical proposition in the form of a warrant. *Third*, select from these warrants the ones you think are most relevant to your case and can be embedded within an argument. *Last*, carefully pair claims with grounds that "call forth" these warrants without having to state them explicitly. For instance, let us take the position of the young couple who decide to get married while hitchhiking through Europe. How do they explain their decision to the husband's practical-minded father? They might assume that he might accept the causal warrant that "Marriage tends to produce maturity." In that case, they carefully put together a claim and a ground that would stimulate this warrant in the father: "We got married because it is time for me to grow up." This simple process of thinking *through* the audience instead of *at* the audience is the most essential step in creating a trusting rather than an antagonistic relationship. Logic, in other words, is first and foremost an *ethical* practice when it comes to rhetoric, for it requires us to think first of others before we speak to them about their fears, desires, and interests.

To understand what makes a "legitimate" argument, then, it is helpful to also know what makes an "illegitimate" one. **Fallacies** represent arguments that, when analyzed in isolation, do not "hold up," in the sense of maintaining logical coherence. Practically, logical fallacies are precisely those quotes that, when taken out of context and broadcast on the news, force politicians and celebrities and other public figures to explain themselves. This demand on the part of the public for such speakers to "justify" their fallacious statements is central to understanding the nature of fallacies. Although it is often common to hear fallacies defined as "errors in logic," it is more accurate to describe them as incomplete arguments that have attempted to do too much in a short amount of space. Logician Charles Peirce, for example, denies that there are such things as purely false logical fallacies. Rather, "logical fallacies produce propositions, false, indeed, as they were intended, but yet with a modified meaning, [they can be made] true" and that "human errors are always those which addition or amendment will rectify."[7] In other words, even the most ridiculous statement can be corrected by filling in all the gaps that had initially been left empty.

The determination of a fallacy should thus address the following questions:

1. Understood purely on the level of symbolic relationships, do the assertions contained in warrant, claim, and grounds add up to a coherent whole? (For example, there is no simple warrant that connects the claim "I should buy a cat" with the grounds "because I hate animals." However, this might make more sense if the person explained he or she is trying to learn to love animals and that a cat seems easier to take care of than a dog.)

2. Understood as a practical tool to address a problematic situation, does the argument conscientiously address the realities of the situation? (For example, the argument "You should take a risk, because life is short" [invoking the warrant from the principle "those with short lives should take risks"] may be reasonable advice for a person planning a trip to France, but it is highly unethical to say to a child who wishes to dive off a bridge.)

3. *Understood as an empirical claim, does the argument invoke a valid warrant or refer to verifiable grounds?* (For example, the argument "You should eat more candy because you want to stay healthy" invokes the causal warrant "candy increases health," which is clearly false [except under extraordinary circumstances], and the argument "People are Gods because they never die" is clearly false because people are mortal [unless this argument is to be taken metaphorically].)

Perhaps the simplest way to identify a fallacy from a rhetorical standpoint is simply to ask which arguments, when taken in isolation, simply don't make sense to an audience or strike them as absurd. It is the responsibility of the rhetor to make claims that an audience can understand and then act upon. Speaking without having understood the facts of the situation, having properly analyzed the audience, and having taken the time to construct arguments that are internally consistent and ethically responsible leads to misunderstanding at best and misdirection at worst. Therefore, each examination of the forms of reasoning will also include mention of common fallacies associated with each form.

DISCUSSION

One of the best ways to understand the function of a warrant is through jokes. A major component of humor is how we are able to participate in constructing absurd arguments that somehow make sense. For instance, take the bad joke: "A man walked into a bar and said 'ouch!'" In effect, this can be rewritten as an argument: "A man said 'ouch' (the claim) because he walked into a bar (grounds)," thus invoking the causal warrant "walking into a hard metal object causes pain" instead of the expected warrant concerning what happens when one walks into a place that sells alcohol. What other jokes can you think of that rely on unspoken warrants for their humor?

▶ PRINCIPLE

Argument by principle draws on widely shared maxims, definitions, and norms that categorize whole classes of people, events, objects, and actions according to their shared properties and characteristics. A **principle** is defined as a universal law, doctrine, or definition that helps guide judgment in particular cases by telling us what to expect from a class of things. In effect, it tells us that "should you encounter one of these, this is the qualities it will possess." Of all forms of argument, principle is by far the most common. The reason is that principles are the most available thing to access in any culture. We learn principles in school, in places of worship, in the home, amongst our friends, and from literature and works of art. Such principles might include "All dogs are loyal" or "The California beaches have the best surfing" or "Smart phones are distracting" or "Internet trolls are abusive" or "Democracies honor civil liberties" or "All monotheistic religions believe in one God." Any time you start with a category of objects and attach to that a quality that they all have in common, you have a principle.

Principles are valuable because they answer one fundamental question about a person, an event, or an object: "What can I expect of it?" A principle asserts that a certain thing (an "S") has certain properties ("P") because of its nature as a specific *type* of thing. Argument by principle is almost always used as a strategy of *labeling*. Consequently, argument by principle rarely makes explicit the warrant being used. What counts is that the speaker labels a specific person, object, event, or action as belonging to a certain category of things whose qualities we all know. For instance, one of the early health debates about cigarettes concerned precisely whether they were "carcinogens" or not. For a critic to assert the grounds that "A cigarette is a carcinogen" leads to the claim that "A cigarette is a cancer-causing agent" based on the warrant that "All carcinogens contain cancer-causing agents." In this case, the definition of a carcinogen is not at issue. What is controversial is whether a cigarette does or does not belong to this category of objects.

In other words, usually the controversy surrounds whether or not one accepts the assertion of the *grounds*. Take, for instance, the following "grounds" for argument by principle: "An embryo is a human being," or "Massachusetts is a British colony," or "The violence in Rwanda was a genocide," or "Those two women are married," or "That shooting was a terror attack," or "This product is grown organically." To understand the significance of argument by principle, one simply needs to ask what properties or qualities are attached to that subject (S) because it belongs to that specific category. The question is then whether or not the audience will accept that label or will reject it because they feel that the subject possesses different properties. If the speaker thinks that the warrant needs to be expressed explicitly, often it is because the warrant may itself be called into question, it is not completely clear to the audience what it means, or because stating the principle out loud is a way to rally support for a commonly held view. For instance, there is a difference between saying "An embryo is a human being, therefore it has human rights" and saying "All human beings by nature have inalienable human rights, and an embryo is a human being." In the first one, the warrant is left unspoken in the assumption that the audience will fill it in. In the second one, the speaker makes the warrant explicit and by doing so attempts to reaffirm a commitment to that principle before drawing consequences about the nature of embryos.

The most common fallacies are those that are fallacies of principle. This is because the majority of our arguments invoke a warrant in the form of "All S's are Y," a type of warrant that notoriously leads us to make broad and unjustified claims about a whole class of people or objects or events. Although there are numerous fallacies associated with argument from principle, the most common fallacy is **stereotyping**, which invites us to treat a diverse group of things as if they all were the same, thereby reducing a complex population to a simple and monolithic entity. Any time we claim that "All members of a group have this property," we are treading very close to stereotyping. One must also be careful about slipping into an **either/or** fallacy. This fallacy comes to an erroneous conclusion that if anything does not belong to one category, then it must be the exact opposite. The claim that "You are with us or you are against us" is the embodiment of the either/or fallacy. Simply because we might associate good things with a certain category of people, ideas, or actions, does not mean that everything that is not included in that category is somehow in conflict with or contradictory to it. Our principles must always be stated with some degree of humility and an understanding of the diversity and plurality of human experience.

When an argument by principle is structured as one of your main points, the purpose of the argument is usually to prove the grounds—namely that a certain subject matter belongs in a certain category that carries with it certain properties. Take, for instance, the arguments that "We should outlaw abortion because it is murder," or alternately, "We should legalize abortion because a woman has a right to make choices about her own body." Both of these arguments rely on proving either that abortion belongs in the category of "all acts of killing" or that abortion belongs in the category of "all reproductive choices." If an argument by principle is a main point, the rest of the paragraph is usually focused on providing reasons why a certain subject matter should be defined in a certain way.

Kailash Satyarthi: "All the Great Religions Teach Us to Care for Our Children"

Arguments from principle are the bread and butter of persuasion. Principles are the foundations of moral action as they give us not only definitions to make sense of our world but give us a list of imperatives that, as certain types of people in certain circumstances, we should or should not do. Often our principles are tied to moral authorities as well. It is to these authorities that Kailash Satyarthi appealed during his Nobel Prize speech when he used this platform to support the rights of children. Satyarthi is an activist who gave up a lucrative career as an electrical engineer to launch a crusade against child servitude, founding the single largest civil society network for the most exploited children, the Global March Against Child Labor. This excerpt from his speech not only used the power of narrative examples, but also appealed to the widest possible spectrum of religious authorities to condemn the exploitation of children across the globe on principle:

> Twenty years ago, in the foothills of the Himalayas, I met a small, skinny child labourer. He asked me: "Is the world so poor that it cannot give me a toy and a book, instead of forcing me to take a gun or a tool?"

> I met with a Sudanese child-soldier who was kidnapped by an extremist militia. As his first training lesson, he was forced to kill his friends and family. He asked me: "What is my fault?"

> Twelve years ago, a child-mother from the streets of Colombia—trafficked, raped, enslaved—asked me this: "I have never had a dream. Can my child have one?"

> Friends, all the great religions teach us to care for our children. Jesus said: "Let the children come to me; do not hinder them, for the kingdom of God belongs to them." The Holy Quran says: "Kill not your children because of poverty." Friends! There is no greater violence than to deny the dreams of our children.[8]

DISCUSSION

It is in the closing lines that we hear the declaration of principle: " 'Let the children come to me; do not hinder them, for the kingdom of God belongs to them.'" Restated as a syllogism, it runs as follows: "All children possess the kingdom of God. They are children. They possess the kingdom of God." The rest of the argument asks us to consider whether or not we are acting on the basis of that principle in our actions. Do we keep children as if they owned the Kingdom of God? Do we recognize their authority? Consider a time when you have taken a *principled stand* on something by labeling something in a controversial way. Did it have positive or negative consequences for you? In retrospect, do you think you were correct in your argument?

▶ GENERALIZATION

Rhetors use arguments from generalization when they try to draw general conclusions from either a series of examples or a single powerful anecdote. **Generalization** therefore entails drawing a general conclusion about a class of people, events, objects, or processes based on specific examples drawn from experience. In other words, the claims made in arguments from generalization therefore always demand that we treat a great number of things in a certain way, and the grounds for this sweeping judgment is that a single case can stand in for the whole. For instance, "My grandfather witnessed the devastation of World War II. So I believe all wars devastate the civilian population." The claim invites us to treat all wars the same way (as devastating to civilians) based on the particular experience of a particular person in a particular war. The warrant for this claim is that "My grandfather's experience with one war is representative of what all wars are like." Clearly, however, this warrant would likely be challenged by military veterans who may have fought in more modern wars, which tend to use precision weapons and avoid at all costs mediated images of civilian deaths. They might respond, "Wars have changed since your grandfather's day," thereby challenging the representativeness of his experience.

One way to think about arguments from generalization is to think of the grounds in terms of an individual spokesperson for a larger group. The question for the audience, then, is why they should trust *this particular* spokesperson. What makes he/she/it such an authority? Clearly, not all particular things can stand in for the whole. Simply accepting any case as representative leads to the worst type of stereotyping. For instance, if I am walking down the sidewalk and a man in an "I love NY" T-shirt rudely bumps into me without apologizing, I do not then blurt out the argument, "All people from New York are rude because that guy in the T-shirt was rude to me!" The warrant that "This one man in an 'I love NY' T-shirt stands in for the entire population of the state of New York" is absurd. However, if I buy a particular make of car and it constantly has engine problems due to no fault of my own, there seems justification for saying, "This make of car is terrible because I bought one and it kept having engine trouble." Because a manufacturer produces each car effectively the same way, there is warrant for assuming that "My car is representative of every car of this make." The difference between these two examples is simply that whereas no two people are ever alike, two industrially manufactured products are virtually identical. The challenge with making arguments from generalization is therefore to determine how reliably a single example can stand in for multiple examples.

As with arguments from principle, the warrant for arguments from generalization are very rarely made explicit, although it does occur. Most frequently, arguments from generalization begin with the claim and then are proven by the grounds. For instance, one might argue, "All tyrants wish to rule a great empire. Just look at Caesar or Hitler." Or perhaps, "All low-carb diets are conducive to weight loss. I tried a low-carb diet and lost 40 pounds!" In both cases, the claim is made that all members of a certain class of things have a certain property because one or a number of individuals in this class had that property. The essential part of this argument relies on the strength, therefore, not of the *principle* but of the *example*. Although usually the warrant is left unspoken, there are times when making the warrant explicit can be useful—namely if there is any doubt in people's minds that the examples are representative of the whole. So, for instance, the argument that weight loss on a low-carb diet is effective because of one's own experience can be bolstered by making explicit that "I am just an ordinary person who has had the same experience as thousands of other people trying to lose weight." This reassures an audience that the example given is not an extraordinary or isolated case.

The most frequent fallacy associated with warrant from generalization is, predictably, **overgeneralization**. Overgeneralization is simply when one makes too broad a leap from the particular to the general, such that the warrant "S_1 stands for all S's" simply does not hold up. Simply because a person has the bad luck to pick a rotten apple out of a bin does not mean that the entire selection of apples is rotten. Similarly, simply because one has met a single person who is associated with a certain group (or has seen such a person represented in the media) does not mean that he or she represents the entire group. Unfortunately, overgeneralizations are easy to slip into because single cases might be so vivid and powerful that they capture our imagination and our emotions in a way that distorts our judgment. Oftentimes, a single powerful anecdote has the potential to motivate people in a way that even the most accurate statistics can never do. Consequently, the fallacy of overgeneralization becomes the foundation for stereotypes.

When an argument by generalization is structured as a main point, this part of the speech usually focuses on providing one or a number of specific cases that are not only shown to be representative of a general state of affairs, but which also carry with them a great deal of narrative power and pathos. A main point structured as a generalization might be, for instance, "We see the great benefits of universal healthcare policies by the success of the Canadian and German systems." Once the claim is made, an in-depth investigation of the specific cases then follows. However, the strength of the argument is then clinched at the end by making broad and universal claims concerning *all* such policies. The end of a main point structured as an argument by generalization should always be itself a principle.

Patrick Buchanan: "These People Are Our People"

A standard use of generalization in political speeches is the use of a specific citizen or community to stand in for a whole class of people. In 1992, for example, conservative commentator and author Patrick Buchanan delivered a speech at the Republican National Convention in order to highlight economic hardship that he felt resulted from Democratic policies that overlooked the needs of average working Americans. To make his point, Buchanan spoke about a specific encounter he had at James River Paper Mill in New Hampshire that he felt encompassed the struggles of factory workers:

> There were those workers at the James River Paper Mill, in Northern New Hampshire in a town called Groveton—tough, hearty men. None of them would say a word to me as I came down the line, shaking their hands one by one. They were under a threat of losing their jobs

at Christmas. And as I moved down the line, one tough fellow about my age just looked up and said to me, "Save our jobs." Then there was the legal secretary that I met at the Manchester airport on Christmas Day who came running up to me and said, "Mr. Buchanan, I'm going to vote for you." And then she broke down weeping, and she said, "I've lost my job; I don't have any money, and they're going to take away my little girl. What am I going to do?". . .

My friends, these people are our people. They don't read Adam Smith or Edmund Burke, but they come from the same schoolyards and the same playgrounds and towns as we came from. They share our beliefs and our convictions, our hopes and our dreams. These are the conservatives of the heart. They are our people.[9]

DISCUSSION

One can see from this example how a political and rhetorical use of generalization is often paired with a strategy of identification to create a common bond amongst an audience by exploring a single representative example. Buchanan describes the qualities of the citizen in one small town, in effect defining the grounds (the example) as "The workers of the James River Paper Mill are tough, hearty people." The claim is then "These people are our people," meaning in effect that "All conservatives are tough, hearty people." The warrant is "The workers of the James River Paper Mill are representative of all conservatives." Now think back upon the many myths associated with the founding of any nation, city, or tribe. How do these single examples operate by the logic of generalization to represent larger social groups or institutions? What are the positives and negatives to this rhetorical strategy?

▶ ANALOGY

Arguments from analogy invite us to accept a claim by inviting us to treat something unfamiliar as we would treat something more familiar. An **analogy** warrants us to treat two essentially unlike things the same way because they share a vital similarity that is particularly relevant to the case at hand.[10] Importantly, arguments from analogy do not argue the *reason* why we should treat two things similarly. They simply draw a comparison and tell us to treat one thing as we treat this other thing. What makes arguments from analogy persuasive is that they allow the audience to transfer the qualities from something very familiar—which ideally contains some striking quality or characteristic that immediately comes to mind—to some other thing that might be unclear or confusing. It is like the old strategy that people use to try to get others to try new foods: "If you like chicken, you'll like alligator." In an argument from analogy, we simply switch out S_2 for S_1 and act as if it is like the other object. In this case, the warrant is simply, "We can treat alligators in the same way we treat chickens." Other times, an argument from analogy makes a more explicit claim concerning the specific properties or characteristics that are shared. For instance, one might argue, "The human race will not exist forever. Even the dinosaurs died out." In this case, the warrant remains in the same form: "We can treat the human race as we treat the race of dinosaurs." But the analogy is more explicit about the quality—namely their finitude—they have in common.

Unlike argument by principle and by generalization, it is actually quite common for arguments from analogy to make the warrant explicit. Arguments from analogy really come in two common forms. The first generally leaves out the warrant and makes a rather common comparison in order to make the unfamiliar into something familiar. Any argument that suggests "we should (or should not) do this thing because it is very much like this other thing" or "that it is going to turn out the same way that this other thing turned out" uses argument from analogy by simply drawing a comparison without having to explain that they should be treated identically. For instance, "We should not build a wall on our own borders because the East Germans built a wall around Berlin." In this case, the warrant is left out because most people are familiar with why the comparison is being made—building walls suffocates freedom. However, the second kind of argument which makes the warrant explicit usually does so because there is a sense of humor or surprise to the comparison. In this case, it is the claim that is often left unsaid. For instance, "The Earth's atmosphere can be treated a lot like a greenhouse. A greenhouse heats up primarily because it doesn't allow heat to escape." This leaves the unsettling conclusion to be filled in by the audience—that our planet, like a greenhouse, is warming because we do not allow the heat to escape.

False analogy is the fallacy associated with this form of argument. Put simply, false analogy either makes logically absurd or ethically dubious associations between two things that have very little relationship to one another, such that the warrant "We can treat S_1 like we treat S_2" simply makes no sense. Sometimes the fallacy is due to lack of understanding. The skeptical argument that "I'm not going to see a doctor because I don't believe in magic" invokes the (false) analogical warrant "We can treat modern medicine as we treat magic." Other times the fallacy is clearly not meant to be empirically true but is nonetheless ethically dubious because of the connotations of the comparison. During times of war or within tyrannical regimes, for instance, often specific "out-groups" are compared with all manner of terrible things—diseases, animals, barbarians, and the like. "Name-calling" of this type is effectively an argument by analogy, of the most despicable kind.

A main point structured as an argument by analogy is similar to an argument by generalization, but differs because it refuses to make universal claims concerning *all* of a subject. Instead, argument by analogy simply says that we can understand an unfamiliar case by comparing it to a more familiar case, whether it is a realistic comparison or a metaphor. For instance, a main point that is an argument by analogy might be "We should not restrict the right to bear arms in this country because it is well-known that the Nazis used gun-control laws to oppress minorities." In this case, the main point relies on an exclusive comparison between the present situation and another, analogous situation. The burden of proof here falls on showing the similarity between the two specific cases, unlike generalization, which focuses more on proving a "rule" rather than a similarity.

John Lewis: "We All Live in the Same House"

John Lewis has represented Georgia's 5th congressional district in the U.S. House of Representatives since 1987. However, he is perhaps most well known for being the former chairman of the Student Nonviolent Coordinating Committee, which played a key role in the struggle to end legalized racial discrimination and segregation. Lewis was also a Freedom Rider, spoke at 1963's March on Washington, and led the demonstration that became known as "Bloody Sunday." In his 2016 commencement address to Washington University in St. Louis, Lewis used an experience from his childhood of visiting his aunt's "shotgun house" in Alabama during a wind storm as an analogy for the global political and social situations we face in the twenty-first century:

> On one Saturday afternoon, we were playing in her dirt yard and an unbelievable storm came up. The winds started blowing, the thunder starting rolling, the lightning started flashing, the rain started beating on the tin roof of this old shotgun house. She thought it was going to blow away. She got all of us little children to come inside. . . . One corner of this old house appeared to be lifting, so she had us walk to that side to try to hold the house down with our little bodies. . . . As children, as humans who live on this little planet we call Earth, let's never leave the house. Call it a house of Washington University. Call it a house of St. Louis. Call it the house of Atlanta, Georgia. The house of New York. The house of Africa. The house of the Middle East. The house of China. We all live in the same house. We all must be part of that effort to hold down our little house. If you see something that's not right, not fair, not just, do something about it. Say something. Do something. Have the courage. Have the backbone to get in the way. Walk with the wind. It's all gonna work out.[11]

DISCUSSION

The essence of an argument from analogy is simply that we can treat one thing as we treat another similar thing—in this case, that we can treat the Earth, our nations, or neighborhoods as if we were in a shotgun house. Specifically, the argument from analogy appears in the middle of this passage: "We were little children walking with the wind, but we never, ever left the house. As children, as humans who live on this little planet we call Earth, let's never leave the house." Simplified, this argument runs as follows: "We can treat our little planet as if it were the same as my grandmother's house. We never abandoned my grandmother's house. We should never abandon our little planet." Once we accept this comparison, arguments from a principle or cause then tell us what to expect from living in a shotgun house—namely having the loyalty and the courage to defend the house. In this case, in what ways does this analogy make sense and in what ways does the analogy fall apart? How would the analogy be different if he lived in an apartment or a two-story home? How important is it to find the "right" analogy?

▶ SIGN

Arguments from signs infer the existence or discern the identify of something from some kind of visible or otherwise empirically verifiable evidence. In other words, it defines what we cannot see by what we can see. Therefore, **sign** warrants encourage us to accept a state of affairs by careful reading of external clues or indicators. Arguments based on signs are usually called for in situations when people are concerned with identifying the nature of some part of a situation. They answer the questions: "What is it?" and/or "What is or was here?" For instance, the perception of crumbs on a counter and an open lid are signs that lead us to infer that a person was in the kitchen and has taken a cookie from the cookie jar. Similarly, a college-age individual wearing a hat and shirt bearing a specific logo and colors of a university is a sign that leads us to identify that person as a student at that university. Naturally, arguments from sign are most commonly used either in forensic argumentation that deals with proving the guilt or innocence of a person based on what the evidence shows the individual has done in the past, or in deliberative policy discussions that require us to diagnose the present situation by the reading of present indicators. In almost all popular crime shows, there are scenes in which investigators walk onto the scene of a crime and read signs ordinarily gone unnoticed that reveal some important aspects of what happened and who committed the crime. But forensic investigation also deals with how we determine whether or not a lake is polluted, whether the economy is growing, or whether some foreign power is preparing for war. All of these arguments tell us "what is the case" based on a gathering together of clues and evidence and facts that point to a specific conclusion.

Argument by sign operates the exact opposite of argument by principle. An argument by principle defines all of the properties of a given class of objects and predicts the property that we will encounter when we experience one of those objects. For instance, an argument by principle based on the warrant "All dogs are loyal" tells me that if I get a dog, it will be a loyal pet. An argument by sign goes in the opposite direction. It presents us with a series of qualities and has us infer the nature of the subject. For instance, if a person says, "I love my pet because she is so loyal to me," I am justified in claiming that "You must have a dog" based on the warrant that "The property of loyalty in a pet is an indication that it is probably a dog." Arguments by sign are akin to games in which we close our eyes and have someone put an object in our hand and guess what it is based on what it feels like.

Arguments from sign follow a very simple pattern. The claim always makes a tangible statement that some state of affairs exists, and the grounds support this claim by pointing specifically to particular things that are either incontrovertible facts or phenomena that are readily available to sense perception. These claims usually come in one of two forms. In the first case, the argument is that a certain event happened in a certain way based on available evidence. For instance, the prosecution in a court trial might argue: "This knife was the murder weapon (claim) because the bloodstain on the knife matched that of the victim (grounds)." In this case, there are actually two arguments by sign compressed into a single claim. The first argument is based on the warrant that "If this test on a blood sample matches the same test on another sample, they both belong to the same individual and no other." This argument justifies using blood samples as evidence. The second warrant is that "The presence of the victim's blood on a knife indicates the fact that this knife was used to stab the victim." Note that the second claim could be refuted by the defense attorney by saying that the blood was planted on the knife as a way to frame the defendant. This argument would, in effect, challenge the legitimacy of the warrant.

The second type of argument by sign declares the identity of something based on visible signs. In this case, we are not being asked to reconstruct some past event, as in a courtroom, but rather to identify something that we are actually observing. For instance, when we see a person approaching from far away, we often cannot tell who it is right away. As they approach, we are able to discern certain shapes or colors or markers that we begin to interpret until we recognize a pattern that suggests a specific identity. Or when someone knocks on our apartment door and we look through the peep-hole, we try to size up the person's identity—whether or not the individual is a friend, a neighbor, a salesperson, a thief, a fundraiser, or one's roommate—as a way of determining whether or not we should open the door. In politics we often have to read the signs of our enemies and allies in order to determine their motives. And much of the future of our environmental and energy policies are going to be determined by how we interpret the signs of global warming and climate change in the future.

The fallacy associated with this warrant is a **faulty sign**. A faulty sign is simply an appeal to an indicator that does not actually point to what the rhetor claims that it does. One way faulty signs are effective is when they appeal to unreflective commonsense associations to either advance or reject intricate diagnoses of situations of incredible breadth and complexity. The claim that "Our nation's morals are declining because of all the violence on television police dramas" implies the faulty sign that "Rising violence on television is indicative of rising violence in actual life." Another way they are effective is when they are used as shorthand indicators of value based on price or packaging or popularity. The popular **bandwagon** fallacy is a variant on faulty sign that takes the form of the warrant "The popularity of a thing is a sign of its value." Whenever we purchase a product because it is the "#1 Bestseller" and comes in an attractive package, we purchase it because we believe these things are indicators of its worth.

An argument by sign is exclusively focused on proving the existence of a certain state of affairs that either exists currently or has happened in the past. It offers proof and evidence that such a state of affairs is present and not merely a fiction or illusion. For instance, a main point structured as an argument by sign might be structured as "Rising temperatures, increasing desertification, and melting glaciers all signal that we are currently in the midst of a major shift in global climate." In this main point, the focus becomes first of all proving that these signs are indisputably real by using scientific research or testimonies, and second of all demonstrating why these are all signs of this particular state of affairs. Arguments by sign are thus typically the most heavily researched and "technical" of the main points.

Pamela Meyer: "We Think Liars Won't Look You in the Eyes"

As human beings, the signs we are most attentive to in our everyday life are the signs that we read from other people's nonverbal expressions. From them, we perceive whether a person is hostile or well-meaning, amused or angry. We also try to read facial expressions as signs of whether a person is telling the truth or not. In one of the most popular TED talks of all time, American author, certified fraud examiner, and entrepreneur Pamela Meyer explains the meaning of signs and what to look for when someone is lying:

> Now this brings us to our next pattern, which is body language. With body language, here's what you've got to do. You've really got to just throw your assumptions out the door. Let the science temper your knowledge a little bit. Because we think liars fidget all the time. Well guess what, they're known to freeze their upper bodies when they're lying. We think liars won't look you in the eyes. Well guess what, they look you in the eyes a little too much just to compensate for that myth. We think warmth and smiles convey honesty, sincerity. But a trained lie spotter can spot a fake smile a mile away. Can you all spot the fake smile here? You can consciously contract the muscles in your cheeks. But the real smile's in the eyes, the crow's feet of the eyes. They cannot be consciously contracted, especially if you overdid the Botox. Don't overdo the Botox; nobody will think you're honest.[12]

DISCUSSION

The logic of signs is always that the perception of one thing tells us about the presence of something that is not immediately present. Arguments by sign always appeal to some kind of visible evidence that can be interpreted as indicating one thing over another. What signs does Meyer pick out as indicative of someone lying? What other signs do you typically pick up on to spot a liar in your own experience? Think also more generally about how facial expressions are signs of certain attitudes. Today, we often see specific still shots of movies used as "memes" for one thing or another. What are some of these memes and what do you think they are "signs" of independently of the words people paste on top of them?

▶ CAUSATION

Causal arguments are used to predict or explain the effects that certain objects, processes, or events have on other entities under specific conditions. For instance, a new parent might say, "My daughter was just born yesterday (grounds), and I am simply tired out (claim)." The warrant for this claim is that "Newborn babies make their parents exhausted." Strictly speaking, arguments from **causation** assert that certain consequences or effects will naturally follow some specific interaction of elements in a situation. Some common causal warrants might include

"Eating too many calories will lead to weight gain," "Appeasing dictators will only increase the possibility of aggression," "Increased carbon dioxide in the atmosphere increases global temperature," or "Online bullying increases the rates of suicide." In rhetorical argumentation, however, these causal claims are almost always stated in the context of some normative suggestion of what we should or should not do. For instance, "You should reduce calorie intake if you want to lose weight," or "If we want to stop foreign aggression, we must meet it with military force," or "We must reduce carbon emissions in order to prevent global warming," or "To reduce teenage suicide, we must stop online bullying."

Causal reasoning is thus employed wherever we are encouraged to act (or not act) based upon *accepted* beliefs about cause-and-effect relationships. Causal arguments do not introduce new explanatory concepts, but rather rely on explanations already in place. Superstition, for instance, relies heavily on accepted causal accounts, no matter how fallacious. "Don't step on that crack if you don't want to break your mother's back" invokes the warrant "Stepping on cracks causes your mother's back to get broken." As arguments become more complex, the type of audience that is influenced by causal warrants becomes more specialized. For instance, a conservative economist might argue, "We need tax cuts on capital gains in order to increase investment in new business." The warrant for this claim is simply that "Capital gains tax cuts increases investment." But a liberal economist might argue, "Without government stimulation of a depressed economy, consumer confidence will continue to decline." The warrant for this claim is "Government stimulation of the economy increases consumer confidence." Both of these arguments would be applauded when delivered to friendly audiences that willingly "fill in" the warrant to connect the claim and the grounds. When delivered to unfriendly audiences, the warrant is immediately exposed and challenged: "Cutting capital gains only gives away money to the rich" or "Government stimulation only increases the debt to pay for wasteful projects." Consequently, speeches that use causal reasoning for a mixed audience almost always rely on expert research to establish their accuracy. Once a causal argument is made, rhetors almost always try to justify the warrant that has been invoked using testimony or statistics.[13]

The fallacy of **false cause** occurs any time a causal argument is made that invokes a clearly incorrect or exaggerated causal sequence. As it has already been pointed out, the most pervasive arguments from false cause occur in superstition. The claim that "I knew my good luck would come to an end because I didn't knock on wood" invokes the causal warrant that "Failing to knock on wood produces bad luck." But more serious cases of false cause often occur when people act on the basis of traditional and prescientific causal attributions, such as arguments that one should consume ground-up rhinoceros horn in order to increase sexual potency or that interracial marriage should be outlawed in order to protect children from psychological harm. As with the fallacy of faulty signs, however, those of false cause are attractive precisely because they provide easily comprehensible explanations for sometimes bewilderingly complex affairs. The frequent explanation that various plagues or diseases (such as AIDS) have been caused by some type of moral failing or divine retribution is indicative of the human craving for simple explanations.

Two common variants of the false cause fallacy are the slippery slope and scapegoating fallacies. The **slippery slope** fallacy takes the form of an argument that claims we must not make an even incremental step in a certain direction if we are to prevent a dramatic slide and decline into a terrible state of affairs. For instance, one very popular slippery slope argument takes this form: "We cannot allow even one handgun to be banned, because then we would inevitably end up completely defenseless and unarmed." The warrant for this is: "A slight compromise on handguns will produce a complete capitulation." The fallacy of this type of argument is that it assumes an unstoppable domino theory of cause and effect that removes human agency from the equation. The **scapegoating** fallacy takes the form of an argument that claims that the reason some undesirable state of affairs has come about is because of the existence or actions of a particular group of people who are on the margins of society and are easy to blame. For instance, the argument that "We need to deny health services and education to illegal immigrants if we want to hope for a balanced budget" invokes the causal warrant "The presence of illegal immigrants causes an excessive drain on the budget." What makes this argument a fallacy is not that it makes the reasonable claim that state services go to illegal immigrants, but rather that this sole factor is responsible for the entire state's budget crisis. In both cases, plausible causal sequences are exaggerated to such a degree that they become fallacies.

Main points that are structured as arguments from causation are almost always focused on documenting the effects that are desirable or undesirable from the presence of something or the implementation of some policy. In a problem–solution arrangement, for instance, one might begin with a main point that documents the negative effects of some current situation. For instance, "Because so much of our personal data is now stored online in corporate and government databases, identity theft has become rampant in today's society." In this case, the causal claim diagnoses the effects of a certain technological condition. The main point structured as a solution might then argue, "In order to make ourselves safe from identity thieves, we must seek to reduce our online presence while at the same time creating a number of different passwords that do not overlap." In both cases, however, the paragraph that follows from these main points are actually further causal claims that focus more on the finer details of the processes. To make causal main points effective, in other words, one should feel as if one had "opened the hood" to the causal mechanisms so we can understand why something has happened or will happen.

Caitlyn Jenner: "The Power of the Spotlight"

For most of her life, Caitlyn Jenner was known as Bruce Jenner, perhaps the most famous Olympic gold medal-winning decathlete in American history, whose picture adorned the Wheaties cereal box for many years. Later, Jenner worked in television, film, writing, auto racing, business, and even appeared as a Playgirl cover model. But in April 2015, she revealed her identity as a transgender woman and changed her name from Bruce to Caitlyn. For her subsequent advocacy, she earned the 2016 ESPY award (Excellence in Sports Performance Yearly), and on receiving her award argued that she has an important role to play to help others like herself fight for their rights:

All across this country, right now, all across the world, at this very moment, there are young people coming to terms with being transgender. . . . They're getting bullied, they're getting beaten up, they're getting murdered and they're committing suicide. . . . Every time something like this happens, people wonder, 'Could it have been different if spotlighting this issue with more attention could have changed the way things happen?'. . . If there's one thing I do know about my life, it is the power of the spotlight. . . . I know I'm clear with my responsibility going forward, to tell my story the right way, for me, to keep learning, to reshape the landscape of how trans issues are viewed, how trans people are treated.[14]

DISCUSSION

To make a claim of cause is to predict the future effect from the presence of some object or event. In this case, Jenner is talking about the effects that follow from an individual being in the public spotlight. To be in the spotlight is to be able to alter public opinion. However, it is important to point out that Jenner's ethical imperative derived from an argument by principle. To be in the spotlight is to have the potential to change the opinions of others, but the duty or responsibility that comes from that is determined by one's moral principles. In what other ways do causal arguments bring about questions of moral principle? In other words, how does our determination of how things *actually* affect one another impact the ways in which we think we *should* act?

▶ SUMMARY

In rhetoric, logos represents not only the art of reasoning, but also the art of crafting one's arguments to make those reasons persuasive. Perhaps the most important aspect of this art is to know what to leave out. More often than not, amateur speakers put in too much rather than too little. They pile arguments on top of arguments as if persuasion occurred by the sheer weight of argumentation. However, a good speech will actually include only a few actual arguments, with each argument in effect representing a main point. The rest of the speech will then focus on providing backing for those arguments in various ways, including resources from ethos, pathos, and style.

The most important thing to remember about a good argument from logos is that it often—but not always—leaves out the warrant that serves to bridge the claim and the grounds, and that this warrant has been chosen specifically because the speaker knows it will be subconsciously granted by the audience without it having to be made explicit. Although this point has been made numerous times, it bears repeating that the warrant is not an extra argument or defense of the claim. It does not add a great deal of "new" material. It simply acts as a basis of inference that allows us to connect a claim with its grounds in a way that makes sense to us. For instance, we do not agree with the argument "I decided to put on my jacket because I was hot" not because we know anything special about that situation, but because we reject the causal warrant "Wearing a jacket makes one cool" on logical grounds. By saying a warrant acts as a "bridge," it simply means it gets us from one side of the argument to the other on the basis of an inference that is stable enough to stand on. The art of crafting arguments is to therefore appeal to those premises that the audience already believes and are eager to use to help a speaker establish his or her claims. This means that a good argument from logos begins with an understanding of the audience, proceeds to making explicit the premises that they will readily assent to, and then finally to building arguments that invoke those premises without needing to verbalize them.

Let us take, for example, a woman who is advocating for universal health care and is speaking to a variety of different audiences:

- ▶ First, she speaks to a group of college graduates who she knows are anxious about being on their own. She makes the argument: "Without universal health care we are all at risk, as we have seen in the story of one student who was forced to abandon her long-term career goals because of the debt incurred by the injuries caused by an uninsured motorist," invoking the warrant from *generalization*: "This recent graduate represents the possible fate of all recent graduates."

- ▶ Second, she speaks to a group of economists who are mostly concerned about the effect of universal health care on long-term economic growth. She makes the argument: "We are headed down an economic spiral without health care, as we have seen from the rise in personal debt and bankruptcy caused by health costs," invoking the warrant from *sign*: "Increased debt and bankruptcy are signs of future economic decline."

- ▶ Third, she speaks to the executives of multinational corporations familiar with different forms of health care across the globe. She makes the argument: "The American system needs to move to a single-payer system because of the success we have seen in European nations," invoking the warrant from *analogy*: "We can treat the American health care system like we treat the European health care system."

- ▶ Fourth, she speaks to a group of working parents concerned about both costs and securing the future of their children's health. She makes the argument: "Universal health care is absolutely necessary if we are to avoid condemning our children to a life of poverty simply because they had the bad fortune to get sick while looking for a job," invoking the warrant from *cause*: "Universal health care will help keep children out of poverty."

- ▶ Last, she speaks to a group of constitutional scholars familiar with the Bill of Rights and the Declaration of Independence. She makes the argument: "We cannot shirk our responsibilities to cover those who become sick because that is a violation of the right to life," invoking the principle from the Declaration of Independence that "All human beings should be guaranteed the right to life."

One should think of arguments from logos as establishing an initial bond between speaker and audience in which the speaker provides a framework that the audience completes by filling in the missing warrant. This generates a sense of participation that does not have the same effect as when the speaker spells out every single part of an argument. By leaving out essential aspects that the audience can contribute on their own, it makes them more willing to consider the subsequent backing for that claim that constitutes the rest of the speech.

Speakers slip into fallacies when they use warrants that appeal to misinformation or stereotypes that do not effectively or logically bridge the claims to the grounds. Fallacies, in other words, take the form of logical argumentation without providing the substance. Fallacies can take two forms. On the one hand, they might appeal to blatantly false warrants. To borrow an example from Plato, a candy maker might reason with a group of children that "They should not eat fruits and vegetables because they taste bad," invoking the warrant from principle that "One should not eat any food that tastes bad." This is a fallacy primarily because the principle is simply false. On the other hand, they might construct arguments that simply make no sense if they are examined closely. A *non sequitur*, for instance, represents any type of argument that simply does not have any sense of coherence and "does not follow." For instance, that same candy maker might say, "You should eat candy because I am dressed like a funny elephant." The only way this argument makes any sense is by authority: "You should always trust things told to you by someone dressed like a funny elephant." This hardly even makes enough sense to be comprehensible, yet it is the verbal parallel of most techniques of advertising to children by using cartoon characters to sell medicine. But this example also shows that fallacies can be very effective persuasive techniques if they appeal to the unthinking impulses and biases of an audience in the guise of reason.

▶ CHAPTER 8 EXERCISES

1. **IMPROMPTU:** In order to experiment with how arguments can build on one another, write an impromptu argument with exactly five claims. First, use argument by sign to establish the existence of a problem. Second, use argument by causation to show how this problem will produce negative effects. Third, use argument by generalization to give a specific example that shows why all such problems should be treated the same way. Fourth, use argument by principle to assert our moral responsibility to deal with this problem. Last, use argument by analogy to give us a positive image of what will happen if we do the right thing.

2. **DEBATE:** Choose a conventional debate topic over some ethical question—for instance, capital punishment, euthanasia, censorship, gun control, or abortion. Have each side specifically answer these questions about this topic using forms of reasoning. Sign: What is the evidence that this issue is a problem? Cause: What are the consequences of doing or not doing certain actions? Principle: What are the moral principles at stake concerning what class of things or actions are good or bad? Analogy: What can this moral problem be compared to

using some kind of metaphor? Generalization: What specific instances can you think of that have actually happened that prove the nature of the general case?

3. **GROUP:** Come up with a deliberative topic that addresses some specific situation that is common to everyone in the class at the present moment. Divide into groups and articulate a position on this issue using as many forms of reasoning as you can. Have each group present their position and then vote on which position was the most persuasive, with each group ranking the position of the other three groups from 1 to 3 (and not ranking their own).

4. **TAKE HOME:** Look at arguments or jokes made on Twitter that demonstrate specific forms of reasoning. Choose one and rewrite the tweet in a way that makes explicit the claim, the grounds, and the warrant. Identify the type of warrant being used. Present your findings to the class.

5. **VIDEO:** Explore the power of using argument by sign by actually videotaping yourself in front of an actual phenomenon that acts as evidence for a claim. For instance, if the problem is the lack of bike racks on campus, videotape yourself in front of a series of overcrowded bike racks that act as evidence for your claim. On the video, make sure you interpret the findings and make clear your conclusions.

▶ NOTES

1. For the various meanings of *logos*, see George B. Kerferd, *The Sophistical Movement* (Cambridge, UK: Cambridge University Press, 1981), 83.

2. John Dewey, "Logic," in *John Dewey: The Later Works*, vol. 8, ed. Jo Ann Boydston (Carbondale: Southern Illinois UP, 1986; original work published 1933), 4.

3. Charles Peirce, "Harvard Lecture 1, 1865," in *The Writings of Charles S Peirce: A Chronological Edition*, vol. 1, ed. Max Fischh, (Bloomington: Indiana University Press, 1982), 175.

4. Charles Peirce, "The Fixation of Belief," in *The Philosophy of Peirce*, ed. Justus Buchler (New York: Harcourt, Brace, and Co., 1950), 5.

5. Charles Peirce, "The Fixation of Belief," 5.

6. This model is elaborated in Stephen Toulmin, *The Uses of Argument* (Cambridge, UK: Cambridge University Press, 1958). See also Wayne Brockriede and Douglas Ehninger, "Toulmin on Argument: An Interpretation and Application," *Quarterly Journal of Speech* 46 (1960), 44–53.

7. Charles Peirce, "Private Thoughts Principally on the Conduct of Life," in *The Writings of Charles S Peirce: A Chronological Edition*, vol. 1, ed. Max Fischh (Bloomington: Indiana University Press, 1982), 5.

8. Kailash Satyarthi, "Nobel Lecture," available at www.nobelprize.org/nobel_prizes/peace/laureates/2014/satyarthi-lecture_en.html (accessed 20 August 2016).

9. Patrick Buchanan, "Address to the Republican National Convention," available at www.americanrhetoric.com/speeches/patrickbuchanan1992rnc.htm (accessed 20 August 2016).

10. For more on argument by analogy, see James R. Wilcox and Henry L. Ewbank, "Analogy for Rhetors," *Philosophy and Rhetoric* 12 (1979), 1–20; James S. Measell, "Classical Bases of the Concept of Analogy," *Argumentation and Advocacy* 10 (1973), 1–10.

11. John Lewis, "Commencement Address to Washington University in St. Louis," available at https://source.wustl.edu/2016/05/john-lewis-2016-commencement-address-washington-university-st-louis/ (accessed 20 August 2016).

12. Pamela Meyer, "How to Spot a Liar," available at www.ted.com/talks/pamela_meyer_how_to_spot_a_liar/transcript?language=en (accessed 20 August 2016).

13. For a discussion of causal inferences, see David Zarefsky, "The Role of Causal Argument in Policy Controversies," *Argumentation and Advocacy* 13 (1977), 179–191.

14. Caitlyn Jenner, "Speech at the ESPY Awards," available at www.washingtonpost.com/news/morning-mix/wp/2015/07/16/watch-caitlyn-jenners-powerful-speech-at-espys/ (accessed 20 August 2016).

9

Pathos

This chapter explores the ways of constructing appeals to emotion based on charged descriptions of people, objects, events, or actions. Whereas logos persuades based on cognitive beliefs derived from claims of fact, pathos persuades based on affective orientations derived from feelings of like and dislike, desire and fear, and pain and pleasure. The concepts employed thus come in opposite pairs relating to the attractive (+) and repulsive (–) spectrum of emotions, and they are organized according to their relationship to people (saint and sinner), objects (idol and abomination), events (utopia and wasteland), and actions (virtue and vice). The goal of this chapter is to demonstrate how, within certain problematic situations, to attract people to certain things that are beneficial while repelling them from others that are harmful. If logos persuades an audience as to what is the best course of action based on belief, pathos motivates them to actually pursue that course of action out of fear or desire.

In the Greek rhetorical tradition, **pathos** refers to the use of emotional appeals to persuade an audience. Whereas *ethos* persuades by the character and *logos* persuades by reasoning, *pathos* persuades by producing an emotional response in an audience that makes it favorable to one thing and unfavorable to another. In his *Rhetoric*, Aristotle offers a definition of emotions (*pathē*) that remains an important resource for understanding their function in rhetoric. He writes:

> The emotions are those things through which, by undergoing change, people come to differ in their judgments and what are accompanied by pain and pleasure, for example, anger, pity, fear, and other such things and their opposites. There is need to divide the discussion of each into three headings. I mean, for example, in speaking of anger, [one should describe] what is their state of mind when people are angry, and against whom are they usually angry, and for what reasons.[1]

Emotions, for Aristotle, are those psychological feelings of pain or pleasure we associate with things in our environment about which we must make a judgment. To understand someone's emotions, according to Aristotle, we only need to ask that person to describe three things: (a) his or her state of mind; (b) the people, objects, events, or actions that produce the state of mind; and (c) the reasons he or she feels this way. Once we know these things, we can then reproduce these emotions in others by speaking about those same people, objects, events, or actions in such a way that brings about that state of mind. In other words, emotional appeal does not simply tell us: "Be angry at this thing." It describes the type of thing that makes a certain audience, for example, angry, and the emotion is evoked on its own.

Although often maligned as an "irrational" means of persuasion, emotional appeal is an inevitable and necessary part of any persuasive act. Although people's emotions can certainly be manipulated for irrational ends, the use of emotion in persuasion is no more or less ethical than the use of credibility or logic. Indeed, the relative importance of *pathos* in rhetoric is exemplified by the fact that Aristotle, despite his apparent reservation about excessive use of emotional appeals and persuasion, nonetheless felt the need to spend almost a third of his book defining what he considered the most important emotions. This is because, far from "distorting" our judgments, emotions are what make judgments possible by giving us the motive to prefer one thing over another. Without emotional involvement in our surroundings, all the reason and credibility in the world would not encourage us to expend the least bit of energy to accomplish a task. That is why people who are "apathetic" (or "without pathos") are those who have an incapacity to make a judgment. In Aristotle's treatise, he offers a definition of the following emotions:

Anger	An impulse to inflict punishment on a specific individual in response to the pain of a conscious, obvious, unjustified slight with respect to oneself or one's friends and which is accompanied by the pleasure of imagining revenge.
Mildness	The pleasurable settling down and quieting of anger due to the elimination of the perceived threat or the subordination of one's enemy.
Love	Wishing good things for a person you consider to be good, and wishing them for the other person's own sake and not your own, accompanied by the pleasure in imagining their happiness.
Hate	To despise and wish evil upon a general class or group that one does not like and wishes to eliminate, accompanied by pain at knowing they exist and by pleasure at wishing their elimination. Hate is unlike anger because whereas anger is excited by offenses that concern an individual and a specific slight, hate is directed at a category of things and is more difficult to remedy.
Fear	A pain or disturbance arising from a mental image of impending evil of a painful or destructive sort that one believes might actually occur in the near future.
Confidence	Confidence is the pleasure of anticipation of future things conducive to safety because one imagines them near at hand, and it allows one to act freely and without fear.

Shame	A pain or disturbance regarding that class of evils, in the present, past, or future, which we think will tend to our discredit and which are judged as evil in comparison with some established norm or principle.
Shamelessness	A certain contempt or indifference regarding the acts which bring about shame and the pleasure that accompanies willful rejection of virtue.
Benevolence	The pleasure in imagining oneself performing disinterested kindness in doing or returning good to another or to all others.
Pity	A sense of pain at what we take to be an evil of a destructive or painful kind, which befalls one who does not deserve it, and which we think we or our loved ones might be susceptible to in similar circumstances.
Indignation	A pain at the sight of undeserved good fortune due to the fact that such fortune could have been bestowed upon a worthier individual.
Envy	A disturbing pain directed at the good fortune of an equal, felt not because one desires something, but because the other person has it.
Emulation	A pain at the presence of persons who are by nature like us who have goods that are desirable and are possible for us to attain, accompanied by the pleasure of anticipating that one can possess them.
Contempt	The antithesis of emulation, a feeling by those in a position to be emulated to feel pleasure at one's own superiority and a painful disregard or disgust for those who do not possess the virtues or goods because of their perceived unworthiness.

One thing that becomes clear from Aristotle's category of emotions is that they are far more complicated than what we would call mere "feelings." Whereas a feeling can simply be a sensation (such as the feeling of being burned when touching a hot stove), an emotion is something more complex that relates to our entire reaction to that sensation (such as fear of being burned). In other words, emotions are different from feelings because they are tied up with our likes and dislikes, our hopes and fears, and our relationship with ourselves and others. **Emotions** are therefore dramatized feelings that orient us to things within our immediate environment that stand out as significant, accompanied by feelings of pleasure and pain. Calling them "dramatized feelings" recognizes that emotions are still related to feelings insofar as emotions either produce or anticipate bodily sensations. When we look forward to a vacation, we both "feel" pleasure in the moment and also look forward to the feeling of the sand and the sun and the water. But the emotion is not simply these feelings. They are *dramatized* feelings because we play them out in our imaginary narratives in which we envision either how we will relate to something in the future or how something happened in the past. Emotions are therefore always objective and dramatic; they involve our active relationship with things either in the real world or in our imaginations.[2]

It is because of the "dramatic" character of emotions that they are tied so closely to our capacity for judgments. According to John Dewey, a sense of judgment always lurks behind any emotion because "emotions are attached to events and objects in their movement . . . toward an issue that is desired or disliked."[3] Emotions arise in the midst of objective situations and tell us how to orient ourselves to particular parts of that situation (as when we enter a strange room and try to determine who is a possible ally and who is an antagonist). Furthermore, we tend to feel the strongest emotions in those situations that are in flux and uncertain. He goes on:

> The rhythm of loss of integration with environment and recovery of union not only persists in man but becomes conscious with him; its conditions are material out of which he forms purposes. Emotion is the conscious sign of a break, actual or impending. The discord is the occasion that induces reflection. Desire for restoration of the union converts mere emotion into interest in objects as conditions of realization of harmony.[4]

Put another way, emotions are intelligent insofar as they inform us of ruptures in our environment and signal their possible restoration. Emotions tell us what we need to support, what we need to reject, what we need to be concerned about, and what we can trust. It is thus the ethical function of rhetoric to try to direct emotions toward the right objects in the right way in order to bring about a "realization of harmony."

As indicated by Dewey's remark about liking and disliking, because emotions always involve a dramatic relationship between ourselves and other things, they can be effectively divided into emotions that *attract* us to things (and therefore have a positive orientation) and ones that *repel* us from them (and therefore have a negative orientation). **Attracting emotions** draw us closer to somebody or something; we associate such attracting emotions with love, curiosity, pity, generosity, envy, trust, respect, obsession, or greed. Clearly, not all attracting emotions are "good" ones. Sometimes we are attracted to the wrong things for the wrong reasons. The mark of an attracting emotion is simply that, when something is present, people tend to want to "get closer" to it and to preserve it. **Repelling emotions**, by contrast, push us negatively away from somebody or something; we associate such negative emotions with anger, fear, shame, guilt, embarrassment, anxiety, disgust, or cowardice. The characteristic response of a repelling emotion is something like a "fight-or-flight" reaction in which we either try to avoid something or decide to face up to it in order to get rid of it. Of course, emotions do not always demand immediate action. Often we may love somebody and yet never talk to them, and we may be angry at those whom we must, by necessity, obey. But the lasting presence of such repelling emotion usually makes us try to get out of that situation, just as attracting emotions usually draw us toward something over time.[5]

The power of rhetorical discourse is often based upon its ability to harness this motivational power of emotions to encourage new beliefs and actions. The first step is to connect the right emotion to the right things. A rhetor who wishes an audience to reject something will inspire repelling emotions, while attracting emotions will be directed toward the object of the rhetor's preference. Usually, both of these effects are produced by loading up certain objects with positive or negative feelings. One of the basic strategies of advertising, for instance, is simply to show a product in association with pleasurable sensations (attractive people, a clean house, fresh breath, a healthy body) while associating its competitor with negative sensations (ugly people, a dirty apartment, bad breath, disease). These feelings then are bundled together in a particular way to make us desire or fear certain products and consequences. We then imagine ourselves owning this product through an imagined drama that culminates in us being popular, powerful, healthy, and wealthy. Our emotional attachment to this vision then leads us to buy a product.

After relating certain emotions to certain things, the second step is to either amplify or diminish the salience, or relative strength, of our emotional response. **Amplification** increases salience by exaggerating something and making it "larger than life" so that it stands out as important and demands our attention. This can be done both to attract us to something and to repel us from something. For instance, nations that go to war inevitably amplify the great virtues and material rewards that will come from victory, promising both glory and riches in order to attract soldiers to the battlefield. By contrast, pacifist critics amplify the inevitable consequences of war, including the death of civilians, the traumatic effects of war on soldiers, and the rise of militarism at home, in order to repel us from war. Likewise, **diminution** reduces something, pushes it into the background, and makes it insignificant and trivial. Naturally, diminution has an inverse relationship to attraction and repulsion than amplification. To encourage attracting emotions, diminution actually seeks to reduce the level of threat in order to make something seem benign and therefore harmless. For example, investors in a controversial plan for a nuclear energy plant to be built next to a nature preserve will diminish the possible impact of the plant on the environment (while amplifying its economic benefits). By contrast, to encourage repelling emotions, diminution will downplay the benefits in order to make an alternative not very worthwhile to pursue, as a critic of nuclear power might do when showing how the energy benefits are meager over the long-term compared to a more sustainable investment in wind and solar energy.

Pathos works in rhetoric, then, by dramatizing feelings and amplifying or diminishing aspects of our environment in such a way that we are actively attracted to or repelled by four categories of things—people, actions, events, and objects. **People** represent both individuals and groups (Rosa Parks, the National Academy of Sciences, the European Union); **actions** refer to conscious behavioral choices made by people (eating fast food, declaring war, philosophizing); **events** stand for time-bound, complex, moving situations that have a beginning, middle, and an end (a car accident, the Middle Ages, the Apocalypse); and **objects** represent entities that can be understood and named as discrete things. Objects might include physical entities, real and fictional (trees, unicorns, Africa, atoms, Dante's *Inferno*, a satellite, Pluto), or conceptual objects or ideas (justice, the law of gravity, Judaism, the Bill of Rights, gay marriage). To make us feel something strongly about something, then, a rhetor must make it stand out from our general environment and endow it with particular qualities that make it worthy of our attention and concern. That is why pathos is necessary in rhetoric. Out of the infinite aspects of our environment, a rhetor must select those things that are vital to address in any effort at a successful resolution. One must necessarily *amplify* and *exaggerate* these things in order for them to stand out and attain salience. Poor efforts at pathos will simply name emotions and tell us to feel them, as if emotions could simply be brought forth on command; effective uses of pathos will call them forth without needing a name. Rhetoric uses graphic examples to inspire emotions that make an audience turn away from one thing and toward another.

In other words, the essence of pathos is vivid description, not logical exposition. Whenever one gives formal reasons, detailed accounts, or logical analysis, one is using logos; the appeal is to one's cognitive belief structure based in propositions and facts. Pathos, by contrast, gives "life" to those beliefs. For example, a speaker can use logos to give a formal cost-benefit analysis for why addressing poverty helps people's lives at the same time that it improves the economy and cuts crime. But one can also describe the squalor of living in a slum, the diseases that beset a hungry child, the lost potential of dying addicts, and the success story of a person who discovered their inner potential through the help of a teacher. Pathos thus incorporates elements of narrative and style to sculpt powerful images that live in people's imaginations and make them *feel* ideas that logic can only *explain*. The best rhetoric, then, will always balance the use of pathos with a more reasonable logical analysis. There is nothing wrong with exaggeration when it is done for the purposes of getting an audience engaged and enthusiastic about an issue that it may have otherwise thought unimportant. One must simply supplement this enthusiasm with the kind of practical judgment that can be produced only through long and careful forethought and analysis.[6]

Fortunately, a good narrative can easily combine reason and emotion in such a way to reconcile the tension between logos and pathos. As many of the examples used in this book have shown, public speakers rarely restrict themselves to making explicit claims that are grounded in empirical data and warranted by logical reasoning. More often than not, their claims are embedded in narrative stories. These stories may be personal, moral, historical, fictional, or demonstrative, but *as stories* they all share a common aim—to give meaning to ideas by showing how they function over time in people's lives and in the environment in a way that is both pleasing as a story and plausible as an account. A narrative is thus more than a mere stringing together of events in chronological order. Even the timeline of someone's life, insofar as it has a beginning and an end, is not a narrative. A **narrative** is a dramatic story that creates a desire in an audience and then fulfills that desire by describing the interaction among agent, scene, act, purpose, and agency in such a way that brings about an emotional and cognitive unity.

The rhetorical aspect of narrative becomes clear once we are forced to choose between the validity of competing narratives about the same situation. In our interpersonal lives, we are constantly faced with this choice whenever we find ourselves caught in a dispute between mutual friends. Political situations are no different. When faced with competing narratives, an audience must decide which narrative is more "rational" to follow. Earlier we distinguished between **narrative fidelity**, or how accurately a narrative represents accepted facts, and **narrative probability**, or the coherence of the narrative as a story apart from the actual facts. The most effective narrative from a rhetorical standpoint should have both high narrative probability *and* high narrative fidelity. By presenting an argument in a form of a story that accurately represents reality in a coherent, engaging, and powerful manner, a speaker invites an audience to vicariously participate in a new vision of reality. Especially when narratives are broad in scope, these narratives can completely alter an audience's basic worldview. The narratives we tell of our common histories have particular power in structuring our social organizations, our self-conceptions, and our relationships with other groups. Logical rationality plays a crucial role in structuring these things as well, but more often than not they begin and end in narratives whose lasting impact is usually emotional.

The strategies in this chapter are therefore based on the premise that pathos is most persuasive when a rhetor attaches an attracting or repelling emotion to a specific type of "target" (a person, action, event, or object) and then amplifies that emotion through a dramatic narrative. Each of these strategies has been given a name, as follows:

Target of Pathos	Attracting Strategy (+)	Repelling Strategy (−)
People	Saint	Sinner
Actions	Virtue	Vice
Events	Utopia	Wasteland
Objects	Idol	Abomination

In each of the strategies, a rhetor has embedded a person, action, event, or object and made it a central factor (for good or evil) in a dramatic narrative that has both fidelity (insofar as it reflects reality) and plausibility (insofar as it tells a good story). Combining both fidelity and plausibility within a narrative is no easy task. A narrative that has fidelity without plausibility tends to reduce to an uninspiring recounting of details, whereas a narrative that has plausibility without fidelity is interpreted as a merely entertaining fiction. Only when an audience receives our stories as being both realistic and well told do they bring about the pathos that becomes a motive for action. It is therefore an ethical responsibility on the part of the speaker to create stories that actually represent a state of affairs and do not to slip into easy exaggeration and melodrama that play to the biases of an audience for the sake of short-term persuasive victory.

DISCUSSION

A major component of the art of interviewing is being able to amplify one's good qualities and diminish one's negative qualities, thereby bringing about attracting emotions in the interviewer concerning your status as a future employee. What was one of the most successful narratives that you told about yourself in an interview context (or any other situation in which you had to "impress" someone)? What was amplified and what was diminished? And what type of response did you get that told you it had been a success?

▶ UTOPIA

A utopia is a vision of a perfect event, understood as a state of affairs. This event can be personal and momentary, such as the moment parents witness the birth of their first child; it can be shared and historical, such as one's memories of a Golden Age; and it can be shared and futuristic, such as one's visions of the Promised Land. In all cases, the event is portrayed as the culmination of hopes and desires that we yearn to recapture in memory or in actuality. To employ **utopia** is to use the power of an ideal to reveal the limitations of one's actual situation and inspire hope that future "perfect" events will occur. Ronald Reagan, for instance, was famous for referring to the United States in such utopian terms, referring to it as a "Shining City on a Hill." Whenever rhetors engage in this form of amplification in which they outline some noble dream for the future or nostalgia for the past in order to inspire action, they are engaging in utopia.

This is not to say that utopia is always employed for noble sentiments. Some of the worst crimes in history have been perpetrated by those who use the power of utopia to justify acts of terror and oppression. Hitler used utopia when he went into ecstatic praise of his vision of a Third Reich that would last 1,000 years, and the medieval church used utopia when it inspired its Children's Crusade. Yet to abuse a tool does not condemn the tool. The speeches of the most adored and humane leaders of the twentieth century equally make use of utopia to liberate and empower. By creating a sense of dissatisfaction with one's present state of affairs and inspiring hope for the future, utopia is one of the most powerful manifestations of pathos. There is no social movement at any time that has not inspired its followers by envisioning a perfect state of affairs that will be brought about through struggle and effort on the part of the people. Consequently, although utopia can be something that spurs on the powerful to seek more power, utopia actually has the most direct impact for oppressed audiences that confront the direst of situations. When people feel they have nowhere to go but up, utopia inspires in them the hope that they can finally lift themselves up out of their conditions.

Emotions connected with utopia tend to cluster around hope, joy, patience, gratitude, and courage. Because utopia in rhetoric is almost always projected into the future, the glorious events that are promised to come generate in hearers a great pleasure in reveling in the act of imagining the images of what is to come. If the events are inevitable, there may be joy, patience, and gratitude. If the events, however, are still in doubt, then courage and hope are produced in order to ensure that this utopian future will come to be—emotions that carry with them an element of pain insofar as there remains a possibility that the utopia will be thwarted.

Tawakkol Karman: "In the End, This New World Will Inevitably Emerge"

One of the utopian movements of the early twenty-first century was the "Arab Spring." Sparked in 2010 by the Tunisian revolution, protests erupted all around the Arab world to resist dictatorships and struggle for new freedoms. Today we know that the Arab Spring was soon eclipsed by the horrors of the Syrian Civil War, but in 2011 there was still a sense of great hope in the air. Yemeni journalist and human rights activist Tawakkol Karman, founder of the organization Women Journalists Without Chains, expressed this utopian hope in her Nobel Peace Prize speech in 2011. She had been awarded the prize in order to recognize her work in nonviolent struggle for the safety of women and for women's rights in Yemen. In her speech, she recognized the challenges ahead but expressed that utopian optimism for inevitable victory that is common to all who struggle for social change:

> The revolutions of the Arab spring in Tunisia, Egypt, Libya, Yemen and Syria . . . in terms of motivation, driving power and objectives, didn't take place on isolated islands cut off from all the rapid and astonishing developments and changes which our world is witnessing. The Arab people have woken up just to see how poor a share of freedom, democracy and dignity they have. And they revolted. This experience is somewhat similar to the spring that swept throughout Eastern Europe after the downfall of the Soviet Union. The birth of democracies in Eastern Europe has been difficult and victory emerged only after bitter struggle against the then existing systems. Similarly, the Arab world is today witnessing the birth of a new world which tyrants and unjust rulers strive to oppose, but in the end, this new world will inevitably emerge.[7]

DISCUSSION

In light of subsequent history, do you think Karman's utopian optimism is misplaced, or do you believe that the inevitability of the birth of a new world will simply take more time? This is often the ethical question that lies behind the strategy of utopia. When is it appropriate to guarantee to an audience that a new world is dawning when one cannot, in actual fact, determine the future? Does the motivation and inspiration it provides in the present have subsequent drawbacks when hopes do not come to fruition?

▶ WASTELAND

The opposite of utopia is wasteland. Instead of playing on hope, it draws its power from disgust and fear produced by amplifying qualities in events that we find repulsive. Specifically, **wasteland** portrays a horrific event or state of affairs that we either wish to escape (if we are in it) or to avoid (if we are not). In other words, if utopia envisions Heaven, wasteland dramatizes Hell. Not surprisingly, especially for anyone who has seen Michelangelo's *The Last Judgment* or read Dante's *Inferno*, portrayals of wasteland are more graphic, more violent, more dramatic, and generally more exciting than portrayals of utopia. This is because whereas utopia presents a perfect state of affairs that typically has resolved all tensions, wasteland presents a state of affairs that is full of conflict and uncertainty. Thus, despite the fact that we yearn for utopia, when we are in it, there just isn't much to talk about. But we talk unendingly about our problems, which are full of suspense and shock and climax and struggle. Hence the discourse of wasteland is often paradoxically more prevalent and attractive than utopia because it is so graphic.

There are three types of situations in which wasteland is usually employed. First, wasteland can be used to motivate action by portraying one's current situation as so terrible as to be intolerable. To live in a wasteland is by necessity to seek utopia. Second, wasteland can be used to inhibit a path of action much as the slippery slope fallacy functions in logic. By picturing a horrible fate should one adopt the wrong path, wasteland warns against certain routes of action that will result in destruction. Consequently, this second form of argument is most effective in the opposite situations of the first. In these cases, wasteland most appeals to audiences who either are content with the current situation or are wary of making the wrong decisions because they have much to lose. Third, wasteland can be used to describe a past situation from which we have escaped, thereby making us content with our current lot by comparison. The first strategy motivates us to change, the second makes us fearful of change, and the third makes us content with the status quo.

Wasteland emphasizes the emotions of fear, sorrow, frustration, sadness, or regret. When the wasteland that is portrayed is one's present situation, emotions that accompany it are the pain of sorrow, frustration, sadness, and regret—all of these emotions dealing with something immediately present or recently passed that we wish could be otherwise. However, when wasteland is projected into a possible future—namely a future that will come to pass if we do not make the right decisions—then the primary emotion is one of fear and of a striking, visceral pain of imagining the terrifying events on the horizon. Predictably, then, wasteland remains one of the most powerful rhetorical techniques in generating fear as a motivating factor in rhetorical decision-making, for good or for ill.

Rachel Carson: "Everywhere Was a Shadow of Death"

For those who are passionate about the preservation of the environment, no strategy is more familiar to spark action than that of prophesizing a wasteland that is to come. With the threat of global warming looming over so much of the environmental debate today, it is important to recall that concern for the state of the global environment is a relatively recent phenomenon. It was only after 1962 that the environmental movement took on a much broader agenda of regulating human behavior so as to prevent large-scale ecological disaster. The key to this shift was Rachel Carson's book *Silent Spring*, which specifically warned of the dangers of using chemical pesticides and more generally argued for a wholesale shift in how we conceptualize our relationship to the natural environment. Her primary rhetorical strategy, as indicated by the title, was to predict the wasteland that would come about should we not alter our current practices. This is an excerpt from chapter 1 of her book, titled "A Fable for Tomorrow":

> There was once a town in the heart of America where all life seemed to live in harmony with its surroundings. The town lay in the midst of a checkerboard of prosperous farms, with fields of grain and hillsides of orchards where, in spring, white clouds of bloom drifted above the green fields. . . . Then a strange blight crept over the area and everything began to change. Some evil spell had settled on the community: mysterious maladies swept the flocks of

chickens; the cattle and sheep sickened and died. Everywhere was a shadow of death. . . . There was a strange stillness. The birds, for example— where had they gone? Many people spoke of them, puzzled and disturbed. The feeding stations in the backyards were deserted. The few birds seen anywhere were moribund; they trembled violently and could not fly. It was a spring without voices. . . . The roadsides, once so attractive, were now lined with browned and withered

> ## DISCUSSION
>
> If the strategy of utopia often risks raising false hopes, the strategy of wasteland is often criticized for a pessimism bordering on apocalypticism. Once again, as with utopia, the long-term effectiveness of one's rhetoric when it concerns events is how well one's predictions match up to future realities. Is it ethically justified to paint a horrific picture of a possible future which is unquestionably exaggerated if, indeed, it prevents people from making bad decisions that would have negative consequences?

vegetation as though swept by fire. These, too, were silent, deserted by all living things. Even the streams were now lifeless. Anglers no longer visited them, for all the fish had died.[8]

▶ VIRTUE

Whereas events are things that happen outside of our control, actions are things that we do with conscious intent and are connected specifically with our choices and our physical behaviors. If one volunteers to throw a party, that decision and its subsequent performance is an action. But the party itself, with all its unpredictable happenings and complex interactions, is an event. Actions are thus more specific and have a much more limited scope than events. But this limitation is also an advantage. It is only because we can focus our attention on particular types of actions that we can also improve them through care and skill and practice. The strategy of **virtue** is thus employed to help us identify the nature of specific types of actions that we find worthy of praise and to generate passionate commitment to cultivating these virtues. Usually, speakers draw from numerous instances of these actions, performed by a variety of usually ordinary individuals, each of whom shows how a specific type of behavior brings about some good consequence both in practical life and in the development of character. For instance, the biblical parable of the Good Samaritan praises the virtues of courage and charity by embodying these praiseworthy actions in such a way that is both memorable and powerful.

Usually we encounter this rhetorical strategy in educational environments, first in childhood and then in various religious environments. However, virtue also has rhetorical significance when a particular type of virtue needs to be called upon in a specific exigence in order to produce the necessary change to solve an urgent problem. In this case, the virtue might be present in an audience, but only in latent form. The rhetor thus needs to call upon these "reserves" of virtue by showing how the only way to overcome an obstacle is by harnessing the power of a specific type of virtue whose performance can meet short-term challenges and/or accomplish long-term goals. For instance, if a previously oppressed population is suddenly called upon to stage a mass protest against a violent regime, they will most certainly need to have the courage to withstand the inevitable crackdown that will follow. However, if their revolution is successful, the short-term necessity for courage will need to be tempered by a more long-term commitment to patience and humility if the revolution is not to simply continue the cycle of violence. It is therefore a sign of practical wisdom to know which virtue is the most important to call upon in any particular problematic situation.

Virtue focuses specifically on how we praise actions that arouse emotions of pride, humility, courage, guilt, and contentment. Virtue may, for instance, be used to praise the audience itself, as when a coach might praise the team for the victory by highlighting the virtues of teamwork. In this case, the emotions are of pride and contentment at achieving a level of virtue. However, more often than not, rhetoric in the context of persuasion often establishes ideals of virtue by which to motivate an audience that has not yet attained them or perfected them, as for instance when a team loses and the coach instead praises the virtues of the other team. In this case, praising the virtues produces a sense of humility, guilt, and courage insofar as the audience recognizes the degree to which it has failed to live up to the standards of virtue but is nonetheless committed to attain that level of excellence.

Pope Francis: "You Carry Out Your Work Inspired by Fraternal Love"

Pope Francis, formerly the Argentinian Cardinal Jorge Mario Bergoglio, became Pope in 2013 to great expectations. Being the first Pope named from a developing country, many hoped his Jesuit background and his work with the poor of South America would stimulate the mission of social justice in the Catholic Church. Since becoming pope, Francis has emphasized more than any of his predecessors the duty to help the poor and disenfranchised in the world that are left behind by global capitalism. In his speech at the Second World Meeting of the Popular Movements at the Expo Feria Exhibition Centre in Santa Cruz de la Sierra, Bolivia, in 2015, Francis praised the virtue of love as one of the most important tools for stimulating popular movements for reform across the globe:

> As members of popular movements, you carry out your work inspired by fraternal love, which you show in opposing social injustice. When we look into the eyes of the suffering, when we see the faces of the endangered campesino, the poor laborer, the downtrodden native, the homeless family, the persecuted migrant, the unemployed young person, the exploited child, the mother who lost her child in a shootout because the barrio was occupied by drugdealers, the father who lost his daughter to enslavement. . . . When we think of all those names and faces, our hearts break because of so much sorrow and pain. And we are deeply moved. . . . We are moved because "we have seen and heard" not a cold statistic

but the pain of a suffering humanity, our own pain, our own flesh. This is something quite different than abstract theorizing or eloquent indignation. It moves us; it makes us attentive to others in an effort to move forward together. That emotion which turns into community action is not something which can be understood by reason alone: it has a surplus of meaning which only peoples understand, and it gives a special feel to genuine popular movements.[9]

DISCUSSION

What is rhetorically significant about Pope Francis's praise of love is that he does not simply praise it as an abstract emotion or feeling; he defines it as a practice that is actualized only in our actions and behaviors toward others. How does his use of examples make his praise of virtue more concrete and more powerful? Can you think of other virtues that you often hear praised, and can you give concrete examples of how they might also be expressed rhetorically?

 ## VICE

The opposite of virtue is **vice**, a strategy that repels us from certain concrete actions by making them morally offensive and/or practically harmful. Even young children are familiar with the long list of vices that they are taught to shun by reading Aesop's Fables. From "The Boy Who Cried Wolf" (lying), to "Little Red Riding Hood" (disobedience), to "The Fox and the Crow" (vanity), each of these stories is meant to attach a stigma to certain types of actions in the hope that children will avoid the temptations that often culminate in self-destructive and socially condemned behaviors. Without such a consensus about vices (alongside necessary virtues), no society could hold together for very long. And like virtue, vice is also a strategy used to guide behavior in specific rhetorical situations. In these contexts, vice usually has two functions. First, it complements virtue by telling the audience what kind of actions they should avoid if they wish to meet the challenges of the hour. Usually this list includes such devices as selfishness, vengeance, pride, impulsiveness, and the like. Second, it creates motivation through polarization by condemning the vices of an opposing group; these vices almost always including some combination of arrogance, greed, corruption, and ignorance. Combined, these two strategies justify an audience's opposition to another group while instructing them on what actions to avoid if they are not to fall into the same vices as their opponents.

Not surprisingly, vice can be easily abused as a rhetorical strategy by all sides. As indicated in the discussion on polarization, nothing comes more naturally to social groups than the feeling of their own superiority and the inferiority of others. Just as those in power often see dissenters as ungrateful and disruptive agitators, those resisting power see themselves as noble martyrs standing up to the forces of evil. Consequently, it is extremely common to find two opposing parties accusing each other of the exact same vices. As with all rhetorical appeals, however, the ethics of the strategies is determined by the strength of their evidence and warrants. Pathos appeals, including even accusations of the most horrific vices, are ethical if they are backed by stories grounded in narrative fidelity, meaning that they come from legitimate sources and can be verified by third parties. Unfortunately, many of the most successful propaganda campaigns were based on stories of vice that were completely fabricated. In World War I, the British made great gains in public opinion through false stories of German soldiers who stabbed babies with bayonets and crucified Canadian soldiers on crosses. The sad irony is that the cynicism produced in the public by the realization that they had been manipulated made actual stories of even worse atrocities by the Nazis three decades later impossible to believe. There is, then, something to be said for the fable of the boy who cried wolf. The more we abuse the strategy of vice for short-term gain, the less effective it is when we must confront genuine "evils" in actual life.

The strategy of vice arouses the emotions of shame, shock, disappointment, disgust, and hate. Like that of virtue, the strategy of vice can be used in two ways. When a child has developed a series of bad habits at school, for instance, a parent uses a strategy of vice to produce a painful feeling of shame, disappointment, and perhaps even shock in the child who maybe had not realized how far they had fallen. But an alternative strategy can be used to try to warn the child ahead of time to avoid the bad effects of peer pressure by giving examples of vices that produce a somewhat pleasurable feeling—because the child stands above it—of disgust and even a hatred of such behavior so that they never fall into the habits. This sort of rhetoric is particularly common in athletic teams, the military, the family, and corporate environments in which teambuilding exercises centered around particular practices are essential to a properly functioning social group.

Steven Spielberg: "It Is All One Big Hate"

Few other artistic genres make use of exaggerated virtues and vices better than the Hollywood movie. Steven Spielberg is perhaps one of the most widely known and successful screenwriters, directors, and producers in Hollywood, earning early fame by exploiting such contrast between virtue and vice in his movies such as *Jaws, Raiders of the Lost Ark*, and *E.T.* However, his later films adopted a more serious and sober examination of human vices, particularly as they manifested in history. Movies such as *Schindler's List, Amistad, Saving Private Ryan*, and *Lincoln* all explored how our vices have played out in actual events. It is not surprising, then, that the topic of our vices—particularly the vice of tribalism—played a central role in his commencement address to Harvard University in 2016:

> As a kid, I was bullied—for being Jewish. This was upsetting, but compared to what my parents and grandparents had faced, it felt tame. Because we truly believed that anti-Semitism was fading. And we were wrong. Over the last two years, nearly 20,000 Jews have left Europe to find higher ground. And earlier this year, I was at the Israeli embassy when

President Obama stated the sad truth. He said: "We must confront the reality that around the world, anti-Semitism is on the rise. We cannot deny it.". . .

Now, I don't have to tell a crowd of Red Sox fans that we are wired for tribalism. But beyond rooting for the home team, tribalism has a much darker side. Instinctively and maybe even genetically, we divide the world into "us" and "them." So the burning question must be: How do all of us together find the "we"? How do we do that? There's still so much work to be done, and sometimes I feel the work hasn't even begun. And it's not just anti-Semitism that's surging—Islamophobia's on the rise, too. Because there's no difference between anyone who is discriminated against, whether it's the Muslims, or the Jews, or minorities on the border states, or the LGBT community—it is all one big hate.[10]

> **DISCUSSION**
>
> Almost any individual recognizes that the use of "us versus them" logic is a pervasive and problematic vice that is shared by almost all human cultures. However, we often find ourselves repeating this vice in different ways, usually offering reasons why our particular criticism of a "them" is both morally just and practically necessary. What are some of the ways in which we convince ourselves that our own "tribal" biases are more rational and justified than the biases of some other groups? How do we make our own vices exceptions to the rule?

▶ SAINT

There is a subtle but important difference between praising a person and praising a person's action. When praising a type of action (a virtue), the *specific* person performing the action does not make that much difference. It only matters that the character has certain general qualities that make him or her a certain *type* of person. For instance, in the story of the tortoise and the hare, we only need to know that the tortoise is a slow creature and the hare is a fast one so that, when they race, we are able to learn that the slow and steady runner will always beat the fast and fickle one. Consequently, one of the indicators of the strategy of virtue is that the characters are easily replaceable by other characters with similar qualities. For instance, one might tell the story of the farmer and the Wall Street banker and learn the same lesson as from the tortoise and the hare, when after a few years the farmer develops a successful organic fruit company while the Wall Street banker makes and then loses $10 million in an insider trading scheme. In virtue, the person doing the action is merely a placeholder for the activity and is effectively replaceable by other people with similar qualities.

To praise a person means to praise a specific individual (or a specific group of people acting as if they were an individual) with a unique combination of characteristics that makes him or her stand out as someone who cannot be replaced. The strategy of **saint** therefore holds up a particular person as worthy of our special attention, praise, and emulation both for his or her own sake as well as for our self-advancement. What makes the strategy of saint similar to that of virtue is that the reason we wish to honor this person is precisely because of his or her unique virtues. If we give a eulogy to one of our parents, we will highlight his or her acts of love and generosity and sacrifice and humor and courage that made that parent special. However, the point is not to praise any particular virtue or set of virtues; it is to highlight the manner in which a person embodied these virtues, which was greater than the sum of its parts. In other words, there is something "ineffable" about our saints that makes them impossible to ever completely define. We cannot, for example, go to great length praising the Good Samaritan precisely because the only thing we know about the Good Samaritan is that he was a Samaritan who stopped to help an injured person by the road. The only thing we can do is praise the action. A person, therefore, is more than the sum of a couple of virtues. A person embodies an infinite number of unique details and a host of contradictions that make him or her irreplaceable in the world.

Rhetorically, saint is used for one of two purposes. First, saint is used to legitimate authority by creating heroic images of leaders who stand above and apart from the everyday citizenry. This function has existed since the most ancient human civilizations and has also provided the impetus to create some of the most enduring monuments, such as the Egyptian pyramids. Although democratic political movements have significantly undermined the legitimacy of such grandiose strategies, one still finds exaggerated efforts at turning leaders into saints any time one encounters a relatively closed society or institution. Second, and more commonly, saint is used as a strategy to create identification by praising a particular individual with whom an audience feels a connection and feels it possible to emulate. This strategy is common to both families and to nations. Eulogies for beloved matriarchs or patriarchs of a large family perform the same function as eulogies to heroic or noble citizens who stood for the best that a country had to offer. Those who listen to such commemorative speeches are not made to feel that sense of divine awe, often combined with fear, that is produced by praising a superhuman leader; rather, they feel a unique kinship that comes with familiarity and affection, feelings that produce in an audience a desire to emulate this person and to be as much like them as they can.

To praise a saint is to make an audience feel a sense of love, charity, sympathy, pity, gratitude, or respect toward that person or group. The emotion we feel towards saints usually come in one of two forms. The things we hold up as exemplars for us to imitate and honor produce in us pleasurable feelings of love, gratitude, and respect that encourage us to seek them out as authorities. However, many of our saints are also ones who suffer because they are, as it were, too good for their environment. For these we feel charity, sympathy, and pity—combining both pleasure and pain—as we do when we hold up as examples individuals like Anne Frank, the young Jewish girl who survived in an attic for many years and left us a diary of her thoughts before finally being taken by the Nazis during World War II. Consequently, we wish to follow and emulate the first type of thing and honor and save the second type.

Lonnie Ali: "He Wanted Us to Use His Life and His Death as a Teaching Moment"

When boxer Mohammed Ali died in 2016, the world lost arguably one of the most recognizable and celebrated athletes of all time. Born Cassius Clay, Ali gained early celebrity by winning the gold medal in boxing at the 1960 Summer Olympics and then following this up by defeating Sonny Liston and earning the heavyweight title in 1964. Already controversial because of his outspoken and charismatic personality, he then sparked even more controversy by converting to Islam and changing his name to Mohammed Ali in 1964—a name that many sports announcers refused to recognize, with the notable exception of Howard Cosell. Then, in 1967, Ali was convicted and sentenced to five years in prison for publicly refusing to be conscripted into the U.S. military to fight in the Vietnam War, citing his religious beliefs and opposition to foreign war. Finally exonerated by the Supreme Court in 1971, Ali had become a symbol of courage and principled resistance for millions of people. At his funeral, his wife Lonnie recalled how her husband wished to set himself up as a role model for others—a "saint"—so that he might inspire young people to do great things:

Some years ago during his long struggle with Parkinson's in a meeting that included his closest advisers, Muhammad indicated that when the end came for him, he wanted us to use his life and his death as a teaching moment for young people, for his country and for the world. In effect, he wanted us to remind people who are suffering that he had seen the face of injustice. That he grew up under segregation, and that during his early life he was not free to be who he wanted to be. But he never became embittered enough to quit or to engage in violence. It was a time when a young black boy his age could be hung from a tree. Emmett Till in Money, Mississippi, in 1955, whose admitted killers went free. It was a time when Muhammad's friends, men that he admired, like brother Malcolm, Dr. King, were gunned down, and Nelson Mandela imprisoned for what they believed in. For his part, Muhammad faced federal prosecution. He was stripped of his title and his license to box, and he was sentenced to prison. But he would not be intimidated so as to abandon his principles and his values.[11]

DISCUSSION

It is notable that Mohammed Ali, despite being one of the most successful boxing champions of all time, wanted himself to be remembered for his integrity and courage in standing up for what he believed religiously, politically, and socially. How many other celebrities or public figures do we make "saints" for something other than what they had become famous for? By contrast, how many people do you know that you would consider "saints" but who practice their virtues quietly and behind the scenes? How would you praise such people if you had the opportunity to do so?

▶ SINNER

The counterpart of saint is sinner. In **sinner**, another person (or group that we feel justified in treating as if it were an individual) is portrayed in a negative light in order to make that person repellent to an audience. The strategy of sinner is a component of all polarization strategies that seek to divide the sheep from the goats by portraying the character of a particularly bad goat. As with saint, the key to this strategy is to make the "sinner" as unique a character as possible in such a way that makes him or her stand out as particularly reprehensible (even amongst sinners!). If the person is not described in detail, the strategy ends up becoming one of vice and becomes focused on a type of action rather than person (or type of person). There is a big difference between condemning the vice of violent persecution and condemning Hitler. A vice is something that anybody can do, but Hitler is a person that only Hitler can be. It is this level of detail that makes sinner an interesting rhetorical strategy. That is why stories about Satan, particularly in Hollywood movies, are far more interesting to us than hearing warnings about vices. Although we know what a vice is and produces, one never quite knows what Satan is going to do.

The rhetorical function of sinner is the opposite of saint. First, sinner undermines the legitimacy of authority by portraying the so-called "saints" in power as corrupt, cruel, and stupid. In relatively closed and oppressive societies, these rhetorical expressions often take the forms of underground literature or anonymous graffiti, whereas in relatively open and democratic societies, they take the form of ubiquitous negative advertising and political harangue. In both cases, however, the strategy is simply to de-legitimate current leadership. However, sinner is also used by the powerful to demonize the opposition, often through show trials and prosecutions that ideally force "confessions" by would-be sinners. Second, sinner is used for identification through polarization, creating specific images of the "not-us" so that groups know whom they are fighting against and whom they do not wish to become. In these cases, a particularly "bad apple" is held up as an example of the whole group and is often then, literally or proverbially, "hanged in effigy." As with all strategies using repelling emotions, the ethics of when to use sinner is very complicated. There are certainly times when a leader or representative of a group can be legitimately held up for condemnation and ridicule, but these times are usually rare. Most of the time, people are more mistaken than cruel, and attempts at understanding are usually more fruitful than melodramatic attempts to divide human beings into good and evil.

To employ the strategy of sinner is to make people feel anger, shame, contempt, disgust, or hate. We feel shame when we identify the sinner in some way with ourselves, as often happens in religious rhetoric when the aim is to produce in an audience a feeling of their own inadequacy and need for redemption. In this case, the pain of feeling shame is somewhat compensated by the hope of eventual redemption through utopia. But it is more frequent in political discourse that the sinner is located in an "out group" identified by the strategy of polarization. In this case, a sinner is held up as the embodiment of everything we should not be and who stands as a symbol for everything we are not or should not be. In this case, the pleasures and pains are reversed, the pain coming from the feelings of anger, contempt, disgust, or hate we feel toward that other person or group which is compensated by the pleasure in our own feelings of being superior to that other individual.

Camille Paglia: "I'm Sick and Tired of These New Historicists with Trust Funds"

Criticisms of university professors as privileged and out of touch have perhaps been around as long as the university itself. The metaphor of the "ivory tower," of professors from on high looking down at a world in which they do not participate or engage with, is today popular even amongst university professors. Camille Paglia has sought throughout her career to engage the public directly in different media, often appearing in *Salon* or *Time* magazine. Social critic, author, libertarian, and Professor of Humanities and Media Studies at the University of the Arts in Philadelphia, she has made a career of staking out controversial positions and criticizing popular trends in academia. In this extemporaneous talk, sponsored by M.I.T.'s Writing Program in 1991, Paglia lashed out at what was then a new trend in academics in order to reconsider traditional histories from a perspective that explicitly critiqued established powers and sought to recover previously marginalized voices—not necessarily because the endeavor was wrong, but because its practitioners were what she called "phonies":

> The problem of the last twenty years is that people think that "liberal" and "conservative" mean something. The liberal and conservative dichotomy is dead. The last time it was authentic was in the Fifties, when there really was an adversarial voice coming out of people I really respected, the New York Jewish intellectuals like Lionel Trilling and the people of Partisan Review. There was an authentic liberal versus conservative dichotomy at that time. But my generation of the Sixties, with all of our great ideals, destroyed liberalism, because of our excesses. We have to face that. And we have to look for something new right now.
>
> The situation right now is that we have on one side people who consider themselves leftists but to me, as far as academe is concerned, are phonies, people who have absolutely no credentials for political thinking, have no training in history, whose basic claim to politics is simply that nothing has happened to them in their

DISCUSSION

One can see from her language how the strategy of sinner often overlaps with that of vice. The difference is that sinner concentrates on the figure of the person who possesses those vices, whereas vice is an abstract process or action on its own. In this case, the "New Historicists" possess vices, but they are nonetheless specific people who do specific work and are recognizable as distinct human beings. Compare her language to that of the excerpt from Steven Spielberg, however. Do you think her language falls into the same "vice"? When is it appropriate to pick out an individual or class of people for specific ridicule in this way?

lives. A lot of these people have money. I'm sick and tired of these New Historicists with trust funds. I'm so sick and tired of it. And because they're pampered, their whole lives have been comfortable, because they've kissed asses all the way to the top, they have to show they're authentic by pretending sympathy for the poor lower classes, the poor victims.[12]

▶ IDOL

When we refer to objects, we refer to any identifiable and tangible part of our environment that is stable and familiar enough to label with a noun. Objects, therefore, do not simply mean discrete *physical things* such as trees and tables and pencils; they also include *organizations* such as schools and parliaments, and *processes* such as recycling and judicial review. Anything that we can define as a class of thing, with certain predictable characteristics associated with a common name, is an object. To make an idol out of an object is therefore to invest a common class of things with extraordinary qualities and powers that make those things worthy of reverence and worship. For instance, when we think of idols, we think of golden statues that possess magical forces that can be harnessed and used by the ones who possess them. The rhetorical strategy that goes by the name idol effectively is that which makes us feel this worshipful attitude toward objects. **Idol** is the attempt to invest an object with such attractive qualities that an audience seeks to possess, preserve, and/or use that object. For example, ads that lead us to believe that a car will make us sexy, computers will make us powerful, energy drinks will make us athletic, and cell phones will make us worldly all make use of idol. But idol is also used to justify "family values" policies by idolizing the two-parent middle-class home, to respond to an economic downturn by idolizing progressive tax increases on corporations, or to defend military aggression against a dictatorial state by idolizing parliamentary government. Any time a type of "thing" is held up as a solution to a problem because of its unique properties, one finds the strategy of idol.

There are three rhetorical situations in which idol is effective. First, idol is vital to any preservationist argument that wishes to protect something from being undermined or destroyed by changes in society. Here, idol invests an object with enough *intrinsic* value that people will seek to protect it, thereby making it a crucial strategy to defend the existence of things that may not have immediate utilitarian value, including buildings, works of art, nature preserves, social organizations, and many cultural traditions. Second, idol imagines a type of perfect object that might be created by ingenuity and effort, much as one might imagine a space station on Mars or a perfectly functioning democratic Congress. In this case, idol motivates us to action by setting forth the possibility that we might create something new in the world. Third, idol can be effectively used in rhetorical situations that require a choice from among objects that can be used as practical tools to achieve success. For example, debates over modern military strategy often come down to rhetorical battles over competing idols. Should we rely on smart bombs, air power, or boots on the ground? In politics, the Constitution often functions as an idol, as do institutions, political parties, and even bureaucratic procedures. Any time a *thing* (including laws and processes) is held up as a solution to some specific practical problem due to its instrumental value, one is employing idol to make a case.

Idol turns our attention to specific objects and makes us feel respect, interest, surprise, curiosity, or gratitude toward them. The emotions we feel about an idol often are not as strong as the other strategies of pathos. Idols are things we possess or benefit from in some way, so the feeling tends to be more utilitarian. Nonetheless, the things we praise as idols are often necessary for our way of life, as when we praise the Constitution, free speech, the rule of law, democratic institutions, smart phones, and text messaging. Sometimes we are surprised and curious about our idols, particularly when we realize the benefits that we gain from things that we often take for granted, like electricity. But most of the time we feel respect, interest, and gratitude, for all of the objects around us that help us achieve a level of happiness.

Malala Yousafzai: "The Extremists Are Afraid of Books and Pens"

Although the term "idol" may have a negative connotation, many objects should, in fact, be idolized in the sense of being praised and respected for what they are and can produce. Indeed, many social movements are actually motivated in part by idols. Take the case of Malala Yousafzai, a young girl from Pakistan who became known worldwide after being shot in the head by a Taliban assassin in 2012 in retribution for advocating for girls' education. Ironically, her survival from the shooting gave her an even more powerful platform to advance her agenda for educating young girls not only in Pakistan but throughout the developing world. For her work, she was awarded the Nobel Peace Prize in 2014, becoming the youngest person to receive it. In her speech, she praised a very simple idol—books and pens—as the key to social reform in Pakistan:

The wise saying, "The pen is mightier than sword" was true. The extremists are afraid of books and pens. The power of education frightens them. They are afraid of women. The power of the voice of women frightens them. . . . I remember that there was a boy in our school who was asked by a journalist, "Why are the Taliban against education?" He answered very simply. By pointing to his book he said, "A Talib doesn't know what is written inside this book." They think that God is a tiny, little conservative being who would send girls to the hell just because of going to school. . . . Pashtuns want education for their daughters and sons. And Islam is a religion of peace, humanity and brotherhood. Islam says that it is not only each child's right to get education, rather it is their duty and responsibility.[13]

> ### DISCUSSION
>
> What does it mean to praise the power of an object like a "book"? How do we look at objects differently when we praise them in this way and give them a kind of agency on their own. What other objects do we often idolize in our everyday life? Certainly, advertising makes a business out of idolization. However, what are some of the subtle ways that we idolize common objects to ourselves or even to each other?

▶ ABOMINATION

The opposite of idol is **abomination**, which is the attempt to make an object seem so repellent that an audience ignores, shuns, discards, or destroys it. If the idol is what gives one special power by possessing it, an abomination is something that gives one a demonic power or actively drains power away from a person. A perfect example of an abomination in literature is the "One Ring" from J.R.R. Tolkien's *Lord of the Rings* trilogy, a ring that promises its wearer great power while at the same time isolating and weakening its wearer until he or she becomes a mere wraith. Abominations make up that special class of objects that often appear to us as benign or beneficial but in fact damage us or our environment by their use. For example, cultural critics often define objects such as pop music, television, video games, pornography, and fast food as abominations that suck the life out of the young generation. Likewise, critics of political culture use abomination to categorize laws, governing bodies, corporations, political parties, or even symbols as things that impede human progress. An abomination, therefore, is not simply something that we don't like and that has distasteful qualities; it is a thing that is an active threat to our well-being and is seductive enough to warrant special condemnation.

Abomination performs the exact opposite rhetorical functions as idol. First, instead of attempting to preserve objects, it seeks to point out the things in our environment that need to be eradicated or at the very least controlled and regulated. It is an old story that the idols of the young generation are the abominations of the older generation, a story that is not soon to end. Second, abomination warns against pursuing certain goals because of what might be produced as a result. For instance, pursuit of cloning is not necessarily done by sinners or engaged in as a vice, as this research is done by scientists undertaking technical research in the hopes of scientific progress, but that particular line of research might end up with various "abominations," such as a father's daughter who grows up to look like his deceased wife. Third, abomination tells us to avoid using certain tools because of their disastrous effects, much as demonic idols, once used, take over the user and bring about devastation in the form of a wasteland.

To use abomination is to make people feel disgust, fear, aversion, indifference, worry, annoyance, or hate about an object. Abominations bring about more powerful emotions than idols precisely because they are perceived as threats to our well-being. We also tend to see in abominations certain nefarious intent, thereby tending to anthropomorphize objects and make them more menacing. For instance, almost all new technologies at some point have been turned into abominations because they threaten established ways of life—consider how the telephone, the radio, and the television broke through the wall of the home and disrupted the Victorian family. The fear brought down by abomination is thus almost always tied to a fear of bringing about a wasteland insofar as the object then becomes responsible for creating the event, as when science fiction projects a wasteland into the future based on the horrific consequences of some technological development such as artificial intelligence. Abomination thus brings about acute pain at imagining a certain object in the midst of one's habitat and a visceral pleasure in imagining it destroyed.

Wael Ghonim: "My Online World Became a Battleground Filled with Trolls"

Today, technology has most certainly become an idol. With the ubiquity of digital media and smart phones, our utopian visions are more often than not influenced by our faith in technology. However, there are always dark sides to technologies. Wael Ghonim has experienced both sides of the story. In 2011, he became an international figure after spending 11 days being incarcerated and interrogated by Egyptian police after helping to create a Facebook page called "We Are All Khaled Said" to honor a young Egyptian man who had been tortured and killed by that same police force. This Facebook page helped energize pro-democracy demonstrations in Egypt, and the experience eventually led Ghonim to write an optimistic book, *Revolution 2.0: The Power of People Is Greater Than the People in Power*. However, his subsequent experience in Egypt was less than utopian, and in a reflective TED talk in 2016 Ghonim described how the very social media that had sparked the revolution had become something of an abomination afterwards:

The post-revolution events were like a punch in the gut. The euphoria faded, we failed to build consensus, and the political struggle led to intense polarization. Social media only amplified that state, by facilitating the spread of misinformation, rumors, echo chambers and hate speech. The environment was purely toxic. My online world became a battleground filled with trolls, lies, hate speech. I started to worry about the safety of my family. . . . It became clear to me that while it's true that polarization is primarily driven by our human behavior, social media shapes this behavior and magnifies its impact. Say you want to say something that is not based on a fact, pick a fight or ignore someone that you don't like. These are all natural human impulses, but because of technology, acting on these impulses is only one click away.[14]

DISCUSSION

What are the ways in which objects like the smart phone and its accompanying social media apps influence or even determine the behavior of individuals and groups? Do you ever feel that the mere presence of an object within a social environment determines how people interact with one another? Do certain objects license certain behaviors while preventing others? How can our praise or blame of objects help create environments that are more productive for deliberation and creating meaningful shared experiences?

▶ SUMMARY

Pathos represents a form of proof that legitimates our attitudes toward objects, events, people, and actions in our environment based on how we feel about them. Although often criticized for being "irrational" forms of persuasion, pathos arguments are both unavoidable and necessary. In the first case, they are unavoidable because our language is always loaded with emotional connotations and judgments that influence the way we describe our environment. It makes a world of difference, for instance, whether or not we introduce someone as a "friend" or a "boyfriend/girlfriend." Both of these terms might be technically accurate, but our selection of one over the other carries with it significant emotional significance about how we feel about this person. Moreover, to think one can escape from pathos simply by speaking in purely technical jargon is not to leave pathos behind, but to show oneself as "apathetic," or without emotional concern—itself an emotional proof. In the second case, pathos arguments are necessary because we cannot form elaborate rational judgments based on statistically good evidence about every single thing in our environment. Most of our behavior toward the people, objects, events, and actions that we encounter in our world is guided by largely emotional judgments of liking and disliking rather than true and false. Without the complex of emotional judgments about our world, we would have no background framework to make the careful logical judgments that are required in specific affairs.

We generate proofs of pathos largely by constructing narratives that show the object of interest interacting in a situation that produces an emotional response. To say that "I met an evil man yesterday" does not produce pathos simply because one labels a person with the epithet "evil." One has to show how this man interacts with his world in order for us to form an emotional judgment about him. There is a big emotional difference, for instance, between a description of a man who is poisoning a stream because he carelessly discharges wastewater from his chemical factory and a man who poisons a stream because he wishes to kill all the people in a village. We may have warrant to label both men as being "evil," but the emotions are different based on the different narratives. We may feel that the first man is evil because he is greedy and indifferent to the pain of others, whereas the second person is evil because he is cruel and inhuman. Either way, the dramatization of the *way* in which we think he is evil is what produces the emotion, not the label itself. In fact, it is often better in pathos arguments to leave the "labeling" of the emotion or characteristic to the audience. This allows them to participate in the construction of the argument without simply following the words of the speaker.

Each pair of pathos arguments generates attracting or repelling emotions to a certain type of thing. *Utopia* and *wasteland* produce emotional responses to discrete events or more enduring situations. In other words, we celebrate or condemn certain specific events in our lives, such as the moment we caught the touchdown pass or the day we heard about the death of a loved one, much in the same way that we celebrate or condemn whole eras in history, such as the Golden Age of Rome or the horrors of World War I. Each of these examples represents a certain state of affairs that we either wish to reproduce or hope never happens again, and has as its rhetorical function to validate or condemn certain courses of action that will produce these states of affairs. *Virtue* and *vice* share with utopia and wasteland a focus on activity, but these arguments emphasize the worthy or unworthiness of the action being performed by people rather than by the quality of the events produced by those actions. In virtue and vice, we either admire certain habits of action for their own intrinsic value or condemn habits of action for their complete lack of it, often regardless of the consequences. For instance, it is a virtue to courageously stand one's ground, and it is a vice to always cowardly flee resistance, even if the first might kill you and the second save your life in specific situations. But we usually believe that virtue brings about long-term goods nonetheless, and that those goods include not just practical survival but the goods of feelings of self-worth and the development of character. Rhetorically, then, the power of virtue and vice is to help cultivate the types of practices that we find valuable in society and that we believe are necessary for the development of culture and civilization.

The third pair of pathos arguments differs from the first two because it focuses on our feelings about specific, tangible things rather than types of events or activities. With *saint* and *sinner*, we are encouraged to respect or condemn specific people or more general types of people who can be considered collectively as an individual. For instance, politicians during the Red Scare might praise Joseph McCarthy as a saint while condemning the generic "Communist" as a sinner, therefore justifying their allegiance to McCarthy as he attempts to identify the various "sinners" in the State Department. Rhetorically, the point of this strategy is to populate our environment with friends and enemies, to tell us whom to trust and whom to avoid, and generally to say whom we should emulate and whom we should condemn. Last, *idol* and *abomination* arguments perform the same function for the various "things" in our world, including not only physical things such as books and televisions but also procedural things such as laws and constitutions, and conceptual things such as evolutionary theory or Christianity. Anything we think we can describe as a discrete or general thing with stable qualities that we can define is an object. Rhetorically, idol and abomination therefore tell us what kinds of things we should think about and surround ourselves with in order to produce a good life and a good character.

Overall, then, the function of pathos is to make us feel like we are in a specific situation with specific types of people doing specific types of actions with specific kinds of objects. The more we can graphically dramatize the situation in which we are in, the more we feel an emotional connection to that situation and the more we are motivated to act or think in a specific way. Without emotions, we might be able to logically construct reasons for why things happen or what we should do, but these reasons are not intimately connected to us personally in a way that makes us care about them. These explanations would simply exist for us like any number of graphs or charts or line drawings or pictures. Pathos is what brings a situation to life and makes us passionate about it; the absence of pathos, then, is not "reason" but barrenness.

▶ CHAPTER 9 EXERCISES

1. **IMPROMPTU:** Practice all of the different strategies of arousing pathos. Imagine all the people, objects, actions, and events that are associated with a family household. Assign a different strategy to each student in the class. Now imagine the different emotions, positive or negative, that we might associate with each of the four categories. For instance, what objects in the house tend to be conducive or destructive to family coherence? What individual (or type of individual) can you praise or blame? What habits and actions tend to produce harmony or dissension? And what types of events go on in a household as a result of all of the factors that are desirable or undesirable? Write a very short speech answering these questions based on your assigned strategy.

2. **DEBATE:** Divide the class into two and consider the topic of whether the object of the "smart phone" has been a net benefit or a net detriment to a happy social life and productive political culture. Then subdivide each group to develop three separate argumentative strategies, the first dealing with whether or not the smart phone is an idol or abomination; the second dealing with whether the actions that we associate with smart phones are virtues or vices; the third dealing with whether culture as a whole has become a utopia or wasteland. Have each subgroup take turns presenting their arguments pro and con and take a vote at the end of class.

3. **GROUP:** Break into groups and have each group design and develop a new "product" to put on the market that fits some urgent need for students. Develop a sales pitch that touches on all four strategies of pathos. First, develop an idol to praise for its intrinsic qualities and excellence. Second, create a saintly persona for this object who praises himself or herself for having had the wisdom to choose such an object. Third, praise the actions that one can perform with this object that make one virtuous. Last, imagine the utopia that arises once this object becomes a part of your life.

4. **TAKE HOME:** Search for a recent editorial in a major newspaper by looking online. Find an editorial that makes use of pathos to make its argument. Circle the passages in which the author makes an emotional appeal and label it. Present your findings to the class by reading out the specific passage and asking the class to identify the strategy.

5. **VIDEO:** Identify a particular "virtue" that you possess that you think makes you somewhat distinctive. This virtue can be any type of action worthy of praise, whether it is simply a good habit, such as always picking up litter that one sees along the roadside, or whether it is a particular skill or practice in which you demonstrate excellence, such as cooking, musical performance, or athletics. Make a short video in which you talk about this virtue and demonstrate it in practice while at the same time trying to seem humble and grateful.

▶ **NOTES**

1. Aristotle, *On Rhetoric: A Theory of Civic Discourse*, trans. George Kennedy (Oxford, UK: Oxford University Press, 1991), 1378a.

2. This makes emotions different than **moods**, which tend to be pervasive qualities of a person's personality that affect his or her cognitive processing in all situational contexts (as when a "depressed" person

always interprets things differently than one who is an "optimist"). Emotions, by contrast, are always specific. We love some*body* and we fear some*thing*. Emotions do not simply exist in a void. They are always responses to some aspect of our environment. Richard J. Davidson, "On Emotion, Mood, and Related Affective Constructs," in *The Nature of Emotion: Fundamental Questions*, ed. Paul Ekman and Richard J. Davidson (Oxford, UK: Oxford University Press, 1994), 51–55.

3. John Dewey, *Art as Experience* (New York: Perigree Books, 1934), 20.

4. Dewey, *Art as Experience*, 41.

5. For a review of different perspectives on emotion, see Randolph R. Cornelius, *The Science of Emotion: Research and Tradition in the Psychology of Emotions* (Saddle River, NJ: Prentice Hall, 1996).

6. For the relationship between reason and emotion, see John M. Cooper, *Reason and Emotion: Essays on Ancient Moral Psychology and Ethical Theory* (Princeton, NJ: Princeton University Press, 1999).

7. Tawakkol Karman, "Nobel Prize Speech," available at www.nobelprize.org/nobel_prizes/peace/laureates/2011/karman-lecture_en.html (accessed 20 August 2016).

8. Rachel Carson, "A Fable for Tomorrow," available at http://core.ecu.edu/soci/juskaa/SOCI3222/carson.html (accessed 20 August 2016).

9. Pope Francis, "Speech on the Poor and Indigenous Peoples," available at http://time.com/3952885/pope-francis-bolivia-poverty-speech-transcript/ (accessed 20 August 2016).

10. Steven Spielberg, "Commencement Speech to Harvard University," available at www.entrepreneur.com/article/276561 (accessed 20 August 2016).

11. Lonnie Ali, "Eulogy for Muhammed Ali," available at www.nytimes.com/2016/06/11/sports/lonnie-billy-crystal-bill-clinton-eulogies-for-muhammad-ali.html (accessed 20 August 2016).

12. Camille Paglia, "Crisis in the American Universities," available at http://gos.sbc.edu/p/paglia.html (accessed 20 August 2016).

13. Malala Yousafzai, "Speech at the United Nations," available at https://secure.aworldatschool.org/page/content/the-text-of-malala-yousafzais-speech-at-the-united-nations/ (accessed 20 August 2016).

14. Wael Ghonim, "Let's Design a Social Media That Drives Real Change," available at www.ted.com/talks/wael_ghonim_let_s_design_social_media_that_drives_real_change/transcript?language=en (accessed 20 August 2016).

10

Eloquence

This chapter defines the ultimate goal of a speech as the accomplishment of eloquence. It describes eloquence as a quality not so much of the speech but of the experience produced by the speech, an experience defined in terms of the ability to address the particular demands of a situation while also pointing to more universal values, goals, and truths that inspire people to greater thoughts and feelings. It then proposes two methods for producing eloquence. The first method is to structure the speech around a dramatistic symbol that provides a coherent and recognizable narrative form. Often making use of analogical reasoning, a dramatistic symbol draws parallels between a specific exigence and a more familiar character or situation in order to clarify its meaning and establish purpose. The second method is to use one of the major poetic categories of the heroic, the tragic, or the comic in order to try to give an overarching dramatic structure that helps portray characters and plot in a coherent way. The goal of eloquence is to combine all of the previous methods of persuasion into a powerful dramatic telling that advances a prudent judgment while encouraging the audience to look to broader horizons of meaning.

The mastery of eloquence is the culmination of the art of rhetoric. As it was introduced in the introduction to this book, eloquence is something more than just pretty-sounding words; **eloquence** is a type of experience produced when an oration achieves the heights of aesthetic form in such a way that carries an audience beyond itself while simultaneously bringing illumination to the particulars of the audience's situation. The way that eloquent rhetoric addresses us can best be explained by pointing to the speech that is consistently ranked as the greatest oration in American history: Martin Luther King Jr.'s "I Have a Dream" speech. What gave that speech such unique power was King's ability to take the particular challenge of civil rights reform in the United States and see it as part of a larger historical and spiritual journey of the nation toward universal freedom for all, all the while drawing from vivid metaphorical imagery that made his "dream" tangible to the audience's imagination.

Eloquence thus achieves more than simply confronting a particular rhetorical exigence with prudence and timeliness, as important and as necessary as is that function. All rhetoric involves advocating choices in moments of uncertainty and urgency. However, eloquent rhetoric attempts to expand the boundaries of meaning to encompass more than the immediate appearances that trouble us, thus moving us from a concern for immediate action to a capacity for reflective thought. This means eloquent rhetoric makes us look at the situation from a distance and see it in the light of history, of truth, of beauty, and of the higher values that inspire us to think great thoughts and perform great deeds. In summary, eloquence is the effect of great rhetoric that (a) emerges in a moment of uncertainty or contingency, (b) addresses the particular appearances at issue, and (c) appeals to the critical judgment and ordinary convictions of others, while at the same time (d) offering a breadth of vision that inspires an audience to dwell in a more general sphere of thought, meaning, and reflection. For example, when King delivered his "Dream" speech, he spoke at a time in which segregation and racial violence remained a reality in the country and when the possibility of civil rights legislation was still unrealized. He addressed the particular "appearances" at issue when he addressed the sights, sounds, and feelings that constantly confronted African Americans at the time—police batons, jail cells, "whites only" signs, poverty, and the ghetto. He appealed to the critical judgment when he called upon Americans to condemn acts of racial injustice and support laws enforcing equality of opportunity. But most importantly, he offered a breath of vision that soared over the natural and social geography of the nation, its valleys and mountains and streams as well as its many diverse racial, ethnic, and religious communities, bringing all of these elements into a narrative whole that roused the appetites of the audience and carried them through a drama that satisfied their desire to envision and pursue a better world.

We have defined eloquence, in effect, as an ability to wed together particular realities and appearances with more universal meanings and possibilities. A **particular reality** means a discrete entity that is unique in the world, usually indicated by words like "this" or "that." For example, although there are many schools in the world, you may attend *this* particular school with all of its unique history and idiosyncratic qualities. A **particular appearance**, then, refers to a unique way in which a particular reality shows itself to a person at a particular time and place. "Appearance" is thus not the opposite of "reality," but rather signifies the way a reality reveals itself and encountered by someone. For instance, although the school is a particular reality, one might encounter it through multiple appearances, such as sitting in one of its classrooms, driving past it in a car, or finding its doors locked. By contrast, a **universal meaning** is an abstract concept, embodied in a language, that is used to interpret and conceptualize a large number of things. The word "school" is used to describe an infinite number of particular realities in order to define its general character as a place in which children are educated. A **universal possibility** is thus a shared general meaning that might not exist yet in reality but that we believe we might be able to achieve through imagination, cognition, and effort. For instance, at the time of King's speech, it was still only a possibility in many parts of the country, despite efforts at desegregation, that black and white children could attend school together and judge one another not by the color of their skin but by the content of their character.

Eloquence is thus an hortatory term that we give to a type of speech that lifts us out of the ordinary, that connects our individual lives and experiences with something larger than ourselves and which inspires us to be better than we are. Eloquence thus tries to navigate between two competing poles of rhetoric. On the one side, there is a technical, formulaic, pedantic kind of rhetoric that lists details, facts, statistics, individual experiences, personal opinions, and current affairs in such a way that makes us think only about our specific moment in the present, our idiosyncratic fears and desires, our mundane lives. This is a kind of rhetoric that overemphasizes particularity. On the other side, there is a rhetoric that tries to achieve uplift and grandiosity but which largely dwells in the abstract, the theoretical, the mystical, the overly poetic, the vague and obscure, and the cliché. This is a rhetoric that overemphasizes universality. To achieve eloquence, however, is not simply to combine both of these elements so that one goes back and forth between a laundry list of particularities and a host of vague maxims and metaphors. Eloquence is a way of making us feel more powerfully about our particular experiences by investing them with universal meanings and significance. In short, it is a way of reminding an audience that each of its members plays an important role in history and that all of us are connected in a way that makes life more noble.

▶ FORM

As discussed in the chapter on arrangement, great rhetoric is the product of form, in which form represents a dramatic progression that rouses an audience's appetites, gradually moves them through a logical and narrative structure, and cumulatively builds toward a resolution that satisfies their appetites. Usually this means beginning with the particulars of a situation, putting those particulars in relationship to other particulars, and then gradually showing how the interaction of these realities and appearances reveals more universal meanings and possibilities that open up a grander vision of a situation that had not been previously recognized. To better grasp the meaning of form, we can look at two types of form defined by Kenneth Burke in his discussion on rhetoric:[1]

1. **Syllogistic form** is a form of a logical sequence, each step leading to the next in a predictable and causal order. Often associated with legal and scientific reasoning, syllogistic form is produced when a conclusion (E) is asserted in the introduction and then followed by a clear sequence of stages that go from A to E through stages B, C, and D. In syllogistic form, the pleasure comes in using logical reasoning to trace out the consequences of an action or to determine the cause of why something came to be. In popular culture, the genres of the detective story and the crime drama make use of syllogistic form to show how all the pieces fit together in a series of "if-then" statements.

2. **Qualitative form** occurs when certain qualities in a work of art prepare the way for another quality that is emotionally satisfying but without logical determination. This can best be understood by interpreting "quality" and "state of mind" to mean an emotional state brought about by experiencing a part of a work of art, as when a person opening a door in a horror movie brings about suspense and when the final encounter with the villain produces excitement. By qualitative form, Burke thus means an arrangement of scenes whereby each emotion prepares the way for the next one, as when suspense produces relief, relief gives way to calmness, calmness sets the stage for curiosity, curiosity prepares us for fear, and fear makes us ready for courage.

The interaction of syllogistic and qualitative form in a work of art gives it logical coherence and emotional continuity, respectively. Syllogistic form puts the pieces in order so that we understand why one thing led to another thing and produced a final result. Qualitative form gives us emotional variety while at the same time giving it a "flow" that allows emotional transitions without jarring effects and gaps. In a speech, syllogistic and qualitative form carries us from the beginning to the end in a way that rouses and satisfies our curiosities and desires.

The challenge of eloquence is therefore to find a way to reveal universal significance within particular situations by rousing and satisfying an audience's appetites through the cumulative development and consummation of form. Although this task is a daunting one, it can be made more accessible by approaching it methodologically rather than by simply assuming that eloquence is a product of "genius." Eloquence does not spring readymade from the mind of genius. It is produced through hard work and a dedication to craft. This chapter will focus on two central methods of producing eloquence—the creation of a dramatistic symbol and the employment of poetic categories. These strategies are introduced in this final chapter because they require mastery of all the other skills beforehand. Until one has completely understood the nature of a rhetorical situation and the structure of ethos, pathos, and logos, attempts at eloquence will fall flat and reduced to one of the two types of failed rhetoric. Only after mastering the parts can we finally constitute a meaningful whole.

Thomas Jefferson: "We Hold These Truths to Be Self-Evident, That All Men Are Created Equal"

The Declaration of Independence is commonly cited as one of the most eloquent expressions of the desire for political liberty ever written. Its words have continually been called upon by subsequent rhetors across the globe to advocate for all manner of causes, not the least of which have been civil rights and women's rights. Not only is it eloquent itself, but it has inspired innumerable acts of eloquence, both in the United States and internationally. One of the reasons for its eloquence is precisely its ability to create a meaningful and active relationship between a particular situation and universal meanings. Jefferson chooses neither to simply enumerate, in legalistic fashion, the specific injustices done by the King of England, nor to pronounce, in philosophical fashion, the abstract principles on which good government must be founded.

Instead, he invokes radical universal principles in order to justify a specific act of revolution in response to an immediate exigence, thereby appealing simultaneously to our practical wisdom, which seeks prudent action in the present, and our contemplative reason, which aspires to grasp transcendent laws. Jefferson begins by defining the universal meanings and possibilities relevant to the situation:

> When in the Course of human events, it becomes necessary for one people to dissolve the political bands which have connected them with another, and to assume among the powers of the earth, the separate and equal station to which the Laws of Nature and of Nature's God entitle them, a decent respect to the opinions of mankind requires that they should declare the causes which impel them to the separation.

> We hold these truths to be self-evident, that all men are created equal, that they are endowed by their Creator with certain unalienable Rights, that among these are Life, Liberty and the pursuit of Happiness, that to secure these rights, Governments are instituted among Men, deriving their just powers from the consent of the governed, that whenever any Form of Government becomes destructive of these ends, it is the Right of the People to alter or to abolish it, and to institute new Government, laying its foundation on such principles and organizing its powers in such form, as to them shall seem most likely to effect their Safety and Happiness. Prudence, indeed, will dictate that Governments long established should not be changed for light and transient causes; and accordingly all experience hath shewn, that mankind are more disposed to suffer, while evils are sufferable, than to right themselves by abolishing the forms to which they are accustomed. But when a long train of abuses and usurpations, pursuing invariably the same Object evinces a design to reduce them under absolute Despotism, it is their right, it is their duty, to throw off such Government, and to provide new Guards for their future security. Such has been the patient sufferance of these Colonies; and such is now the necessity which constrains them to alter their former Systems of Government. The history of the present King of Great Britain is a history of repeated injuries and usurpations, all having in direct object the establishment of an absolute Tyranny over these States. To prove this, let Facts be submitted to a candid world.[2]

The universal meanings are the radical principles that Jefferson set forth that he believes are applicable to all people at all times—that all men are created equal, that people have the right to abolish an oppressive government and institute a new one of their own choosing, and that the end of government is not simply security or material profit but life, liberty, and the pursuit of happiness. The universal possibilities he imagines grow out of these universal meanings. No government at any time, either at that point in history or today, has ever achieved such ends in their pure form, although one can argue that we have certainly approached a closer approximation. Nonetheless, believing that such possibilities can be achieved by any people with the courage to pursue them is inspiring, particularly when such possibilities are grounded in self-evident truths. Then, having lifted his audience to the height of universal perspective, Jefferson returns to the particular realities and appearances that confronted the colonists at that point in time and that

Jefferson attributes to the direct actions of the King of England. Here are just a few of the more graphic examples he uses:

> He has abdicated Government here, by declaring us out of his Protection and waging War against us.

> He has plundered our seas, ravaged our Coasts, burnt our towns, and destroyed the lives of our people.

> He is at this time transporting large Armies of foreign Mercenaries to compleat the works of death, desolation and tyranny, already begun with circumstances of Cruelty & perfidy scarcely paralleled in the most barbarous ages, and totally unworthy the Head of a civilized nation.

> He has constrained our fellow Citizens taken Captive on the high Seas to bear Arms against their Country, to become the executioners of their friends and Brethren, or to fall themselves by their Hands.[3]

Once again, the difference between a particular reality and a particular appearance is merely one of degree. Particular realities are things that we know exist and are facts that we can confirm. That the King of England is transporting armies of mercenaries, that he has ordered colonists to work on English ships against their will, and that he has burnt buildings in certain towns are facts that can be proven true or false. Particular appearances are ways that realities appear to us when seen in a certain light. Through his detailed use of language, Jefferson makes the king of England appear to be a barbarous brute and dictator and calls up horrific images of colonists being forced to execute their brothers on the high seas because of the threat of death. Jefferson thus does not seek to enumerate the facts on the ground; he wishes these facts to appear to us in a certain way so that we are disgusted and repulsed by them, thereby calling forth pathos. The final rhetorical gesture appears in the conclusion, when he declares

DISCUSSION

It was not soon lost on many readers of the Declaration of Independence that its universal possibilities were contradicted by the particular realities of the United States, not only in the eighteenth century but also up until the present. Thomas Jefferson directed his complaints to Great Britain, but at the time slavery remained an institution in the colonies, women remained without many of the rights of men, and Native Americans were being systematically forced from their lands. Yet the Declaration has remained a touchstone of the highest ideals of human freedom both in the United States and around the world. Given these contradictions, how does one have to read the Declaration of Independence today in order for it to achieve "eloquence" without, at the same time, ignoring the complicated realities that seem to tarnish its legacy?

the United States of America free from Great Britain and makes a commitment on their behalf: "And for the support of this Declaration, with a firm reliance on the protection of divine Providence, we mutually pledge to each other our Lives, our Fortunes, and our sacred Honor." Here is a practical judgment made in a rhetorical situation in light of universal meanings and possibilities that inspire courage and faith.

▶ DRAMATISTIC SYMBOL

Although eloquence can occur without them, most eloquent speeches either create or make use of a dramatistic symbol to narrate for their audience a way of acting or responding to a specific type of rhetorical situation. A dramatistic symbol is thus different than simply a verbal or written symbol. At its most *general* level, a **symbol** is anything that represents something other than itself to some other person who understands this representation. At this level, all words and popular icons operate as symbols insofar as they mean more than their sound or their marking. To communicate anything to anyone is to use symbols. We are awash in symbols every day, from the most trivial to the most sublime, and as human beings, it is virtually impossible to escape their influence. So, to say that the use of symbols is important to public speaking is a truism; saying anything to anyone at any time or thinking of the most elementary thought requires the use of symbols. A **dramatistic symbol**, by contrast, stands out as a way of identifying the core elements of a representative type of situation that recurs throughout time while at the same time identifying an orientation, attitude, or pattern of response that arises in response to that type of situation.

As with many of the concepts in this book, it is from Kenneth Burke that we derive this definition. Burke thought there was a place for a definition of a symbol which was more than simply any sign that referred to something other than itself. Inspired by his fascination with great literature, he thought of a symbol in terms of its dramatistic function—by which he meant how it contributed to the way we understood our relationship to the world around us as if it were a dramatic story that narrated how some agent (the "who") within some scene (the "where") performed some act (the "what") for some purpose (the "why") through some agency (the "how"). Consequently, his understanding of a symbol explicitly concerned the behavior of agents—usually well-known literary, historical, or religious figures—within specific scenes. For instance, most English classes make use of the idea of the "Christ figure" to interpret works of literature, namely by identifying certain characters who, despite their virtues, must be "sacrificed" for the redemption of other characters in the novel. But one could also find examples of "Robin Hood figures," or "Gandhi figures," or "Rosa Parks figures," or "Julius Caesar figures," or "Joan of Arc figures," or "Confucius figures" in literature just the same. In each case, one is simply looking for a type of behavior consistent with, and summed up by, a particular famous person (real or fictional) who has come to embody that particular way of acting, feeling, and behaving.

For Burke, a dramatistic symbol therefore represents not a multiplicity of meanings but a specific *formula* that stands for a recognizable pattern of experience. To understand this definition, one has to clarify the distinction between three types of experience. A **universal experience** is a type of experience that all human beings are capable of having, no matter where they live or when they lived. In other words, it is an emotion or mood that all people can experience simply because they are human beings—for instance, pleasure, pain, joy, despair, anger, excitement, and the like. By contrast, a **mode of experience** is a specific relationship between an individual and an environment that is particular to a specific place, time, and culture. For instance, all human beings are capable of feeling fear. However, each of us feels this universal experience only in a particular mode. A child experiences fear when he is lost in a department store. A CEO feels fear when she sees sales numbers decline. A Roman Emperor feels fear when he sees his enemies conspiring against him. Our modes of experience account for our uniqueness, while our universal experiences provide the context for our unity. Last, a **pattern of experience** represents our recognizable and habitual ways of adjusting to a recognizable type of situation—to a familiar mode—that is often accompanied by a certain type of emotion—a universal. For instance, a young child reacts to a situation of being lost by adopting a pattern of crying loudly. A CEO adopts the pattern of cost-cutting and reorganization. A Roman Emperor adopts a pattern of systematically executing all of his potential enemies. What matters in a pattern of experience is not that it is wise, productive, or thoughtful; what matters is simply that it is a consistent way of adjusting to a type of situation that we can first recognize and then either imitate or condemn.

A dramatistic symbol therefore is a name we give to a pattern of experience that we believe is significant enough to identify and give a name. It also represents a formula. In sum, this formula runs as follows: "When an agent of type A is faced with recognizable situation S and feels universal experiences E, that agent responds by adopting a certain pattern of action P, which produces results R." For instance, during the "March Madness" college basketball tournament, it is not uncommon to characterize a lower ranked team who pulls off a stunning upset to be characterized as a "Cinderella" team at the "Big Dance." Put into our formula, it might go as follows: "When a team that nobody ever heard about enters a competitive environment in which a team is given no chance of success, and when that team feels a combination of fear and anxiety, it actually shows its extraordinary virtue by doing everything it can to overcome obstacles and prove all of its detractors wrong by winning with excellence and grace." Rhetorically speaking, however, having to explain this formula to an audience would make for a long and boring commentary. Instead, the sports commentator simply shouts, "What a Cinderella story!" and everybody knows what it means.

But a speaker need not only rely on preexisting symbols, such as the often used "David and Goliath" symbol to give courage to people who feel they are faced with overwhelming odds. A speaker can also actually transform the subject of a speech into a dramatistic symbol, particularly when it comes to commemorative speeches in which an individual's character and actions are held up for praise, often with the explicit purpose of imitating his or her virtues. For instance, when Abraham Lincoln sought to commemorate the fallen soldiers at Gettysburg during the Civil War, he used the opportunity to translate their actions into a symbol of those willing to sacrifice their lives to defend the democratic experiment:

It is rather for us to be here dedicated to the great task remaining before us—that from these honored dead we take increased devotion to that cause for which they gave the last full measure of devotion—that we here highly resolve that these dead shall not have died in vain—that this nation, under God, shall have a new birth of freedom—and that government of the people, by the people, for the people, shall not perish from the earth.[4]

Indeed, it was Lincoln's ability to transform the soldiers into symbols that made the Gettysburg Address such a monument of the democratic spirit. The most effective commemorative speeches use such strategies.

Symbols can perform six functions, as defined by Kenneth Burke.[5] Furthermore, it is important to keep in mind that a symbol can serve any number of these functions in a speech, often at different points. How many functions it serves depends on how extensively the symbol is put to use within the speech as well as the different audiences it may be addressing. The six functions are as follows:

1. *Produce "artistic" effects*: On a purely stylistic level, a dramatistic symbol can provide an opportunity for a speaker to "inhabit" the symbol much as an actor performs a part on stage. An **artistic symbol** addresses the question, "How might I perform this?" Burke explains that a symbol which performs an artistic function allows an artist to put on a "virtuoso" performance, much as a Shakespearean actor uses the character of Hamlet to show their dramatic range of emotion. In other words, a symbol provides an opportunity for a speaker to act "in character" usually for the sake of making some exaggerated actions. For instance, Martin Luther King Jr. often used the symbol of "Moses on the Mountaintop" when he wished to talk about the Promised Land.

2. *Interpret a situation*: In a rhetorical situation marked by confusion and uncertainty—an unclarified complexity—a dramatistic symbol can function to give it order and meaning. An **interpretation symbol** addresses the question, "What exactly is going on here?" The important thing to keep in mind is that an *interpretation* is not simply a novel description of something we already know about. It must act to create order out of disorder—otherwise it only fulfills the artistic function of imaginative play. A symbol that serves an interpretive function reveals underlying causes or motives that become clear insofar as they are similar to the causes or motives that characterize the situation of a familiar symbol. For instance, imagine that the police were puzzled by the success of a criminal who seemed able to rob people at will, and yet none of the community was willing to turn him in or testify against him. Characterizing this individual as a modern-day "Robin Hood" would help clarify that his success came from the fact that he was responding to a situation of vast inequality in wealth by redistributing money to the poor.

3. *Force acceptance of things we had previously denied*: This function can only occur when there is a *preexisting* undesirable or threatening aspect of a situation that we have been unable to emotionally accept because it is too difficult to admit. An **acceptance symbol** addresses the

question, "How can we come to terms with this?" Reacting to a state of denial, a dramatistic symbol of this kind can therefore act to establish a relationship between the audience and the danger that it has ignored, usually by giving the audience a feeling of power it had not previously experienced. These types of symbols usually come in two forms, tragic or comic. A tragic symbol helps us come to terms with a threat by making us feel more noble in our suffering—or even in our defeat. For instance, the symbol of the Spartan soldiers at Thermopylae, popularized by the movie *300*, would be an effective tragic symbol for soldiers who know they are likely facing death in battle, thereby admitting this possibility by making them feel noble and courageous. On the other hand, a comic symbol helps us come to terms with a stressful or threatening situation by making it seem somewhat harmless or absurd. For instance, the symbol of "Chicken Little," who ran around thinking that the sky was falling, can be used to make light of our own anxieties and put them into perspective.

4. *Imagine more perfect situations that "correct" for what we lack in the present*: Oftentimes we want our symbols simply to provide us an opportunity for imagining that we are somewhere other than our current place and time. A **corrective symbol** addresses the question, "What would be a better life?" A dramatistic symbol of this type offers a vision of possibility that helps correct the imbalances of the present. However, these visions need not be practical or even necessarily possible. Burke mentions that fictional romances or fantasy stories are the ideal representative of this type of symbol. That is to say, corrective symbols appeal to us simply because they offer an appealing utopia in which to inhabit. In rhetoric, therefore, sometimes corrective symbols can be dangerous, as when the symbol of the Roman Emperor ruling his empire inspired Mussolini and his movement of Italian fascism. But it can also provide inspirational images of a potential future, as Martin Luther King Jr.'s symbol of Moses and the Promised Land.

5. *Encourage the expression of "submerged" emotions*: Dramatistic symbols allow people to vicariously experience powerful emotions that they would otherwise suppress. These symbols often have the power to arouse deep emotions, either as symbols of cruelty and horror or as symbols of hope and love. An **emotional symbol** thus addresses the question, "What can I feel in this situation?" Notably, emotional symbols do not necessarily mean we have to act in any particular way. Its purpose is simply to arouse a powerful emotion. For instance, people go to horror movies simply as an excuse to feel terrified, not in order to commit violent acts. Similarly, speakers can make effective use of emotional symbols in their speeches in order to evoke emotions of pity, fear, anger, sorrow, or love—an effect often seen in religious rhetoric when speakers refer to "martyrs for the faith" as exemplars of sacrifice and virtue.

6. *Emancipate or condemn certain types of action*: Last, dramatistic symbols have the unique power to invert our moral codes, thus making the better into the worse and the worse into the better. An **emancipation symbol** addresses the question, "What should be our new standards of virtue?" By using these symbols, behavior otherwise thought immoral and shameful can come to be seen as noble and courageous in a new light, while actions previously praised can be condemned. These types of symbols are particularly present in contexts of social conflict

or revolutionary action, such as that which occurred during the movements for abolition or women's rights. For instance, the symbol of St. Paul in his "Letter to Philemon," in which he suggests freeing a slave and treating him as a brother, became a powerful emancipation symbol during the abolition movement.

To grasp the function of a dramatistic symbol, a comparison with the use of metaphor may be helpful. The difference between a dramatistic symbol and a metaphor is simply one of degree. A metaphor performs all the functions of a dramatistic symbol except that of scope and depth. Figurative metaphors are usually used to creatively define particular aspects of a situation and to engage people's imaginations. A dramatistic symbol is used to structure our view of an entire rhetorical situation, to guide action in the long- and short-term, to help "identify" both a speaker and audience as having a certain character, and, most importantly, to structure the organization of the entire speech from beginning to end. It gives audiences a single, coherent image that will stick in their memories after the oration is over. Ralph Waldo Emerson highlights this particular quality of eloquence:

> The orator must be, to a certain extent, a poet. We are such imaginative creatures that nothing so works on the human mind, barbarous or civil, as a trope. Condense some daily experience into a glowing symbol, and an audience is electrified. They feel as if they already possessed some new right and power over a fact which they can detach, and so completely master in thought. It is a wonderful aid to the memory, which carries away the image and never loses it. . . . Put the argument into a concrete shape, into an image—some hard phrase, round and solid as a ball, which they can see and handle and carry home with them—and the cause is half-won.[6]

The dramatistic symbol is precisely this "glowing symbol" that compresses a complex situation into a concrete shape, a "hard phrase round and solid as a ball, which they can see and handle and carry home with them." In other words, a dramatistic symbol is a metaphor extended over the length of the speech because the speaker believes it grasps some essential aspect of the rhetorical situation that warrants such strategic simplification.

Many speeches, of course, do not have dramatistic symbols. They use a multiplicity of metaphors as seem appropriate to the specific argument at the time, and the speeches are structured using the conventional models as we defined in the canon of organization. Eloquent speeches, however, seek to transcend the more rigid designs and allow a speaker to weave a more complex narrative story that follows the logic of the symbol rather than that of a template. Of course, beginning speechwriters cannot simply leap over mastering the logic of templates and all the specific strategies that go with them. Usually, such efforts result in a confusing mess. However, once these basic skills are mastered, one can begin experimenting with speeches that grow out of a more poetic sensibility that seeks not just to inform and persuade but also to bring about an experience of transcendence that is a rare accomplishment in the world.

Elizabeth Cady Stanton: "Even Jesus of Nazareth, in These Last Sad Days on Earth, Felt the Awful Solitude of Self"

In 1892, at the age of 76, long-time women's rights activist Elizabeth Cady Stanton delivered what has come to be her most famous address, "The Solitude of Self." First delivered to the House Judiciary Committee, and later that evening to the National American Woman Suffrage Association (NAWSA), the speech was in one way her "retirement" address, delivered at the moment that she had resigned from the presidency of the NAWSA. But it was also, more importantly, a speech that concerns the importance of looking at the women's rights movement in broader terms than simply suffrage, as important as that was. As the title indicates, her address was concerned with establishing women's rights on an "existential" basis; that is to say, it was a statement concerning what it means to be a human individual. For Stanton, what it meant to be human was to be forced into a condition of self-reliance. No matter how much individuals work to together, how much they wish to help one another, ultimately each individual had to overcome their most important struggles alone. Therefore, the ultimate goal of the women's rights movement was neither to take things from others nor to be taken care of by others; it was rather to give each individual woman the resources by which she could become truly self-reliant. To make this argument, she uses the dramatistic symbol of Jesus during his last days, when he had to suffer conviction and crucifixion alone. This symbol, for her, becomes the pattern of experience that all individuals, both men and women, had to imitate in their goal of becoming truly independent:

> Nothing strengthens the judgment and quickens the conscience like individual responsibility. Nothing adds such dignity to character as the recognition of one's self-sovereignty; the right to an equal place, everywhere conceded; a place earned by personal merit, not an artificial attainment, by inheritance, wealth, family, and position. Seeing, then, that the responsibilities of life rests equally on man and woman, that their destiny is the same, they need the same preparation for time and eternity. The talk of sheltering woman from the fierce storms of life is the sheerest mockery, for they beat on her from every point of the compass, just as they do on man, and with more fatal results, for he has been trained to protect himself, to resist, to conquer. Such are the facts in human experience, the responsibilities of individual sovereignty. Rich and poor, intelligent and ignorant, wise and foolish, virtuous and vicious, man and woman, it is ever the same, each soul must depend wholly on itself.

> Whatever the theories may be of woman's dependence on man, in the supreme moments of her life he can not bear her burdens. Alone she goes to the gates of death to give life to every man that is born into the world. No one can share her fears, no one mitigate her pangs; and if her sorrow is greater than she can bear, alone she passes beyond the gates into the vast unknown.

> From the mountain tops of Judea, long ago, a heavenly voice bade His disciples, "Bear ye one another's burdens," but humanity has not yet risen to that point of self-sacrifice, and

if ever so willing, how few the burdens are that one soul can bear for another. In the highways of Palestine; in prayer and fasting on the solitary mountain top; in the Garden of Gethsemane; before the judgment seat of Pilate; betrayed by one of His trusted disciples at His last supper; in His agonies on the cross, even Jesus of Nazareth, in these last sad days on earth, felt the awful solitude of self. Deserted by man, in agony he cries, "My God! My God! why hast Thou forsaken me?" And so it ever must be in the conflicting scenes of life, on the long weary march, each one walks alone. We may have many friends, love, kindness, sympathy and charity to smooth our pathway in everyday life, but in the tragedies and triumphs of human experience each moral stands alone.

> ## DISCUSSION
>
> For different audiences, encountering this address in different circumstances, the symbol of Jesus suffering in solitude may function in different ways. For instance, for a person who is faced with great suffering and has tried to deal with the emotional stress by simply trying not to think about it or "looking on the bright side," the symbol can facilitate acceptance by making them realize that they are not alone in their suffering. For which audience does it function as in interpretation symbol or as an emancipation symbol? Also, read carefully how Stanton defines the attitudes and actions that she associates with the solitude of self. How can this be interpreted in terms of modes of experience, universal experiences, and patterns of experience? And how does Stanton herself translate herself into a symbol during this speech?

But when all artificial trammels are removed, and women are recognized as individuals, responsible for their own environments, thoroughly educated for all the positions in life they may be called to fill; with all the resources in themselves that liberal thought and broad culture can give; guided by their own conscience and judgment; trained to self-protection by a healthy development of the muscular system and skill in the use of weapons of defense, and stimulated to self-support by the knowledge of the business world and the pleasure that pecuniary independence must ever give; when women are trained in this way they will, in a measure, be fitted for those hours of solitude that come alike to all, whether prepared or otherwise. As in our extremity we must depend on ourselves, the dictates of wisdom point to complete individual development.[7]

▶ POETIC CATEGORIES

Although rhetoric is not the same as dramatic art, an advanced public speaker is able to make use of dramatic resources in order to more powerfully deliver a message. These resources can be termed poetic categories. For Burke, a **poetic category** represents a way of telling a certain type of story that organizes the plot and characters in a certain predictable sequence and produces specific emotional responses. When we go to see a classical Greek tragedy on stage, for instance, we may not know which play we will see, but we can be assured that there'll be a great hero brought to ruin by some twist of fate, and when we see a Shakespearean comedy, we will know there will be a host of motley characters constantly scheming harmlessly against one another until chance brings everything into the open and people make up and fall in love. However, poetic categories are more than simply general templates for organizing fictional events and people into a coherent stage drama; they are also ways of interpreting actual events in real life. As Burke explains, a poetic category can be understood as a rhetorical way of making meaning of our lives in history. In other words, it makes a great deal of difference whether we write ourselves into tragedies or comedies as we try to play our role in the drama of existence.

Poetic categories are therefore similar to dramatistic symbols insofar as they represent a sort of formula for action. However, poetic categories are more general than dramatistic symbols, as they represent something closer to a genre than a specific pattern of experience. For example, even though both Macbeth and Hamlet are characters in Shakespearean tragedies, they represent different dramatistic symbols. Macbeth represents a pattern of experience whereby an ambitious hero brazenly kills all who stand in his way in order to retain power, whereas Hamlet represents a pattern of one who attempts to enact just revenge upon an enemy by employing overly intellectual and complicated maneuvering. Dramatistic symbols are therefore far more particular than poetic categories. At the same time, however, one's choice of dramatistic symbol often indirectly makes use of the resources of poetic categories. To choose, for instance, the symbol of the great European explorers as a dramatistic symbol for space exploration is also to make use of the poetic category of the heroic drama. The best speeches therefore often make use of both dramatistic symbols and poetic categories in concert to craft inspiring narratives. Of the many poetic categories that are available, we will look at three of the most important that frequently occur in rhetorical discourse—the heroic, tragic, and comedic.

The Heroic

Perhaps the most common poetic category used in rhetoric is that of the **heroic**, which calls an audience to courageous and committed action in the name of some higher ideal that has been revealed through the actions of a hero, living or dead. Importantly, heroic dramas do not simply narrate and praise great and noble deeds, as one might think of ceremonies that praise the heroism of firefighters who run into a burning building or ordinary citizens who tackle a would-be murderer. When we talk about a "hero," we mean a particularly exceptional type of person who accomplishes deeds and achieves revelations that are unavailable to everyday people. According to Joseph Campbell,

> a hero ventures forth from the world of common day into a region of supernatural wonder: fabulous forces are there encountered and a decisive victory is won: the hero comes back from this mysterious adventure with the power to bestow boons on his fellow man.[8]

Interspersed in this journey are stages where the hero rejects his calling, then comes to accept it after a traumatic event and challenge, dies only to be reborn, and finds allies along the way to help him toward redemption and conquest. For instance, Luke Skywalker in the *Star Wars* movies follows the hero's journey on his way from being a mere mechanic on a desert planet to being the last Jedi who teaches the ways of the Force to the galaxy.

What makes these heroes important rhetorically is that their deeds give them ethos, which gives them credibility and an audience, whereas their revelations provide new principles of action, which their audiences are prepared to follow. According to Bill Butler,

> among the chief characteristics of the hero is his right to establish the laws of Heaven on Earth, and the concurrent right to break any of those laws, including the most serious injunctions against murder, with impunity. For that is partially what a hero is: like the gods, both law-*maker* and law*breaker*.[9]

The paradigmatic biblical hero, for instance, is Moses, who journeys to the mountaintop to receive the Ten Commandments and then returns to the people to pronounce the new principles that shall lead them to the Promised Land. Essential to its rhetorical function, then, is the ability of the heroic drama to provide (a) an ideal vision of a better future, (b) new principles on which to act in the name of that future, and (c) courageous leadership to inspire collective action. Virtually any time groups feel they must strike out in new directions and confront new obstacles and/or enemies, some form of heroic rhetoric is not far behind. Already in this textbook we have seen numerous examples of heroic rhetoric, from Sojourner Truth to Eugene Debs, and virtually any summer blockbuster will feature at least one character making a heroic speech in a time of crisis. Heroism is what inspires us to do things that we might not otherwise have the courage to do, and as a result, it makes for great drama.

Dolores Ibárruri: "We Are Here. Your Cause, Spain's Cause, Is Ours"

During the Spanish Civil War between the Republican Government and the Fascists led by Francisco Franco, one of the most powerful voices in defense of the Republic was Dolores Ibárruri, better known by her pseudonym La Pasionaria (or "the passion flower"). The eighth of eleven children, she was born in Spain to a family of miners, she later married a miner, and she first took on a public role when she started writing for a miners' newspaper to advocate for better wages and working conditions. Over the years, she rose to prominence in the Spanish Communist Party (which came to play an important role in the Republican administration), but it was during the war that she truly developed her heroic rhetorical persona. Often delivering fiery speeches at rallies or on the radio, she became famous for coining the phrase "*No Pasaran!*" ("The fascists shall not pass!), as well as telling a meeting of women that "It is better to be the widows of heroes than the wives of cowards!" One of her most famous addresses was given in farewell to the "international brigades," foreign volunteers that came from Europe and the United States to fight on behalf of the Republican government. During the end of the war, when it was clear that the military cause was lost, the brigades were released from their duties and La Pasionaria gave them a heroic farewell in Barcelona, Spain, on November 1, 1938, calling on all mothers and women to tell stories of the international brigades after the war was over:

Recount for them how, coming over seas and mountains, crossing frontiers bristling with bayonets, sought by raving dogs thirsting to tear their flesh, these men reached our country as crusaders for freedom, to fight and die for Spain's liberty. . . . They gave up everything . . . they came and said to us: "We are here. Your cause, Spain's cause, is ours. It is the cause of all advanced and progressive mankind."[10]

> ## DISCUSSION
>
> As demonstrated by the speech, a hero remains a hero even when the cause he or she may have fought for has lost. A hero, therefore, is not determined by whether or not one wins or loses. It is determined by the spirit in which the cause is defended. One of the interesting qualities of this speech is how La Pasionaria exploits the opportunity to praise the international brigades to actually celebrate the cause of Republican Spain itself, while condemning those who would not defend the Republic as "vile and accommodating"—in this case, referring specifically to France, Britain, and the United States. Can you think of other speeches, ceremonies, or awards that a nation or group uses to praise individual heroes as a means by which to celebrate the overall goals and values that the nation or group stands for?

The Tragic

Tragedy tends to arise in the opposite rhetorical situations as that of heroism. Heroic rhetoric is fitting for moments in which individuals or groups must ready themselves for a hard journey ahead, to give them confidence in their success despite sometimes overwhelming odds. Tragic rhetoric, by contrast, almost always follows on the heels of disaster, after one's path has ended in pain, suffering, death, or failure. Whereas heroic rhetoric looks eagerly to a great future, tragic rhetoric reflects soberly upon an unfortunate past. The goal of tragedy, however, is not to lament one's fate and wallow in misery and pity. Quite the opposite, the goal of tragedy is to wrench meaning out of suffering to answer the lingering question, "Why did this have to happen?" In tragedy, "one learns by experience" such that "the suffered is the learned."[11] *Tragedy* is therefore not synonymous with words like *horrific, violent,* or *sad,* despite their frequent combination. The unforeseen or accidental death of a loved one may be traumatic for those still living, but that does not make it tragic. A tragic death is one that, despite bringing intense suffering, also produces a kind of wisdom.

The purpose of employing the poetic category of tragedy in rhetoric is to help an audience achieve **catharsis**, which Aristotle defined as the sense of wisdom that follows upon the purging of pity and fear brought about by the trauma of witnessing the suffering of others whom we love and respect. What an audience wants, in other words, from a tragic speech is not more images of trauma but the opposite—words that will help us overcome our traumas and their sufferings with dignity and wisdom and courage. Whereas the emotions of pity and fear focus our attention on particular people and things, tragedy expands our vision to a wider universe in which those things are embedded; tragedy thus purges pity and fear by turning our gaze from the object of suffering before us to the night sky above us, thus subsuming particular realities and appearances under universal meanings and possibilities.

One should not therefore confuse the meaning of tragedy with that of elegy. In poetry, the **elegy** is a mournful, melancholy, or plaintive poem, often presented as a funeral song or a lament for the dead. Like tragedy, elegy often focuses on the magnitude of human suffering; yet unlike tragedy, does not redeem suffering through wisdom or some higher purpose. The embodiment of the elegy is the perfected technique of complaint; it is a "wailing wall" that invites people to express their suffering in public in such a way that emphasizes how small they are in confrontation with immense forces. The goal of the elegy, in other words, is to condemn the magnitude of injustice in the world and appeal to some higher moral law to help the helpless and give strength to the powerless. In rhetoric, the elegy is often employed by individuals or groups who feel they have been unjustly oppressed by an illegitimate power. It expresses itself in a "Woe is me!" type of lament. Yet there is no catharsis in elegy. There is only lamentation and the reward of giving expression to one's pain.

The peculiar nature of tragic pleasure, by contrast, comes precisely from the act of bearing witness to universal truths about the world through particular images of traumatic suffering. That is to say, tragedy neither dwells on particular suffering nor simply ignores it by offering nice-sounding platitudes. Instead, tragedy goes *through* those particular appearances and tries to find the universal meanings within them. Most often, these meanings deal less with the individual who has suffered than with the environment that has brought about that suffering. The pleasure that accompanies catharsis is therefore the pleasure of having gained a greater wisdom and recognizing that such wisdom can only come through great suffering. It is the task of rhetoric to bring forth this wisdom and to produce a community of affiliation grounded in its acceptance.

Robert F. Kennedy: "To Tame the Savageness of Man and Make Gentle the Life of This World"

On April 4, 1968, Robert F. Kennedy, then senator from New York but also candidate for the Democratic presidential nomination, learned that King had been assassinated in Memphis, Tennessee. He had just arrived in Indianapolis, Indiana, for a political rally that would be attended primarily by an urban, African-American crowd. At the time, news had not reached most of the public, and nobody at the rally was aware of King's death. Wary of the volatility of the situation, his aides suggested that he cancel the appearance, but instead Kennedy chose to announce King's death to the crowd and speak extemporaneously on the subject from hastily composed notes. Dramatically standing on the back of a pickup truck, he used the poetic category of tragedy to try to make sense of what was, on its face, a senseless and violent act. It has gone down as one of the greatest political eulogies of all time. Less than two months later, Kennedy was assassinated in Los Angeles:

> I'm only going to talk to you just for a minute or so this evening, because . . . I have some very sad news for all of you, and, I think, sad news for all of our fellow citizens, and people who love peace all over the world; and that is that Martin Luther King was shot and was killed tonight in Memphis, Tennessee.
>
> Martin Luther King dedicated his life to love and to justice between fellow human beings. He died in the cause of that effort. In this difficult day, in this difficult time for the United States, it's perhaps well to ask what kind of a nation we are and what direction we want to move in. For those of you who are black . . . you can be filled with bitterness, and with hatred, and a desire for revenge.
>
> We can move in that direction as a country, in greater polarization . . . filled with hatred toward one another. Or we can make an effort, as Martin Luther King did, to understand, and to comprehend, and replace that violence, that stain of bloodshed that has spread across our land, with an effort to understand, compassion, and love. . . . We have to make an effort in the United States. We have to make an effort to understand, to get beyond, or go beyond these rather difficult times.

DISCUSSION

The fact that Kennedy chooses to quote Aeschylus at this moment—one of the greatest of the Greek tragic poets—demonstrates precisely the rhetorical value of tragedy to help people make difficult judgments in times of suffering or despair. Indeed, the passage he selects captures exactly the lesson of tragedy, namely that we often have to suffer pain before we can truly grasp the lessons of a certain type of difficult wisdom. Note, also, how different this lesson would be had he chosen instead the heroic frame. Whereas the death of a tragic figure brings about reflection and wisdom, the death of a hero is often followed by action and resolve. How do you think the audience would have acted differently if he had chosen the heroic as his poetic category? And can you think of any other national trauma in which the tragic frame, rather than the heroic frame, was the more appropriate response?

My favorite poem, my favorite poet was Aeschylus. And he once wrote: "*Even in our sleep, pain which cannot forget / falls drop by drop upon the heart, / until, in our own despair, against our will, / comes wisdom / through the awful grace of God.*" What we need in the United States is not division; what we need in the United States is not hatred; what we need in the United States is not violence and lawlessness, but is love, and wisdom, and compassion toward one another, and a feeling of justice toward those who still suffer within our country, whether they be white or whether they be black.

So I ask you tonight to return home, to say a prayer for the family of Martin Luther King . . . but more importantly to say a prayer for our own country, which all of us love—a prayer for understanding and that compassion of which I spoke. We can do well in this country. We will have difficult times. We've had difficult times in the past . . . and we will have difficult times in the future. It is not the end of violence; it is not the end of lawlessness; and it's not the end of disorder.

But the vast majority of white people and the vast majority of black people in this country want to live together, want to improve the quality of our life, and want justice for all human beings that abide in our land. And let's dedicate ourselves to what the Greeks wrote so many years ago: to tame the savageness of man and make gentle the life of this world. Let us dedicate ourselves to that, and say a prayer for our country and for our people.[12]

The Comic

Whereas the heroic is appropriate at the *beginning* of something and tragedy is appropriate at its *end*, **comedy** is the most appropriate while in the *middle* of something. Specifically, comedy always situates characters within a complex *deliberative* situation, in which **deliberation** means a communicative activity by which multiple parties, each with different perspectives, goals, and interests, attempt to come to a common practical judgment about some pressing issue. Obviously, then, comedy as it is being used here refers not to the art of making people laugh but a way of telling a dramatic story. Comedy, after all, was the counterpart of tragedy on the Greek stage. But instead of portraying the heroic suffering of individual heroes who were more noble and greater than ourselves, comedy portrayed the absurd antics of a multiplicity of exaggerated characters less virtuous and stupider than ourselves. In both Shakespearean plays and Hollywood films, the plot of a comedy usually revolves around an initial misunderstanding or deception that magnifies to absurd proportions until some chance event reveals what is truly going on to everyone involved, such that an amicable reconciliation between parties becomes possible. In comedy, the end does not come with the triumph of the hero over the villain (as in an epic) or with the noble death of the hero in his or her struggle for greatness (as in a tragedy); it comes with the resolution of misunderstandings made possible by humility and forgiveness.

The essence of dramatic comedy is therefore not the "joke" but the "situation." In both stand-up comedy and in dramatic comedy, there is certainly **humor**, which can be defined as that burst of spontaneous laughter produced by the momentary violation of expectations and the absurd juxtaposition of incongruous things in such a way that also produces some new insight. For instance, it is funnier to throw a pie in the face of the king wearing ermine robes than it is to see a pie thrown in the face of a peasant child, precisely because the shocked expression of the king covered with cream reveals all the great trappings of royalty to be merely superficial covering on an ordinary person as capable of shock and embarrassment as the rest of us. With the child there is no such contrast, and hence this act would be interpreted merely as being cruel. The difference is that jokes bring about humor through condensed and usually stereotypical stories or phrases, whereas dramatic comedies bring forth humor by developing certain character types and showing how they interact with others in a complicated deliberative context. If a joke simply has us imagine a king getting hit with a pie, a dramatic comedy shows all the wild machinations that go into a group of oddball conspirators trying to bring about that event, inevitably resulting in a final scene in which all the characters are in the castle at the same time and end up in a pile laughing at each other and covered in cream pies.

In rhetoric, the poetic category of comedy is therefore most useful in deliberative situations that have become so polarized (usually by competing heroic narratives) that collective judgment has become virtually impossible. During these moments, comedy replaces a heroic narrative that pits good against evil with comic narratives in which multiple parties, each with the best intentions, are needlessly clashing with each other because they have not understood each other's perspectives and have exaggerated their own virtues and victimhood. Comic rhetoric is thus deliberative because comedy always portrays people as agents of change attempting to make the best judgment (often out of a bad situation) in collaboration or competition with many people unlike themselves.

In rhetoric, then, comedy is often used as a way of resolving disputes, easing tensions, and giving people broader perspective on issues through a combination of witty observations and enlightened interpretations. In comedy, one does not laugh *at* others but *with* them, often concerning foibles for which he or she is responsible. Consequently, comedy is often used in speeches of introduction, identification, enrichment, and administration in which the goal is a feeling of voluntary participation in a shared experience. Rather than seeking to magnify the glory of the end and the virtue of suffering, as with tragedy, comedy looks at suffering largely as the unnecessary consequence of ignorance, exaggeration, and narrow-minded partisanship and seeks to avoid it through mutual understanding and acceptance of differences. The reason that comedy is "funny," therefore, is twofold: first, it is funny to see how ridiculous people are when they take themselves too seriously; second, the most important way to overcome our own self-importance and try to work together with others (despite previous tensions) is to be able to laugh at ourselves.

Shazia Mirza: "These People Want to Live"

Born in Birmingham, England, Shazia Mirza is a British stand-up comedian who was born of Pakistani parents, and who also happens to be a Muslim. Although at first she worked as a science teacher, she eventually found that stand-up comedy was her true talent. Rhetorically speaking, she found that drawing attention to her unique persona as a British citizen and a Muslim woman gave her a unique perspective on culture and politics that allowed her to be provocative and insightful in a way that other comedians could not, namely by pointing out and exposing our many cultural stereotypes that we use to make sense of a complicated political environment. In one of her essays that she wrote in the wake of the European migrant crisis that followed in the wake of the Syrian Civil War, Mirza used a comic touch on a serious issue of how to confront serious economic and social problems while at the same time adjusting to an influx of migrant populations. Her strategy is to use the comic frame not necessarily to diminish the enormity of the challenges that we face but rather to highlight the central lesson of comedy, namely that the only way to get through a crisis is to recognize our own frailty in each other's basic humanity:

> When people are unhappy, discontent and disillusioned with their own life, they want someone to blame. Once we blamed Yoko Ono. Now we blame refugees. . . . [But] refugees are not coming to Britain for the food, weather and £65.45 a week. . . . They're not coming because they want to find Harry Potter, drink tea and watch drunk people rolling down every high street looking for their teeth on a Friday night.
>
> No. These people want to live.[13]

DISCUSSION

If the heroic launches us on new expeditions and the tragic brings wisdom out of the inevitable suffering that such journeys bring, comedy helps us make our way day by day in the everyday world of human affairs by reminding us that we are just one of thousands or millions of ordinary people trying to make our way through a difficult and confusing environment. In her essay, Mirza criticizes our natural human tendency to simplify problems and place the blame on an easily identifiable group, a strategy that is at the essence of scapegoating. Her strategy is, on the one hand, to make fun of the idiosyncrasies of British culture that few people would envy—such as the weather—while on the other hand empathizing the simple desires that motivate most migrants, namely the desire to simply live in peace. What do you think is the rhetorical benefits and drawbacks of using comedy in this way to address such a serious political problem? Are there times when you think that comedy is simply inappropriate?

▶ SUMMARY

Eloquence in a speech is not synonymous with pleasant-sounding words and delivery in a comfortable situation. Eloquence, rather, is produced when an audience within a rhetorical situation encounters a speech that is capable simultaneously of prudence and transcendence, in which **prudence** means the capacity to make a practical judgment about a particular matter of concern, and **transcendence** means the capacity to move through the particular matter at hand and thereby experience meanings that are grander and more universal than those that are immediately present. Importantly, transcendence does not mean ignoring the particular realities and appearances of the exigence and simply spouting maxims and clichés and grandiose abstractions. It means showing how universal meanings and possibilities are revealed *through* and *within* the specific events, people, actions, and objects that make up a rhetorical situation. This is why we feel that the words of the Declaration of Independence are thought to be eloquent:

> Despite the fact that they were written for a specific context, Jefferson managed to give universal expression to the desire of human beings to feel at home within a political system. The preamble deals neither with what has been or what will be, nor with philosophical principles stated in the abstract. It deals with what exists within the common world we inhabit together through time, which includes infinity.[14]

In other words, Jefferson helped create a feeling of what it meant to be "American" by advocating a specific judgment of prudence in the moment—to declare revolution—while also revealing universal meanings and possibilities in a form of popular government based on the preservation of life, liberty, and the pursuit of happiness.

The first step in the construction of eloquent speech is therefore to identify a relationship between particular realities and appearances and universal meanings and possibilities. We identify *particular realities* when we simply define all of the specific people, events, objects, and actions that are significant in a rhetorical situation. Particular realities are all the definable "things" we must take account of. *Particular appearances* are the *ways* that we encounter all of these things. Appearances are the way a reality shows itself to us under a "certain light" and in a certain place and time. For instance, racial segregation certainly existed as a reality in the South, but it took many appearances, from segregated lunch counters to water fountains to school systems, and with those specific places looking different depending on how they were experienced and by what form of media they were represented. *Universal meanings* thus represent more general types of things we can say about these particular realities as a way of categorizing them and broadening their significance. Even though Southern segregation was a particular reality in the United States, it also has general meaning as a form of oppression and violence that makes it a part of a larger history of the abuse of power. Finally, *universal possibilities* refer to general types of meanings or values that are not actually present in the particular situation but might nonetheless be valuable to us as ends-in-view, as guides for future action based on our hopes and imaginations. The irony of history is that we often glimpse universal possibilities through particular appearances of great suffering, as when children being sprayed with fire hoses makes us imagine what true freedom might mean.

Rhetors can also structure a speech using one of the major poetic categories that represents a certain genre of storytelling rather than a specific story itself. Although there are numerous poetic categories, the three major categories used in rhetorical speeches are the heroic, the tragic, and the comic. In the *heroic* category, a speaker attempts to rally an audience to courageous action by disclosing universal possibilities that will turn into a reality if they only follow a certain path that has been revealed to the speaker, usually by some higher authority. Heroic rhetoric thus accomplishes eloquence by showing how a particular obstacle must be overcome in order to achieve a universal possibility, usually in the form of a utopia, while making a saint of the leader. In tragedy, a speaker attempts to wrest meaning out of suffering, whether that suffering is by a hero or by a victim. Instead of advocating for heroic initiative, tragedy reflects upon past pain or failure in order to make sense of our particular suffering by revealing its universal meaning and perhaps even its universal possibility. In other words, when our heroic ventures fail, we look to tragedy to help us understand why they failed and what we can learn from that failure. Last, in comedy, a speaker tries to make the best of a complicated and contentious deliberative situation by helping all parties laugh at themselves just enough to make a limited judgment that benefits everyone. Unlike the heroic and the tragic, the comic tends not to dwell as much in the universal as it does in the particular, preferring prudence over transcendence. In this way, comic rhetoric often is not as "eloquent" as heroic or tragic rhetoric, but when done well, it nonetheless can produce powerful feelings of relief, camaraderie, and optimism that produce their own sense of self-transcendence.

Finally, eloquence shows us the power and importance of public speaking even in our electronic age. It is difficult to experience eloquence sitting in front of a video screen or reading a newspaper. We experience eloquence when we are with others in a situation of uncertainty and urgency and when we hear words spoken to all of us with charisma, wisdom, and passion. These moments leave a lasting impression upon us that changes us in a way that other forms of communication find difficult to achieve. Human beings are social and political animals, born to live with others and to communicate with them using all of our bodily senses. Rhetorical public speaking at its best channels all of these energies and impulses and focuses attention on particular matters that require our agency to change. Of course, we cannot use a single speech to transform the globe— but neither can a single viral video, no matter how popular. History is written by an infinite number of particular acts by people pursuing the universal possibilities inherent within their own situations. The experience of eloquence is produced when we finally are able to break the bounds of our finitude and catch a glimpse of a meaningful world just beyond our reach yet potentially within our grasp. It is the responsibility of the engaged citizen to keep pushing those boundaries so that we can expand the horizon of human possibilities in a fragile and changing world.

▶ CHAPTER 10 EXERCISES

1. **IMPROMPTU:** Select one of the functions of a symbol (with the exception of "artistic effects") and choose your symbol from a popular character in movies that is also associated with a particular pattern of experience. Now create a short speech that tries to address some problem common or at least familiar to people in the class, using the symbol to suggest a way of responding that is consistent with the function of the symbol you have selected.

2. **DEBATE:** One of the great ethical and rhetorical challenges that a nation faces is how to respond to acts of violence. It is during these times when the importance of poetic categories in rhetoric takes on a heightened significance. For instance, after the terror attacks of September 11, 2001, which destroyed the World Trade Center in New York City, there was a considerable debate about when it was appropriate to be "funny" again. Discuss the issue of whether or not comedy is ever an appropriate response to attacks of such magnitude. When we respond to situations in which people have been killed, are our only options tragedy or heroism?

3. **GROUP:** Divide yourselves into groups and assign each group a poetic category. Now write a eulogy to a popular character in movies or literature that can be fit into that genre. If the character is fictional, speak as if the character were real and the action in the movie or book were true.

4. **TAKE HOME:** Find a popular "meme" to which people often attach funny quotations. Without reference to any specific use of this meme, interpret it according to the functions of a symbol. What is the pattern of experience that this meme represents? And what is the typical function that this particular meme is used for? Present your findings to the class.

5. **VIDEO:** Deliver an eloquent speech of praise that makes explicit use of a "particular appearance" of a "particular reality" that you often encounter in your everyday experience. Make sure to connect that particular object to a "universal meaning" and a "universal possibility". The more exaggerated its significance, the better.

▶ NOTES

1. For more on form, see Kenneth Burke, *Counter-Statement* (Berkeley: University of California Press, 1968).

2. Thomas Jefferson, "The Declaration of Independence," www.archives.gov/exhibits/charters/declaration.html (accessed 12 November 2012).

3. Thomas Jefferson, "The Declaration of Independence," www.archives.gov/exhibits/charters/declaration.html (accessed 12 November 2012).

4. Abraham Lincoln, "The Gettysburg Address," http://myloc.gov/Exhibitions/gettysburgaddress/Pages/default.aspx (accessed 15 July 2012).

5. For more on symbols, see Burke, *Counter-Statement*.

6. Ralph Waldo Emerson, "Eloquence," www.rwe.org/complete-works/vii-society-and-solitude/chapter-iv-eloquence (accessed 7 May 2010).

7. Elizabeth Cady Stanton, "The Solitude of Self," available at http://voicesofdemocracy.umd.edu/the-solitude-of-self-speech-by-ecs-to-the-house-judiciary-committee-speech-text./ (accessed 23 March 2017).

8. Joseph Campbell, *The Hero with a Thousand Faces* (Princeton: Princeton University Press, 1949), 23.

9. Bill Butler, *The Myth of the Hero* (New York: Rider and Company, 1979), 9.

10. Dolores Ibárruri, "Farewell to the International Brigades," available at www.english.illinois.edu/maps/scw/farewell.htm (accessed 24 November 2016).

11. Kenneth Burke, *A Grammar of Motives* (Berkeley: University of California Press, 1969), 39.

12. Robert F. Kennedy, "Remarks on the Assassination of Martin Luther King," available at www.americanrhetoric.com/speeches/rfkonmlkdeath.html (accessed 24 November 2016).

13. Shazia Mirza, "On the Culture of Hate," available at www.newstatesman.com/politics/uk/2016/09/shazia-mirza-culture-hate-once-we-blamed-yoko-ono-now-we-blame-refugees (accessed 25 November 2016).

14. Nathan Crick, *Democracy and Rhetoric: John Dewey on the Arts of Becoming* (Columbia: South Carolina University Press, 2010), 173–174.

Glossary

Abomination   The attempt to make an object seem so repellent that an audience ignores, shuns, discards, or destroys it.

Acceptance symbol   A symbol which functions when there is a preexisting undesirable or threatening aspect of a situation that we have been unable to emotionally accept because it is too difficult to admit.

Actions   A category of subject matter referring to conscious behavioral choices made by people.

Actual examples   Descriptions of real things that exist or have existed, that happen or have happened.

Administration speeches   Speeches that are delivered by officials of a group or institution to an audience whose presence is usually mandatory in order to justify policy decision and improve the procedures and communication structures of an organization.

Advocacy speeches   Speeches that persuade an uncommitted audience to place certain beliefs and attitudes at the top of a hierarchy of needs by showing how they are necessary to achieving ideal ends.

Agent   A type of persona who speaks on behalf of some institution as a spokesperson of legitimate authority, thereby standing as a "representative" of a recognized institution or social group.

Alliteration   The use of words that begin with the same consonant sound.

Amplification   Increasing salience by exaggerating something and making it "larger than life" so that it stands out as important and demanding of our attention.

Analogy   Treating two essentially unlike things the same way because they share a vital similarity that is particularly relevant to the case at hand.

Antithesis   When two similarly phrased, but contradictory, ideas are consecutively expressed in order to favor one over the other.

Apologist   A type of persona employed when speakers wish to rebuff attack, including both attacks on one's personal character and more often on one's position.

Appearance   The way one physically appears to an audience, ideally not only to please the eye but also to identify oneself to an audience as a certain type of person who will deliver the message in a certain type of way.

Appropriateness   How "fitting" the speech is to all of the particular elements and unique circumstances of the speech.

Arrangement   The canon of giving order to a speech in anticipation of giving it form.

Artistic symbol   A symbol that can provide an opportunity for a speaker to "inhabit" the symbol much as an actor performs a part on stage.

Attracting emotions   Emotions that draw us closer to somebody or something; we associate such attracting emotions with love, curiosity, pity, generosity, envy, trust, respect, obsession, or greed.

Audience   Any person, or group of people, who hears, reads, or witnesses any communicative event.

Bandwagon   A fallacy based on the idea that the popularity of a thing is a sign of its value.

Belief   A statement of fact on which a person is prepared to act.

Catharsis   The sense of wisdom that follows upon the purging of pity and fear brought about by the trauma of witnessing the suffering of others whom we love and respect.

Causation   Asserting that certain consequences or effects will naturally follow some specific interaction of elements in a situation.

Claim   The primary position or conclusion being advanced by a speaker that represents the "payoff" of the reasoning.

Comedy   A poetic category that usually revolves around an initial misunderstanding or deception that magnifies to absurd proportions until some chance event reveals what is truly going on to everyone involved, such that an amicable reconciliation between parties becomes possible.

Commemorative speeches   Speeches that establish or reinforce bonds between audience members by praising something or someone that the speaker believes reflects their shared values.

Comparison   A way of taking two different things and putting them side by side to show their similarities and differences.

Conclusion   The final section of a speech that satisfies an audience's desires and make them feel as if the speech has come together as a whole and therefore achieved qualitative unity in form.

Concrete word Specific and readily identifiable qualities or actions in order to give an audience a more vivid experience of some thing or an event.

Constraint Any counterforce that stands between us and the attainment of our interests.

Content The specific arguments, stories, or facts that a speech contains.

Contested exigence An exigence that not everyone agrees is an actual problem.

Contingency Some unexpected obstacle, perplexity, or problem.

Conventions Shared, normative habits.

Corrective symbol A symbol which provides us an opportunity for imagining that we are somewhere other than our current place and time.

Counterpublic A public that develops outside of and counter to the established mechanisms of the state.

Criticized audience A group antagonistic to the rhetor's interests, such as another political party, or simply a demonized audience that is used as a convenient foil.

Decentralization The ability for organizations or groups to operate without any central organizing structure.

Definition Approaching a subject by asking and interrogating its definition.

Deliberation A communicative activity by which multiple parties, each with different perspectives, goals, and interests, attempt to come to a common practical judgment about some pressing issue.

Deliberation speeches Speeches that occur when an audience wishes to hear a diverse group of speakers give different perspectives on how to address a common topic in order to come to an informed judgment about a matter of common concern.

Deliberative speech In the Classical period, speech which occurred in the assembly, dealt with the future, and addressed matters of the expedient and the inexpedient.

Delivery The manner in which a speaker physically performs the speech through the crafted use of the voice and gesture.

Desire A concrete energetic ideal that propels people to action in pursuit of some value or pleasure.

Dialect   A local phrasing common in a particular group but not used universally.

Digital rhetoric   A type of public speaking in which individuals speak directly to the audience but do so not from a conventional public speaking context but from more intimate or on-site locations that imitate more traditional journalistic techniques.

Diminution   Reducing something, pushing it into the background, and making it insignificant and trivial.

Distinction   The attempt to establish credibility by the possession of special knowledge and/or unique experience that are superior to those of the audience.

Division   A way of taking something that seems to be a "whole" and breaking it into its constituent parts or combining disparate parts into a whole.

Dramatic irony   When an audience is aware that something is going to happen, but the characters in a narrative do not.

Dramatistic symbols   Symbols that organize other symbols into coherent dramatic structures that establish relationships and help us interpret and regulate our world.

Either/or   A fallacy that comes to an erroneous conclusion that if anything does not belong to one category, then it must be the exact opposite.

Elegy   A mournful, melancholy, or plaintive poem, often presented as a funeral song or a lament for the dead.

Eloquence   A type of experience produced when an oration achieves the heights of aesthetic form in such a way that carries an audience beyond itself while simultaneously bringing illumination to the particulars of the audience's situation.

Emancipation symbol   An emancipation symbol has the unique power to invert our moral codes, thus making the better into the worse and the worse into the better.

Emotional interpretant   The feeling produced by the sign and that which comes closest to what is conventionally called the connotative meaning, or what qualities we associate with the object.

Emotional symbol   Emotional symbols allow people to vicariously experience powerful emotions that they would otherwise suppress.

Emotions   Dramatized feelings that orient us to things within our immediate environment that stand out as significant, accompanied by feelings of pleasure and pain.

Encouragement speeches   Speeches that focus on arousing a greater commitment and enthusiasm to a group identity already formed, usually to meet some challenge or create excitement for being together.

Energetic interpretant   The appropriate action or effect produced by the sign and that which corresponds to what we might call the pragmatic meaning of a word, or how it affects our behavior.

Engaged citizen   An individual who is an active participant in the democratic process of debate, deliberation, and persuasion as it relates to issues of public concern.

Enrichment speeches   Speeches that satisfy an audience's desire to successfully pursue preexisting interests by giving lively and engaging instruction about objects, events, processes, or concepts that promise to benefit the audience members' lives in some way.

Enthymeme   A rhetorical form of the syllogism which leaves out one or more premises that the speaker can rely upon the audience to "fill in" or "supply" on their own.

Epideictic speech   In the Classical period, speech which occurred at ceremonial events, dealt with the present, and addressed matters of praise and blame.

Ethics of rhetoric   How well the speaker has fully considered the broader consequences of his or her actions beyond the immediate moment and has acted conscientiously with respect to that evaluation.

Ethos   The sense of public character that is recognized by an audience and influences their reception of the speaker's arguments.

Events   A category of subject matter referring to time-bound, complex, moving situations that have a beginning, middle, and end.

Evoked audience   The attractive image that the rhetor constructs of and for the audience.

Example   Stories that include descriptions of actual or hypothetical events, people, objects, or processes that can embody an idea or argument in a concrete form so that audiences can "see" what it means.

Exigence   Any outstanding aspect of our environment that makes us feel a combination of concern, uncertainty, and urgency.

Expert testimony   Quotations from individuals who may not have directly experienced something but who know a considerable amount about the subject matter due to extensive research.

Extemporaneous speaking   Using notecards, which includes key points, quotes, and transitions drawn from a larger outline, while leaving the speaker to fill in the gaps during the actual delivery of the speech.

External constraints   The people, objects, processes, and events that may physically obstruct any productive action even if persuasion of an audience has occurred.

Eye contact   The degree to which a speaker actually looks at members of the audience while speaking.

Fact   A condensed empirical claim that tells us about some facet of the world that we can rely upon to be true.

Fallacies   Arguments that, when analyzed in isolation, do not "hold up," in the sense of maintaining logical coherence.

False analogy   A fallacy that either makes logically absurd or ethically dubious associations between two things that have very little relationship to one another.

False cause   A fallacy in which a causal argument is made that invokes a clearly incorrect or exaggerated causal sequence.

Faulty sign   A fallacy that appeals to an indicator that does not actually point to what the rhetor claims that it does.

Feedback   The return messages that are constantly being sent by the other people involved in the communicative process.

Feeling   A sensory response to some environmental stimulation or physical state.

Fictional examples   Descriptions of events that are only imagined to have happened in the past, present, or future.

Figurative style   Specific elements of the speech designed to capture the attention and seduce the ear of the audience, thereby making it engaged with what is being said and creating more of a feeling of continuity and unity.

Figure   A series of signs designed to produce emotional interpretants based on an appeal to the ear.

Final outline   The last stage of your speech preparations that precede the actual writing or delivery of a speech and is useful both for evaluation purposes and to allow the speech to be performed again.

Forensic speech   In the Classical period, a speech which occurred in law courts dealt with the past and addressed matters of the just and unjust.

Form   The entire arc of temporal experience produced by symbols that first arouses and then fulfills desires and appetites in an audience.

Form of communication   The overall structure and means of expression of any communicative act.

Form of delivery   Ways of communicating that reveal character by using phrases, words, accents, or gestures commonly associated with certain character types.

Formal style   The overall tone and feel of a speech in its totality.

Generalization   Drawing a general conclusion about a class of people, events, objects, or processes based on specific examples drawn from experience.

Genre   A coherent and recognized arrangement of elements in a composition or discourse that is appropriate to certain occasions and that creates audience expectations that constrain and guide a speech's content, style, and delivery.

Goodwill   The presence of conscious and thoughtful consideration of the audience's well-being, as we would expect from a good friend.

Grounds   The supporting evidence for the claim that represents the "proof" for the conclusion.

Habit   A learned sequence of behavior in which mental and physical energies work relatively effortlessly together to accomplish a familiar task.

Hero   A type of persona who is willing to actively confront power in the name of helping others even if it means that great suffering might come upon him or her.

Heroic   A poetic category that calls an audience to courageous and committed action in the name of some higher ideal that has been revealed through the actions of a hero, living or dead.

Humor   A poetic category that can be defined as that burst of spontaneous laughter produced by the momentary violation of expectations and the absurd juxtaposition of incongruous things in such a way that also produces some new insight.

Hyperbole   Using extreme exaggeration to highlight a specific quality or idea.

Identification   The strategy of creating a common bond with an audience by drawing parallels between the characteristics of speaker, audience, and the subject matter of the speech.

Idol The attempt to invest an object with such attractive qualities that an audience seeks to possess, preserve, and/or use that object.

Immersion The sense that everybody is deeply involved in everyone else's lives and activities all at once.

Implosion The impression that everything far away can be brought close to you in an instant.

Impromptu speaking Speaking without preparation on a subject given to you at the moment.

Inferences The act or process of deriving conclusions from premises known or assumed to be true.

Inherited ethos The actual reputation that rhetors "carry with them" because of an audience's acquaintance with past behavior.

Interests Things that people enjoy doing, want to know about, or desire to attain.

Internal constraints The beliefs, attitudes, and values of an audience that must be changed if persuasion is to occur.

Internal preview A sentence within the speech that lets an audience know what they are about to hear.

Internal summary A sentence that reminds an audience what they have heard so as to reaffirm some important point.

Interpretant A more developed sign that mediates between the sign and its object that explains why they should go together.

Interpretation symbol In a rhetorical situation marked by confusion and uncertainty—an unclarified complexity—an interpretation symbol can function to give it order and meaning.

Introduction The beginning of a speech that should arouse some desire or appetite in the audience to hear the remainder of the speech.

Introduction speeches Speeches that seek to establish a relationship with an audience of strangers by using narratives to disclose central aspects of one's character that the speaker believes he or she shares with others.

Invective speeches Speeches whose only function is to provoke an audience to self-reflection by directly attacking and ridiculing its most valorized conventions, values, attitudes, and beliefs by judging them in light of a higher ideal.

Invention   The canon of discovering something to say.

Irony   When the apparent or expected meaning is the opposite of its actual or consequent meaning.

Lay testimony   Quotations from ordinary people who have had relevant experience with some issue.

Logical interpretant   Analogous to the dictionary definition and corresponds to what is conventionally called the denotative meaning of a word, or what "thing" it objectively refers to.

Logical reasoning   The use of inferences and proofs to establish relationships among propositions that warrant specific conclusions.

Logos   The use of rational arguments and evidence to persuade an audience of the reasonableness of one's position.

Main points   The most important claims made by the speech that are intended to support the main thesis.

Manuscript speaking   Writing out every word of a speech and delivering it as written.

Mass communication   The dissemination of a message received simultaneously by multiple parties in a different environment than that in which it was produced.

Maxim   A short, pithy statement expressing a general truth or rule of conduct that is commonly accepted by culture and used to justify a variety of beliefs and actions.

Meaning   The interaction between the tenor and the vehicle in a metaphor.

Memory   The fourth canon of rhetoric that refers to the ability to memorize a text and to reproduce it in a manner that seems natural rather than artificial.

Memory delivery   To write a manuscript first and then rehearse it until one knows it by heart and can deliver without a manuscript.

Metaphor   Describing one thing by using language that is normally used to describe something seemingly unrelated in order to imply that they share some essential underlying quality.

Metonymy   A way we represent a purely abstract idea, a notion, or concept by treating it as if it has a purely physical existence.

Mode of experience   A specific relationship between an individual and an environment that is particular to a specific place, time, and culture. For instance, all human beings are capable of feeling fear.

Mood   Pervasive qualities of a person's personality that affect his or her cognitive processing in all situational contexts.

Monroe's motivated sequence   A special sequence designed for policy speeches that encourage immediate action.

Mosaic form   A mode of presentation that places multiple things next to each other simultaneously, as in a hyperlinked website.

Motive   Any conscious psychological or physiological incitement to action within a particular situation.

Myth   An emblematic story from the past that captures and expresses both a moral lesson and an understanding of historical origins and destiny of a particular group or nation.

Narrative   A dramatic story that is more complex than an example, and that captures and holds the attention of an audience by promising that, through the unfolding of the plot and character, something new and satisfying will be produced at the end.

Narrative fidelity   How accurately a narrative represents accepted facts.

Narrative probability   The coherence of the narrative as a story apart from the actual facts.

Notecards   Abbreviated parts of the final outline put on small cards used for extemporaneous speaking as a means of reminding the speaker of the order and content of material to be presented.

Object (of sign)   What is represented by the sign.

Objects   A category of subject matter representing entities that can be understood and named as discrete things.

Occasion   The specific setting shared by speaker and audience whose circumstances determine the genre, the purpose, and the standards of appropriateness of what is said.

Online communication   Text, image, audio, and video messages sent and received by individuals on computer-aided technologies and capable of being received simultaneously by an infinite number of users, and also being recalled by those users at any time.

Opinion   A conscious personal belief expressed as a commitment to a certain matter of fact or value.

Orientation   How we stand in relationship to a thing, whether we are attracted to or repulsed by it.

Outlining   A way of summarizing and organizing the "highlights" of a speech into sections and putting them into a linear progression of beginning, middle, and end.

Overgeneralization   A fallacy in which one makes too broad a leap from the particular to the general.

Oxymoron   Placing two terms together that seem contradictory in order to highlight their tension.

Paradox   A statement of an apparent contradiction that nevertheless contains a measure of truth.

Parallelism   The repeated pairing of different, usually opposing, ideas in a rhythmic "couplet" within the same sentence.

Particular appearance   A unique way in which a particular reality shows itself to a person at a particular time and place.

Particular reality   A discrete entity that is unique in the world, usually indicated by words like "this" or "that."

Partisan   A type of persona who represents neither a group nor institution but an idea or ideal.

Pathos   The use of emotional appeals to persuade an audience.

Pattern of experience   A recognizable and habitual way of adjusting to a specific set of stimuli.

Pauses   Adding a patient and conscious silence between words or thoughts in a way to stimulate thought or generate tension.

People   A category of subject matter representing both individuals and groups.

Persona   The constructed ethos that a rhetor creates within the confines of a particular rhetorical context.

Personal stories   Narrations of one's life experience that provide insight into the speaker's practical wisdom, virtue, or goodwill.

Personification   Describing abstract or nonhuman objects as if they possessed human qualities.

Persuasion   The ability to change the beliefs of others through symbols.

Pitch   A musical term that refers to the ability to speak each word as if it was a separate note in a melody, moving up and down the scale.

Poetic category   A way of telling a certain type of story that organizes the plot and characters in a certain predictable sequence and produces specific emotional responses.

Polarization   The strategy of dividing an audience into a positive "us" and a negative "them" in order to create unity through difference.

Position   How a speaker orients his or her body with respect to the audience, including the choice of whether to stand behind a podium, walk around, or sit down.

Practical judgment   The act of defining a particular person, object, or event for the purposes of making a practical decision.

Practical wisdom   A proven ability to size up problematic situations and make judgments that show prudence and forethought.

Prestige testimony   Quotations from famous and well-respected individuals who may have nothing directly to do with an issue but whose words provide inspiration and insight.

Primary audience   Those people actually assembled together to hear the speech as it is delivered in person by the speaker.

Principle   A universal law, doctrine, or definition that helps guide judgment in particular cases by telling us what to expect from a class of things.

Pronunciation   Speaking a word such that it is correctly spoken and each syllable stands out.

Prudence   The capacity to make a practical judgment about a particular matter of concern.

Public   A group of citizens who recognize each other's interests and have developed habits of settling disputes, coordinating actions, and addressing shared concerns through common communication media.

Public memory   The storehouse of social knowledge, conventions, public opinions, values, and shared experiences that a speaker can appeal to within a speech and feel confident that they will resonate meaningfully with that audience.

Public opinion   The percentage of people who hold certain views to be true about public affairs.

Public speaking   Acts of speaking that are delivered within a shared space that includes both the words and the total environment in which they are uttered.

Public speech   An oral communication delivered by an individual to a public audience gathered in a shared physical environment to listen collectively and respond to that message in the present.

Purpose   The reasons for and circumstances under which an occasion occurs.

Qualitative form   A form that occurs when certain qualities in a work of art prepare the way for another quality that is emotionally satisfying, but without logical determination.

Qualitative unity   The feeling that one can sum up an entire arc of experience within a single term.

Rate   The dynamic between rapidly and slowly spoken parts of the speech.

Relationship   Putting two or more things in causal relationship to one another in order to understand how something was produced.

Repelling emotions   Emotions that push us negatively away from somebody or something; we associate such negative emotions with anger, fear, shame, guilt, embarrassment, anxiety, disgust, or cowardice.

Repetition   The repeated use of a key phrase to begin a series of sentences whose endings vary.

Rhetor   A conscious instigator of social action who uses persuasive discourse to achieve his or her ends.

Rhetorical background   The larger environment that defines the historical and social context for any particular rhetorical event.

Rhetorical constraints   Those obstacles that must be overcome in order to facilitate both the persuasive and practical effects desired by the speaker.

Rhetorical exigence   An issue that generates concern and uncertainty for some organized or semi-organized group that can be resolved, in whole or in part, by persuading an audience to act in a way that is actually capable of addressing the situation.

Rhetorical foreground   The specific and salient aspects of a common situation as it affects or interests some audience at a particular moment in time, including the motives of the audience itself.

Rhetorical public speaking   The art of addressing pressing public concerns by employing deliberate persuasive strategies before a public audience at a specific occasion in order to transform some aspect of a problematic situation by encouraging new forms of thought and action.

Rhetorical situation   A situation that occurs when public contingencies generate concern and uncertainty within a public audience and give force and effectiveness to persuasive discourse that encourages collective action.

Rhythm   Composing words such that, when spoken and heard, they follow some kind of musical pattern that is recognizable and predictable and helps an audience move along with the words.

Saint   Holding up a particular person as worthy of our special attention, praise, and emulation both for his or her own sake as well as for our self-advancement.

Salience   How strongly an emotion is felt within a particular situation.

Scapegoating   A fallacy that takes the form of an argument that claims that the reason some undesirable state of affairs has come about is because of the existence or actions of a particular group of people who are on the margins of society and are easy to blame.

Secondary audiences   All those people who encounter the speech either through some other media or secondhand through the spoken word of another person.

Second-person fictional examples   Descriptions which place the audience in a hypothetical situation that asks them to envision doing something.

Semiotics   The study of signs.

Sign   An argument that encourages us to accept a state of affairs by careful reading of external clues or indicators.

Signpost   A short phrase that marks a path along the way and lets them know your location.

Simile   Highlighting a specific quality of a thing by explicitly comparing it to a like quality in something unrelated.

Sinner   Holding up another person (or group that we feel justified in treating as if it were an individual) and portraying him or her in a negative light in order to make that person repellent to an audience.

Situation irony   When someone's actions produced the very opposite effect than what they had intended.

Slippery slope   A fallacy which takes the form of an argument that claims we must not make an even incremental step in a certain direction if we are to prevent a dramatic slide and decline into a terrible state of affairs.

Social knowledge   A culture's conventional wisdom and practical judgment as expressed in maxims, generally held beliefs, and value judgments.

Solicitation speeches   Speeches that persuade an audience to adopt some policy, object, process, or attitude based on the perceived rightness or utility of the subject matter.

Sources   Those people, books, research, media, testimony, and the like which help you discover something new to say that is persuasive, reliable, and novel.

Special knowledge   The kind of knowledge one receives by learning technical discourses and procedures, such as the knowledge one receives from attending a university.

Specific purpose   An expression of an interest in a particular goal that the speaker finds interesting and that may have value for an audience.

Speech anxiety   When standing physically in front of a group of people to give a speech makes us feel all the more vulnerable, nervous, and exposed.

State   The instrument that the public uses to address consequences that it deems important enough to manage.

Statistics   Mathematical generalizations that help us make predictions about certain types of objects or events.

Stereotyping   A fallacy that invites us to treat a diverse group of things as if they all were the same, thereby reducing a complex population to a simple and monolithic entity.

Style   The art of putting material together in such a way that it adds up to an attractive and meaningful unity.

Surprise   That which appears suddenly, unexpectedly, and shockingly and without preparation.

Suspense   That which has been promised to appear but whose actual qualities have been kept secret.

Syllogism   A complete form of reasoning with all parts clearly defined and explicit.

Syllogistic form   A form of a logical sequence, each step leading to the next in predictable and causal order.

Symbol   Anything that represents something other than itself to some other person who understands this representation.

Synecdoche   A way of representing a larger complete whole by describing it only in terms of a smaller part or microcosm.

Tactile   A type of experience that involves the profound and unified interplay of the senses.

Target audiences   Those individuals or groups in either the primary or secondary audiences who are able to be persuaded and are capable of acting in such a way to help resolve the exigence.

Technical situation   A situation that exists when we confront problems with a proven discourse and method to guide us.

Tenor   The underlying quality or property that is intended to be highlighted in a metaphor.

Testimony   Direct quotations from individuals who can speak with some authority on a certain state of affairs.

Thesis   An explicit and detailed argument that seeks to achieve a specific purpose.

Third-person fictional examples   Descriptions of the actions of other people as if they actually happened until usually revealing at the end that it is just a story.

Topics of invention   Specific ways of placing material into relationships that ideally bring about new questions and new insights.

Tragedy   A poetic category in which the pursuit of a high ideal produces suffering for a hero and which brings about learning in those who witness it.

Transcendence   The capacity to move through the particular matter at hand and thereby experience meanings that are grander and more universal than those that are immediately present.

Transition   Short phrases or words that provide a bridge that connects two ideas and helps an audience proceed from one to the other.

Trope   A series of signs designed to produce complex logical interpretants based on appeal to the mind.

Uncontested exigence   An exigence that everyone acknowledges to be a pressing problem that demands to be addressed.

Unique experience   The kind of expertise one acquires by having directly experiencing an event in a particular way.

Universal experience   A type of experience that all human beings are capable of having, no matter where they live or when they lived. In other words, it is an emotion or mood that all people can experience simply because they are human beings.

Universal meaning   An abstract concept, embodied in a language, that is used to interpret and conceptualize a large number of things.

Universal possibility   A shared general meaning that might not exist yet in reality but that we believe we might be able to achieve through imagination, cognition, and effort.

Utopia   Using the power of an ideal to reveal the limitations of one's actual situation and inspire hope that future "perfect" events will occur.

Value   An abstract ideal quality that guides our behavior across a variety of situations.

Vehicle   How the tenor is embodied and expressed in a specific figure within a metaphor.

Verbal irony   A variant of sarcasm in which case one says the opposite of what one actually means.

Vice   A strategy that repels us from certain concrete actions by making them morally offensive and/or practically harmful.

Virtue (ethos)   An established habit of doing good, of performing particular activities that are held in high regard and embody the best cultural values.

Virtue (pathos)   Honoring the nature of specific types of actions that we find worthy of praise and generating passionate commitment to cultivating these virtues.

Visual aid   Graphics which supplement the verbal component of a speech by effectively condensing complex material or conveying meanings that cannot be captured with language itself.

Volume   The dynamic between softly and stridently spoken parts of the speech.

Warrant   The inferential leap that connects the claim with the ground, usually embodied in a principle, provision, or chain of reasoning.

Wasteland   Portraying a horrific event or state of affairs that we either wish to escape or to avoid.

Working outline   A tentative plan for the speech that allows a speaker to experiment with different arrangements before exerting the time and energy required to finalize the speech.

Written speech   The primary media of print rather than handwriting insofar as print privileges sequential ordering of parts, a specific point of view, an explicit logical progression, a complex arrangement of information, and a spirit of objective detachment.Discussion

Index